The Archaeology
of Colonial Encounters

**Publication of the Advanced Seminar Series
is made possible by generous support from
The Brown Foundation, Inc., of Houston, Texas.**

**School of American Research
Advanced Seminar Series**

George J. Gumerman
General Editor

The Archaeology of Colonial Encounters

Contributors

Susan E. Alcock
*Department of Classical Studies and Kelsey Museum of Archaeology,
University of Michigan*

Terence N. D'Altroy
Department of Anthropology, Columbia University

Michael Dietler
Department of Anthropology, University of Chicago

Janine L. Gasco
Department of Archaeology, California State University, Dominguez Hills

Kent G. Lightfoot
Department of Anthropology, University of California, Berkeley

J. Daniel Rogers
*Department of Anthropology, National Museum of Natural History,
Smithsonian Institution*

Katharina Schreiber
Department of Anthropology, University of California, Santa Barbara

Michael W. Spence
Department of Anthropology, University of Western Ontario

Gil J. Stein
Oriental Institute, University of Chicago

Peter van Dommelen
Department of Archaeology, University of Glasgow

The Archaeology
of Colonial Encounters

Comparative Perspectives

Edited by Gil J. Stein

School of American Research Press
Santa Fe

School of American Research Press

Post Office Box 2188
Santa Fe, New Mexico 87504-2188
WWW.SARPRESS.SARWEB.ORG

Director: James F. Brooks
Executive Editor: Catherine Cocks
Manuscript Editor: Carol Leyba
Design and Production: Cynthia Dyer
Proofreader: Ellen Cavalli
Indexer: Catherine Fox

Library of Congress Cataloging-in-Publication Data:
The archaeology of colonial encounters : comparative perspectives /
edited by Gil J. Stein.— 1st ed.
    p. cm.
Includes bibliographical references and index.
ISBN 1-930618-43-3 (cloth : alk. paper) — ISBN 1-930618-44-1 (pbk. :alk. paper)
1. Archaeology and history. 2. Ethnoarchaeology. 3. Acculturation—History.
4. Colonization—Social aspects—History. 5. Colonies. I. Stein, Gil, 1956-

CC77.H5A715 2004
909'.09719–dc22

   2004023519

Library of Congress Catalog Card Number
International Standard Book Number 978-1-930618-44-2 (paper).
First edition 2005. Second paperback printing 2011.

Cover illustration: Chapel and old Russian well, Fort Ross State Historic Park, California.
Photograph © Daniel F. Murley.

Contents

Figures

Tables

Acknowledgments

It is a pleasure to acknowledge the many talented people who made this book possible. First and foremost, my colleagues and I thank Dr. Douglas Schwartz, the now-retired president of the School of American Research, for his vision in establishing the advanced seminar program as a uniquely effective way to foster in-depth examinations of significant research problems in anthropology. Our seminar, titled "The Archaeology of Colonies in Cross-Cultural Perspective," was held March 19–23, 2000. Nancy Owen Lewis, the director of academic programs, and the staff of SAR were wonderful hosts, providing our group with everything we needed to make our stay in Santa Fe comfortable and extraordinarily productive. I especially wish to thank my nine co-participants in the seminar—Sue Alcock, Terry D'Altroy, Mickey Dietler, Jan Gasco, Kent Lightfoot, Dan Rogers, Mike Spence, Kathy Schreiber, and Peter Van Dommelen—for presenting such insightful and thought-provoking analyses of their own research areas as they related to more global issues of anthropological theory. I can honestly say that the combination of paper presentations, debates, and discussions was one of the most extraordinary intellectual experiences I have ever had. I think that all of us emerged from our week in the seminar house with a deeper and far more nuanced understanding of the complexities of ancient colonial encounters.

I also want to express my colleagues and my own appreciation to Joan O'Donnell, James F. Brooks, and Catherine Cocks from SAR Press, all of whom helped us tremendously in the various stages of transforming our seminar papers into book form. We thank the two anonymous reviewers for the press who provided us with insightful comments, critiques, and suggestions for improving our manuscript. Similarly, we appreciate the careful editing work of Carol Leyba.

Finally, I want to thank my family for their forbearance during the long gestation of this book.

GJS, Evanston, IL, 2004

To my daughters Abby and Hannah

The Archaeology
of Colonial Encounters

1

Introduction

The Comparative Archaeology of Colonial Encounters

Gil J. Stein

For we who were Occidentals now have been made Orientals. He who was a Roman or a Frank is now a Galilaean, or an inhabitant of Palestine. One who was a citizen of Rheims or of Chartres now has been made a citizen of Tyre or of Antioch. We have already forgotten the places of our birth; already they have become unknown to many of us, or, at least, are unmentioned.... Some have taken wives not merely of their own people, but Syrians, or Armenians, or even Saracens who have received the grace of baptism.... The one and the other use mutually the speech and the idioms of the different languages. Different languages, now made common, become known to both races, and faith unites those whose forefathers were strangers. As it is written, "The lion and the ox shall eat straw together." Those who were strangers are now natives; and he who was a sojourner now has become a resident.

> *Fulcher of Chartres, Medieval Chronicler of the Crusades*
> A.D.*1127 (Krey 1921:280–81)*

Colonial encounters are a widespread, cross-cultural process having far-reaching effects on the economy and political organization of prehistoric and historically documented societies in both the Old and New Worlds (Algaze 1993a, 1993b; Champion 1989; Dyson, ed. 1985; Lyons and Papadopoulos, eds. 2002; Rowlands, Larsen, and Kristiancen, 1987). As illustrated by the quote above from Fulcher of Chartres, a twelfth-century participant in and chronicler of the Crusades, these colonial encounters also had profound transformative effects on the cultural identities of all groups involved. Archaeologically documented colonies were established by state societies such as Teotihuacan (Santley, Yarborough, and Hall 1987) and Oaxaca (Rattray 1990b, 1993; Spence 1992); by polities of Andean South America such as Wari (Schreiber 1992), Tiwanaku (Goldstein 1993), and the Inka Empire (D'Altroy 1992; Pease 1982); by Uruk Mesopotamia (Algaze 1993b; Rothman, ed. 2001; Stein 1999b), Egypt (W. Adams 1984; S. T. Smith 1998), Assyria (Larsen 1976), Greece (Boardman 1980; Dietler 1998; Tsetskhladze and De Angelis 1994); Phoenicia, and Carthage (Aubet 1993; van Dommelen 1998); by the empire of Alexander the Great and his Hellenistic successors (Descoeudres 1990); and by Rome (Alcock 1989, 1993; Haselgrove 1987; Millett 1990; Wells 1998). However, to date there has been no real effort to synthesize this large body of accumulating evidence into a general theoretical understanding of colonial encounters in cross-cultural perspective. Gosden (2004) proposes a comparatively oriented model for the archaeology of colonialism. Gosden's approach explicitly focuses on the materialization of symbolic power between regions, and not on colonies per se (2004:3). As such, it complements the approach taken in our own volume, which examines the dynamics of symbolic, political, and economic interaction in relation to identity in colonial encounters. This is particularly important because the common model of colonies is grounded in the experience of European colonialism in the sixteenth to nineteenth centuries A.D. By focusing on non-Western and precapitalist networks from both the Old and New Worlds, we can broaden our perspective to develop a more realistic, synthetic understanding of colonial encounters.

Despite the intellectual centrality of colonial encounters in the anthropology of complex societies, there is still no consensus among anthropologists about (1) what colonies are, (2) how and why colonies vary one from another, (3) how colonies function as social, economic, and political entities, (4) what colonial relations are like with indigenous host communities, and (5) how ethnic identities are transformed in colonial situations. Most significantly, researchers disagree on the fundamental foci of analysis—are we studying *colonies, colonization,* or *colonialism?* Overall, our understanding of these important phenomena suffers because we have no theoretical framework within which to understand colonial encounters as a cross-cultural phenomenon. I am using the term "colonial encounters" in the title of the book and in the discussion below as a way to avoid the semantic baggage of other constructs, while at the same time emphasizing the dynamic nature of these processes of cultural interaction.

This chapter attempts to identify some of the main research issues involved in developing a comparative archaeology of colonial encounters. My goal is to highlight key debates and emerging themes in the ways we conceptualize this form of interaction. The theoretical framework employed here explicitly recognizes the cultural uniqueness of specific historical conjunctures while at the same time maintaining a comparative perspective aimed at identifying both variation and cross-culturally recurring processes in colonial encounters. This book presents revised versions of papers discussed at a conference on the archaeology of colonization in cross-cultural perspective, held at the School of American Research in Santa Fe (NM), March 19–23, 2000, as part of the SAR advanced seminar program. The contributors to this volume examine prehistoric, precapitalist, and early historic colonies of the Old and New Worlds in an attempt to develop a more synthetic understanding of colonial encounters as a form of interregional interaction characteristic of ancient state societies and/or their constituent social groups.

COMPARATIVE ARCHAEOLOGICAL RESEARCH ON COLONIES

Colonies, colonial encounters, and colonialism have emerged as an important focus for converging lines of research by social anthropologists, ethnohistorians, and anthropological archaeologists. This is entirely appropriate, since colonialism has played such a crucial role in shaping the complex societies and enduring structures of political economies in both the ancient and modern worlds. At the same time, as postcolonial theory has emphasized, the practices of colonialism have had a pervasive and transformative impact on the cultures of all groups involved in colonial encounters. Colonialism has furthermore played an important and often implicit structuring role in Western intellectual traditions, not least in anthropology and archaeology.

As Dietler points out (this volume), archaeology can contribute significantly to our understanding of colonies, colonial encounters, and colonialism for several reasons. First, it generates material data that are fundamentally different from, and independent of, the textual record on which most colonial and postcolonial theory is based. Archaeological data illuminate the unconscious processes and *habitus* of daily life, thereby complementing the ideologically charged information provided by historical sources. Archaeological data also allow us to examine those ancient, non-Western, and precapitalist colonial encounters that fall outside the scope of the written word, whether for geographical, chronological, or contextual reasons. Thus archaeology can provide a wide range of case studies that can contribute to more general theory because they differ markedly from the standard, better-known episodes of colonial expansion by Greece, Rome, and the European states in the Age of Discovery.

Archaeologists have studied colonies for more than a century (all Roman archaeology in Britain and early historical archaeology in the United States could be regarded as the archaeology of colonies). However, the explicitly *comparative*, theoretically informed study of historical, ancient, and non-Western colonies and colonial encounters is a relatively recent development (see, for example, Dyson, ed. 1985; Descoeudres 1990; D. H. Thomas 1991; Cusick, ed. 1998; Gosden 2004; Lyons and Papadopoulos, eds. 2002). This book complements and builds on the comparative work to date in two significant ways. First, the focus of analysis is shifted here from analyses of colonialism to analyses of colonial encounters as a concept that does not have implications about specific power relations among the interacting groups. Second, the current volume is the first to bring case studies from the prehispanic New World into explicitly comparative analyses of colonial encounters. The latter is particularly important as a corrective for our discipline's tendency to build theoretical models of colonial encounters based on either Greco-Roman or European colonialism.

A related set of theoretical, methodological, and empirical developments suggests that now is an ideal time to attempt a new synthetic appraisal of ancient colonial encounters. At the theoretical level, archaeologists have been able to identify a broadly recurring pattern of colonization as a strategy of expansion in ancient state societies (Algaze 1993a). Sociocultural anthropologists have come to recognize the importance of indigenous agency in colonial systems—that is, the idea that local groups play a key role in structuring interaction. At the same time, anthropological archaeologists have begun to question the universal applicability of the European-based world-system model to non-Western and precapitalist colonial networks (for example, Dietler 1998; Stein 1998). In other words, the dominant role of the colonizer has been effectively challenged (see, for example, Blaut 1993). Concurrently, anthropologists have developed methodological frameworks to examine the roles of indigenous groups in colonial interaction and the ways their identities are transformed (for example, Deagan 1998; Hannerz 1987; van Dommelen 1997a). Finally, we now have an extremely rich database of high-quality empirical research on both colonies and colonial-local interaction in a variety of Old and New World complex societies.

COLONIAL ENCOUNTERS AND EVOLVING PARADIGMS OF INTERREGIONAL INTERACTION

Colonial encounters form part of the broader phenomenon of culture contact or interregional interaction. A number of related theoretical developments in both historical and prehistoric archaeology have led to an emerging consensus that we can reasonably call a new paradigm for interregional interaction (Stein 2002b). Archaeologists have come to recognize that a focus on agency (for example, Dobres and Robb 2000), practice (for example, Lightfoot, Martinez, and Schiff 1998), and social identity (for example, van Dommelen 1998; Wells 1998) can greatly clarify our understanding of how complex societies function and evolve. More specifically, researchers have been revising their models to incorporate the idea that the recursive relationship between social structure and the strategic actions of individuals or small groups plays a major role in reproducing and changing the social organization of complex societies.

The second major development leading to a fundamental rethinking of interregional interaction has been the increasing dialogue among prehistoric archaeologists, archaeologists working with textually documented ancient societies such as Mesopotamia, Egypt, Greece, and Rome, and historical archaeologists dealing with the European expansion in the Age of Discovery (see, for example, Lightfoot 1995).

Recognizing that the world systems and acculturation models apply to only a small subset of culture contact situations, researchers are now making a conscious effort to define interregional interaction in ways that incorporate a broad range of variation including long-distance trade, colonial situations, and military expansion. By doing this, we can now start to move beyond simple typologies of interaction, and instead we can start to focus on the variables and processes that explain why the organization and effects of culture contact can be expected to vary under different structural conditions and historical contingencies (Schortman and Urban 1998; Stein 1998).

This emerging perspective on interregional interaction consists of seven interrelated elements (Stein 2002b). First and fundamentally, the current research combines processual and post-processual approaches. From pos-tprocessual theory, we see a concern with agency, practice, ideology, the active role of material culture in negotiating cultural identity, and the importance of historical contingency. Key processual elements include a recognition of the importance of political economy, a comparative analytical framework, and a concern with explicit, replicable methodologies that use data to evaluate broader theoretical propositions.

Second, the new framework rejects unilinear models such as acculturation and world systems as being limited to only a narrow range of the possible forms of interaction. Third, this framework is, in Kent G. Lightfoot's words, "multiscalar"(Lightfoot 1995; Lightfoot, Martinez, and Schiff 1998:199). In contrast with the world-systems model's structural overdetermination at the interregional level, current approaches see the organization of culture contact as the composite outcome of processes at both the intra- and inter-polity levels.

The fourth key element of this new paradigm is its explicit recognition of patterned variability in the power relations of the polities linked by an interaction network. Under some conditions, more developed "cores" can control less developed "peripheries" on the lines of world-systems/acculturation models. In many other cases, interaction can take place on a more equal footing. Some of the major factors that can affect the interregional balance of power are (1) distance and transportation economics; (2) technology (especially military and transportation technologies); (3) population size and composition (especially in the primary zone of culture contact); (4) disease; (5) military organization; and (6) the degree of social complexity in each polity.

The fifth aspect of this framework is the explicit recognition that the interacting complex societies must be seen as heterogeneous entities, composed of different groups whose interests, goals, and social strategies are often in conflict. Group identities are defined by categories such as ethnicity, class, and gender (Lightfoot, Martinez, and Schiff 1998). These groups overlap, so that membership in each is differentially expressed depending on social context. Interregional interaction also creates entirely new categories of identity through ethnogenesis (Deagan 1998).

The heterogeneity of the interacting polities brings out a sixth main aspect of the new interaction paradigm: the importance of internal dynamics. In other words, the diverse economic, political, social, and ideological processes inside each polity are as important as external processes (such as long-distance trade or colonization) in shaping the overall organization of the network.

Finally, the seventh aspect of this new framework is an idea that permeates the other six. This is the principle that human agency is as important as macroscale political economy in the organization of interregional interaction networks. Agency plays a crucial structuring role in all parts of these systems—not just in the highly developed core areas. This contrasts markedly with the world-systems and acculturation models' treatment of less developed peripheral polities as passive recipients of unidirectional influences from the core.

The combination of theoretical developments and an improved knowledge base of more representative archaeological case studies makes this an ideal opportunity to reexamine colonial encounters within this emerging new perspective on interregional interaction. Our goal in this book is to elucidate recurring mechanisms and processes in colonial encounters, rather that engage in a futile attempt to develop a single global model.

WHAT ARE COLONIES?

Definitions and definitional debates are irritating, pedantic, and unfortunately necessary. As C. Wright Mills noted, "The purpose of definition is to focus argument upon fact, and...the proper result of

good definition is to transform argument over terms into disagree-
ments about fact, and thus open arguments to further inquiry" (Mills
1959:34).

The basic question "What is a colony?" is surprisingly contentious.
In historians' usage, the traditional view of colonies is almost completely structured by the European experience. In one of the few
attempts to develop a typology of colonies, Finley argues that we should
continue to follow the eighteenth- and nineteenth-century usage and
restrict the term "colony" to only those implanted settlements characterized by (1) large-scale emigration from the homeland, (2) the
appropriation of local lands through the subjugation of local peoples,
(3) colonial control of the local labor force, and (4) formal political
and economic control of the implanted settlement by the homeland or
metropolis (Finley 1976:184). Central to Finley's model is the idea,
drawn from European colonialism, that the implanted settlements
dominate indigenous peoples, who are seen as "technically backward,
small scale in their political organization, incapable of concerted
action, as compared with their European conquerors. Above all they
were . . . hopelessly outclassed in their ability to apply force" (Finley
1976:184). Inequality and domination are thus inherent in every level
of the model, in a chain of domination where homelands control
colonies and the latter in turn control the indigenous host communities around them. As a result, Finley's overrestrictive definition
excludes Greek, Phoenician, Hellenistic, Crusader, Venetian, and
other important historical and ethnographic cases from his definition
of colonies because they do not reflect foreign domination over local
communities (Finley 1976:177).

However, any definition that excludes this many archaeological
and historical cases impedes rather than helps us in our goal of understanding the comparative dynamics of ancient colonial encounters. We
need a more neutral definition of colonies that subsumes, but is not
limited to, European colonialism. For purposes of cross-cultural comparison, I suggest that a colony can be provisionally defined as

> an implanted settlement established by one society in either
> uninhabited territory or the territory of another society. The
> implanted settlement is established for long-term residence
> by all or part of the homeland or metropole's population

and is both spatially and socially distinguishable from the communities of the indigenous polity or peoples among whom it is established. The settlement at least starts off with a distinct formal corporate identity as a community with cultural/ritual, economic, military, or political ties to its homeland, but the homeland need not politically dominate the implanted settlement (Stein 2002a:30).

The corporate nature of the foreign community and its formalized ties with its homeland are important elements that provide a significant distinction between colonies and episodes of migration by individuals or families. This definition treats the nature of power relations between the colony and the host community, and between the colony and its homeland, as open issues to be determined empirically, rather than assuming a priori that these are structured along the lines of European colonialism.

This reformulated definition has several advantages. First, it encompasses the sixteenth- to twentieth-century European expansion while also allowing us to compare a wide variety of ancient, non-Western and/or precapitalist networks of colonies within a single general framework. Second, the recognition of variation in power relationships forces us to investigate the dynamics of historically specific interactional situations, while also focusing our attention on investigating the broader-scale structural determinants of these relationships. The definition of colonies proposed here accords substantially with that suggested by Dietler (this volume).

As the case studies in this volume show, colonies can be established for a variety of often-overlapping purposes. Exchange and/or resource extraction, usually in conjunction with other functions, is probably the single most common reason for the establishment of colonies. Other important colonial functions, usually combined with exchange and resource extraction, are (1) colonies as military or administrative outposts connected with direct conquest, such as Roman provincial colonies (Alcock this volume; Schreiber this volume); (2) colonies as refuges, such as the Puritan Massachusetts Bay colony; (3) "settler colonies" as so-called safety valves to resettle excess population in order to defuse social conflict or land shortages in the homeland, such as the Greek colonies or Australia; (4) colonies as outposts for the spread of a specific ideology, such as the Spanish missions in California (Lightfoot this volume); (5) colonies as capital investments in agriculture, such as the early English colonies in Virginia; and (6) colonies as points of resettlement for the conquered populations of empires, such as the Inka *mitmaqkuna* settlements (D'Altroy this volume).

The ancient Greeks distinguished between at two different kinds of colonies—*apoikea* (a settlement colony that reproduced the key features of its founding *polis* or city-state) and *emporion* (trading outpost). We have also noted above Finley's (1976) attempt to develop a typology of colonies. Although it is important to recognize that colonies can be founded for different reasons and operate in a variety of contexts, we should be careful not to reify these distinctions. The contributors to this volume were unanimous in arguing that typologies of colonies only obscure the tremendous range of variation in the reasons for the establishment of these settlements, and in the ways that they actually functioned.

The establishment of colonies appears to be a process uniquely characteristic of complex societies—almost exclusively states and empires. We can speculate that some possible reasons for this might include the following:

1. States function at a larger scale and have a higher demand for goods, both commodities and prestige goods. High levels of long-term demand may well be a key factor leading to colonial enterprises as a way to supplement or reorganize exchange in order to obtain these goods.

2. States have the degree of economic specialization and what we might call the "organizational technology" to carry out the large-scale movements of people and materials involved in the process of colonization.

3. Only states would have the large standing armies necessary to establish and maintain long-term garrisons (in those cases where the establishment of colonies has a military component).

4. It is necessary to have the corporate structure of a colony when dealing with host communities that are in themselves complex societies.

In an important 1993 article in *American Anthropologist*, Guillermo

Algaze (1993a) suggested that colonies founded by the earliest pristine states differed markedly from those founded by later secondary states, because the former enjoyed tremendous superiority over their less developed neighbors. By contrast, once secondary states began to establish colonies, the developmental asymmetries between colonies and host polities were much less pronounced, leading to more balanced power relationships between the two. Algaze's model is worth considering in the light of the case studies in this volume, since we are dealing with colonies established by both pristine and secondary states. Related to this is the observation that colonization is often associated with secondary state formation in the host polities, either through local resistance to colonization or through the disruptive effects of external trade in prestige goods or other commodities.

The contributors to this volume were in general agreement that colonies must be considered within their regional and interregional context. Colonial encounters take place in a social space that consists of at least three key focal points: the colonies themselves, their homelands or metropoles, and the indigenous host societies in whose midst the colonies are established. Cooperation and competition among these three very different nodes defines the organization of the interregional interaction network as a whole. As a result, we need to examine each node explicitly to develop a realistic understanding of colonial encounters. For this reason, the contributors to this volume focus not only on the colonies themselves, but also on interaction and the role of indigenous groups as active agents in these networks.

POLITICAL ECONOMY

We can no longer automatically assume that colonies dominate the preexisting indigenous polities or communities among whom they are founded; nor can we assume that colonies directly reflect the interests of their colonial homelands. Given this conceptual shift, what is the range of variation in the power relations linking the colonies, homelands, and host communities that make up a colonial network, and how does it influence the developmental trajectories of colonial encounters?

A concern with the political economy of colonization requires that we examine a series of different relationships among the three aforementioned "nodes" of the colonial encounter: homelands, colonies, and host polities. When examining the relationship between homelands and colonies, one important question is, "Who controls colonies?" Greek and Old Assyrian colonies seem to have been state sanctioned but privately run; we can reasonably guess that Phoenician colonies were not state controlled. Other colonies were directly organized and controlled by centralized state institutions. How does the degree of state control (or lack of control) affect the organization of colonies and their relations with host communities? As part of this examination, we must recognize that colonies and their homelands often diverge rapidly in their political and economic interests.

A second dyadic power relationship among the three nodes of the colonial encounter concerns interaction between the colony and the host polity. One can suggest that colonists can pursue three main strategies: (1) domination, (2) long-term competition, and (3) alliance (see also Rogers this volume, for a discussion of different strategies of expansionist control over other societies). The implicit "European colonialist" model has led most studies of colonial-local interaction to focus on domination and, to a lesser degree, competition as the main strategies for interaction. We need to investigate the strong possibility that *alliance* strategies may have been extremely important in ancient, non-Western, and precapitalist colonial networks, particularly when colonizing groups were dealing with populous and/or already-complex local polities whom they could not militarily dominate.

Clearly, this revised definition of colonies and the recognition of the complexities involved in colonial encounters require us to rethink as well the way we conceptualize the material signatures of colonies in the archaeological record.

The Recognition of Colonies in the Archaeological Record

The identification of colonies in the archaeological record is surprisingly difficult, not least because it is closely related to the problematic issue of recognizing ethnicity through material culture (see, for example, Emberling 1997; S. Jones 1977). In general, one can identify as colonies those settlements whose architecture, site plan, and material culture assemblage are identical to those of another region but are located as spatially discrete occupations surrounded by settlements of the local culture. One would expect colonies to be founded as completely new settlements on previously unoccupied land. Alternatively, if founded in a preexisting settlement, a colony should show sharp architectural and artifactual discontinuities with earlier occupations (see Stanish 1989). Artifactual similarities to the homeland should reflect a broad complex of material culture used in a variety of contexts, rather than being limited to a single category such as ceramics.

Santley, Yarborough, and Hall argue that the ethnic identity of the inhabitants in a colonial enclave should be expressed in material culture connected with two different levels of social inclusiveness: the enclave as a whole, and the more restricted domestic level (1987:87). At the enclave-wide level, the identity of the foreigners is expressed and reinforced through public rituals; these are often centered on a ceremonial structure whose architecture generally incorporates the style or symbolic elements of the homeland. Common language, styles of dress, the wearing of particular badges or emblems, and burial customs are also enclave-wide ways to express the foreigners' separate identity.

At the domestic level, the members of an enclave generally live together in a spatially contiguous area, distinct from local and other groups. Food preferences, preparation procedures, and the material culture associated with these practices should both differ from local patterns in the host community while resembling the cultural practices of the homeland. In addition, the foreigners' distinctive ethnic identity will often be reflected by the use of raw materials or styles from the homeland in the ritual paraphernalia used for household rituals (Santley, Yarborough, and Hall 1987:87–88).

It is important to consider alternative interpretations for the presence of foreign styles of material culture in the sites of a different culture, rather than automatically assuming that this material culture reflects the existence of a foreign enclave. The use of multiple criteria combined with contrastive patterning between the foreign and local assemblages is necessary to distinguish the actual presence of foreign settlers from either (1) intercultural trade in the absence of a colony or (2) emulation by groups of local elites who are simply adopting status-related aspects of foreign material culture (through either importation or imitation). Trade, emulation, and the presence of trade colonies should leave different archaeological signatures. If interaction is limited to trade without the presence of a foreign enclave, then we would expect to see only portable trade items in the local settlement; foreign public and residential architecture would be absent, as would be evidence for foreign food preferences in spatially discrete contexts. If interaction consists of local elite emulation of foreign styles, we would expect to see these imports or imitations limited to high-status households, while lower-status groups retained local customs. In most cases, the elite households would show a distinction between the emulation of foreign styles in public contexts and the retention of local styles in domestic life.

Colonial Encounters and Identity

Many sociocultural anthropologists and archaeologists refer to the "colonial entanglement" as a way to emphasize the complexities and ambiguities of power relationships and identities of colonizers and their host communities in colonial encounters (for example, N. Thomas 1991; Dietler 1998). Work by Lightfoot, Deagan, and others has shown that the interregional interaction networks within which colonies are founded bring multiple groups into contact not just colonizers and host communities. In these encounters, the social identities of colonizers, other foreign communities associated with the colonizers, and host communities can all change.

Much, if not most, attention has focused on identity transformations in the host communities, often implicitly or explicitly relying on the traditional "acculturation" model of culture contact. This model assumes a unidirectionality in which the dominant colonizing "donor" culture transforms the more passive indigenous "recipient" culture of the host community. Similarly, archaeologists have traditionally viewed the social identity of the colonizing group as essentially static, mirroring the culture of the homeland in both ideology and material culture. If items of material culture did not exactly mirror the material culture of the colonial homeland, then they were assumed to reflect a process of local emulation, in which elites (and others) in the host community selectively appropriated high-status symbols and items of colonial material culture.

We now recognize that the political interests, economic goals, and social identities of colonizing groups diverge rapidly from those of their homelands. Even when the colonizing group dominates its host community politically, militarily, and economically (as in the case of Spanish colonies in the Americas), it is clear from the work of Deagan (1998), Cusick (ed. 1998), and others that rather than speaking of unidirectional processes such as "acculturation" (by the host community), or "assimilation"/"going native" (by the colonizers), what occurs instead is a bidirectional or multidirectional process in which diasporic cultures can form entirely new, composite identities through what has been termed transculturation, ethnogenesis, creolization, or hybridization. We need to understand this transformative process in relation to the political economy of colonization and the dynamics of power relations among colonies, host communities, and colonial homelands.

At the same time, we should explicitly recognize that continuities in social identity by either colonizing or host groups are phenomena worthy of study, since they may have played important roles in either domination by one group or resistance by another. Rogers's (1990) pathbreaking study of Arikara selective appropriation of Euro-American material culture provides an important example of the ways that artifactual evidence can serve to illuminate the development of new identities in colonial encounters. By studying transformations or aggressive nontransformations of identity, we can understand how colonial-local interaction actually worked, while monitoring change in the developmental trajectories of colonies as social entities. Finally, to study identity and its transformations more accurately, we need to develop finer-grained, contextually sensitive perspectives on colonies and indigenous groups. These analyses need to focus carefully on chronological variation and change, as well as on variation in behavior and symbolic activity in public versus domestic social contexts (see, for example, Deagan 1983, 1993; Lightfoot, Martinez, and Schiff 1998).

COMPARATIVE ANALYSES OF COLONIAL ENCOUNTERS

The contributors to this volume examine colonial encounters from two complementary perspectives: (1) a "top-down" approach that focuses on local, regional, or interregional political economy, and (2) a "bottom-up" approach that emphasizes individual or small group agency as it relates to identity and its transformations. Clearly, these analytical foci are always intertwined at a fundamental level; both are necessary in order to develop a nuanced, holistic understanding of the complexities of colonial encounters. In fact, one might argue that the very disjunctures and ambiguities that so characterize colonial encounters provide an ideal context for understanding the intersection of political economy and identity. The chapters in this book reflect these complementary approaches.

The contents and format of this volume reflect three broad areas of discussion. The first section presents a series of theoretical frameworks and issues that structure modern analyses of ancient colonial encounters. Michael Dietler discusses the ways in which the development of European understandings of the Greco-Roman world have exercised a pervasive influence on European intellectual traditions, thereby structuring Western conceptions of colonies and colonialism in both the modern and the ancient worlds. Using as a case study the interaction between the Greek colony of Massalia (modern Marseille) and the local groups of the lower Rhône Valley in southern France, Dietler critiques the commonly used Hellenization perspective and world-systems model for their structural overdetermination, their unidirectional view of power relations, and their inability to account for local agency in the natives' selective appropriation of Greek material culture.

Janine Gasco presents an overview of the Spanish conquest and colonization of the Americas—perhaps the crucial historical case that implicitly frames our understanding of all other historically and archaeologically documented colonial encounters. Gasco shows that one cannot understand Spanish colonial agendas and practices in the New World without situating them within the historic context of fourteenth- and fifteenth-century Spanish history. Specifically, the centrality of religious ideology and the administrative structures imposed on native populations in the Americas can be directly traced to the militaristic Christian ideology and political strategies used by Aragon and Castile in the reconquest of the Iberian Peninsula from the Muslim Moors. Through an analysis of the cacao economy in the Soconusco region in Mexico, Gasco also makes the important point that Spanish colonial rule and its impact on local populations differed significantly from region to region as a negotiated outcome of conflict and accommodation with native American groups. Thus, contrary to the general perception of Spanish dominance, local groups in Soconusco showed a high degree of agency and autonomy by retaining control over the production of cacao, arguably one of the most important commodities in the colonial economy.

Peter van Dommelen argues for the utility of postcolonial theory, notably the concepts of "hybridity" and "hybridization," for our understanding of ancient interaction and the development of new, colonial identities. Through a comparative analysis of the first millennium B.C. Phoenician and Punic colonization of Sardinia, Andalusia in southern Spain, and Ibiza, van Dommelen shows that it is misleading to talk about colonial enterprise as a unitary phenomenon. Instead, the goals, nature, and outcome of these colonial encounters varied markedly, depending on the specific regional context and the nature of the indigenous societies in whose midst they settled. He also shows that colonial agendas and the intensity of colonial-local interaction changed significantly over the course of three centuries. Perhaps most significantly, van Dommelen suggests that new colonial identities developed on Sardinia through a hybridization process (Bhabha 1992) in which the indigenous groups showed great selectivity in their appropriation and transformation of Punic material culture.

The second section of this volume presents a series of archaeological case studies from the Old and New Worlds to emphasize variation and contingency in the colonial encounters, as well as the need to situate these processes of interaction within their historical and regional contexts. Gil J. Stein's chapter analyzes the roles of smaller-scale social groups in the sociopolitical organization of both the colonial homeland and the indigenous societies as factors structuring the political economy of colonial encounters. This analysis compares two episodes of Mesopotamian colonial encounters in Anatolia (modern Turkey): the Old Assyrian trading colonies of the eighteenth century B.C. and the colonial network of the Uruk expansion in the fourth millennium B.C. In both cases, the fragmented, factionalized political landscape of the metropole, combined with surprisingly high levels of indigenous social complexity in Anatolia, led to an essential symmetry in power relations between the Mesopotamian colonies and their Anatolian host communities.

Kent G. Lightfoot contrasts two more or less contemporaneous eighteenth- and nineteenth-century European colonial encounters with similar native Californian hunter-gatherer groups: the Russian colony at Fort Ross in the north and the Spanish mission system along the southern coast. Lightfoot demonstrates that the differing colonial agendas of the two competing European powers, combined with a significant difference in the duration of the colonial encounters, led to markedly different outcomes for native Californian demography, identity, and cultural cohesion. The Spanish mission system in southern California lasted for more than a century and was directly focused on the relocation, control, and religious conversion of indigenous groups, with correspondingly drastic effects on the demography and cultural identity of the native southern Californians. By contrast, the short duration and secular, commercial focus of the Russian trading outpost at Fort Ross had considerably less impact on the composition and cohesion of local Pomo groups in northern California.

Finally, Michael W. Spence applies Abner Cohen's (1969, 1971) ethnographically based "trade diaspora" model of interregional interaction to Classic-period Mesoamerica, through an analysis of the Zapotec ethnic enclave of Tlailotlacan in the urban center of Teotihuacan, circa A.D. 200–650. Although clearly Oaxacan in character, this enclave does not appear to have been sponsored by the Monte Albán state. Spence argues for a more generalized version of the diaspora model in order to deemphasize the role of trade per se, while paying closer attention to the ways in which this small diasporic community of an estimated 800 merchants and their families maintained and reproduced its distinctive cultural identity within an enormous cosmopolitan urban center of up to 150,000 inhabitants. Spence also constructs important bridging arguments to specify criteria for the archaeological identification of an ethnic enclave. Taking a practice theory approach (analogous to that used by Lightfoot, Martinez, and Schiff in their analysis of a multi-ethnic community at Fort Ross), Spence focuses on *habitus* in the productive technology, style, and use of material culture as a key element in forging a Zapotec diasporic identity. Spence also shows the utility of an archaeological focus on two important (but often overlooked) processes through which a community of foreigners reproduces itself physically and culturally: marriage and the socialization of children. By combining artifactual and bioarchaeological lines of evidence, Spence shows that the small reproductive population of Tlailotlacan maintained its identity by exchanging marriage partners with other Zapotec diasporic communities. In parallel, stable isotope evidence from human bone and teeth shows that both male and female members of the Tlailotlacan enclave traveled widely outside of the city of Teotihuacan, probably residing for significant periods in other diaspora enclaves. This analysis emphasizes the need to consider colonial encounters within a broad regional context, a view shared by virtually all the contributors to this volume.

The third section of this volume presents Old and New World case studies of imperial colonial strategies, which seem, on the face of it, to have differed significantly from the colonial encounters of smaller-scale, less centralized polities. Katharina Schreiber contrasts the colonial strategies of the Wari Empire of the later first millennium A.D. Middle Horizon. By examining the three nodes of the colonial encounter—metropole, colony, and local population—Schreiber shows that imperial agendas and expressions of local agency both changed markedly over time. Equally important, Schreiber's comparative regional analysis demonstrates that the form, function, purpose, and constituent population of Wari colonies varied significantly between the Nasca region on the Peruvian south coast with the Sondondo Valley of the central highlands. Wari colonies were founded for administrative purposes, for military control over the local population, for specialized resource procurement (coca production), and even as a way to transform the indigenous ritual landscape into one centered on Wari religious ideologies. This variation in imperial colonial strategies was greatly affected by the nature of the local groups in the conquered areas, notably their degree of sociocultural complexity and capacity for resistance.

Terence N. D'Altroy presents a detailed analysis of the Inka *mitmaqkuna* system of forced resettlement and colonization. Like the historically known Neo-Assyrian Empire of the first millennium B.C. in the Near East, the Inka Empire used mass deportations and resettlement of conquered peoples as a fundamental tool of statecraft, economic organization, and imperial control. The scale of this process was staggering, even by modern standards; the Inka Empire resettled an estimated three to five million people out of a total population of ten to twelve million. Entire provinces or towns of colonists called mitmaqkuna were relocated to new areas, sometimes as far as 2,000 kilometers away from their original homelands. The Inka organized these mass resettlements for two reasons: to disperse groups who posed a threat of rebellion, and to create settlements of economic specialists whose productive output was controlled by the state. By isolating these groups within larger local populations, the Inka insured their loyalty to the state and minimized potential resistance. One of D'Altroy's most significant observations is that Inka administrators were well aware of identity politics and its material correlates; to insure the social isolation and dependence of the colonists, the Inka required mitmaqkuna colonists to retain their traditional, ethnically distinct styles of clothing, and they required them to retain their "official" residential affiliation with their homeland, regardless of their actual place of (forced) residence. D'Altroy's chapter also provides us with a sobering reminder of the limitations of archaeological data in that, despite its astounding scale, the mitmaqkuna system is known only from historical documents. Communities of this sort can only be recognized by the presence of Inka material culture, and not by any artifactual indicator of the ethnicity of the deported groups.

Susan E. Alcock examines the divergent developmental histories of two Roman imperial colonies in Greece (Corinth and Patras) and two in southwest Anatolia (Pisidian Antioch and Cremna). Her analysis reinforces the point that Roman colonial strategies and goals differed markedly by region and were in every case structured as much by local factors as by deliberate imperial strategies of political, economic, and military control. As in other case studies presented in this volume, the Roman colonies were multiethnic in character and highly stratified socially, with the result that they can in no way be treated as homogeneous communities. Alcock demonstrates that the organization and cultural identity of the inhabitants of these Roman colonies changed over time in regionally distinctive ways. In the case of Corinth and Patras, one can document the gradual reassertion of a Greek identity, while Pisidian Antioch and Cremna developed a more complex creolized identity in which a Roman colonial identity remained important, along with indigenous Anatolian and Hellenized aspects. Alcock emphasizes the contextually dependent nature of these new colonial identities, and the fact that their constituent elements were not mutually exclusive:

> Polyphonic identities, with different contexts determining choices made in self-presentation and cultural allegiance, would seem to have become the elite norm at this time, rather than any strict exclusivity between Greek and Roman positions.... These communities could see themselves, and sell themselves, as both Roman *coloniae* and Greek *poleis*, as context and need dictated (Alcock this volume).

The final chapter in this volume is J. Daniel Rogers's synthetic overview of some of the key theoretical issues in examining the archaeology of colonial encounters. Rogers emphasizes the importance of local agency, indigenous systems of meaning, and historical context for the understanding of these processes. Rogers argues for the utility of an essentially semiotic approach to material culture as a way to monitor those transformations of identity that play such a key role in colonial encounters. Rogers proposes that archaeologists can study the linkages between cultural memory, identity, and material culture by examining three kinds of sign structure: indexes, symbols, and signs. Each type of sign has a different temporal valence and set of linkages between object and identity. Thus, for example, icons refer to past time, while symbols are more forward looking due to their polysemic character. By deconstructing the symbolic aspects of material culture in this way, it becomes possible for archaeologists to monitor changes in the cultural coherence of a group, and in the processes through which new creolized/ hybridized identities emerge over the course of a colonial encounter.

EMERGING THEMES IN THE ARCHAEOLOGY OF COLONIAL ENCOUNTERS

The chapters in this volume present different case studies from at least ten different colonial encounters in the Old and New Worlds. They include not only "canonical" cases of colonization by Greece, Rome, and Europe, but also non-Western, precapitalist, and even prehistoric colonial episodes. The authors are unanimous in emphasizing the astonishing degree of variability in colonial organization, and consequently all reject the utility of colonial typologies as tools for research.

Instead, all emphasize the importance of following historically situated analyses of the key *processes* involved in colonial encounters. Though rejecting globalizing frameworks such as world-systems theory, the contributors to this volume all see great value in comparative analyses that still recognize the unique character of specific culture histories. The case studies and theoretical overviews presented here emphasize a number of shared perspectives. I outline below some of the themes that I believe to be the most significant for current and future research on the comparative archaeology of colonial encounters.

1. *The problematic nature of the term "colonialism" and its intellectual baggage.* Most of the contributors to this volume agree on the need to disentangle the concept of colonies from that of colonialism. Dietler (this volume) defines colonialism as "the projects and practices of control marshaled in interactions between societies linked in asymmetrical relations of power, and the processes of social and cultural transformation resulting from those practices." It is thus a form of unequal social relations between polities and entails the idea of political, military, and/or economic dominance by intrusive foreign groups over local populations (Osterhammel 1997:4). However, colonialism is not just an abstract concept; it is embedded in a culturally specific historical experience. In Western thought, the central defining case of colonialism is the expansion of early capitalist Europe to extend its control over the Americas, Africa, South Asia, and Southeast Asia from the sixteenth through the mid-twentieth century. The connection between colonialism and the last four centuries of Western history is so deeply rooted that a number of scholars in different disciplines have argued that the European colonial encounter continues to structure not only Western intellectual conceptions of other cultures (including the discipline of anthropology and the culture concept; Dirks 1992:3), but even the West's very definition of itself as a distinct entity (Said 1978). Colonialism is inextricably bound up with notions drawn from the European experience, such as "domination of an alien minority, asserting racial and cultural superiority, over a materially inferior native majority; contact between

a machine oriented civilization with Christian origins, a powerful economy, and a rapid rhythm of life and a non-Christian civilization that lacks machines and is marked by a backward
economy and a slow rhythm of life; and the imposition of the
first civilization upon the second" (Emerson and Fieldhouse
1968:1; see also Balandier 1951:75).

We can only start to develop a more synthetic archaeology of
colonial encounters by bringing non-Western and precapitalist
colonial networks into our comparative analyses in a way that
does not assume a priori colonial dominance of the recent
European kind. At the same time, we must examine the
colonies themselves, their homelands, and the indigenous host
communities as the three main institutional actors whose interaction defines a colonial network.

2. *The myth of the colonizer-colonized dichotomy.* The chapters by
Lightfoot, Schreiber, van Dommelen, and Alcock show clearly
that traditional analyses have vastly oversimplified a complex
reality by treating colonial encounters as a simple dichotomy
between "the colonizers" and "the colonized" (see also Stoler
1989). At a minimum, the colonial encounter should be treated
as having three nodes: (1) the colonial homeland or metropole,
(2) the colonies themselves, and (3) the indigenous societies
in whose midst the colonies are established. One recurring
pattern is that of a rapid divergence between the interests and
agendas of the metropole and its colonies. It is important to
emphasize that while the political and economic interests of
colonies may rapidly split off from those of the metropole, at
the same time colonists often emphasize (sometimes hyper-
trophically) their cultural ties to the homeland in order to
assert a distinct, superior identity in their interactions with
indigenous groups. Each of the three nodes in the colonial
encounter is best understood as having a heterogeneous composition. As van Dommelen (this volume) notes, "By ignoring
the much more nuanced and complicated social and economic
divisions at the grassroots level, in which criteria such as gender,
age, and class intersect with the colonial-indigenous distinction,

dualist representations not only assert the dominant position of the colonizers, but they also overlook much of the social dynamics of a colonial situation."

Many, if not most, colonial encounters have been multiethnic entanglements in which "the colonizers" consisted of several distinct cultures, with differing identities, power structures, value systems, and agendas. At the same time, the local "colonized" node emerges as a multifaceted congeries of distinct, often conflicting ethnicities.

3. *Problematic comparisons with the Classical world and the European expansion.* Michael Dietler's chapter in this volume forcefully reminds us of the degree to which the pervasive influence of Rome and Greece on Western thought leads many archaeologists to develop anachronistic interpretations of ancient colonial encounters. Similarly, D'Altroy (this volume) notes, "A more subtle bias also pervades the study of ancient colonies— namely, the deference paid to intellectual traditions whose motivations and practices are expressed through documents.... [W]e need to be wary of systematically interpreting past colonization through Rome-colored glasses."

It is particularly important to proceed with caution when considering precapitalist and/or non-Western colonial encounters in the light of the European expansion in the "Age of Discovery." As Lightfoot (this volume) points out, a consideration of European colonial practices can be useful for understanding similarities and differences in colonial ideologies, dominance structures, political strategies, interethnic relationships, and local ("native") agency.

However, at the same time, we must recall that the European expansion into the Americas certainly differed from other colonial encounters due to historically unique factors such as (1) the tremendous technological differences between the Europeans and indigenous peoples, (2) the biological vulnerability of the indigenous peoples of the Americas to Old World pathogens, and (3) the vast difference in cultural traditions and religious ideologies between the Europeans and their native

American counterparts. If precapitalist situations are so different that we cannot uncritically apply concepts drawn from the European expansion, then is it still possible to undertake a comparative study of ancient/historic colonial encounters?

The risks of comparison are compounded by the fact that much of the existing literature on the archaeology of colonialism tends to oversimplify European colonialism into a single homogeneous model. As the papers by Lightfoot, Gasco, and Rogers all demonstrate, there existed tremendous variation in European colonial practices, power relations, and modes of interaction with native peoples. These contrasts existed not only between the colonial enterprises of different colonizing polities such as Spain, Portugal, England, France, Russia, and the Netherlands, but also *within* the colonial policies of these states, depending on the areas they colonized and the specific cultures with whom they interacted. To paraphrase the aphorism of American political life, all colonization is local.

Thus one cannot uncritically apply a single unitary model of European colonialism to the archaeological record. Conversely, we should not automatically assume that comparisons with European colonialism(s) have nothing to tell us about precapitalist and/or non-Western colonial encounters. As Gasco observes (this volume), "The comparative study of colonies, colonization, and colonialism should be designed precisely to sidestep these assumptions and explore in a systematic way how and why ancient and more recent colonial situations are similar and different."

4. *Colonial encounters engender the development of new forms of cultural identity.* Closely related to the need to reject the dualistic oversimplification of the "colonizer-colonized" dichotomy are two key processes that must be taken into account in the analysis of colonial encounters: the mutability of identity, and the common, if not universal, process of *new* identity formation in the course of long-term colonial interaction. Anthropologists and archaeologists have long recognized the importance of these processes but have always analyzed them through the use of

unidirectional, core-dominant models such as acculturation theory (for a history and critique of the acculturation concept, see Cusick 1989b; for Classical archaeologists' models of "Hellenization" and "Romanization," see critiques by Dietler and Alcock, both this volume).

A number of convergent, alternative understandings have allowed researchers to develop a more nuanced, realistic understanding of the transformations of identity in colonial encounters. Instead of acculturation, anthropologists have begun to examine the idea of transculturation or ethnogenesis (Deagan 1998), the linguistically derived concept of creolization (Hannerz 1987), and the concept of hybridity, drawn from postcolonial theory (Bhabha 1992). All three related concepts focus on the idea of new, composite identities that emerge as negotiated outcomes in which local agency and colonial structures play important creative roles. Van Dommelen (this volume) argues for shifting the analytical emphasis from hybridity (as an outcome) to *hybridization* as a dynamic process through which new identities are negotiated: "Studying hybridization suggests a different perspective on the colonizers, emphasizing, on the one hand, the local roots and local interests of at least part of the colonial community while, on the other hand, also acknowledging their extraregional involvement in a colonial network." The key shared element in all three alternative concepts is the emphasis on local agency, rather than seeing indigenous peoples as passive recipients of these changes. These concepts have direct archaeological implications in allowing us to better understand the cultural meanings associated with the selective appropriation and fusion of different material culture styles in colonial encounters.

5. *Variation in the "colonial programs" of colonizing polities.* The case studies presented by Schreiber, D'Altroy, Lightfoot, Gasco, and Alcock all agree in showing that colonizing polities—especially empires—showed great variability in their colonial programs, depending on the specific local contexts in which a given colony was established. This variation reflects not only the importance of homeland ideologies in structuring what

Schreiber calls "imperial agendas," but also represents a composite, negotiated outcome of interaction, accommodation, and resistance by the local groups in any given colonial encounter. It is noteworthy that this variation was not just characteristic of the various European colonizing powers of the Age of Discovery, but also applied to precapitalist or non-Western empires such as Rome, Wari, or the Inka.

6. *The need to focus on variation in modes of interaction, rather than on colonial "types."* Lightfoot (this volume) represents the unanimous view of the contributors to this volume when he states that "given the tremendous range of variation in colonial programs…we do great injustice to the study of cross-cultural variation by attempting to pigeonhole our case studies into a few discrete colonial types." Instead, we should focus on understanding the contextually dependent variation in the modes of interaction (at the macro scale) and in the processes of identity transformation (at the micro scale) over the course of a colonial encounter.

7. *The non-universality of world-systems theory.* For the last twenty-five years, world-systems theory (Wallerstein 1974; Hall and Chase-Dunn 1993; Kardulias 1999) has played a dominant role in anthropological/archaeological theories of interregional interaction systems, including colonial encounters. The attraction of this construct derives from its claims to cross-cultural applicability as an explanatory model. However, as Dietler (this volume) notes, "World-systems models exhibit a tendency toward mechanistically reductionist, structurally overdetermined, functionalist explanations and an emphasis on core determination of process in the periphery. They are unable to accommodate culture or local agency and, in their uniformity, they deny the fundamental historicity of colonialism." This theoretical problem is further compounded by evidentiary biases. An overreliance on textual data tends to privilege core agency, since the core, not the periphery, writes the histories. Even though recent research has argued that world-systems theory is not universally applicable (see, for example, Dietler 1998; Gasco this volume; Stein 1998, 1999b), we should not reject the idea of cross-cultural

comparison altogether. Other comparative models have explanatory utility, such as Abner Cohen's trade diaspora model (see, for example, Spence this volume) or Homi Bhabha's hybridity concept (see van Dommelen this volume). As Gasco notes, the key element that needs to be included in comparisons of this sort is the recognition of the importance of local agency and local systems of meaning as crucial factors structuring interaction and trajectories of change. The papers in this volume show that one can still see recurring commonalities in colonial practices, modes of interaction, and the dynamics of changing identity, without recourse to either the classic or more recent reformulations of the world-systems model.

8. *Colonial interactions change over time.* Colonial encounters and their organization are not static. As the chapters by Schreiber, Alcock, and van Dommelen demonstrate, colonial encounters show marked diachronic change in colonial agendas, political economy, cultural identities, and above all, in power relations. It is a mistake to regard inherently unstable, changeable modes of interaction as if they were temporally invariant. Quite often, our perceptions of a given colonial case are skewed by our tendency to project our understanding of the later stages of the sequence onto the earlier phases of the encounter. As a result, researchers often impute major power asymmetries onto the initial structure of interaction, which might have been far more evenly balanced (Dietler 1998:298). Conversely, as Alcock shows in her comparative analysis of four Roman imperial colonies, strong imperial control over colonies was often subverted over time by the local realities of geopolitics and indigenous cultural identity.

9. *The importance of local agency.* In rejecting the determinative role of colonizers and colonialism, we necessarily must recognize the importance of the other social actors in this arena of interaction. The case studies in this volume are unanimous in stressing the importance of local agency in structuring the dynamics and historical trajectories of colonial encounters. As Rogers (this volume) points out, "Native cultural logics and percep-

tions of events play an essential role in how interactions have been structured." The case studies presented here provide numerous examples of the ways in which local decision making, local power structures, and local cultural schemes repeatedly modified and even subverted colonial agendas, so that the outcome was in almost every case composite, heterogeneous, and negotiated rather than predetermined. The correlates of this interaction can be seen in the emergence of new, creolized or hybridized identities, artifactual styles, and forms of social organization—all phenomena that can be studied in the archaeological record.

Taken together, the data, theoretical perspectives, and areas of debate and consensus that emerge from the chapters in this volume present a cross-sectional view of promising current approaches to the study of ancient colonial encounters. The sheer complexity, contextual contingency, and degree of diachronic variation in the organization of colonies and their interacting groups make any effort at comparative analysis daunting indeed. However, the analyses presented here are surprisingly consistent and complementary in the approaches they suggest as the most useful ways to investigate the problem. More than anything else, these comparative studies show the significance of this topic for anthropological research, and the nuanced complexity of this ancient and recurring process of cultural interaction and transformation.

2

The Archaeology of Colonization and the Colonization of Archaeology

Theoretical Challenges from an Ancient Mediterranean Colonial Encounter

Michael Dietler

"Let each man be a Greek in his way! But let him be one," implored Goethe at the dawn of the nineteenth century. A couple of generations later, the prolific British man-of-letters John Addington Symonds insisted that "All civilized nations, in all that concerns the activity of the intellect, are colonies of Hellas" (1880:401). Similarly, in the mid twentieth century, at the twilight of the British Empire, the classicist Gilbert Murray wistfully asserted that "the continent of Europe has been our modern Hellas....And surely we may without self-flattery claim that in the high civilisation which Europe has inherited and passed on to her kindred across the oceans, is a Hellenism which the barbarian rejects but still longs to understand and assimilate" (1953:52–53). These quotations, which were chosen from hundreds of other possible examples echoing identical sentiments, serve admirably to introduce a paradox in the investigation of ancient colonial situations: undertaking an archaeology of colonization requires first understanding the colonization of archaeology. This problem is particularly acute in the study of the ancient Mediterranean, the region of my own research. However, the implications of this issue are by no means limited to this situation, but reverberate throughout the archaeology of colonies, colonization, and colonialism in general. Later discussion will make clearer the basis of this claim, as well as suggesting a few possibilities for dealing with some of the problems that inhere from this predicament.

But first things first. Let me begin by explaining what I mean by the "colonization of archaeology." This intentionally provocative trope encapsulates an extremely complex historical process explored in greater detail elsewhere (Dietler n.d.). However, in brief, I am arguing, first, that the discursive foundations of modern European identity and colonialist ideology and practices were largely grounded in selective interpretations and interpolations of the texts of two *ancient* colonial powers: Greece and Rome. This curious appropriation produced a limited and doubly inflected representation of the ancient encounters engendered by Greco-Roman expansion. But what is more, because of the European etiological mythology of Greco-Roman cultural ancestry that developed out of the Renaissance and the resulting structures of "cultural capital" (Bourdieu 1984, 1990) that developed within the academy and European society in general, such perceptions have become part of the doxic, implicit foundations of Euro-American culture. This, of course, includes the academic discursive framework within which archaeology was constituted as a professional discipline. Hence, without a critical awareness of the complex referential loops involved in this process, archaeologists attempting to study ancient Greek and Roman colonialism (or, indeed, ancient colonialism in general) risk unconsciously imposing the attitudes and assumptions of ancient colonists, filtered and reconstituted through a modern interpolating prism of colonial ideology and experience and absorbed as part of the Western intellectual *habitus*, back onto the ancient situation. Ironically, this would constitute a kind of second colonization of the non-Greco-Roman peoples of the ancient Mediterranean, but one even more pervasive than the first in that all access to indigenous experience of the encounter would have been finally suppressed under a hegemonic interpretive discourse.

Consequently, this chapter first attempts to demonstrate and disentangle the complex recursive interrelationship that has developed between the prolonged colonial encounter initiated by Greeks and Romans in the ancient western Mediterranean and modern European culture and colonialism. In particular, it shows both how this *ancient* Mediterranean colonial situation came to exert such a profound influence in the construction of cultural capital and colonial ideologies in *modern* Europe and America, and how those features have had a pervasive reciprocal influence in structuring the teleological discourse of modern scholars engaged in the archaeological exploration of these (and many other) ancient colonial encounters. This analysis indicates that, given its role as the symbolic reservoir for modern colonial ideology, there is an especially pronounced need for critical analytical scrutiny of ancient Greek and Roman colonialism by archaeologists. However, it also suggests that it is impossible to evaluate and improve upon current understandings of this particular ancient colonial encounter (or others treated in this volume) without situating our approaches to the archaeology of colonialism within a simultaneous critical sociohistorical examination of the role that the ancient encounter played in both the development of modern European culture and the institutional context in which the discipline of archaeology has been formed. Circumventing the structural determinisms and naturalized teleological assumptions arising from this recursive relationship is by no means easy. However, the chapter also suggests how a focus on consumption, theoretically grounded in the anthropological literature of colonial and postcolonial studies, may provide a means for restoring agency and contingency to the archaeological analysis of colonialism and reasserting the fundamental historicity of the phenomena clustered under this rubric. Due to limitations of space, I have excluded all but a passing mention of the archaeological case in southern France that generated the largely theoretical discussion presented here and that illustrates its utility. Hence, those seeking further clarification must look elsewhere (see Dietler 1990b, 1997, 1998, 2004, n.d.).

RECURSIVE COLONIZATIONS, ANCIENT AND MODERN

Perhaps the most intriguing and consequential case of "invented traditions" in European history involved a sweeping "colonization" of modern consciousness by the ancient Greco-Roman world. This process was launched several centuries ago, and its evolving manifestations have been a pervasive feature of European culture ever since. The passages cited at the beginning of the chapter are illustrative of this curious cultural conquest of the present by the past, although many other examples easily could have been substituted to make this point (see Dietler 1995, n.d.). More important in the present context, however, is to examine the nature of, and reasons for, the historical development of this referential and reverential engagement with the ancient "classical" world and, especially, to reveal its connection to the intimate and problematic relationship between ancient and modern colonialisms that I posited above.

This issue is of particular concern in dealing, as my own research does, with the colonial encounter in the western Mediterranean during the Early Iron Age. That is because this encounter constitutes the seminal episode in the colonial process through which the indigenous peoples of the territories that would eventually spawn the dominant colonial powers of the modern world—France, England, Spain, Portugal, and Germany—first became entangled with the Greco-Roman world that would later come to play such an obsessional role in the collective ancestral imagination of these imperial nations. Hence, it is a moment of pregnant significance for modern discourses of imperialism and anti-imperialism. This feature also indicates both why there is such a pressing need for a critical archaeological reanalysis of this encounter and why situating that analysis from a position that attempts to dislodge the encounter from its discursively embedded context is simultaneously so desirable and difficult.

This modern infatuation with ancient Greece and Rome stems from a particular moment in European history, the so-called Renaissance of the fifteenth century, when a new myth of European cultural ancestry was constructed. Not coincidentally, this was a period that also witnessed the first phase of modern European colonization beyond the Mediterranean (Mignolo 1995; Quinn 1976).

Here, I am principally concerned to do several things. First, I examine the ways in which the development and embellishment of this ancestral myth was linked to the production of both a field of "cultural capital" (Bourdieu 1984, 1990) marshaled in processes of class differentiation within European societies and an imperialist discourse providing an ideological engine for European colonialism abroad. I then show how both of these closely interrelated features subtly have conditioned and constrained the interpretive perspectives of archaeologists engaged in the study of ancient Mediterranean colonialism and explain why it is so critical to "decolonize" our intellectual habitus, to the extent that this is possible. Finally, I briefly suggest an approach that points the way toward circumventing some of these vexing problems.

The Renaissance was not so much a "rebirth" as an invention, a self-conscious attempt to link the present directly to a long-dead and poorly understood period of the past by negating a millennium of intervening history and a wide variety of other cultural influences. As the movement began in Italy, it is not surprising that ancient Rome provided the initial ancestral "golden age" and that Roman culture was the first focus of adulation and emulation. The imperial legacy of Rome was not the least of its attractions that inspired imitation, and this movement rapidly spread to other parts of Europe as well, including especially France, Spain, and, eventually, England (Pagden 1995; Quinn 1976). Liberally reinterpreted visions of Roman culture inspired facsimiles and established the canons of taste in everything from architecture to literature, art, political philosophy, furniture and clothing styles, and gardens (for example, see Auslander 1996; Haskell and Penny 1981; Kostof 1995; Mukerji 1997). Some of these borrowings were deliberately historicist, while others were based upon supposed timeless, universal aesthetic principles that the classical world was believed to have distilled and codified. Latin was expanded and transformed from its monastic role as the language of the church to attain an even more elevated status as the universal language of secular rational intellectual discourse; and the works of Roman poets, orators, and historians were studied as stylistic models and sources of moral and philosophical inspiration. The lingering aura of prestige that Latin acquired during this time is reflected in the fact that most universities in the United States, thousands of years and miles away from any connection to ancient Rome, have Latin mottoes on their crests.

A widespread fascination with the ancient Greeks did not develop until several centuries after the debut of the Renaissance. It was not until the eighteenth century that the Greeks began their sudden rise from obscurity to the level of a pan-European cultural obsession and were retrieved from relegation to the decadent "Orient" to be rehabilitated as the quintessential ancestor of "the West." This dramatic transformation stemmed largely from a romantic humanist vision developed in Germany during the eighteenth century and especially popularized by a scholar named Johann Joachim Winckelmann (Butler 1935; Marchand 1996; Wohlleben 1992). This romantic aesthetic fixation on the Greeks originated partly as a reaction against the rationalist Enlightenment tradition of "Augustan" neoclassicism that had become particularly associated with France. Although Winckelmann never actually visited Greece, he became convinced through his reading and observation of art that "good taste...had its origin under the skies of Greece " (1987:3) and that ancient Greek culture represented the pinnacle of human development in the quest for universal standards of absolute beauty and truth. For Winckelmann, emulation of Greek culture, or what he rather imperfectly understood it to be, was almost a moral obligation. This version of passionate philhellenism, which Wohlleben (1992) has aptly labeled "Graecolatry" and "Graecomania," was adopted by Goethe, Schiller, Schlegel, and other influential German writers and intellectuals who came to believe that becoming Hellenized was the only possible path for someone seeking personal development (*Bildung*). Hence Goethe's dictum, "Let each man be a Greek in his way! But let him be one." This virulent strain of Graecomania soon infected France, England, and other countries as well (Webb 1982; Zuber 1992), leading to Shelley's famous battle cry of Romantic Hellenism in its waning days, "We are all Greeks" (Shelley 1822).

By the nineteenth century, the Greek colonization of modern European (and Euro-American) culture was at its apogee. Political philosophy, art, architecture, and education were permeated by appeals to the ancient Greeks (Grafton 1992; Jenkyns 1980; Marchand 1996; F. M. Turner 1981). Would-be Greek temples such as La Madeleine in Paris, the Altes Museum in Berlin, the British Museum in London, the Field Museum in Chicago, or the "Parthenon" in Nashville are impressive architectural testaments to the ideal of a monument thought to be uniquely expressive of "high culture" on both sides of the Atlantic during the nineteenth and early twentieth centuries. However, the kind of Hellenism that informed European life after the early nineteenth century was quite different from the Romantic Hellenism of Winckelmann and Shelley. As Marchand has noted for Germany, the earlier Graecophiles

> borrowed their ideals—self-cultivation, disinterested con-
> templation of the beautiful, good and true, admiration of

the ancients—from aristocratic models; but the incorporation of nineteenth-century philhellenism into the founding
of Prussia's new research universities, secondary schools,
museums, and art academies after 1810 universalized these
values and in effect imposed them on generations of mid-
dle-class Germans.... As the century progressed, philhellenism became more and more the conventionalized
predilection of the educated middle class (*Bildungsbürgertum*),
inextricably linked to the academy and state bureaucracy
(1996:xviii–xix).

Rome by no means disappeared as a cultural ancestor in the face of
this rampant Graecolatry. It still remained a powerful source of inspiration in terms of legal, institutional, and architectural models, and the
legacy of its imperial conquests continued to provide a standard of reference and ambition for modern European nations (Koebner and
Schmidt 1964; Vance 1997). But the relationship between the Greek
and Roman legacies was the subject of a broad range of complex, and
often contradictory, interpretations. The characteristics of the two civilizations were often contrasted, with the Greeks dominating a clear
hierarchy of cultural superiority and the Romans getting the nod for
military and administrative prowess. However, the best aspects of Rome
itself were often considered to be a product of its own Hellenization. As
Murray succinctly summarized this view, "Roman civilization, as it
became more perfect, became more Hellenic" (1953:13). Given that
Rome (or at least its ruling elite) had been heavily influenced by Greek
art, architecture, philosophy, and science, it was often seen to have
been actually carrying out a historic mission as a middleman in bringing the superior moral and intellectual enlightenment of Greek civilization to the "barbarians" it incorporated into its empire. Hence, the
European myth of cultural ancestry in the nineteenth century
enshrined both Greece and Rome as hallowed progenitors with complementary characteristics and roles.

The same processes of institutional embedding that Marchand
noted for nineteenth-century Germany were in operation in England
and France as well, albeit with variations appropriate to the different
political histories and educational systems of these nations. In all three
nations, a knowledge of, and a cultivated appreciation for, the "classics"

became a powerful form of "cultural capital," in the sense of Bourdieu (1984, 1990), by which members of the ruling class (now essentially the wealthy bourgeoisie) were able to embody and symbolically assert their cultural and moral superiority. Access to this specialized cultural competence was acquired in the universities and the institutions of secondary education that were available only to the privileged and that formed the elite class of each country: the English "public school" and the tellingly named German "*Gymnasium*" and French "*lycée*." The curricula of these schools tended to be heavily dominated by the study of Greek and Latin language, literature, and history, as contact with these idolized ancient civilizations was thought to have powerful transformative effects in the development of character and taste (Ringer 1979, 1992). As Gerard (1982:357) has remarked, the lycée student of the late nineteenth century was "a little citizen of the ancient classical world" who learned the history of his own country only as a brief episode in the history of Rome.

Likewise, as Bowen (1989) noted for England, the public schools were designed to fashion an elite ruling class that included both a remnant of the traditional aristocracy and a wealthy and powerful segment of the bourgeoisie. Their mission was to impart the traits of aristocracy to those who had not inherited them and to enhance the patina of superiority for those who had. "In the nineteenth century that had been the task of Hellenism; its content provided the appropriate ideology, while its vehicle, the Greek language, served an essential mystifying function, since the express purpose of arcane learning is to exercise domination over the uninitiated" (1989:183). Moreover, for the Victorian public school boy, in training for his role in ruling an empire, "intelligence mattered less than the acquisition of 'character,' and intellectual activity was largely restricted to otiose and repetitive exercises in the languages of two former imperial powers, Greece and Rome" (James 1994:206–7). The public schools took their lead in this obsessive focus on classical education from Oxford and Cambridge, the prestige universities of Victorian England, which the public schools were designed to service. The classics dominated the curricula of these universities, and admission to them depended upon having acquired the proper training in Greek and Latin.

To a certain extent, the hierarchical vision of the relationship between Greek and Roman culture noted earlier also came to reflect and reinforce finer class distinctions within the English bourgeoisie. At least a smattering of Latin was diffused more widely through the middle class via the grammar schools, whereas Greek continued to be the preserve of "expensively and extensively educated males" of the public schools (Vance 1997:15; see also Grafton 1992). In brief, knowledge of Greek was a prime source of cultural capital in the cultivation of diacritical "distinction" of the kind analyzed by Bourdieu (1984). The fashionable practice of the "grand tour" visit to the Mediterranean became, from the eighteenth century on, another important element in developing the cultural capital of classical cultivation, one that was available only to those wealthy enough to undertake such an expensive voyage to see the landscape and statuary of their classical "ancestors" (Constantine 1984; Fox 1978). As even that archtypically insular Englishman, Dr. Johnson, noted, "A man who has not been to Italy is always conscious of an inferiority" (quoted in Fox 1978:45).

The barriers to social mobility for those who were not in a position to acquire this cultural competence (that is, to become Romanized and, especially, Hellenized) were more than simply social conventions. They were also increasingly institutional. In France, Germany, and England during the nineteenth century, a knowledge of Greek and Latin was not only necessary to enter university, but the entrance examinations for the civil service all began to require a strong competence in these ancient languages (Bowen 1989; W. B. Cohen 1971; Marchand 1996). This feature also assured that politicians and upper-level administrators of the empires controlled by these countries all had in common the feature of having been steeped in the classics. From Bismarck to Gladstone, Napoléon III, and the graduates of the École Coloniale, they shared an exclusive common bond of tastes, values, and implicit cultural references lodged in esoteric access to an idolized and idealized ancient culture. The British prime minister, William Gladstone, for example, who wrote an influential book on Homeric Greece (Gladstone 1858), expressed a sentiment common to his class in stating, "The state of Athens at its climax, that is of human nature at its climax..." (quoted in Livingstone 1935:43).

Even if many elite schoolboys managed to acquire only a veneer of classical learning, their education provided them with (1) a conviction that the cultural ancestry of their own country lay in ancient Greece and Rome; (2) a belief in the inherent attractiveness and superiority of Greek "civilization" in an absolute, universal hierarchy of cultures; and (3) an assurance that the personal cultivation of Hellenized tastes that their schooling imparted was a sign of their own superiority and an appropriate diacritical mark of their class and its destiny to lead others. However, the legacy of the classics was not simply one of Bildung, of personal cultivation and the pursuit of beauty (and the embodiment of class distinction). From Athens to Alexander, Caesar, and Augustus, it was also a legacy of colonization and colonialism. This legacy was interpreted by each of the modern European states that saw itself as the legitimate heir to Greco-Roman civilization as a mandate to continue an inherited mission to "civilize" the "barbarian" world and as an ideological model for its own imperial practices.

An institutionalized infatuation with the ancient "classical" world was by no means confined to the European powers; it also had an influential role in those colonies that were settled by large, dominant European populations, such as the United States (Macarthur 1943; I. Morris 1994). Even a cursory reflection on the monumental architecture of the nation's capital city and the capitol buildings of most state governments, not to mention countless museums, courthouses, banks, and other major institutions, should be sufficient to appreciate the impact of Greco-Roman models in America. This pervasive phenomenon is to a large extent the result of a self-conscious attempt by the "classical class" of the former colonies, including especially Thomas Jefferson, to fashion an independent national taste that would express and inspire a sense of historical destiny for the new republic. Jefferson quite explicitly saw the newly independent United States as a new Greece developing in the wilderness of America, and he turned directly to ancient Athens and, especially, the Roman Republic for appropriate architectural models (Kostof 1995:624). Moreover, the rigidly geometric land-demarcation system imposed on the newly acquired territory west of the Appalachian Mountains bears an uncanny resemblance to the cadastration practices imperial Rome used to restructure the landscape of its colonies.

As this last example suggests, the multifarious roles that Greco-Roman colonialism played in the development of the discourse of modern imperialism and the practices of modern colonialism are difficult to overestimate. At the most basic level, it involved an axiomatic absorption of the fundamental Greco-Roman hierarchical dichotomization of the world into "civilized" societies and "barbarians," a perspective that would have far-reaching effects in the development of modern imperialism (and, as we shall see, in archaeological interpretive models). But the specific manifestations of the ideological relationship between ancient and modern colonialisms were both varied and pervasive.

Initially, from the fifteenth through the seventeenth centuries, Rome was the nearly exclusive source of imperial models. As Pagden has noted, "It was, above all, Rome which provided the ideologues of the colonial systems of Spain, Britain and France with the language and political models they required, for the *Imperium romanum* has always had a unique place in the political imagination of western Europe" (1995:11). Of course, the Italians also shared in this discursive project: Machiavelli's influential writings, for example, are permeated by advocacy of colonization on Roman models. In fact, ultimately, all the European empires made continual symbolic and discursive reference to the Roman Empire (Brunt 1965; Mattingly 1996; Pagden 1995; Quinn 1976; Seed 1995; Tulard 1997). However, this Roman legacy, known mostly through the ancient texts of writers such as Cicero, Polybius, Strabo, Caesar, Livy, Virgil, and Sallust, and the remnants of its monuments, was interpreted in an astonishing variety of ways. For example, Seed (1995) has demonstrated that, from the fifteenth through the seventeenth centuries, the major European colonial powers all based their "ceremonies of possession" in the New World, by which they claimed sovereignty over land and peoples, explicitly upon their understandings of ancient Roman practices, although these understandings were radically different in character from one another.

Greek colonization and imperial politics were also gradually incorporated into imperialist discourse and became particularly influential in Victorian England and Prussia: seeing themselves more as enlightened modern Athenians than Romans, the Athenian Empire of the fifth century B.C. became the analogy of choice (Jenkyns 1980; Marchand 1996:24). But the Romans also retained a very powerful role in imperialist discourse. This was especially true in France (for example, Napoléon III 1866), although the numerous books comparing the British and Roman Empires (for example, Bryce 1901; Cromer 1910;

Lucas 1912) attest to the allure of this legacy in England as well. Roman precedents and analogies also permeated debates in the British Parliament and in newspaper editorials (Brunt 1965; Vance 1997). Moreover, Rome also provided a source of models for the practices and vocabulary of colonialism. Such "investigative modalities" and technologies of control as the Roman colonial census, taxation, and cadastral land restructuration practices, as well as ethnographic surveys, all had their derivatives in, for example, British India (Cohn 1996). Greek and Roman colonial models were, in fact, both contrasted and combined in a variety of complex ways. Murray's opinion that "at home England is Greek, in the Empire she is Roman" (quoted in Jenkyns 1980:337) exemplifies some of these analogical complexities and paradoxes.

Whatever the relative Greek/Roman emphasis, what is strikingly clear is that ancient Greek and Roman versions of colonialism were seen as axiomatic points of reference for modern situations. As Livingstone noted, "These ages, with which we have spiritual affinities and which have anticipated our problems, have a special interest and instructiveness for us. They are our Doppelgänger. We recognize our faces in theirs" (1935:117–18). This was no less true in the matter of colonialism than in other aspects of life. Examples illustrating the pervasive and symbolically powerful operation of such analogies are innumerable, beginning most obviously with the adapted term of supreme rulership for the new "empires"—"Empéreur" for the Napoléons, "Kaiser" (Caesar) for the Prussian Wilhelm, "Empress of India" for Victoria, and Czar (Caesar) for the Russian court.

In France, modern imitations of triumphal arches built by the Romans to celebrate victories in their wars of conquest are found in cities ranging from Paris to Lyon and Marseille; and these were erected by governments as diverse as those of Louis XIV and Napoléon I to the Third Republic. Indeed, the recently constructed Grande Arche de la Défense in Paris is a modernist interpretation of this same tradition. According to Hautecoeur, Napoléon I insisted that public monuments "ought always to be in the style of the Romans. His empire ought to be the continuation of that Empire which spread from Egypt to the British Isles" (quoted in Ridley 1992). To further this project of symbolic association, Napoléon had himself portrayed in Roman garb as a bronze statue atop a monumental column in the center of the Place Vendôme, imitating precisely the Roman Emperor Trajan's Column at Rome.

A major aspect of this invocation of ancient empires was the representation of modern colonialism as the continuation of a civilizing mission that had been inherited from one's cultural ancestors. Colonization could thus be portrayed almost as an unavoidable altruistic duty imposed by history. This idea was often quite explicitly articulated, as in the French colonial doctrine of the *mission civilisatrice*. The English equivalent was Kipling's famous "white man's burden," which the classicist Gilbert Murray would refer to half a century later as "the fine work of the better colonial governments in performing their 'sacred trust'" (1953:59). This hierarchical classification of cultures was, of course, frequently undergirded by racist ideology, a prime example being Sir Francis Galton's (1869) scientistic scalar classification of the natural intellectual ability of various regional, national, and racial groups, in which "the negro" ranked several grades below the Englishman and ancient Athenians topped even the English.

I manifestly do not mean to imply in this brief and necessarily schematic discussion that the invocation of the classical past was a homogeneous phenomenon: on the contrary, it was richly riddled with complexities, contradictions, and controversies. As I suggested earlier, the character of the Greek and Roman legacy evolved considerably from its manifestations in the early Renaissance, through the Enlightenment, to the Romantic humanism of the eighteenth century and its bourgeois bureaucratic incarnation in the nineteenth and twentieth centuries. Moreover, within each of these periods, Greek and Roman precedents were selectively marshaled to argue all sides of a given philosophical or political issue. They were invoked both as a self-satisfied endorsement of the status quo and as a critical appeal for reform (as, for example, in the famous debate between the "Ancients and Moderns" in France: Perrault 1979). Nor can the invocation of the Greco-Roman past be reduced simply to a cynical manipulation to rationalize imperial ambition and greed. In fact, Roman and Greek antecedents were often invoked to criticize current imperial policies and practices as much as to justify them (for example, Hobson 1902). But what was common to all sides of these debates was a fundamental implicit acceptance of the direct relevance of ancient Greco-Roman colonialism to modern cases, and the assumption of a common "Western" cultural heritage in the civilizations of ancient Greece and Rome. There was, in other words, a shared discourse that implicitly defined the terms of discussion by shaping the boundary between the taken-for-granted and the unthinkable.

The overtly hegemonic grip of the classics on European culture has gradually diminished in the wake of the sundering of the Victorian world produced by the catastrophic trauma of the First World War. Indeed, it has been said that Hellenism died on the battlefields of Flanders (Bowen 1989:183). Rather, I would suggest that, although it was perhaps mortally wounded, this death has been a long and slow affair. It is true that "classics" departments now occupy more the intellectual periphery than the center of European and American universities; but they still vastly outnumber those dedicated to the study of any other ancient culture; and, indeed, no university feels complete without one (contrast this situation with, for example, departments of Celtic studies). Moreover, the privileged status of classical scholarship within academia persisted even more strongly in some countries than it did in the anglophone world—the prime examples being Germany and France (Marchand 1996; Ringer 1979). But even in the anglophone academic world, our common operational vocabulary and specialist jargons are still permeated by terms (colloquium, symposium, syllabus, anthropology, archaeology, etcera,...) that derive from and subtly reinforce an implicit hierarchy of valuation in which terms of Greek or Roman origin (preferably hybrids of the two for neologisms) have greater symbolic capital than their Anglo-Saxon analogs. Interestingly, this phenomenon seems to be at least as characteristic (if not more so) of postcolonial scholars, whose manifest political project involves challenging the hegemony of the classical cannon, as it is of defenders of the centrality of "Western civilization."

What is more, although the field has been changing rapidly, within classics departments generally there are still deeply entrenched conservative Hellenist perspectives (involving hierarchical assumptions about ancient cultures) and disciplinary practices that have influenced and constrained the exploration of the classical past in subtle and not-so-subtle ways (Dyson 1989; Hingley 1994; Marchand 1996; I. Morris 1994; Shanks 1995; van Dommelen 1998). Finally, although it is clear that cultural capital within the academy and in society at large no longer is linked to an ability to read Greek, nevertheless the myth of cultural ancestry created in the Renaissance and the hierarchies of cultural superiority engendered by this tradition have persisted as a profoundly embedded, implicit part of popular consciousness. Although an overt concern with the classics is now the preoccupation of only a relatively small body of academic specialists, many of the tenets of the Renaissance, Enlightenment, Romantic, and Victorian engagements with the Romans and Greeks have been absorbed subtly, as implicit unarticulated attitudes, into the consciousness of people who know and care little about ancient history. They have become a taken-for-granted part of a popular habitus that operates at the level of unquestioned assumptions about the "natural" order of things, a kind of discursive landscape of the axiomatic in which we live.

Goudineau's (admittedly informal) recent survey shows, for example, how persistent the ideology of the civilizing mission of colonization and the cultural hierarchy of "civilization" and "barbarians" that informed Napoléon III's interpretation of the Roman conquest of Gaul (see Dietler 1994) have been, even among well-educated French people in the postcolonial era. More than 85 percent of those he interviewed considered the Roman conquest of Gaul to have been "beneficial," and almost 60 percent thought of it as "a model to reproduce." Almost 70 percent of those who considered it positively did so because it was responsible for bringing "civilization" (Goudineau 1990:17–18).

I would suggest that this subterranean groundwater of Graecolatry and Romanophilia is what lies behind the angst and heated conservative resistance to multiculturalist challenges to the central place of courses on the "foundations of Western civilization" (understood essentially as the heritage of Greeks and Romans rather than, for example, the equally plausible Celts, Iberians, Germans, Phoenicians, and so on) in the curricula of American universities. The recent book by Hanson and Heath (1998), which combines a nostalgic call for a kind of neo-*Bildung* Hellenism with a bilious harangue against those recent scholars who have dared to view the Greeks as simply another interesting ancient society worthy of critical analysis rather than as the deified Western ancestor, emphatically underscores the emotional weight that this assumption of cultural superiority still carries in many quarters.

TOWARD A REFLEXIVE ARCHAEOLOGY OF THE COLONIAL

Given this deeply embedded "colonization" of modern European consciousness by the classical world, what implications does it have for the central problem addressed in this volume—the archaeology of colonization and colonialism—and, most particularly, for my own research investigating the colonial encounter in Iron Age France? The answer is both complex and subtle, and it can best be at least suggestively revealed in the following critique of interpretive models that have guided research on this latter colonial situation. But one of the most obvious points that can be made at this stage is that archaeologists, and the discipline of archaeology, have also been formed within this broader discursive field. Indeed, archaeology (particularly the archaeology that deals with this episode of colonialism) developed as a professional discipline largely as a result of the antiquarian desire stimulated by this infatuation with the ancient classical world, and it has been frequently implicated in the concomitant process of modern colonialism (Marchand 1996; I. Morris 1994; Schnapp 1996). The museums of northern Europe and North America are now filled with treasures of Greek and Roman sculpture, architecture, bronzework, and ceramics as a result of the acquisitive urge that motivated the development of archaeology as a means of bringing back the tangible relics of an ancestral past; and the archaeology of Rome, for example, was born of Napoléon's conquest of Italy and his obsession with its colonial legacy (Ridley 1992). These objects, in turn, have formed the basis for the development of connoisseurship, one of the forms of "distinction" (Bourdieu 1984) that became an important element of the cultural capital of cultivated tastes. It is also clear that archaeology, as a European invention exported to the colonies, frequently served as one of the cultural techniques of domination by which the pasts of colonized societies were defined, systematized, and controlled (Anderson 1991; Cohn 1987, 1996; Guha 1997; Said 1978). Hence, ultimately, we need to think not only about the archaeology of colonization and the colonization of archaeology, but also about archaeology as colonialism. That, however, is a dimension that space demands be left to other venues (for example, see Abu El-Haj 1998, 2001, Dietler n.d.; Holl 1990; Trigger 1984) in order to return to the main theme of this chapter.

It is important to emphasize that the previous discussion is decidedly not intended as an indictment of classicists, nor to imply that archaeologists are unreflective products of a single, uniform hegemonic discourse, or that archaeology as a discipline has been a static instrument of such a discourse in any simple, straightforward way. Rather, what I wished to indicate is that an understanding of the practice of archaeology requires that it be clearly situated within the evolving cultural history of its institutional landscape and practices.

In the current context, I have suggested that the intimate entanglement of ancient and modern colonial situations presents some severe challenges to archaeologists attempting the crucial work of reexamining and understanding ancient cases. Fusions of vocabulary, for example, have sometimes led to the unconscious imposition of anachronistic motivations and structures stemming from modern colonialism onto the past, as in the treatment of trade in the ancient Mediterranean in terms that derive from the competitive nationalist colonial projects of the nineteenth century (for example, Dunbabin 1948) or, as I will argue later, in the application of world-systems models. What is crucial is the constant questioning of our implicit assumptions and their discursive bases, because these have a great influence in conditioning research goals, interpretation, and evaluation of knowledge claims. Such assumptions may, for example, preclude the asking of certain questions, and they may create uneven standards of plausibility for interpretations. I am not advocating that this be carried to the level of "epistemological hypochondria" that was common in much recent postmodern criticism, but the dangers evident in the palimpsest of colonialisms revealed earlier should require a high degree of vigilance, especially in the case of Greek and Roman colonialism.

Having explained at some length why I feel the archaeology of colonial encounters in the ancient Mediterranean (my own field) is both necessary and difficult, it is also important to say a few words about the value and feasibility of an "archaeology of colonialism" more generally. Why is such an obviously difficult project a worthwhile endeavor at all? And what can archaeology contribute to the broader anthropological and historical investigation of colonialism? The answer to the first question is, I think, fairly easy. Colonialism has been implicated frequently as one of the most significant forces in world history. It has been estimated that, by the early decades of the twentieth century, one-half of the surface of the earth's continents was under some form of colonial domination, and about two-fifths of the population of the world (more than 600 million people) were living under colonial rule (Girault 1921, cited in Osterhammel 1997:25). Few scholars would seriously contend that it is possible to understand the state of the current "postcolonial" world, as well as its various forms of cultural and economic "neocolonialism," without reference to this historical legacy of colonialism. Most would also agree that such understanding requires a comparative exploration of the enormous range of strategies and practices employed in the effort to exert control over other societies around the world and the myriad repercussions of those practices, including forms of resistance.

The discipline of archaeology can contribute to this project in several ways. In the first place, it can aid in understanding the expansion of the Euro-American capitalist "world system" that, from the sixteenth century on, was responsible for the most extensive implementation of colonialism in world history (Braudel 1984; Ferro 1997; Wallerstein 1974; Wolf 1982). It can do this by furnishing kinds of evidence that are qualitatively different from and independent of the colonial texts that constitute the vast bulk of evidence available to historians. Because most colonial powers were literate and most subjects of colonial domination were not (at least originally), the textual evidence for such encounters tends to be highly partial, in both senses of the term. What archaeology offers is access to the *material dimension* of the encounter and to the processes of daily life through which the colonial situation was experienced and worked out by ordinary people. This is by no means a straightforward or unmediated window of access to an indigenous perception of the colonial situation: archaeologists practice an interpretive discipline that has many serious problems with data and epistemology that limit the range and quality of the information they can generate. However, even within cultural anthropology and history, a new appreciation of the significance of material culture in colonial processes has been growing recently (for example, see Comaroff and Comaroff 1991, 1997; Howes 1996; N. Thomas 1991; Turgeon 1998; Turgeon, Delâge, and Ouellet 1996), and this promises new possibilities for fruitful synergistic collaboration with archaeologists in the investigation of colonial history.

Perhaps an even more important contribution of archaeology to the study of colonialism derives from the fact that it is the primary conduit to ancient, precapitalist colonial encounters, for which relevant contemporary texts are far more limited or absent. As noted earlier, understanding colonialism in the encounters generated by the historically recent development of Euro-American capitalist expansion requires that they be set in comparative perspective through examination of the historical dynamics of many different contexts. It is especially necessary to examine the many colonial situations that predate Euro-American colonialism in order to ascertain both the singular and more widely shared features of this already diverse set of recent phenomena that has generated most of our anthropological theory on colonial interaction, as well as to understand its genesis. Without recourse to archaeological data, such fundamental issues could only be subject to speculative surmises.

Archaeological studies of colonialism should also serve to counter an occasional tendency toward temporal myopia among cultural anthropologists and historians for whom modern Euro-American colonialism sometimes seems the only game in town. Although the huge geographical extent of capitalist expansion is undeniable, it is well to recall that, for example, the Roman Empire lasted far longer than any modern empire and, in many ways, its colonial practices had even more profound cultural and social consequences than more recent examples (for instance, in terms of linguistic replacement). Moreover, one frequently cringes to hear certain technologies of control or aspects of colonial practice naively attributed to a unique origin in the logic of capitalism, when they were, in fact, a feature of much earlier colonial systems. As should be clear from the earlier discussion, most of the nineteenth-century European colonial administrators who were responsible for devising and implementing these practices were far more intimately familiar with the history of Greek and Roman colonialism than are many current scholars of colonialism and postcoloniality, and they were acutely aware of the prior origin of the practices they were trying to replicate or adapt. In this vein, it is also relevant to note that the late twentieth century is by no means the first experience of a postcolonial moment in world history. The ancient world had many such episodes (ironically, for reasons that should now be obvious, these have often been referred to as "dark ages").

COLONIZATION, COLONIALISM, IMPERIALISM

At this point, it is also necessary to introduce a brief parenthetical discussion of terminology. Specifically, I want to make clear the senses in which I employ the intersecting terms "colonization," "colonialism," and "imperialism." I raise this issue not out of a pedantic concern to establish a semantic orthodoxy, nor to indulge the kind of typological fetishism for which archaeologists are renowned. Rather, the issue is of concern for two reasons. First, these are all terms about which there is general consensus regarding their importance, yet little agreement about their precise definition. A perusal of even a small sample of the extensive relevant literature (for example, Bartel 1985; D'Altroy 1992; Ferro 1997; Fieldhouse 1981; Finley 1976; Garnsey and Whittaker 1978; Hovarth 1972; Klor de Alva 1995; Koebner and Schmidt 1964; T. Mitchell 1988; Osterhammel 1997; Said 1993; Schreiber 1992; van Dommelen 1998; R. J. C. Young 2001) reveals a wide variety of often-contradictory ways in which the terms are used and in the ways their meanings are seen to intersect or overlap (see Dietler n.d.). Secondly, this issue of terminology serves as a striking initial example of the subtle complexities of the problematic relationship between ancient and modern colonial situations noted earlier. This is because, in fact, most of our modern analytical vocabulary for treating such phenomena derives precisely from this ancient Mediterranean colonial encounter (as did a good part of the operational vocabulary of modern colonialism). For example, the terms "colonization," "colonialism," "colonial," and "colony" all derive from the Latin word *colonia*, and "imperialism" and "empire" stem from the Latin *imperium*. However, the meanings of these words have been significantly transformed as they have been applied over the centuries to a variety of modern contexts and processes (see Finley 1976; Koebner and Schmidt 1964; Pagden 1995). Reapplying them uncritically to the seminal ancient context poses the danger of importing modern meanings back to the past and implicitly rendering the ancient cases simply as variants, or prototypes, of the modern. As should be clear from the earlier discussion, this was precisely the ideology responsible for the original application of these words to modern situations. But Roman "colonies" were not the same thing as nineteenth-century French or British colonies, and it is an analytically crucial move to recognize and make explicit that what has been terminologically constructed as metonymy is actually metaphor.

As postcolonial critics have been especially instrumental in emphasizing, this is not a trivial problem. R. J. C. Young, for example, has noted that "all perspectives on colonialism share and have to deal with a common discursive medium which was also that of colonialism itself: the language used to enact, enforce, describe or analyse colonialism is not transparent, innocent, ahistorical or simply instrumental" (1995:163). As he further emphasized, a failure to challenge the way that colonialism has involved (in addition to its military and economic instruments of control) a permeation of knowledge, risks attempting to understand colonialism through its own discursive products.

Overcoming the problems posed by this terminological palimpsest is not easy, but it is quite important. The strategy frequently employed by cultural anthropologists to signal cultural and historical distinctiveness—that is, using indigenous terms in place of translating them into subsuming "etic" analytical categories—has, by and large, been precluded in the current case precisely because those terms have already been coopted and integrated into our analytical discourse with interpolated semantic content. Moreover, the idea of linguistic reform—of inventing and imposing upon the reader a new analytic vocabulary to deal with ancient cases that avoids all Greco-Roman terms already incorporated into modern discourse—seems a cumbersome and quixotic endeavor at best: the intellectual equivalent of spitting into the wind. Rather, I would suggest that, although we are condemned to pragmatically continue to employ the terms current in the discourse of colonial analysis, we must maintain a self-conscious wariness of the traps of implicit fusion and the dangers of anachronism. Whatever imperfect vocabulary one ultimately decides to employ, vigilant attention must be paid to differences as well as similarities in the colonial contexts and processes that are clustered semantically.

In the face of the terminological disaccord noted earlier, my own pragmatic preference is to reserve the word "imperialism" to indicate an ideology or discourse that motivates and legitimizes practices of expansionary domination by one society over another (what might equally be called "colonial discourse"). The term "colonization" is problematic because it is frequently used to mean the act of establishing "colonies," but in (at least) two very different senses that correspond to two historically different meanings of the word "colony": that is, either a settlement of foreigners established in the territory of others or a subject province ruled by an alien power. Among various potential solutions to this confusion, I choose to use "colonization" to indicate the act of imposing political domination over foreign territory and people, and "founding colonies" to denote the act of establishing new settlements in alien lands. This also implies that I use the word "colony" in a sense that is both narrower than its nineteenth- and twentieth-century usage and broader than its original Latin meaning. "Colony," as used here, encompasses the Greek term *apoikia* and the Latin *colonia* (both originally implied the founding of a settlement in foreign territory, but with quite different relations of dependency within different structurations of the political economy: see A. J. Graham 1964). I use "colonial province" to designate a subject territory that is the product of colonization.

Finally, by "colonialism" I mean the projects and practices of control marshaled in interactions between societies linked in asymmetrical relations of power, and the processes of social and cultural transformation resulting from those practices. Hence, colonization is, ultimately, solidified or maintained through colonialism; but colonialism can also operate without the formal political subjugation of foreign territories that colonization implies. Or it may precede an eventual colonization. The nature and effectiveness of such practices defined as colonialism, and their potential permutations, may be extremely variable from one context to another, ranging from such things as trade, to missionary activities, warfare and raiding, political administration, and education. Similarly, the processes of transformation are highly variable, and they always entail a host of unintended consequences for both indigenous peoples and alien colonists. Both parties eventually become something other than they were because of these processes of entanglement and their unintended consequences.

These definitions of colonization and colonialism are sufficiently broad ones that they cannot be considered analytically precise categorical tools used to demarcate a uniform process or a reified transhistorical phenomenon explicable within a single "theory of colonialism." Indeed, I am in agreement with the growing body of scholars who voice skepticism that such a project is possible (for example, J. L. Comaroff 1997; Cooper and Stoler 1997; Dirks 1992; N. Thomas 1994). Rather, in the sense used here, these terms are pragmatically general (and inherently plural) rubrics employed to focus critical attention and facilitate the comparative discussion and analysis of a range of practices and strategies by which peoples try to make subjects of other peoples in a variety of disparate historical situations, and the complex transformations occasioned by those practices, in the effort to better understand both the similarities and differences in these processes through history.

HELLENIZATION AND WORLD SYSTEMS: SHARED INADEQUACIES

To illustrate some of the ramifications of the previous discussion, let me briefly turn to an examination of two interpretive perspectives that have tended to dominate archaeological investigation in the area of my own research: the colonial encounter in Early Iron Age France. This was an encounter initiated in the late seventh century B.C. by Etruscan merchants trading along the Mediterranean coast of the lower Rhône basin. At the beginning of the sixth century B.C., Greeks from the city of Phocaea in the eastern Mediterranean established the first colonial settlement in the region, the city of Massalia (modern Marseille). Another Phocaean colony was established within a couple of decades at Emporion (modern Ampurias) on the coast of Catalonia. Massalia eventually grew to become the largest settlement in the entire region (at about 50 hectares) and, over several centuries, established a number of very small subcolonies along the coast of southern France. However, unlike the later situation of Roman imperial expansion (Woolf 1998), Massalia was never powerful enough to engage in major colonization. For several centuries, its relations with the surrounding indigenous peoples were primarily characterized by trade and cross-cultural consumption—a form of social and cultural entanglement that I have characterized as "consuming colonialism" (see Dietler n.d.).

The assumption that this encounter had important cultural and sociopolitical consequences for the indigenous societies of western Europe has been firmly entrenched in the archaeological literature for a very long time. In general, two major interpretive perspectives have tended to dominate analysis of the situation. The first, which I will call the "Hellenization perspective," has been an enduring theme since the first discoveries of Greek imports more than a century ago and is still a powerful influence (compare Benoit 1965; Bouloumié 1981;

Jacobsthal and Neuffer 1933; Kimmig 1983). The second approach, which has become increasingly popular in recent years among Anglo-American and some French scholars, consists of various versions of "world-systems" models.

The Hellenization perspective is simply a particularly overt and naive expression of the colonization of modern Western consciousness that I discussed earlier. It is a tautological re-presentation of the past in terms of assumptions about the civilizing mission of modern colonialism and the inherent attractiveness and superiority of Western culture that were constructed precisely on appeals to this ancient encounter. Hence, it hardly seems necessary to dwell at length on its increasingly obvious inadequacies as a way of understanding the past (see Dietler 1990a, 1995; Morel 1983; Whitehouse and Wilkins 1989). Suffice it to say that this rather vague concept has been used to simultaneously describe and explain what was seen as the absorption or imitation of Greek culture (or that of other Mediterranean civilizations) by indigenous "barbarian" societies. This unidirectional process was accepted axiomatically as an inevitable outcome of mere contact between "barbarians" and the "civilized" Greeks and was considered to be self-explanatory. The desire for all things Greek was assumed to be as natural as gravity (or as the analogically assumed desire for modern Euro-American goods by colonial Others): like water, high culture flows downhill. Moreover, the impetus for historical change was seen to lie always among the dynamic Greeks rather than among the passively receptive "barbarians." For scholars steeped in the tradition of "Hellenophilia" described earlier, the superiority and attractiveness of Greek culture were inherently self-evident. It is hardly surprising that archaeologists formed in this tradition have tended to approach the colonial encounter with a heavy baggage of Hellenocentric preconceptions or that scholars who were themselves so actively striving to become Hellenized would have had difficulty understanding a lack of similar desire on the part of the "barbarians" they were studying. Hence, ultimately, the concept of Hellenization says a good deal more about the aspirations and dispositions of modern scholars than it does about the natives of Iron Age France. It is important to recognize that the desires of the latter are not something transparent and inevitable, but rather something that must be explored and defined empirically and explained theoretically. Hellenization is simply a descriptive concept laden with a host of implicit ethnocentric assumptions. Explaining cross-cultural consumption requires a more complex and subtle consideration of the social forces and cultural structures that govern tastes and desires.

What is more, there are empirical difficulties with this concept. The archaeological evidence shows something very different from a general emulation of Greek culture. Rather, one sees a regionally distinctive, highly selective, and consistent demand for a very limited range of goods for several centuries: essentially wine and drinking gear (Dietler 1990b, 2004). It is striking, for example, that in the lower Rhône basin, despite the immediate and avid thirst for wine, such fundamental Greek cultural practices and goods as writing, coinage, olive oil, clothing, weapons, and religious practices were ignored or rejected for hundreds of years (Bats 1988; Dietler 1997). Moreover, when one looks closely, it is clear that patterns of demand for imported Mediterranean goods and their historical paths of consumption differ considerably from region to region. The differences between the Rhône basin (with its generalized consumption of imported wine amphorae and ceramic drinking cups on nearly all settlements) and the more northerly Hallstatt context (in Burgundy and southwestern Germany, with its spectacular imported bronze wine-serving vessels and drinking ceramics limited to a small number of ostentatious graves, and its notable paucity of wine amphorae) are particularly glaring. But equally striking differences are evident in Western Languedoc or Catalonia (see Dietler 1990b, 1997, 1998, 2004, n.d.).

Growing unease with the idea of Hellenization has provoked a number of scholars to explore alternative approaches. Perhaps the most popular theoretically explicit alternative has been the proliferation of "world-systems" models. This is, in part, a reflection of the growing popularity of world-systems models in the archaeology of colonialism in general, although early formulations of this perspective in the Hallstatt/Massalia case have had a seminal influence within archaeology as a whole, especially the pioneering article of Frankenstein and Rowlands (1978). It has been followed more recently by the analyses of Brun (1987, 1992), Cunliffe (1988), Frank (1993), Kristiansen (1994), Sherratt (1993), and others. These approaches differ in many details (including the explicitness of their derivation from the different theoretical visions of Braudel, Wallerstein, and Frank); but they all share the use of macroscale models of structural dependency that emphasize counterflows of raw materials and manufactured prestige goods articulating a regional division of labor. They situate Hallstatt political relations within a broad Mediterranean-centered world system in which Hallstatt chiefs expanded their power by monopolizing a role as intermediaries in a huge Mediterranean-oriented system geared toward draining raw materials (primarily tin and slaves) from temperate Europe. The apparent collapse of the Hallstatt political structure in the mid-fifth century B.C. is held to be the result of shifts in this system resulting in changes in control of access to Mediterranean prestige goods.

The use of world-systems models in archaeology has already been subjected to a substantial recent critique (see Dietler 1989, 1995, 1998, 1999a; Kohl 1987; Stein 1998, 1999b; Woolf 1990), and I will not undertake a detailed rehearsal of these arguments here. Instead, a few comments are offered outlining problems that are more directly related to the gist of the discussion that introduced this chapter. Suffice it to say that, aside from the issue of anachronism, these models tend to suffer from a magnification of all the problems identified with the original versions of world-systems theory that inspired them. Essentially, world-systems models exhibit a tendency toward mechanistically reductionist, structurally overdetermined, functionalist explanations and an emphasis on core determination of process on the periphery. They are unable to accommodate culture or local agency and, in their uniformity, they deny the fundamental historicity of colonialism (see Comaroff and Comaroff 1992; Dietler 1989, 1995, 1998; Dirks 1992; Roseberry 1989; Sahlins 1985, 1994; Stein 1999b; N. Thomas 1991; Wolf 1982). There is considerable irony in the fact that, despite the radically different Marxist roots of the world-systems perspective, archaeological applications of these models replicate Hellenization's denial of agency outside "core" societies (as well as the axiomatic identification of Greeks as the "core"): both approaches assume the inevitability of native demand on the "periphery" (and, ultimately, reinforce a highly Eurocentric vision of historical determinism). At best, world-systems models have sometimes incorporated a generic concept of functional utility for imports in indigenous societies employing a very generalized model of "prestige goods" and their redistribution; but this perspective is incapable of explaining why particular indigenous societies began exchanges with Mediterranean traders at all, and why those exchanges centered on particular objects and practices. Yet these are crucial issues if, as in this case, we seek to understand the inception and early development of the colonial encounter.

What is even more to the point of this chapter, the very use of the analytical concepts of "center" and "periphery" poses some alarming dangers in that it all too easily melds the physical and the metaphysical into a reified landscape of hierarchical binary difference. In other words, it risks reproducing a set of linkages among binary oppositions (center/periphery; civilization/barbarism; dynamic/static; modern/premodern) that were fundamental to colonialist ideology and then smuggling them into a stable geography of power that cartographically inscribes and naturalizes these metaphysical constructs. As a number of postcolonial theorists have pointed out (for example, Chakrabarty 2000), the unintended consequence of the very process of applying a center/periphery model to recent history is that it serves to reproduce and perpetuate a hegemonic project in which Europe was able to define itself as the center, as the cultural and economic engine of world history. The subsequent uncritical projection of this concept into the distant past serves to further naturalize this image by validating the etiological and teleological mythology of European ancestry. The truly radical move that is necessary to break out of this trap is to deconstruct the very idea of a center and to dismantle the entrenched binary categories that undergird the center/periphery concept.

This warning is even more urgent in the archaeological cases where center/periphery models have been applied to ancient situations—and most particularly in the ancient Mediterranean (for reasons that should be abundantly clear by now). One must ask, for example, on what basis the precarious colonial city of Massalia is defined as the center (or part of the center) during the Early Iron Age and the indigenous societies of Gaul as the periphery? In fact, there is precious little evidence to indicate that this fits any of the economic or political criteria that characterize the center in a modern world-systems model. Once again, it is not unreasonable to suggest that this definition hinges upon the various other linked hierarchical binarisms that furnish the implicit subtext of the model—the same set of binarisms that informed the recursive relationship between ancient and modern colonial ideologies. In other words, Massalia is the center because it was "Greek" (whatever that might mean in the sixth century B.C.) and the indigenous peoples of the region were "barbarians" (the Greek Other)—by definition the denizens of the periphery of the Greek world view. Hence, one can assume that Massalia served roughly the same core structural role as modern Europe and thus correspondingly assume the economic evidence that does not exist.

Along with this tacit assumption of an inherent geography of power, the world-systems approach seems to stimulate a predilection for maps with arrows indicating flows of trade goods across Europe (for example, see Brun 1987; Cunliffe 1988). Yet, a critical look at the archaeological evidence indicates good reason to doubt the plausibility of these arrows. Indeed, when treated as an explicit empirical question rather than a premise, the interconnected set of world-systems assumptions about a significant trade between Massalia and the Hallstatt zone, the existence of relations of dependency and regional division of labor at this early date, and the meaning and function of imports in native contexts appears remarkably dubious (see Bintliff 1984; Dietler 1989, 1990b, 1995, 1999b; Gosden 1985; Pare 1991).

Impressive as some of the individual objects are, the quantity of Mediterranean imports found in the Hallstatt area is exceedingly small in comparison with contemporary imports in southern France. There is little to indicate a steady flow of such imports into the region or to show that their redistribution could have played a systemic role in sustaining the Hallstatt political structure or creating dependency, as the world-systems models assume. Indeed, unlike the case with indigenous Hallstatt prestige goods, there is little to indicate that they were redistributed at all. How this handful of objects could have formed the basis for regional systemic dependency is never adequately explained (and this is, after all, the sine qua non of a world system). Additionally, the invocation of counterflows of tin and slaves to the Mediterranean is based not on any evidence, but rather on anachronistic extrapolations from much later periods when the structure of colonial relations had changed dramatically. In brief, a claim of systemic dependency should require, at a minimum, evidence of at least the moderate duration of a relationship, quantitative significance of the goods exchanged, and a functionally crucial role in the political economy for the objects consumed—none of which has been demonstrated in the Hallstatt case.

What is more, this easy invocation of world-systems mechanisms for the Early Iron Age constitutes a peculiar form of Whig (pre)history that threatens to impede historical understanding of the development of the colonial situation and to preclude perception of indigenous agency and experience of the process. As Nicholas Thomas has warned for recent historical colonial contexts, "Although the ultimately exploitative character of the global economy can hardly be overlooked, an analysis which makes dominance and extraction central to intersocietal exchange from its beginnings will frequently misconstrue power relations which did not, in fact, initially entail the subordination of native people" (1991:84). As with many other colonial situations, in the case of Iron Age France it is a serious analytical error to assume that asymmetrical relations or structures of power that ultimately appeared in later periods were necessarily a feature of the first stages of the encounter rather than a product of a subsequent complex history of interaction and entanglement.

CONSUMPTION, AGENCY, AND COLONIALISM

Examination of this initial phase of the colonial encounter in Iron Age France is important precisely because it holds the promise of revealing the specific historical processes that resulted in the entanglement of indigenous and colonial societies and how the early experience of interaction established the cultural and social conditions from which other, often unanticipated, kinds of colonial relationships developed. As Dirks has argued for modern colonialism, "It is tempting but wrong to ascribe either intentionality or systematicity to a congeries of activities and a conjunction of outcomes that, though related and at times coordinated, were usually diffuse, disorganized, and even contradictory" (1992:7). This caveat is all the more apt in the context of the Archaic Western Mediterranean in which the systems of communication and the technologies of control were far less developed. To understand how structures of colonial dependency and domination were gradually created, often in the absence of coercive instruments of power, we must seek to understand the historical complexities of the "colonization of consciousness" (Comaroff and Comaroff 1992:235–63) and the role of material objects in this process. This means that we must first understand how and why some practices and goods were absorbed into the everyday lives of people, while others were ignored, rejected, or turned into arenas of contest, and how those objects or practices triggered processes of cultural entanglement and transformation.

Developing the theoretical tools to accomplish this goal, and to enable a productive archaeology of colonialism, will require coming to grips with the issue of agency in indigenous societies and abandoning teleological assumptions of inevitability that have underlain previous approaches. Given the confusion surrounding the increasingly popular concept of agency in the current archaeological literature, I should perhaps clarify my use of the term in this context. I am decidedly not talking about an attempt to operationalize a notion of Cartesian individualism in archaeology. Rather, I am aiming at a more nuanced, relational understanding of human subjectivity and consciousness in which the conditions for consequential action, and its motivation, are displaced from transhistorical metastructures (particularly crudely economic ones) to socially situated positions and culturally constructed dispositions. My perspective on this version of what might be called situated agency is informed by insights from both theorists of colonial subjectivity (for example, Amselle 1998; Comaroff and Comaroff 1991; Guha 1997; Stoler 1992) and by practice theory, particularly as developed by Bourdieu (for example, 1990). In other words, I wish to avoid both the Scylla of individual autonomy and the Charybdis of what Sahlins has called "a physics of the world-historical forces" (in Kirch and Sahlins 1992, 1:2), that is, forms of reductionist historical determinism in which agency is attributed solely to economic macrostructures of power and the mechanistic articulation of modes of production.

Whatever their heuristic novelty at a prior moment in time, models of colonial relations in which history is determined at the "core" while the "peripheries" simply react in predetermined ways have surely been rendered obsolete by the past quarter-century of anthropological research and postcolonial analysis. Progress in understanding the colonial experience and its unfolding consequences in specific contexts requires recognizing that intercultural adoption of objects or practices, the process that instigated the initial entanglement of the colonial encounter, is not a phenomenon that takes place at the level of cultures or abstract structures. It is an active process of creative appropriation, manipulation, and transformation played out by individuals and social groups with a variety of competing interests and strategies of action embedded in local political relations, cultural perceptions, and cosmologies. People use alien contacts for their own political agendas, and they give new meanings to borrowed cultural elements according to their own cosmologies and schemes of value. Foreign objects must be understood not only for what they represent in the society of origin, but for their culturally specific meaning and perceived utility in the context of consumption. Hence, the colonial encounter must be contextualized in the conjuncture of the different social and cultural logics of interaction and demand of the different parties involved.

It is important to emphasize again that I am not arguing for a romanticized vision of autonomous action, but rather for a balanced consideration of agency and structure as mutually constituting historical forces. Local history and agency must be situated within the larger political economy, but in a way that allows for motivated and consequential human action. One of the main points of my own research in France has been precisely to understand how indigenous and colonizing societies, through the socially situated, and often contradictory, desires of their own members, were drawn into larger fields of economic and political power relations and were transformed in the process.

It is, of course, easier to advocate such a program in the abstract than to carry it out effectively in the analysis of empirical cases. This is especially true for archaeologists, given our peculiar problems with data and epistemology. Nevertheless, I believe we do have the potential to yield significant new insights and substantially improve understanding of colonial situations, providing we strive to develop appropriate theoretical tools and analytical strategies. The chapters in this book demonstrate a variety of productive attempts to move analysis in new directions, each appropriate to particular kinds of colonial situations.

In my own work, I have found that a focus on the process of consumption can provide a particularly useful and sensitive means for penetrating indigenous agency and experience in a wide variety of colonial encounters. This is because, in the first place, patterns of consumption of a very revealing kind are potentially accessible in the archaeological record, given the development of an appropriate analytical strategy (see, for example, Dietler 1990a, 1990b, n.d.; Rogers 1990, this volume). Moreover, consumption is a domain of practice that is increasingly being recognized by anthropologists and historians as fundamental to the operation of colonialism. The literature of the anthropology of consumption (for example, Appadurai 1986, 1996; Baudrillard 1968; Bourdieu 1984; Dietler 1990a, 1990b; Dietler and Hayden 2001; Douglas and Isherwood 1979; Howes 1996; McCracken 1988; Miller 1987) makes it clear that demand is never an automatic response to the availability of goods, and especially not in colonial situations. It must be understood as an aspect of the cultural economy of societies that follows the political logic of consumption in specific historical circumstances. Hence, the evolution of tastes and desires in the realm of consumption is a powerful, although by no means simple, indicator of local experience of more global colonial processes.

But, in order to exploit the analysis of the relationship between consumption and colonialism, one must first appreciate the fact that the phenomena assembled under the rubric of culture are not static or rigid. In fact, not only is consumption structured by cultural categories and dispositions, but, reciprocally, "culture is constructed through consumption" (J. Comaroff 1996:20). This implies two things. In the first place, objects "materialize" cultural order—they render abstract cultural categories visible and durable, they aid the negotiation of social interaction in various ways, and they structure perception of the social world (Baudrillard 1968; Bourdieu 1984; Douglas and Isherwood 1978). The "systems of objects" (Baudrillard 1968) that people construct through consumption serve both to inculcate personal identity and to enable people to locate others within social fields through the perception of embodied tastes and various indexical forms of symbolic capital (Baudrillard 1968; Bourdieu 1984). But more than simply reproducing static systems of cultural categories, consumption constructs culture in a more dynamic sense; and this is especially relevant to the issue of cross-cultural consumption and colonialism (Howes 1996). In effect, consumption is a process of structured improvisation that continually materializes cultural order by also dealing with alien objects and practices through either transformative appropriation and assimilation or rejection. Hence, culture must be understood not only as something inherited from the past, but as a continual creative project: it is a way of thinking, of perceiving, and of solving problems, including the ever-present problems of dealing with alien peoples, goods, and practices (for example, see Sahlins 1985, 1994, 1995). Societies have never existed in a state of isolation and people must always negotiate their lives in relation to external conditions. This is what Amselle (1998:x)—following Ricoeur's (1992) observation that "selfhood" is constructed in a permanent relation with alterity—means in talking about "originary syncretism." Cultures are inherently relational in nature: they have always been both products of *métissage* and in a ceaseless process of construction through métissage. The distinctive feature of colonial contexts is that the particular configurations of colonial relations of power have a marked influence on the nature and structure of the process. Moreover, precisely because of the significance of consumption to the construction of culture, material culture has repeatedly served as an instrument of colonialism.

Given the importance of consumption in constructing culture and social relationships, it should not be surprising that goods have not only been appropriated and indigenized, they have also been used by both parties in exchanges to attempt to control the other—"making subjects by means of objects" (Comaroff and Comaroff 1997:218). This has involved not only attempts to create novel desires for new goods, but also attempts to get people to use imported objects in particular ways, as well as the (usually mistaken) belief that the use of particular objects or technologies would inherently induce certain kinds of desired behavior. For example, it is clear that clothing played a very important instrumental role in the strategies of European missionaries to "colonize the consciousness" of indigenous peoples in various parts of the world. Among the Tswana in South Africa, both clothing and architecture served as vehicles for attempts by missionaries to inculcate European concepts of domesticity and bodily discipline; and they became sites of struggle as the Tswana used these new material forms as an expressive language to structure identity in new ways and contest colonial categories and aesthetics (Comaroff and Comaroff 1997). As this case suggests, such strategies to use material objects as vectors of control always have unintended consequences for all the parties concerned.

Returning to the issue of the cultural and social logic of desire for cross-cultural consumption of goods, historical accounts of colonial encounters in various parts of the world during the period of European expansion demonstrate that European goods were by no means inherently irresistible to indigenous societies. Usually these peoples exhibited highly selective preferences in both the goods they were willing to accept and to give in exchanges with colonial agents, and they sometimes refused to interact at all (see Sahlins 1985, 1992, 1994; N. Thomas 1991). As has been suggested, indigenous demand in Early Iron Age western Europe was equally specific and selective. In the regions discussed in this chapter, for a period of at least two centuries it was largely confined to a desire for wine and drinking paraphernalia, while other objects and practices were ignored or rejected. Although an appetite for importing alcohol might appear straightforwardly "natural" and self-evident, closer analysis shows that this is not the case (Dietler 1990a, 2001). Moreover, a probing analytical focus on such a deceptively transparent consumption pattern can prove to be extremely revealing of both local agency and the structure of linkages in the broader colonial political economy.

The exploitation of such insights in the archaeological investigation of colonial encounters requires careful attention to identifying specific local patterns of consumption and demand. This involves analyzing simultaneously, on both a regional and site-specific scale, the dynamic relationships among several features: (1) *the contexts of consumption* (that is, the range of the kinds of sites on which objects are found versus those where they are not found, the kinds of specific contexts where objects are found within those sites, the nature of their presence and treatment within those contexts, and so on); (2) *the patterns of association* of imported goods (that is, what kinds of objects are found associated in what kinds of contexts); (3) *their relative quantitative representation* (both in specific contexts and regionally); and (4) *their spatial distribution* (both within sites and regionally). It is also crucial to examine the *specific properties of the objects* imported and consumed, rather than treating them as generic exotic imports, or "prestige goods," as has often been done previously. This requires using a comparative ethnographic and historical perspective to derive plausible models of the range of their potential social roles, of the significance of demand, and of the social consequences entailed by their consumption; and evaluating the relative plausibility of those models against the patterns outlined above in a dialectical process of contrast and comparison. Finally, this kind of analysis is most effective when one examines patterns in both their temporal and spatial dimensions—that is, when there is both a focus on historical process and an attempt to compare and contrast local patterns with those of adjacent regions or other societies within and outside a particular system (lacking the space for an empirical demonstration of this approach here, readers are referred to Dietler 1990b, 1998, 2004, n.d.).

CONCLUSION

In conclusion, the intention of this chapter was to suggest both the importance and the possibility of an archaeological contribution to the understanding of colonies, colonization, and colonialism. It was concerned first to establish that such a contribution depends crucially upon a reflexive sociohistorical understanding of the cultural framework of implicit assumptions that underlies our disciplinary discourse. Moreover, it was particularly concerned to show why the colonial encounter in the ancient Mediterranean has played such a pivotal role in the recursive entanglement of modern and ancient colonialism, and why it requires of analysts an especially high degree of self-conscious vigilance. Modern imperialism and the practices of modern colonialism were grounded in a reverential and referential engagement with ancient Greco-Roman cultures and their colonial legacy. That engagement was based upon a heavily interpolated incorporation of a very partial understanding of that ancient context rooted in colonial texts, and the resulting discourse has continued to inform the interpretative dispositions of archaeologists in subtle and not so subtle ways. The chapter was also concerned to suggest (given that limits of space preclude a genuine demonstration) how a strategic focus on the process of consumption offers possibilities for circumventing some of the problems posed by this interpretative conundrum for the development of a viable archaeology of colonial phenomena. A consumption-oriented approach, focused upon the social and cultural logic of desire for alien goods, the relationship between objects and objectives in colonial interactions, and the unintended entangling consequences of consumption, offers the potential of restoring access to indigenous agency and the fundamental historicity of the colonial situation.

Our challenge is to find ways of making the histories of such colonial situations intelligible without making them seem ineluctable. History is not made at the center of a world system, nor can it be reduced to teleological mechanics of global structures of power. Archaeologists interested in contributing to the anthropological understanding of colonial encounters must push beyond reductionist macro-models and find new, more subtle ways of exploring the relationship between local and "global" processes: we must develop methods for coming to grips with local agency, culture, and history in the material record of the past. We must also strive to remain vigilantly self-conscious of our own situation in the history of colonialism and of the discursive fields that structure our intellectual landscape of implicit tenets and teleologies.

Acknowledgments

I owe a double debt of gratitude to the School of American Research: first, for hosting the advanced seminar at which this paper was presented in 2000, and then, for providing me with a delightful sabbatical as a Weatherhead Resident Scholar in 2002–2003, during which I was able to (nearly) finish the long-overdue book from which this chapter was derived. My thanks also to all the seminar participants for stimulating discussion.

3

Spanish Colonialism and Processes of Social Change in Mesoamerica

Janine L. Gasco

Spanish colonialism within the Americas, at first glance, falls neatly into the general category of sixteenth- to nineteenth-century European colonialism, the "implicit model of colonies," to which a wide range of non-Western, precapitalist examples of colonization can be compared in an effort to develop a comparative archaeology of colonies and colonization (Stein this volume). Clearly the study and analysis of specific manifestations of Spanish colonialism can contribute to a broader understanding of colonies, colonization, and colonialism in cross-cultural perspective—and that is my ultimate goal in this chapter. But we need to examine at the outset our implicit assumptions about colonialism in general and, more specifically, about Spanish and European colonialism. How does Spanish colonialism compare to other examples of European colonialism? To what extent can we speak of either European colonialism or Spanish colonialism as single phenomenon? And, more importantly for our purposes here, is European colonialism fundamentally different from other colonization efforts?

Colonialism refers to "the establishment and maintenance, for an extended time, of rule over an alien people that is separate from and subordinate to the ruling power" (Stein this volume; and see van Dommelen 1997a). Although this process has been well documented throughout history and prehistory in many parts of the world, it is the case of European expansion from the sixteenth through the nineteenth centuries that usually serves as the "implicit" model for colonialism.

The development of an "anthropology of colonialism" has been shaped almost exclusively by the experiences and perceptions of ethnographers working in former European colonies (Pels 1997; Stoler 1989). The burgeoning literature on the critical study of colonialism, colonial theory, and colonial discourse intersects the fields of literary criticism, history, and anthropology (for example, Barker, Hulme, and Iversen 1994; Comaroff and Comaroff 1992; Dirks, ed. 1992; Mignolo 1995; Seed 1991); these studies question standard explanations of European colonialism that are derived largely from the point of view of the colonizer and criticize traditional ethnography because of the ethnographer's close links to current or former colonial powers. They reexamine the colonization process in new ways by seeking out new voices and considering complex interrelationships in colonial settings—clearly laudable goals. These approaches have led to new views of colonial situations, views that reject the binary opposition of "colonizer" and "colonized," and where the notion of hybridity has been introduced to account for the entirely new societies created in colonial situations.

An unfortunate aspect of much of this recent literature on colonialism, however, is that it reinforces the notion that colonialism is a uniquely European phenomenon, limited to the past five hundred years. Moreover, most of this literature is even more narrowly focused, dealing primarily with former British colonies in Asia and Africa in the nineteenth and early twentieth centuries. Not only is the concept of colonialism equated exclusively with European colonialism, but the concept of European colonialism itself is derived largely from the late British experience. Archaeologists whose research focuses on earlier examples of colonization have been critical of this narrow view (see Dietler 1998 and this volume; Lyons and Popadopoulos, eds. 2002; Rogers this volume; van Dommelen 1997a and this volume; Wilson and Rogers 1993). Other scholars have argued that European colonialism itself cannot be seen as a single phenomenon, that fundamental differences "preclude lumping together all the symbolic practices of variations of European domination over other peoples and places across five centuries" (Adorno 1993:142), and some have questioned the appropriateness of including Spanish colonialism of the sixteenth and seventeenth centuries within the broad category of European colonialism (Klor de Alva 1992). So, although recent studies like those cited above provide valuable insights regarding the process of colonialism in certain British colonies at certain periods of time, because of their limited scope, these studies, with a few notable exceptions (for example, Mignolo 1995), do not promote a cross-cultural understanding of colonialism.

Another body of theory that is potentially of value to the cross-cultural study of colonies, colonization, and colonialism is world-systems theory, also based on the experiences of European colonialism. World-systems theory, in its original configuration, sought to explain how European expansion over the past five hundred years has created a divide between developed and underdeveloped nations and led to the unequal distribution of wealth and division of labor that we see today among regions that are characterized as cores, peripheries, and semi-peripheries (Wallerstein 1974, 1980). Attempts to apply world-systems models to premodern and precapitalist societies have forced researchers to modify elements of the original model (for example, Blanton and Feinman 1984; Blanton, Kowalewski, and Feinman 1992; Chase-Dunn and Hall 1997; Peregrine and Feinman 1996; Smith and Berdan 2000, 2003), but the practice of modifying the model to better fit ancient situations has drawn the criticism that the model no longer carries any explanatory weight (Stein 1999b). Moreover, the application of world-systems theory to the very time period for which it was intended has not gone unchallenged because it is a very top-down approach, and it has been criticized for ignoring or minimizing the role of local populations and assuming that people in the periphery were passive victims of global forces (Mintz 1977; Nash 1981; C. Smith 1978; 1984; Wolf 1982). There is little room for variability in world-systems models; exploitation is always unidirectional as the core exploits the periphery. In this regard, world-systems models stand in stark contrast to the suppositions advanced in the colonialism literature noted above, in which local agency and negotiated power relations are emphasized and the interpretation of events by various players is shown to vary markedly.

Regardless of the very different perspectives of these two approaches, research derived from both the critical study of colonialism/colonial theory and world-systems theory suffers from implicit assumptions made about European colonialism. Despite some obvious similarities, European colonialism cannot be easily reduced to a single phenomenon that led to predictable and inevitable results. Even if we limit our consideration spatially to the Americas, there were notable differences between the goals and strategies of Spanish, Dutch, English, Portuguese, French, and Russian colonizers, and these goals and strategies changed over time. Moreover, each of these European powers encountered different indigenous groups who also responded to colonial situations in distinct ways (for a comparison of Spanish and Russian colonization in Alta California, see Lightfoot this volume; for other examples of European colonization in North America, see Green 1996; Salisbury 1996; Trigger and Swagerty 1996). Spanish colonialism itself took shape differently in the diverse regions within its empire depending on a variety of factors that included both cultural and environmental conditions (for the situation in Spanish South America, see Saignes 1999; Schwartz and Salomon 1999; Spalding 1999). And colonial strategies of the sixteenth century differed markedly from those of the eighteenth century (see Altman and Lockhart 1976; Carmagnani 1985; Collier, Rosaldo, and Wirth 1982; MacLeod and Wasserstrom 1983).

In short, two implicit assumptions that underlie much of the existing scholarship on colonialism must be challenged. First, a monolithic view of European colonialism or even Spanish colonialism is in need of revision. Second, the process of colonialism is not limited to European expansion in the past five hundred years. Whereas it would surely be a mistake to assume that the establishment of colonies and the process of colonization in the ancient world inevitably led to colonialism of the sort we usually associate with the classic model of European colonialism—itself a flawed concept—it also would be a mistake to assume from the outset that European colonialism—whatever the variety—is necessarily different from all earlier situations. The comparative study of colonies, colonization, and colonialism should be designed precisely to sidestep these assumptions and explore in a systematic way how and why ancient and more recent colonial situations are similar or different.

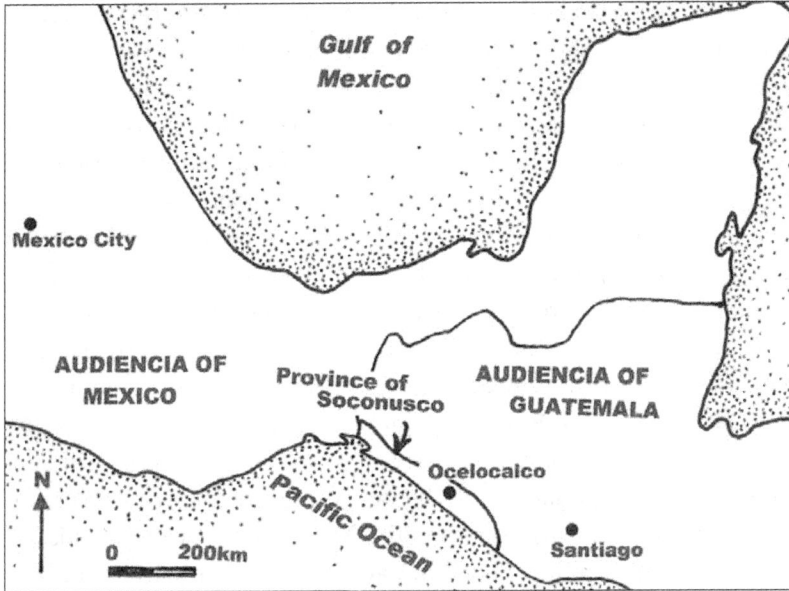

FIGURE 3.1

Soconusco region and Ocelocalco site, New Spain.

In this chapter I present an approach that I hope will both contribute to a more comprehensive understanding of the nature of Spanish colonization in Mesoamerica and provide a useful case study for the comparative purposes of this volume. Following Stein (this volume), who notes that colonies can best be understood "as functioning in a three-fold network that consists of colonies themselves, their homelands, and the indigenous host societies in whose midst the colonies are established," I examine these three nodes for colonial Mesoamerica. I begin with broad background descriptions of Spain (the homeland) and Mesoamerica (the indigenous host societies) that set the stage for the colonial "encounter." I continue with a discussion of the third node: Spain's colonies in Mesoamerica and the process of colonialism. In this section I address specific factors that were influential in shaping the course of colonialism in Mesoamerica. In the final section of the chapter I provide a more close-up view of a single region by reviewing how these factors influenced colonialism in the Soconusco region of Mesoamerica (fig. 3.1).

Whereas in many instances it is necessary for the researcher to determine during the course of analysis whether or not a particular situation can be characterized as an example of colonialism, in the case of Spain's colonies in the Americas (and elsewhere) there is no doubt that we are dealing with a clear-cut case of colonialism (as we are using the term in this volume). Having said that, however, I want to emphasize that characterizing the Spanish colonization effort as colonialism is only the first step; in the same way that the process of colonization has many manifestations, only one of which is colonialism, the process of colonialism also has many manifestations. Although Spain clearly played a dominant role and it exerted a great deal of power in the colonial setting, native Mesoamericans were not passive victims who bowed to the every wish of their conquerors. Because of a complex process of confrontation and negotiation and the varied interpretations of events and institutions on the part of both native Mesoamericans and Spaniards, Spanish colonialism proceeded in ways that diverged sharply from the plan devised by the Spanish Crown and its policy makers.

Anthropologists, ethnohistorians, social historians, and others working in Mesoamerica and elsewhere in the Americas have long been aware of the fact that the indigenous population played an important role in the creation of colonial and postcolonial society (see Deagan 2001), and they have been wary of uncritically accepting Spanish accounts of colonialism (for example, Altman and Lockhart 1976; Boone 1998; Bray 1993; Burkhart 1989; Carmack, Gasco, and Gossen 1996; Chance 1989; Collier, Rosaldo, and Wirth 1982; Farriss 1984; Gibson 1964, 1984; G. D. Jones 1989; Lockhart 1992; MacLeod and Wasserstrom 1983; Mignolo 1995; Ouweneel and Miller 1990; Patch 1993; Restall 1997, 1998; S. B. Schwartz 1994; Terraciano 2001). This recognition on the part of researchers that indigenous Mesoamericans were actively involved in the creation of colonial society is illustrated by the notion of syncretism (Madsen 1967), which has long been used to refer to the fact that the historically distinct traditions of Spain and Mesoamerica became "reinterpreted and transformed" as part of the colonial encounter (Gossen 1996:303). The notion of syncretism has been employed primarily to explain the creation of a new religious system in colonial Mesoamerica and elsewhere that incorporated indigenous and Spanish Catholic elements. The concept of syncretism has been criticized for its ambiguities (see Monaghan 2000), yet this notion that indigenous beliefs played an important role in the creation of a colonial belief system foreshadows by several decades the concept of hybridity noted above.

To understand Spanish colonialism in Mesoamerica, we have the distinct advantage of having not only considerable written documentation from the various Spanish points of view, but also a large corpus of written records from native peoples themselves (also representing many points of view). The field of Spanish colonial archaeology in Mesoamerica is in its infancy, but in certain cases we have some archaeological data to draw on (see Charlton 1972, 1979; Farnsworth and Williams 1992; Gasco, Smith, and Fournier-García 1997; D. H. Thomas 1991), and I provide examples from my own research (Gasco 1987a, 1989a, 1992, 1993), which involved excavation at the abandoned colonial town site of Ocelocalco in the Soconusco region of Chiapas, Mexico (fig. 3.1).

THE SPANISH PERSPECTIVE: POLITICAL, ECONOMIC, AND IDEOLOGICAL BACKGROUND

Spain's underlying motivations and the strategies it employed in the creation of its colonial empire can only be fully understood if we consider the larger context within which Spain and Spaniards were operating at the end of the fifteenth century. Spanish expansion into the Americas was not a random event, but rather an integral part of the region's accumulated historical experience over several centuries. The following account focuses largely on the Spanish state, the force behind Spain's colonization efforts. Yet it is important to keep in mind that Spain in the fifteenth century was a multiethnic society that had, over the previous several centuries, been the focus of invasions and colonization efforts by Romans, Visigoths, and Arabs who had significantly influenced Spanish society.

Once unified as the Roman administrative province of Hispania, the Iberian Peninsula had been invaded and settled by the Visigoths in the wake of Rome's decline. Subsequently the peninsula was invaded by Muslim conquerors and colonizers (Moors) early in the eighth century. Much of the population of the peninsula converted to Islam and adopted elements of Muslim culture. The Iberian population also included other ethnic groups, including a small, but significant population of Jews. One faction within the peninsula remained Christian, however, and they were determined to drive the Moors from the peninsula (Collins 1995; Glick 1979, 1995; MacKay 1977; McAlister 1984; Ramsey 1973).

For the next seven hundred years, Christians and Muslims struggled for control of the Iberian Peninsula in what Spaniards called the *reconquista*. The reconquista was waged initially to reclaim agricultural land and land for pasturage and secondarily to seize booty (including slaves). Religious zeal did not play a significant role in most of the early hostilities; Christian lords frequently fought against each other, and Muslims and Christians showed a degree of tolerance for each other's faith. Beginning in the northwestern portion of the peninsula, the reconquest expanded steadily south, and during centuries of warfare, generations of Iberian Christians acquired the battle skills and ruthlessness that they became noted for in their later campaigns in the Americas. Other strategies developed during this period also were eventually employed during Spain's colonial expansion. One of these practices was resettlement. Once territory was won from the Muslims, it was resettled by a Christian population who created new communities. This concept of repopulation was based on earlier Hispano-Roman law, which held that Christian kings acquired just title to territory that had been taken from infidels or was unoccupied, and they were then free to redistribute these lands to loyal subjects (Hillgarth 1976, 1978; Lomax 1978; McAlister 1984; Ramsey 1973).

The reconquest proceeded in fits and starts, but by the early eleventh century Christian forces were advancing toward Al-Andalus, the much-prized Muslim territory within the Guadalquivir River basin in the southern and eastern part of the peninsula (fig. 3.2). At this point, the struggle was elevated to a holy war. Muslim reinforcements from North Africa and Christian armies, which now included members of medieval military orders, were equally fanatical in their religious fervor. While the Muslims fought to maintain their hold over the Guadalquivir region, the Christians took territories to the west and east. Repopulation now took a more highly structured form; the Christian kings granted charters to new communities that were governed more formally by town councils with the power to give land

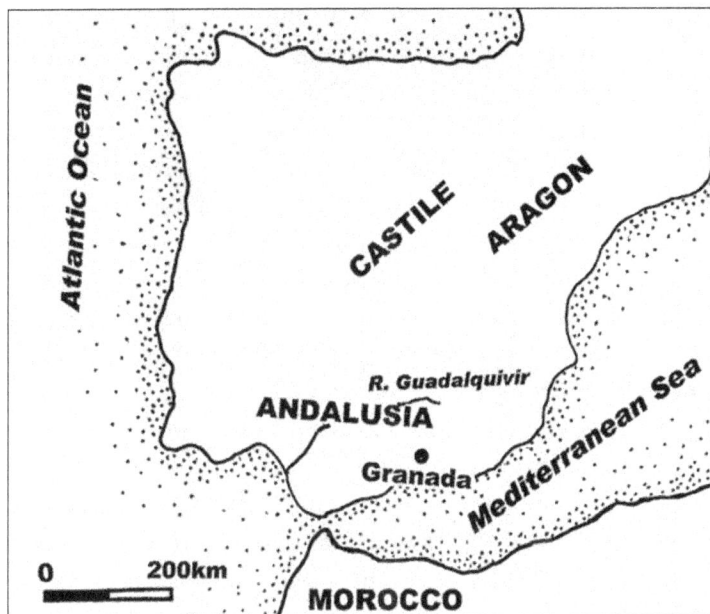

FIGURE 3.2

Iberian Peninsula showing regions mentioned in the text.

grants to citizens and soldiers and to dispense justice (Hillgarth 1976; Lomax 1978; Ramsey 1973).

By the thirteenth century, the balance of power had shifted to the Christian kingdoms, and they were successful in winning territory throughout Al-Andalus (now Andalusia). At the end of the thirteenth century, the last remaining Muslim strongholds were the Emirate of Granada in the far south and several coastal garrisons along the Mediterranean. Yet even as Christian kings gained control over most of the Iberian Peninsula, interest in creating a united Spain was undermined by the aspirations of individual kings, and Spain did not emerge as a single unified political entity until late in the fifteenth century (Hillgarth 1976, 1978; Ramsey 1973).

In 1469, the marriage of Isabella, sister of King Henry IV of Castile, to Ferdinand, heir to the throne of Aragon, set the stage for the creation of the modern Spanish state. Isabella became Queen of Castile in 1474, and in 1479, when Ferdinand succeeded to the throne of Aragon, unification was complete (Liss 1992; Rubin 1991).

The dynamic couple, the "Catholic Kings" (a title bestowed upon Ferdinand and Isabella by Pope Alexander VI), undertook numerous initiatives designed to strengthen the central government and ensure their own control over virtually every aspect of state power (Elliott 1963; MacLachlan 1988; McAlister 1984; Vicens Vives 1969). Other actions led to a growing sense of Spanish nationalism and increased religious intolerance. Within the Royal Council, the highest governmental institution, they created smaller committees who reported directly to the Crown to oversee war, foreign affairs, and justice. Municipalities that had formerly enjoyed considerable autonomy were now politically subordinate to the Crown, and Crown-appointed officers, *corregidores*, were dispatched to many towns to oversee town governance. Other central government staff positions were filled by individuals who were not from the nobility, and whose loyalty lay exclusively with the Crown. Strong measures were implemented to control the economy, including wage and price controls, the creation of monopolistic guilds, and protectionist policies to restrict imports. Standard monetary units also were introduced. Other measures, more closely linked to ideology, included the creation of the Inquisition in 1478 to persecute those whose faith was questioned.

The final assault on the Moors occurred during the ten-year military campaign against the last Muslim center at Granada and culminated in its defeat in 1492. Subsequently, Jews and Moors were expelled from Spanish territory. Related to the growing intolerance within Spain was a new concern with ancestry; Christian Spaniards became obsessed with proving that their blood lines had not been tarnished by Jewish or Moorish blood (*limpia de sangre*) (McAlister 1984:62; Rubin 1991).

Isabella and Ferdinand also took steps to elevate Spain's position in international affairs. They established firm links with other European royalty through marital alliances in which their daughter and son married important figures in the Habsburg dynasty (McAlister 1984:60). Ultimately this alliance with the Habsburgs led to Spain's economic undoing, but in the short term, Spain's emergence as a major European power reinforced the prestige of the monarchy.

The net result of Isabella and Ferdinand's policies was the creation of an absolute monarchy in which all territory, offices, economic affairs, and religious affairs were controlled by the Crown. This was coupled with a growing sense of national pride and religious intolerance. All of these factors contributed to Spain's desire for territorial expansion, and competition with neighboring Portugal only intensified the momentum.

Spain's expansionist policies began with efforts to conquer and colonize the Canary Islands in the late 1470s. In the Canaries, Isabella, as Queen of Castile, implemented many of the same policies that had been employed during the reconquista. She asserted authority over conquered territory, granting the title of *adelantado* to deserving conquistadors and giving them the rights to the booty acquired during conquest (*repartimiento*); and as Queen, Isabella claimed absolute authority over appointments and decisions (McAlister 1984:63–65). In the early 1490s, the Spanish Crown was most concerned with expansion into North Africa; Morocco was, after all, the homeland of the enemy and was considered to be a threat to Christian Spain. But before any North African campaign was begun, Isabella and Ferdinand made what turned out to be a momentous decision. In 1492 they granted a patent to Cristobal Colón, a Genoese navigator, who proposed to make a voyage to the west to discover new territories and locate a new route to eastern Asia, otherwise known as the Indies (Elliott 1963; McAlister 1984).

Colón was granted the right to serve as governor of lands he discovered and was allowed to keep 10 percent of the booty acquired. Colón's voyages led to the establishment of several Spanish settlements in the Caribbean and Panama. The Caribbean colonies proved to be a disappointment to the Crown and to individual Spanish colonists (Elliott 1963; Sauer 1966). The resources Spaniards sought—namely gold—did not exist in large quantities; the indigenous populations were quickly decimated from mistreatment by Spaniards and from introduced diseases. Spaniards soon realized that lands with greater promise lay just beyond the Caribbean Islands, and in the early sixteenth century expeditions began exploring the mainland of Mexico.

In 1519 a young adventurer, Hernán Cortés, set off from Cuba to explore the mainland, and within two years he and his band of conquistadors, aided by thousands of indigenous warriors, were victorious over the Aztec Empire (Burkhart and Gasco 1996; Elliott 1990; J. H. Parry 1966; for an Aztec account of the conquest, see Leon-Portilla 1992). Spanish conquest of the Maya region was more protracted (see Carmack 1981; Clendinnen 1987; Farriss 1984; G. D. Jones 1989; Lutz

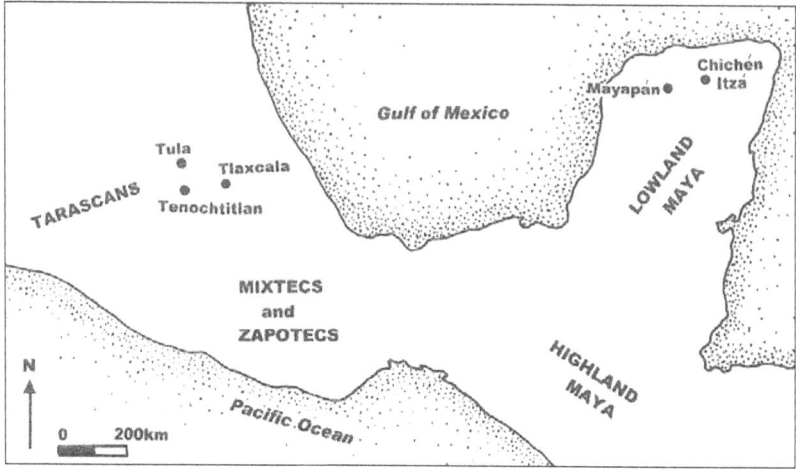

FIGURE 3.3

Postclassic cities and ethnic groups in Mesoamerica.

1994; Orellana 1984), with the final Maya kingdom finally falling to defeat in 1697 (G. D. Jones 1998). With the imposition of Spanish rule, the process of creating a colonial society in Mesoamerica was set into play.

THE INDIGENOUS MESOAMERICAN PERSPECTIVE: POLITICAL, ECONOMIC, AND IDEOLOGICAL BACKGROUND

It is far more difficult to present a brief description of the nature of indigenous Mesoamerican societies because there were so many diverse ethnolinguistic groups who lived throughout the region, each with its own particular historical and cultural background (Figure 3.3). At a very general level, however, it is possible to identify certain traits that distinguished Mesoamerican societies from their neighbors to the north and south (Kirchhoff 1943) and, more importantly for this study, distinguished Mesoamerica from Spain.

Mesoamerican peoples relied on an agricultural system that produced the corn-beans-squash trilogy of plant staples, frequently employing intensive agricultural techniques like raised field (or *chinampa*) agriculture (Blanton et al. 1993; M. D. Coe 1994; Weaver 1993). Mesoamericans had no domesticated large mammals, and this influenced their diet and their agricultural technology. Although meat made up some portion of the Mesoamerican diet in the form of wild game, Mesoamericans acquired much of their protein from plants. Because of the particular corn-processing technique developed in Mesoamerica (the *nixtamal* process where mineral lime is added to the corn, increasing its protein value; see S. D. Coe 1994:14), corn and beans provided complete protein. The absence of domesticated draft animals meant that all agricultural labor was provided by humans. The absence of draft animals may also explain why Mesoamericans never used the wheel except on toys.

Metallurgy was introduced into Mesoamerica sometime between C.E. 600 and 800, but technological advancements and more widespread use of metal goods did not take place until the mid-to-late Postclassic period (circa C.E. 1200–1520). Metal goods, however, were used primarily for adornment (Hosler 1994, 2003); stone remained the most important material for tools. New stone-working technology was developed during the Postclassic period; at this time the bow and arrow were adopted, and arrowheads began to be manufactured (Clark 1989). Large-scale obsidian mining was carried out at the favored sources (Pastrana 1998).

Mesoamericans developed several distinct writing systems, and our understanding of these systems has increased markedly in recent years (Marcus 1992). Unfortunately, the great majority of the pre-Columbian documents that were written on paper, hides, or cloth were destroyed by zealous Spanish priests and colonial officials, so we are left with only a handful of codices and *lienzos* that predate the Colonial period (Robertson 1959). Nevertheless, numerous documents were preserved in other media such as stone and clay, and there are countless documents from the Colonial period, many of them written in native languages (Glass 1975; Nicholson 1975). Reading and writing, however, was the domain of elites, so there are certain limitations that must be recognized when using the written record.

Other common features of Mesoamerican societies included the construction of stepped pyramids, use of a common calendrical system made up of a 260-day ritual cycle and a 365-day solar cycle, playing a ball game that was more closely linked to ritual than to sport, and a shared belief system in which a number of deities were recognized across the entire region and similar rituals were practiced, including human sacrifice (Kirchhoff 1943; Weaver 1993).

The Mesoamerican region was composed of a number of politically independent states, or city-states, at the time of the Spanish invasion (Carmack 1996; M. E. Smith 2003; Smith and Gasco 1996). Although the exact composition of these states was in a constant state of flux, large-scale, expansionistic states had existed in Mesoamerica for more than a thousand years. From roughly the fourth to the eighth century (the Classic period), a few large centralized states (such as Teotihuacan and Monte Albán) dominated much of Mesoamerica, engaging in expansionistic policies that included conquest and at least some colonization (Blanton et al. 1993; Cowgill 1997; Marcus and Flannery 1996; Pasztory 1997; Smith and Gasco 1996; and see Spence this volume). In the southeastern part of the region, a succession of smaller states or kingdoms in the Maya area developed that were never as large as their counterparts to the north, yet they, too, were expansionistic and conquered their neighbors (Culbert 1991; Sharer 1994).

Between the seventh and ninth centuries, the Classic-period states fell into decline, ushering in the so-called Postclassic period.[1] The Postclassic period is generally characterized as a time of political decentralization, and for much of the Postclassic period the Mesoamerican political landscape was made up of competing city-states (Carmack 1996; M. E. Smith 2003; Smith and Berdan 2003; Smith and Gasco 1996). The former domains of Teotihuacan and Monte Albán now consisted of numerous smaller and often antagonistic polities. In central Mexico, Tula became an influential center, although its sphere of influence was much smaller than Teotihuacan's had been (Davies 1977; Diehl 1983). In Oaxaca, small independent polities had relations that ranged between friendly alliances and confederations to outright hostility (Byland and Pohl 1994; Pohl 2003). The Maya kingdoms in the southern lowlands of Guatemala and Belize were largely abandoned; in the Yucatán Peninsula, centralized Maya polities (such as Chichén Itzá, Mayapán) survived, but by the fifteenth century or earlier they, too, had fragmented (Chase and Rice 1985; Kepecs and Masson 2003; Sabloff and Andrews 1986).

Only in the mid-fifteenth century did another large, expansionistic state emerge, with the development in central Mexico of the Mexica-dominated Triple Alliance (Berdan et al. 1996; Berdan and Smith 2003; P. Carrasco 1999; M. E. Smith 1996). This alliance, generally referred to as the Aztec Empire, was created in 1428, and it consisted of the Mexica, whose capital city of Tenochtitlán was located on an island in one of the lakes that once covered much of the Valley of Mexico; the Alcolhua, who dominated the eastern valley from their capital at Texcoco; and a group of Tepanecs whose capital, Tlacopan, was located in the western shore of the lake system. The Aztec Empire began its campaign of expansion by first solidifying its position in the Valley of Mexico; later, under the rulership of Mexica kings Itzcoatl, Motecuhzoma Ilhuicamina, Ahuitzotl, and Motecuhzoma Xocoyotzin, and Alcohua kings Nezahualcoyotl and Nezahualpilli, it expanded into other portions of the Central Highlands, the Gulf coast region, highland Oaxaca, and the Pacific coastal regions of Guerrero, Oaxaca, and Chiapas (Berdan et al. 1996; Berdan and Smith 2003; D. Carrasco 1998; P. Carrasco 1999; M. E. Smith 1996; Townsend 1992). By 1519, the Aztec Empire had conquered much of what is today central and southern Mexico and was exacting tribute from conquered territories.

Another developing centralized state was the Tarascan Empire of west Mexico, although many developments in this region are still not fully understood (Pollard 1993, 2003). It is clear, however, that the Tarascans were a formidable enemy to the Aztecs; the frontier zone between the two empires was heavily fortified, and the Tarascans dealt the Aztecs their most humiliating defeats. Other key areas within the Central Highlands, notably the Tlaxcalan region to the east of the Valley of Mexico, also maintained their independence and were bitter enemies of the Aztecs.

In contrast to Spain, which in the early sixteenth century had recently achieved political unity, Mesoamerica was not unified politically (nor had it ever been). In fact, resentment against the strongest polity—the Aztec Empire—ran high. Aztec control over conquered regions seems to have been tenuous in many cases, and areas often had to be conquered more than once. In addition, several important independent states (for example, Tlaxcala and the Tarascan state), all archenemies of the Aztecs, loomed nearby, creating constant tension (Berdan et al. 1996). Farther south in the Maya region, conflicts between polities were frequent (Chase and Rice 1985; Sabloff and

Andrews 1986). In short, across Mesoamerica there was no single political entity that could rally support to fight a common enemy. Instead, the Spaniards found ready allies among disaffected peoples within the Aztec Empire and among warring states in the Maya region.

Although Mesoamerica was never unified politically, in other respects the region achieved unity as a result of continuous contact among diverse peoples across the region that began as early as 1500 B.C.E. Shared ideology and similar consumer tastes seem to have reached unprecedented levels in the Late Postclassic period, presumably the result of expanding social networks in which goods were exchanged and a common belief system was promoted (Smith and Berdan 2003; Berdan et al. 2003; Boone 2003). The Late Postclassic period was a time of intense commercial interaction, and households across Mesoamerica were able to acquire products from distant lands in quantities that exceeded previous levels (Blanton et al. 1993). In central Mexico and in other regions, markets flourished, craft and agricultural production was intensified, and perhaps for the first time common media of exchange (cacao beans, copper axes, and cotton cloth) were employed for market transactions (Blanton 1996; Brumfiel 1980, 1987; Hassig 1985). Certain goods, such as ceramics and groundstone implements (manos and metates), were mass produced. Even the Aztec tribute system promoted expansion of trade networks, as regions were required to pay tribute in goods that were not produced locally (Berdan 1996; Smith and Berdan 1996).

The process by which commercial networks expanded and a common ideological system developed is not well understood, but it does seem quite clear that it took place independent of the involvement of any particular state. This is not to say that the Early Postclassic states were completely uninvolved in the process, but that it was not engineered by any single polity. All of the trends that characterized the Postclassic period clearly preceded the emergence of the Aztec Empire by two centuries or more. Even under the strong arm of the Aztec state, economic relations were often relatively unaffected by political considerations, and merchants operated as independent agents.

Mesoamerican society was highly stratified in the early sixteenth century, a social process that, like many others, had begun by around 1500 B.C.E. (Carrasco and Broda 1976). Although the details differ among the various regions of Mesoamerica, typically societies had two major divisions: a noble and a commoner class. Membership in these social classes was hereditary, and there was little opportunity for social mobility. In many areas, there was also a category of person that has been translated as slaves—although the meaning of slavery often differed sharply from our own. In Aztec society, for example, individuals could sell themselves into slavery in hard times, but this status did not pass on to one's children.

Several basic beliefs and aspects of world view seem to have been held in common among all of the various Postclassic Mesoamerican groups, suggesting that these notions had deep roots (D. Carrasco 1990; Gossen 1996; Leon-Portilla 1980; Monaghan 2000). Mesoamericans believed in a complex set of relationships among humans, deities, and the universe. The continued existence of order in the universe required the goodwill of the gods, something that could only be achieved if humans engaged in certain activities and abstained from others. There was also a belief that there had been previous worlds or universes that had been destroyed; survival of the current world depended on proper behavior by humans. Proper behavior included not only the required ritual activities, but also appropriate behavior in everyday life; so social, political, and economic behaviors also were shaped by the Mesoamerican belief system. In all aspects of life, Mesoamericans were concerned with order and balance. People were expected to behave in a predictable fashion, one appropriate for their position in life; they were to respect authority, and excess in any activity was to be avoided. Conformity was encouraged, and people felt a deep obligation to their families and to society as a whole.

I do not want to give the impression that we can easily reduce the multiple Postclassic Mesoamerican societies to a single set of behaviors and beliefs—anymore than we can characterize European societies, or even Spanish society, in a simple fashion—and we know that people across Mesoamerica reacted to the imposition of Spanish colonial rule in unique ways. But the general outline provided above is intended to emphasize common features and allow us to better understand some of the basic underpinnings of indigenous belief systems and behaviors that played a role in shaping colonial life and continue to influence life in Mesoamerica today.

By the early 1500s, rumors of mysterious strangers began circulating across Mesoamerica as Spanish presence in the Caribbean intensified and following the first contacts between Spaniards and the Maya of Yucatán and Tabasco (Díaz del Castillo 1956; Scholes and Roys 1968:89; Tozzer 1941). Unable or unwilling to take decisive and unified action against these strangers, most Mesoamericans initially took a cautious approach toward them. Regardless of their strange ways and appearances, Spaniards were generally treated as high-ranking foreigners (Lockhart 1994). Given the state of political affairs, in which tensions were high and there was great dislike for the Aztecs and other powerful polities, many Mesoamerican leaders saw the Spaniards as potential allies, and they engaged in customary activities designed to forge alliances—activities such as feasting and gift-giving. Even when the impending danger became obvious to some, they were unable to convince others that the Spaniards were the enemy.

Cortés's efforts were helped considerably by the cultural knowledge and linguistic skills of Malintzin (Malinche) (see Karttunen 1997). Malinche was a Nahua woman who reportedly had been sold into slavery by her family and who was presented to Cortés by a Chontal-Maya ruler—a typical example of Mesoamerican alliance-building behavior (Scholes and Roys 1968:91). The advantage afforded to Cortés through the information provided to him by Malinche ranks as an important factor that led to the Spanish victory (Todorov 1984). Many other factors also contributed to the Spaniards' success against the Aztec Empire. The most important of these were the Old World diseases that ravaged the indigenous population; the Spanish technological advantages of gunpowder, metal weapons and armor, and horses; the absence of political unity in Mesoamerica; and the willingness of many Mesoamerican warriors to ally themselves with the Spaniards.

THE DYNAMICS OF CONFRONTATION AND NEGOTIATION: SPANISH COLONIALISM IN MESOAMERICA

In the discussion above, I have attempted to provide a broad overview of the long historical processes that created the institutions and prevailing world views in both Spain and Mesoamerica on the eve of contact. I turn now to an examination of Spanish colonialism in Mesoamerica by focusing on six factors that were particularly influential in shaping colonial life. Addressing these factors helps us to understand how and why Spanish colonialism developed in the ways that it did in Mesoamerica, and it also allows us to better understand variability within Mesoamerica. These are factors that might be productively explored in other colonial situations as well.

> To what extent do indigenous and intrusive societies have shared cultural histories?

> What are the technological traditions of indigenous and colonizing societies?

> What are the similarities and differences between political and economic systems of intrusive and indigenous societies?

> What are the similarities and differences between systems of social stratification, ethnic relations, and gender roles?

> What are the similarities and differences between ideological/religious systems?

> What are the objectives of the colonizers, what kind of colonies are established, who are the colonists, and what is the intended role in the colonial enterprise for the host population?

Most of these factors focus on existing conditions in both indigenous and intrusive societies, and as a result they stress the interplay between the two and do not assume that the colonizers can impose their own institutions and ideas unchallenged. Only the last set of factors focuses more exclusively on the colonizing society. Although the give-and-take in colonial situations cannot be ignored, neither should we ignore that colonies, as we are defining them, are implanted settlements in the territory of another society (Stein this volume). The entire process of colonization is set into motion by one party in the encounter: the colonizers. Colonizers who move from their homeland into territory held by another society do so because they have some objective in mind and some idea of how they are going to accomplish it. The extent to which the colonizers can successfully meet their objectives will, of course, depend on other factors, but the variable goals and strategies of colonizers are critical factors to consider because they will create very different colonial situations.

Shared Cultural Histories

Spain and Mesoamerica in the sixteenth century did not have any shared cultural traditions. In every respect, this was nothing less that the meeting of two very different worlds (Crosby 1972, 1986). Although several aspects of Spanish and Mesoamerican cultural systems were similar—notably economic, political, and religious institutions (Lockhart 1994)—colonial Mesoamerica represents a situation in which colonizing and host societies had very different and independent cultural histories. In situations like this, outcomes will be very unpredictable, as both colonizer and host societies often misunderstand each other's motivations and world views. In colonial Mesoamerica this was certainly the case (Hoekstra 1990).

Related to the issue of shared cultural histories is a factor that we might call biological relatedness. This became an incredibly important factor for all of European colonization efforts in the Americas and may be the single factor that distinguishes European colonization in the Americas and the Pacific from other examples of colonization. Indigenous peoples in the Americas had not had contact (or at least not sustained contact) with peoples from the Old World for thousands of years. During these years of separation, certain diseases developed in the Old World that were nonexistent in the New World. Some of these diseases were carried by animals that did not exist in the New World, and others may have disappeared during the course of the migration itself, never arriving in the New World. Over time, Old World populations had built some immunities to these diseases, whereas New World populations had not. This lack of immunity to common diseases introduced by Spaniards (and other Europeans) led to the greatest demographic catastrophe the world has ever seen (Cook and Borah 1971–1979; N. D. Cook 1998; Cook and Lovell 1992; Dobyns 1993; Newson 1985). High indigenous death rates and the ensuing social chaos that it caused contributed substantially to the Spaniards' early success in their American colonies. In fact, the entire series of events may have played out quite differently if it were not for the death of key indigenous leaders and as much as a 90 percent population decline over the first decades of Spanish colonial rule. Throughout the Americas, the entire colonial experience was significantly impacted by the demographic collapse of the indigenous population.

The absence of a shared cultural tradition (which also created distinct material cultures) and the demographic decline among native Mesoamericans meant that the initial contact experience created certain abrupt changes. In Mesoamerica, new materials (for example, metal tools, glass, glazed wheel-thrown ceramics) and new plants and animals were introduced (see discussion on technology below), indigenous population decline was dramatic, and shifts in existing settlement patterns and architecture were swift.

Technological Traditions

Another factor that will influence the nature of a colonial enterprise relates to technology. The extent to which the colonizers initially have a technological advantage over the indigenous society may affect their ability to dominate—or even successfully establish the colony in the first place.

Spain had some obvious technological advantages that helped during the conquest—particularly gunpowder and metal weapons and armor. In the case of Spain in Mesoamerica, however, these technological advantages were not a pivotal factor in the initial Spanish success; the demographic disaster discussed above almost certainly played a larger role.

At another level, Spanish-introduced technologies played an important role in the development of colonial—and contemporary—society in Mesoamerica (G. Foster 1960). Across Mesoamerica, metal tools replaced stone tools, new ceramic technologies were introduced and adopted (the potter's wheel and glazing), new weaving technology was introduced (the floor loom), and, if we consider domesticated plants and animals as part of technology, a wide range of Old World plants and animals were adopted (such as chickens, pigs, sheep, goats, citrus fruits, and bananas). Other material goods and certain introduced plants were not adopted, however (Gibson 1984). Wheat, for example, a mainstay in the Spanish diet, never became widely consumed in indigenous communities because corn was so highly valued as a staple food. The material culture associated with corn preparation and consumption (manos and metates for grinding the corn, *comales* [flat ceramic griddles] for cooking the tortillas) did not change. Textiles continued to be produced on backstrap looms.

This technological element is one that lends itself well to archaeo-logical analysis. It is quite easy to document archaeologically the pres-ence of new materials, although assessing the underlying significance of the adoption of materials introduced by colonizers is a more complex issue. The adoption by host societies of introduced objects in a colonial situation is a subject that has begun to receive increased attention (see Appadurai, ed. 1986; Comaroff and Comaroff 1992; Miller 1995; Rogers 1990; N. Thomas 1991), although the issue has not yet been addressed in any comprehensive way in Mesoamerica. What does the adoption of new technology or material mean? How did people decide whether to incorporate new objects into their lives? Once a new object was adopted, how was it viewed? How should we interpret differential consumption of these new materials? Are people who do not have these new objects in their homes engaging in some form of resistance, or do they simply not have access to them? Whereas we can assume that some objects were forced on Indian communities (for example, many communities were charged tribute in chickens, so chickens had to be raised), the adoption of other objects must have been due to preferences related to percep-tions about those goods. Continued reliance on corn as a staple food, and refusal on the part of Indians to replace corn with wheat, was no doubt a result of the symbolic value of corn and the very deep belief that corn was the essence of humanity (see Sandstrom 1991). But the motives for and implications of adoption of other new materials and objects by indigenous Mesoamericans are difficult to determine. It is also worth mentioning in this regard that Old World societies adopted a number of New World plants that have become thoroughly integrated into regional cuisines across Europe, Asia, and Africa (for instance, chocolate, chile, potatoes, tomatoes). This reverse movement of goods is an important element of the colonial process, but the ideological implications for, say, Italians adopting the tomato have not yet been examined to my knowledge.

Similarities and Differences in Political and Economic Systems

The extent to which the political and economic systems of colo-nizers and host communities are similar will influence the nature of colonization. The political and economic systems of Spain and Mesoamerica were structurally similar in several important respects

(Lockhart 1994), and this allowed the systems to successfully mesh in ways that proved to be impossible in other parts of Spain's empire (such as northern Mexico and the Californias). The political systems of both Spain and Mesoamerica were rigidly hierarchical, resting on control by a hereditary nobility, and entire regional settlement systems were organized in hierarchical fashion with capital cities dominating surrounding towns and villages. Similarly, Spanish and Mesoamerican economic systems had a number of similarities. Both had a tradition of long-distance exchange, both had markets, and both employed a system of taxation or tribute. All of these remained important elements of Spanish colonialism in Mesoamerica.

Other Spanish political and economic institutions did not have counterparts in Mesoamerica, however. Some of the new institutions—such as wage labor, *reducciones* or *congregaciones,* and the *encomienda*—proved to be extremely disruptive to indigenous communities. Other new institutions were willingly or perhaps only grudgingly adopted but were successfully manipulated and modified by indigenous communities to meet local needs.

Briefly, reducciones or congregaciones were the forced resettlement of indigenous communities, hamlets, or homesteads into larger centralized communities that could be more easily monitored by Spanish authorities—primarily the clergy (H. F. Cline 1949; Simpson 1934). Needless to say, forced resettlement represents a serious disruption in people's lives. The congregación program was implemented in various ways, however, and the particular form it took depended on specific Spanish objectives and strategies in a region.

The encomienda system originated in Spain as an institution associated with the reconquista (Simpson 1950). The Crown would commend to a deserving individual—an *encomendero*—the tax revenue and services from the inhabitants of a region consisting of towns, villages, and monasteries within the royal domain for a certain amount of time. Such a commendation did not signify ownership, but rather the temporary rights to collect goods and services from the natives of a specified area. The encomienda system was implemented in the Caribbean, although Queen Isabella was generally opposed to it because she saw it as a potential threat to her own sovereignty. In addition, the system was abused by encomenderos who regarded their charges as slaves. By the time of the conquest of Mesoamerica, King Charles V (grandson of Isabella and Ferdinand) was opposed to the introduction of the encomienda system there, but Cortés ignored the desires of his king and rewarded his men (and himself) with encomiendas consisting of sizable indigenous communities. In the first decades of Spanish rule in Mesoamerica, there was virtually no oversight of encomenderos, and they were free to exact as much tribute and labor as they could. Even after reforms were initiated, they were generally difficult to implement, and in many parts of Mesoamerica the encomienda system and its many injustices endured until the eighteenth century. The encomienda system was unlike anything that Mesoamericans were familiar with because it was such an unreciprocal transfer of goods and services to the encomendero. Although indigenous communities were accustomed to providing their leaders with goods and labor, prehispanic rulers also had obligations to their communities (Hoekstra 1990). Like the congregación program, the implementation of the encomienda system varied across Mesoamerica, depending largely on the nature of Spanish presence in any given area. Its impact has to be evaluated on a case-by-case basis.

Another Spanish imposition was a system of community government that was modeled on the *municipios* of Spain that had developed during the reconquista (Gibson 1984). Although the Spanish Crown intended for Spaniards and Indians to be segregated—officially the Republica de Españoles and the Republica de Indios were recognized as separate systems—municipal governments, whether Indian or Spaniard, were structurally similar. Community officials, consisting of *alcaldes* (mayors or magistrates), *regidores* (councilmen), *alferez* (standard bearer), *alguaciles* (constables), and other minor officials, were to be elected annually. We know now that, in many cases, the Mesoamerican hereditary nobility took advantage of this system, inserting themselves in the highest ranking positions and sometimes restricting voting rights to the nobility (Chance 1986; Farriss 1984, 1986; Haskett 1991; Lockhart 1992:30–44; Restall 1997).

Systems of Social Stratification, Ethnic Relations, and Gender Roles

Spanish and Mesoamerica notions about social stratification, like political and economic systems, had much in common. Both societies were highly stratified, something that Spaniards recognized immediately. The native nobility in Mesoamerica was granted numerous privileges—they could wear Spanish clothing, have horses, and carry arms, activities that were not permitted for commoners (Gibson 1964:155). Spanish policies were implemented in Mesoamerica based on the understanding by both Spaniards and Mesoamericans that native leaders had legitimate authority. On the one hand, indigenous elites were used by the Spaniards to collect tribute and mobilize labor. On the other hand, these elites—or at least many of them—must have seen it as in their own best interest to cooperate with Spaniards. As a result, the indigenous hereditary nobility managed to maintain its privileged position well into the Colonial period in many areas (Chance 1986; Farriss 1984, 1986; Lockhart 1992).

Whereas the traditional structure of social stratification in Mesoamerica was very rigid, one of the unintended outcomes of Spanish colonialism was that for some individuals born into the commoner class, the Spanish colonial world provided the opportunity for social mobility (Lockhart 1992:111 ff.). Not only could people change their status, but they also had access to goods that had previously been the exclusive domain of the elites.

The issue of ethnic identity is quite complex. During the process of political unification in Spain, there was an increasing intolerance of individuals unable to demonstrate that they had no Muslim or Jewish ancestry. Efforts were made to limit emigration to the New World to Castilian Spaniards—efforts that were largely unsuccessful. Nevertheless, at the same time that official policy stressed ethnic purity, the actions of individual Spanish colonists did not strictly conform to that ideal, and many were quick to take Indian women as mistresses and wives, creating a new category of person, the mestizo (P. Carrasco 1997; Mörner 1967). Official Spanish policies reflect great concern with ethnic identity. Under the system of *castas*, parentage determined an individual's classification, which in turn influenced taxation policy and sometimes determined which occupations an individual was eligible to pursue (O'Crouley 1972).

Mesoamericans also had well-defined notions of ethnic identity long before the Spaniards arrived. Within the Valley of Mexico alone, there were several self-identified ethnic groups, each with its own distinct history, patron deity, and style of dress and ornamentation

(Brumfiel 1994; Gibson 1964:9–31). Spaniards failed to perceive or acknowledge these distinctions and found it convenient to lump all Mesoamericans into the single category of "indio." Indians themselves, however, continued—and continue in many areas—to define themselves on the basis of ethnic divisions (Mulhare 2000).

There were some important differences between Spanish and Mesoamerican notions of gender roles. Spaniards brought with them a fundamental belief in the inferiority of women and the notion that women were to be submissive to men (Kellogg 1997; Rosenbaum 1996). The inequality of women was explicitly written into Spanish legal code; women were prohibited from formal participation in political and religious institutions; they could not be judges, lawyers, or priests. Women did have some rights in Spanish law, but only in the context of a patriarchal system where the law supported the power and authority of fathers and husbands.

The nature of gender relations in pre-Columbian Mesoamerica remains a subject of debate; gender complementarity is often identified as a common ideal, but gender hierarchy seems to have existed as well (see Joyce 2001). There is some consensus that the position of women in society was highly regarded overall, even though men dominated public life and, with only a few known exceptions, rulers and the highest ranking priests were males (Schroeder, Wood, and Haskett 1997). Women, however, did occasionally take on high leadership positions in the political sphere, and they also played important roles in the priesthood. Generally there was a sharp division between the work of women and the work of men, but these divisions were not necessarily hierarchical. Among the Aztecs, for example, at birth the midwife shouted war cries to celebrate the successful battle waged by a woman during childbirth; childbirth was equated with success on the battlefield, and giving birth to a baby was equated with taking a captive (D. Carrasco 1998).

Spanish colonialism led to an inevitable clash between the Spanish and Mesoamerican views of gender. In certain respects, the status of Indian women declined during the course of the Colonial period. This change is particularly notable in the colonial legal system where Indian women initially were active participants in court proceedings, but eventually became linked in their legal status to their husbands and treated in the Spanish court system as minors (Kellogg 1995; 1997). Similarly, colonial Indian women were no longer able to participate in religious activities in the same ways they had previously. Whereas in pre-Columbian Mesoamerica women played key roles in the temples, serving as priestesses and teachers, under Spanish rule they were barred from holding these positions.

Despite this decline in the status of women in the more public domain, elements of the pre-Columbian ideals of gender complementarity have survived in many predominantly indigenous communities across Mesoamerica. Ethnographers working in these communities have noted that machismo is largely absent and that husbands and wives seem to approach life with a degree of cooperation that is not seen elsewhere. Interestingly, in Tzotzil communities in highland Chiapas, the word for spouse is synonymous for "my complementation" (Eber 2000).

Similarities and Differences in Ideological/Religious Systems

In the realm of religion and worldview, Spaniards and Mesoamericans had fundamentally different belief systems. Spaniards found certain Mesoamerican religious practices offensive and diabolical, and because they exerted considerable control over public religious life, they were able to wipe out certain of the public rituals that had previously characterized Mesoamerican religion (such as human sacrifice). In addition, thousands of Indians received minimal Christian indoctrination and were baptized. These apparent successes led many Spaniards—as well as some modern researchers who do not question Spanish accounts—to conclude that they had achieved the spiritual conversion of the Indians (Barnadas 1984; Ricard 1966). But the entire process of Christianization—how it was conducted, how Spaniards and Mesoamericans interpreted Christianity, and the issue of syncretism—continues to be studied and debated (for example, Burkhart 1989; E. Graham 1998; Klor de Alva 1982). Some of the issues that now frame the debate include the serious misunderstandings that characterized Spanish-Indian religious interaction and the fact that, despite the tremendous differences in the belief systems of Spaniards and Mesoamericans, there were a number of areas where indigenous ritual behavior could be accommodated within the Catholic Church. So, in spite of the vast differences that initially separated Spanish and Mesoamerican religious systems, the great majority of the indigenous population of Mesoamerica is today nominally Catholic.[2]

Religious intolerance had become an important element of state policy in fifteenth- and sixteenth-century Spain, and the spread of the Christian faith was one of the claimed objectives of Spain's colonial enterprise. Yet Spanish Catholicism of the sixteenth century was full of contradictions, and European Catholicism in general had spread successfully because it was able to integrate pre-Christian beliefs and rituals (E. Graham 1998). Proselytization strategies in Mesoamerica were wide ranging but clearly at times included turning a blind eye to indigenous religious practices (Ingham 1986:35).

But if the earlier claims that Spaniards were completely successful in their efforts to convert Indians to Christianity are now discredited, so too is the notion that Christianity is simply a thin veneer that overlies an intact pre-Columbian indigenous belief system. Instead, as with the other factors we have explored, it is much more useful to consider the give and take that characterized Spanish-indigenous interaction. Particularly in the case of worldview, we need to consider how both Spaniards and Mesoamericans misunderstood each other.

Several examples can be cited that illustrate just how fundamental this misunderstanding was. One important aspect of the Mesoamerican worldview was a monistic orientation, sometimes described as "complementary dualism," in which the whole is made up of complementary and necessary parts (Gossen 1996; Monaghan 2000). The Western propensity to think in terms of dichotomies like good versus evil, male versus female, and life versus death is fundamentally different from the Mesoamerican view, which sees these properties as necessarily bound together. Mesoamerican deities had dual aspects, as did individuals. For example, the Aztec notion of *teotl*, a term that was translated by Spaniards to mean "god" or "sacred," is more accurately thought of as a term meaning "power," but it can refer to both positive and negative power (D. Carrasco 1998; Townsend 1992). Similarly, the Spanish concepts of sin or evil could not be directly translated into Mesoamerican languages because there were no such concepts in the Mesoamerican worldview. For Mesoamericans, a wide range of problems, attributed to sin or evil by Spaniards, were caused instead by disorder and imbalance (Burkhart 1989:38–39; Monaghan 2000). Mesoamerican concepts of soul were also distinctly different from the Spanish one (D. Carrasco 1998; Furst 1995; Monaghan 2000:28–29; Sandstrom 1991:258–60). In each of these cases, Spaniards mistakenly assumed that Mesoamericans understood these terms in the same way that they—the Spaniards—did.

Spaniards also were convinced that spiritual conversion had taken place because of the enthusiasm with which Mesoamericans participated in many of the rituals and ceremonies of the Catholic Church. Christian rituals that included singing, dancing, theatrical displays, processions, offerings, and burning of incense were quickly and willingly adopted (see Burkhart 1998), and Spaniards considered all of this solid evidence of conversion. What they did not recognize, however, was that these displays had also been important elements of pre-Columbian religious ritual, and they provided Mesoamericans with an acceptable way to avoid a total rupture with the past.

Objectives of the Colonizer, Kinds of Colonies and Colonists, and the Role of the Host Population

This is a complex set of related factors that revolve around motivation and strategy of the colonizers. Spain's objectives were territorial expansion, extraction of resources, religious conversion, and domination of conquered peoples. We know about Spain's motives and strategies through the documentary record, but there is also a physical manifestation of Spain's early domination. Physical destruction was associated with the Spanish conquest, certain indigenous settlements were subsequently abandoned, and others were reconstructed with entirely new architectural styles.

In general, colonies can have several possible configurations. In some situations, a few single males are sent to reside only temporarily in the colony to oversee resource extraction, and in others, entire families move to the colony with the intention of staying indefinitely and making a living there. In Spanish colonial Mesoamerica, early Spanish colonists were primarily males, many of whom intended to make their fortunes and return to Spain. Some did exactly that, but others stayed, and many of these individuals took indigenous women as mistresses or wives. Alliance building through establishment of marital ties—a practice familiar to both Spaniards and Indians—continued into the Colonial period, and women from the Mesoamerican nobility frequently married Spaniards (see P. Carrasco 1997).

The entire Spanish colonial enterprise in Mesoamerica was ostensibly controlled by the Spanish state, headed by the Crown and managed by the Council of the Indies in Spain (Elliott 1990; Lang 1975; J. H. Parry 1966). Nevertheless, it is virtually impossible to speak of a single Spanish colonial strategy. Official policies were implemented by colonial officials and bureaucrats who typically resided in the principal cities and towns of Mesoamerica. The interests of Spanish colonists did not always coincide with the interests of the Crown, and this frequently put colonial officials in the difficult position of either enforcing unpopular edicts from Spain, and thus inciting the wrath of fellow colonists, or ignoring the wishes of their king.

Spanish colonists defy simple characterization. In spite of attempts by the Crown to limit emigration to Catholic Castilians with good character, individuals from diverse backgrounds emigrated to the New World for a wide variety of reasons. The largest number were from southern and western Spain, many were poor, and they viewed emigration to the Americas as an opportunity to improve their fortunes (McAlister 1984:108–17).

In addition to the diverse interests of individual Spanish colonists, there were also factions of colonists created by the particular institutional structure of Spain's colonies, and these factions were frequently antagonistic. The clergy constituted one faction, and even within the clergy various groups typically competed against each other. The secular clergy and regular clergy were continually at odds, and members of the different mendicant orders had their own turf wars (Barnadas 1984; Schwaller 1987). A second faction was the Spanish or creole merchants who had to balance their strategies for acquiring personal wealth with the constraining economic policies of the colonial administration that were designed to funnel as much money as possible into the royal coffers. A third faction was made up of large landholders whose interests often conflicted with merchants and the clergy. All of these factions were frequently opposed to Crown policies, and they were able to interfere with the implementation of royal policies.

Spanish colonialism in Mesoamerica was based on the premise that natives would provide the labor for Spanish enterprises. As a result, a self-serving goal for Spaniards was that there *be* a native population to serve as laborers. Although excessive exploitation of native labor was certainly common, there was also a strong desire to keep the labor force alive and accessible.

Apart from these general trends, within Spanish colonial Meso-america there were significant regional differences in terms of Spanish objectives and strategies. In some regions, large numbers of Spaniards settled to live permanently and to engage in extensive exploitation of resources and Indian labor. In other regions, there were few Spaniards in residence and little interest in local resources. Clearly, a major factor that influenced the particular way that colonialism unfolded in any given area was the nature of Spanish presence.

I turn now to a more detailed look at a single region within Mesoamerica to identify how the factors discussed above influenced the process of colonialism under a particular set of circumstances.

CASE STUDY: SPANISH COLONIALISM IN SOCONUSCO

My own interest in Spanish colonialism and its impact on indigenous societies in Mesoamerica has developed over several years as I have conducted both historical and archaeological research in the Soconusco region of what is today Chiapas, Mexico. Initially I set out to examine how the indigenous population of this area was integrated into the Spanish colonial economic system. This research integrated historical records and data from excavations at the abandoned colonial town site of Ocelocalco (see fig. 3.1), a predominantly Indian town occupied between approximately 1560 and 1770 (Gasco 1987a, 1989a, 1992).

Soconusco's main claim to fame in the prehispanic and early colonial eras was that very high-quality cacao (cocoa) was produced in the region. Although the region experienced a cacao boom early in the Colonial period, the prevailing view in the early 1980s, when I began this research, was that with the demise of the indigenous population, cacao cultivation had also fallen into serious decline by the end of the sixteenth century, turning the area into an economic backwater (Gerhard 1993; MacLeod 1973). Contrary to expectations, however, at Ocelocalco we recovered considerable quantities of relatively expensive imported goods such as majolica, lead-glazed earthenware, and metal goods, and smaller quantities of Chinese porcelain. These goods were not isolated but were found in almost every house that was tested

(Gasco 1987a, 1992). The situation at Ocelocalco contrasted sharply with what was known from the few other colonial Indian towns that had been excavated at that time (Charlton 1979; T. A. Lee 1979; Lee and Markman 1979; Seifert 1977).

The archaeological data, together with information that I subsequently gathered from historical documents, revealed that Ocelocalco and the Soconusco region as a whole were not economically isolated but instead were very much involved in the international economy throughout the Colonial period (Gasco 1989a, 1989b). Moreover, Indian families in the Soconusco maintained control of most of the cacao groves until late in the Colonial period (Gasco 1996), which helped to explain how it was possible that so much imported material was found in the houses at Ocelocalco. The documentary evidence that Indian families maintained control over production of the region's most valuable crop did not seem to jibe with prevailing views about Indian-Spanish relations, in which Spaniards inevitably moved to control resources and labor. This study was just one of many carried out in the late 1970s and 1980s that were beginning to identify the wide range of variability and the complexity that characterized Spanish-Indian relations in colonial Mesoamerica (for example, Altman and Lockhart 1976; S. L. Cline 1986; Collier, Rosaldo, and Wirth 1982; Farriss 1983, 1984; Gruzinski 1989; Haskett 1991; G. D. Jones 1989; MacLeod and Wasserstrom 1983). In my initial analysis (1987a), I found that addressing several of the six factors discussed above helped me to identify how the situation in Soconusco compared with that in other parts of Mesoamerica and what accounted for the observed differences.

At Postclassic and Colonial sites in the Soconusco region, there is no mistaking the beginning of Spanish colonial rule. People were either forced or persuaded to abandon their communities and settle in adjacent settlements that were laid out in grid fashion with a church and other public buildings constructed in the town's center (Nuttall 1922). Many new materials and objects were quickly adopted (Gasco 1987a, 1989a, 1992).

At Ocelocalco I have tended to interpret the presence of new objects and materials largely as functional replacements for earlier objects and materials, rather than as a reflection of a significant ideological shift (Gasco 1992). In the archaeological record, I see, for example, that metal cutting implements quickly replaced obsidian ones. Early in the Colonial period, Spaniards dismantled the prehispanic institutions that administered obsidian extraction, production, and exchange (Pastrana 1998). The indigenous families of colonial Ocelocalco shifted to metal cutting tools, and I have no way to know if they felt that this was a great loss, if they grudgingly accepted the new material, or if they enthusiastically adopted it. Similarly, the families of Ocelocalco began to use majolica and lead-glazed serving wares early in the Colonial period. I have suggested previously (1992) that the glazed serving bowls simply replaced the polychrome serving bowls (*cajetes*) that were widely used in the Postclassic period; people were accustomed to eating out of colorful bowls of a certain size (approximately 20 centimeters in diameter) that were imported from outside the Soconusco. In the Colonial period, when these bowls were no longer available, they shifted to colorful bowls (now wheel-thrown and glazed) that were approximately 20 centimeters in diameter and were also imported from outside the Soconusco (Gasco 1987a). Again, I do not know how people viewed this shift.

The mechanics of acquiring imported obsidian tools and imported polychrome bowls in the Postclassic period and imported majolica bowls and metal in the Colonial period were much the same. Local cultivation of cacao, a highly valued product, provided Soconusco residents—during both Postclassic and Colonial periods—with the means to obtain objects brought to the region by professional merchants. I am reluctant at the present time to read too much into the presence of these objects in colonial Ocelocalco households, although I acknowledge that there may be more going on than simple replacement.[3]

For other goods, there was virtually no change from Postclassic to Colonial periods. The same kinds of storage and cooking vessels, which we presume were produced locally in the Postclassic period, continued to be used and produced locally throughout the Colonial period (and to the present day). Similarly, stone manos and metates (the standard grinding implements) continued to be used throughout the Colonial period and up until the mid-twentieth century, when mechanized grinding tools were introduced.

In the Soconusco region, we still have much to learn about Late Postclassic political and economic systems (Voorhies and Gasco 2004;

Gasco 2003a, 2003b). Nevertheless, the region undoubtedly had much in common with the rest of Mesoamerica. A hierarchical political system is reflected archaeologically in a three-tiered settlement pattern (Voorhies 1989), and economically the region was heavily involved in commerce (Voorhies and Gasco 2004; Gasco 2003b). In both political and economic arenas, the Soconusco region had been dominated by the Aztec Empire since the 1480s. Aztec officials and perhaps a colony of soldiers from Central Mexico were stationed in the town of Soconusco (or Xoconochco, the Nahuatl name from which the region gets its name), and towns in the area paid annual tribute in cacao and other products (Gasco and Voorhies 1989; Gasco 2003a).

In the Colonial period, the same basic political structure was maintained in which a regional capital dominated the entire province, and the province was divided into districts where a head town (*cabecera*) dominated outlying villages (*sujetos*). The region continued to be important commercially; the cacao grown in the area was now in demand in the international market. The colonial tribute system was based largely on the existing Aztec system, and the native population paid annual tribute in cacao until the mid-eighteenth century (Gasco 1989b).

At Ocelocalco, there is evidence early in the Colonial period for differential consumption of some introduced goods (mainly the glazed ceramics), and I have interpreted this as a reflection of variable socioeconomic status within the community. Over the course of two hundred years, household consumption patterns became more similar. This trend may indicate a decline in status differences (Gasco 1993, 1996), a pattern that has been noted elsewhere in colonial Mesoamerica. The leveling process that occurred between the late sixteenth century and the mid-eighteenth century, however, was reversed in some communities by the early nineteenth century, a shift I attribute to changing Spanish economic policies and to a growing Spanish population in the Soconusco region (Gasco 1996).

Ethnic identity was transformed during the course of the Colonial period in the Soconusco. Because of the particularly high mortality rates early in the Colonial period among native Soconusqueños (who spoke a Mixe language [Campbell 1988]), Indians from other parts of New Spain moved into the region. By the mid-seventeenth century, at least eight native languages were spoken in the area (Reyes 1961). By the eighteenth century, the majority of the native population reportedly spoke Nahuatl (*mexicano*), suggesting that ethnolinguistic identity may have been more homogenous by this date than it had been in the first two centuries of colonial rule. By the early nineteenth century, a further transformation had taken place; now there was a surge in the proportion of *ladinos* (individuals formerly identified as Indians but who no longer were identified as such)[4] in certain towns within the Soconusco (Gasco 1991, 2005). This process of change in identity from Indian to ladino eventually occurred throughout the entire province, so that today the population of the region is characterized as ladino or non-Indian.

The issue of changing gender relations in colonial Soconusco has not yet been examined in great detail. In a general sense, I assume that the patterns described above for Mesoamerica as a whole were also true for Soconusco, but this is clearly an area that warrants further investigation.

Much of the evidence regarding colonial religious beliefs among native Mesoamericans comes from areas where there is a large corpus of native-language documents, primarily central Mexico and, to a lesser degree, the Yucatán Peninsula. In Soconusco, we have only a very small number of documents written in Nahuatl, and none of the known documents are relevant to the issue of native religion. Spanish-language documents from Soconusco whose authors—usually priests—comment on the natives' faith generally claim that they are good Christians, a claim that deserves some skepticism. We know, for example, that in the late seventeenth century the Bishop of Chiapas, Francisco Nuñez de la Vega, visited Soconusco and discovered a cult devoted to Votan, a pre-Columbian culture hero and calendrical figure. The bishop learned that devotees of the cult worshipped in a cave where they kept sacred objects, including what may have been codices ("*cuadernillos*"), all of which were publicly burned (Nuñez de la Vega [1692] 1988:62). A few decades later, details from a witchcraft trial indicate that entire communities subscribed to "superstitious" (the term used in the document) beliefs. In 1721 several witnesses from the towns of Acacoyagua, Soconusco, and Ocelocalco claimed that certain individuals who were known witches could turn themselves into dogs to frighten others, and these same individuals were responsible for causing illness and death. People who had been harmed by the witches were reportedly cured by other individuals who had special curing powers (BAHD 1983).[5]

The archaeological record has, so far, not provided much evidence about religious belief systems. Within the houses excavated at Ocelocalco, the only recovered artifact with obvious religious significance is a small copper medallion of what appears to be the Virgin of Guadalupe found in a late seventeenth or early eighteenth century house.

Much of the evidence from colonial Soconusco mirrors the more general trends identified across Mesoamerica. One factor, however, played out quite differently in Soconusco than in many other parts of Mesoamerica. A somewhat unique form of Spanish-Indian interaction had a significant influence on the course of colonial development in the Soconusco region. Because of the area's hot, humid climate that was perceived by Spaniards to be unhealthy, few colonists settled in Soconusco. Despite the fact that the region produced cacao, a very valuable resource, cacao cultivation remained in the hands of the indigenous families of Soconusco. Spaniards either had no interest at all in controlling production, or perhaps a few tried and failed (Gasco 1987b, 1989b).

The Spanish civil administration of Soconusco also was somewhat different from that in other regions. Although in the 1520s the entire region was held in encomienda by Cortés and brothers Jorge and Pedro Alvarado, by 1530 the Crown had taken control of the area, and it was administered as a crown encomienda thereafter (Gasco 1987a). There is general agreement that Indians living in Crown encomiendas fared better than those living under individual Spanish encomenderos. This absence of encomenderos, coupled with the small number of other Spanish landowners, meant that until late in the Colonial period most of the land remained in the hands of individual Indians and Indian communities (Gasco 1989b, 1996, 1997).

The Spanish religious administration of the Soconusco region also differed from that in many other parts of Mesoamerica. In Soconusco, religious activities were carried out by members of the secular rather than the regular clergy. The regular clergy were noted for protecting indigenous communities from abuse by other Spaniards, but they also exercised a great deal of control over the communities where they served. The members of the secular clergy, on the other hand, were in general less committed to serving indigenous communities and were not opposed to seeking personal wealth (Barnadas 1984; Schwaller 1987).

The net result of the particular form that Spanish colonial rule took in Soconusco was that Spanish-Indian interaction occurred mainly in the economic sphere, as merchants who traveled to the region, local colonial officials, and the clergy all were involved in the cacao trade. Members of these three factions struggled among themselves to gain access to the valuable cacao grown by indigenous cacao farmers who owned their own orchards and were not subject to the demands of encomenderos. In contrast to many other regions, there was little conflict over land rights, and Spanish landholders were not an important faction until late in the Colonial period (Gasco 1996). Also, in contrast to the many regions where the mendicant orders were heavily involved in indigenous communities, many of Soconusco's secular priests were apparently more interested in commercial activities than in being involved in the communities they served.

Factional fights among members of these three groups dominate colonial documents, making it difficult to arrive at a simple conclusion about what "Spain" wanted in this region. Official Spanish policy emanating from the Crown or the Council of the Indies had little to do with everyday life on the ground. Instead, colonial documents are full of charges and countercharges that one faction or another was mistreating the Indians. It is easy to come away from these documents with the impression that the native population suffered tremendous abuses from Spaniards—and they undoubtedly did. But I think we can get more out of these data. Regardless of the truth of any single charge, it is clear that all the Spaniards recognized that charging your competitors with mistreatment of Indians was a sure way to eliminate the competition. We can safely assume that the native population was well aware of this strategy and did what they could to use it to their own advantage.

One set of documents from the mid-sixteenth century provides us with a glimpse of how native authorities became involved in the factional struggles. On February 22, 1565, the indigenous authorities of several Soconusco towns signed a letter (written in Nahuatl) in which the Spanish governor of the province, Pedro Hordoñez, was charged with numerous examples of mistreatment of the natives of Soconusco. This letter has been published (Anderson, Berdan, and Lockhart 1976;

Paso y Troncoso 1939–1942, 10:62–69) and would seem to be good evidence for misconduct by a high-ranking Spanish colonial official. Nevertheless, in January 1566, the same individuals signed another letter in which they gave their full support for Hordoñez for all the good works he had carried out, and they also noted that the previous year a letter had been written in their names by the governor's enemies.[6] They claimed that this earlier letter (presumably the February 22 letter noted above) was full of lies, and they urged the authorities to ignore it. Perhaps it would be possible to ferret out the truth in this matter from other documents, but a more interesting point is that indigenous leaders were actively engaged in local political intrigue, and they clearly understood that they had leverage over competing Spanish factions.

In summary, by examining briefly the process of colonialism in Soconusco, it is apparent that for most of the factors examined here the situation in Soconusco was quite similar to that experienced elsewhere in Mesoamerica. One factor that distinguished this region from many others in Mesoamerica, however, was the specific nature of the Spanish enterprise in the area. Spanish presence in Soconusco was limited mainly to individuals who were involved in commerce; Spanish-Indian interaction occurred mainly in the economic sphere, as Spaniards—professional merchants as well as colonial officials and the clergy—engaged in trade with indigenous cacao producers. We know that one of the results of this particular form of interaction was that indigenous families consumed a wider range of imported goods than did families in other regions that were less involved in commerce. This form of interaction may have had even broader impacts that have not yet been identified. For example, did extensive commercial interactions between Spaniards and Indians promote the use of Spanish and the decline of native languages in the Soconusco? How was the adoption of new material goods related to changing worldviews? These and other unresolved questions about colonial Soconusco are the focus of ongoing research.

CONCLUSIONS

My goal in this chapter has been to provide evidence from Spanish colonial Mesoamerica that can contribute to a broader understanding of colonies, colonization, and colonialism in cross-cultural perspective.

I have argued that European or even Spanish colonization cannot be easily reduced to a single phenomenon. Not only did the motives and strategies of the various European powers vary, but the nature and responses of the numerous indigenous groups subjected to colonial rule also varied. A similar argument can be made for most of the instances of colonization discussed in this volume, in the sense that we cannot reduce Roman or Inka colonization to a single process. This observation, however, does not mean that we should just throw up our hands and conclude that every colony has its own unique history and that efforts to identify patterns are futile. Instead, for any particular colonial situation, a set of factors that focuses on aspects of both the host and intrusive societies can be systematically examined. This kind of analysis can provide a better understanding of how and why one situation differs from or is similar to another.

In the example I have presented here, we can first see how and why Spanish colonialism in Mesoamerica differed from Spanish colonialism in other parts of the Spanish Empire (in California, for example; see Lightfoot this volume). We might also expect that in yet other parts of Spain's colonies, where indigenous societies were more similar to Mesoamerica in terms of social, political, and economic organization (as in the Andes), that the colonial situation would have had a great deal in common with Mesoamerica (and it did). The analysis can also be undertaken at a more micro level where very specific places, such as Soconusco, can be compared with other specific places within Mesoamerica.

At the same time, by addressing the factors identified above, we can also compare at a more macro level the colonial Mesoamerican situation with other colonial situations. I suspect that much of what is considered unique about Spanish and European colonization efforts in the Americas and the Pacific is due to the several thousands of years of separation between peoples of the Americas (and the Pacific) and peoples of Africa and Eurasia, together with the fact that natural resources (indigenous plants and animals, among others) are so different in the Old and New Worlds. In none of the other cases examined in this volume do we find situations where colonized and colonizers have such distinct cultural and biological heritages and where the repercussions of these differences were so profound. Perhaps European colonization in the New World is unique in this respect. Yet acknowledging this common feature for all of European colonies in the Americas and the Pacific does not help us to understand the very obvious differences that emerged in the various colonial settings across these regions. Dramatic demographic decline and the introduction of new plants, animals, and other materials still led to very different outcomes.

It is clear that there are no adequate global models that can explain the nature of colonies or colonization in all times and places. But anthropologists and historians who advocate a comparative perspective do have within their reach tools that can lead to a more comprehensive understanding of patterns of colonization.

Notes

1. An earlier notion that the "Classic" societies of Mesoamerica represented the pinnacle of cultural and artistic achievement and that the "Postclassic" was a period of decline and decay is now discredited, but the terms are still used to denote the chronological sequence.

2. In more recent times, large numbers of formerly Catholic Indians have converted to Protestantism (see Monaghan 2000).

3. Currently we do not have good data from Postclassic houses that would allow direct comparative contextual analysis of these items in pre- and post-hispanic households. Future work is planned to remedy this, so this interpretation could change as more data become available.

4. A full discussion of the ladino phenomenon is beyond the scope of this paper, but see R. N. Adams 1994; Adorno 1994; Gasco 1991, 2005.

5. Ironically, the Church found the men accused of being witches innocent and the man who admitted to curing people guilty of witchcraft.

6. Letter to the Crown, January 1566, Archivo General de Indias, Audiencia of Guatemala Leg. 44.

4

Colonial Interactions and Hybrid Practices

Phoenician and Carthaginian Settlement in the Ancient Mediterranean

Peter van Dommelen

> The Phoenicians who from ancient times on made voyages continually for purposes of trade, planted many colonies throughout Lybia and not a few in the western parts of Europe, too.
>
> *Diodorus Siculus 5.20.1*

STUDYING ANCIENT COLONIZATION

In modern Western thinking and writing about colonialism, the ancient Mediterranean has always constituted an important point of reference because of its instrumental role in the spread of classical culture over the Mediterranean and into temperate Europe. The numerous Greek settlements in south Italy, in particular, have traditionally been cited as prime examples of ancient colonialism, which figure prominently in both the archaeological record and in many accounts of classical authors. The rise of *Magna Graecia* was nevertheless by no means an isolated or exceptional development in the Mediterranean of the earlier first millennium B.C.E., as large numbers of Greek settlers also ventured into the Black Sea region and found their way to the shores of Mediterranean France and Catalunya. Little attention has similarly been given to the Phoenicians, who sailed from the Levant and Cyprus to the far reaches of the western Mediterranean and established an extensive network of settlements on the islands and eastern and southern coasts of the western Mediterranean. Although the significance of the Phoenician exploits has long been played down by classical archaeologists and ancient historians alike, the Phoenician achievements were explicitly discussed in colonial terms by classical authors, as the above-cited remark of Diodorus Siculus shows. More recent fieldwork in Spain, North Africa, Sicily, and Sardinia has only in the last few decades begun to bring to light their share in the archaeological record of the western Mediterranean. In later centuries, Roman and Carthaginian colonialism, albeit more often labeled as "imperialism," transformed and expanded the colonial impact beyond the Mediterranean regions.

The colonial nature of these Greek and Phoenician settlements has rarely been an object of study in its own right. This assumption has always gone without questioning, because classical authors consistently used colonial terms, and their accounts moreover seemed to be well shored up by the abundant archaeological evidence of Greek and Phoenician settlements throughout the Mediterranean. Following the postcolonial critique of modern colonial representations in a wide range of fields (Pels 1997; Loomba 1998; R. J. C. Young 2003), critical scrutiny of archaeological and historical representations of ancient colonialism has, however, begun to lay bare the implicit associations of the seemingly straightforward colonial terminology. Apart from situations in, for instance, French North Africa, where direct and explicit connections between ancient and modern colonizers have been suggested, the general and unquestioned use of terms such as "colony" and "colonization" has been shown to underlie the implicit application of modern notions to ancient contexts and vice versa (Mattingly 1996; van Dommelen 1997a; De Angelis 1998; Dietler 1998:289–90, this volume). The moral colonial duty to educate and "civilize" the colonized indigenous people is a good case in point. Precisely because this "civilizing mission" had become an integral part of nineteenth- and twentieth-century "imperialism," similar aspirations have implicitly been ascribed to the Greek settlers of south Italy. Such a representation is demonstrably false, however, as Greek overseas settlement was motivated by and represented in quite different terms: the Greek term *apoikia* itself primarily means "being away from home" and does not carry the overtones of conquest and exploitation associated with the word "colonial" (Dougherty 1993; van Dommelen 2002).

Taking further both this archaeological debate and current postcolonial insights regarding the constitution and developments of colonial situations (see below), it is my intention in this chapter to scrutinize the term "colonization" as a unifying notion for large numbers of colonial situations in which Greek, Phoenician, or others played a (supposedly) leading colonial role. To do so, I focus on the lesser-known colonial network controlled by the city of Carthage, which developed out of the earlier Phoenician colonial presence in the western Mediterranean from the middle sixth century B.C.E. onward and which is best exemplified by the Phoenician roots of Carthage itself. My specific aim is to follow up the resemblance and differences between Carthaginian (or more generally Punic) and Phoenician colonial settlement and to gain an insight into the local backgrounds of both colonial and indigenous inhabitants in several different but yet historically related colonial situations. Ultimately, it is my intention to consider the question of whether different colonial situations can meaningfully be grouped together under one (colonial) heading such as "Carthaginian colonization" or whether the specifically local nature of the different colonial experiences and interactions should be emphasized. The archaeological evidence for this discussion is provided by recent work on local colonial interactions in three different regions of the western Mediterranean—namely, west-central Sardinia, southeast Spain, and the Balearics. Chronologically, I shall focus on the final stages of Phoenician settlement and the early centuries of Carthaginian colonial presence in these regions, which roughly coincide with the seventh to fourth centuries B.C.E.

PARTIAL TEXTS AND POSTCOLONIAL HISTORIES

Colonial situations occupy a prominent place in several times and places; probably the most widely studied instances are the European (primarily British) settlements in North America, Australia, and South Africa (seventeenth to nineteenth centuries C.E.) and the Greek and Roman expansion across the ancient Mediterranean. In both of these cases, however, scholarly interest has remained confined to the particular colonial situations of that time and place, without exploring the abstract notion of colonialism in cultural and social terms. It does not come as a surprise, therefore, if the discipline of archaeology as a whole has by and large failed to recognize the importance of colonialism as a recurrent cross-cultural phenomenon of the past.

With regard to the Mediterranean in particular, the general prefer-ence for the active term "colonization" as opposed to the abstract alter-native "colonialism" denotes the view that the latter term refers exclusively to modern European expansion and bears no resemblance to the situations of the ancient Mediterranean (Descoeudres 1990). It is also associated with the long-standing disregard of the colonial roots of the discipline of archaeology in general—although some anthropol-ogists started to explore their own colonial inheritance long ago and occasionally but explicitly have spelled out the archaeological connec-tions (Fabian 1986; Stocking 1991; Bénabou 1976; Trigger 1984). It is only with the quite recent emergence of so-called postcolonial theory and the associated surge of historical and anthropological interest in colonialism that both the colonial past and the limited scope of colo-nization studies in Mediterranean archaeology have been highlighted (Rowlands 1998; Gosden 1999:15–32; Lyons and Papadopoulos 2002).

As the term "postcolonial" itself suggests, postcolonial theory is closely related to the Western decolonization of the so-called Third World. By and large, it can be defined as an attempt to "liberate" for-merly colonized regions, not only politically but also culturally, by reviv-ing or reinventing "authentic" indigenous traditions and achievements and by rewriting history from an indigenous, decolonized point of view. With authors such as Aimée Césaire, Franz Fanon, and Albert Memmi playing a major part in these movements, postcolonial theory first gained academic prominence in literary and cultural studies.

In more recent years, however, postcolonialism has come to refer not only to a specific period in global history characterized by the so-called post-colonial condition,[1] but also to a particular analytical and theoretical perspective on colonialism (Jacobs 1996:22–29; R. J. C. Young 1998, 2003). Although there should be no doubt that postcolo-nialism denotes "the contestation of colonialism and the legacies of colonialism" (Loomba 1998:12), it should equally be clear that, for pre-sent purposes, postcolonialism refers to a particular (Western) way of thinking about representations of colonial situations and structures. As an analytical perspective, postcolonial theory neither assumes any strict similarities between premodern and more recent instances of colonial-ism, nor confines itself to considering only modern colonial situations. To adopt a postcolonial perspective on ancient Greek colonialism is consequently no more anachronistic than any other analysis based on modern insights or indeed technological innovations. In this broader sense, postcolonialism can usefully be defined as "a form of contestatory/oppositional consciousness, emerging from either preexisting imperial, colonial, or ongoing subaltern conditions, which fosters processes aimed at revising the norms and practices of antecedent or still vital forms of domination" (Klor de Alva 1995:245).

Discourse, Context, and Partial Texts

In academic circles, postcolonial theory has been given a sound theoretical grounding by Edward Said in his seminal study *Orientalism* (1978). Drawing on Foucault's work on power and knowledge (1979, 1982), he argued that culture can be a powerful means of domination as effective as economic exploitation and military suppression. He demonstrated this thesis by analyzing a vast array of literary and historical representations, ranging from novels, popular magazines, and films to cabinet minutes and political speeches, which all contributed to confirm the European representation of the East as inferior, unreliable, irrational, and backward. Such continuous and widespread assertions offered tangible "proof" of and effectively sanctioned widespread circulation of simplistic stereotypes, which in turn provided the necessary legitimization and "naturalization" of Western political and military dominance. Backed up by Foucault's insistence that "discourse produces reality; it produces...rituals of truth" (1979:194), Said has explicitly connected discourse to politics, arguing that knowing the "Orient" effectively laid the foundations for a political-cultural framework of Western dominance in the Middle East (Said 1978:3; Loomba 1998:43–48).

In the wake of Said's later analyses of the connections between literary representations and colonialism (1993), postcolonial analysis has practically become synonymous with literary critique and discourse analysis, as is only too obvious from the literary background of virtually all prominent postcolonial scholars and the increasingly numerous handbooks of postcolonial theory. A recent reader of postcolonial studies has even restricted its scope to literary studies in English, thereby suggesting that postcolonial literature is an English-language phenomenon and that postcolonial studies can be equated with literary studies

(Ashcroft, Griffiths, and Tiffin 1995:4; Loomba 1998:96–97; see R. J. C. Young 2003 for a very different kind of introduction).

This strong literary orientation of postcolonial studies has increasingly been criticized as ignoring Said's insistence on the intimate connections between literary and other representations and failing to look beyond literary representations (R. J. C. Young 1998:4–5). Because many discourse analyses of novels pertain only to the colonizers and their home countries—if not just to the upper classes of these societies—they have been criticized as suffering from "weak contextualisations" (L. Turner 1995:204). By ignoring the social and political contexts of colonial situations and by assuming a straightforward relationship between the representations they study and the underlying political reality, many postcolonial studies fail to demonstrate to what extent colonial situations are maintained by cultural, economic, and military means. This neglect of historical context has consequently been denounced as privileging literary production "at the expense of materialist historical enquiry" (R. J. C. Young 1995:161; B. Parry 1987).

Because of their textual bias and their overlooking of the historical and local specificity of colonial situations, most postcolonial studies have contributed to a homogenizing and "monolithic" representation of colonialism (N. Thomas 1994:12). As a corollary, they have consistently overlooked the fact that cultural representations are rooted in specific colonial contexts and that they are thus inextricably related to their economic and political conditions, which is, in fact, a point repeatedly made by Foucault and Said (van Dommelen 1998:26). Although the postcolonial focus on the cultural dimension of colonialism has no doubt added an important feature to colonial studies, it cannot replace analysis of the political and economic aspects of colonialism, since *all* of these made up colonial situations.

Despite these shortcomings, the literary emphasis of postcolonial theory has also become the dominant approach in both anthropology and archaeology as these disciplines have begun to explore postcolonial theory (although anthropologists have long questioned the colonial roots of their disciplinary practice [Stocking 1991]). In archaeology in particular, postcolonial theory is unambiguously identified with discourse analysis and critical scrutiny of literary and academic representations (J. Webster 1996; Gosden 2001). Because there is no shortage of representations that have been created from a one-sided colonialist perspective and in which the colonized are assigned passive parts or in which they do not figure at all, there clearly is much scope in both archaeology and anthropology for studying what Nicholas Thomas has termed "partial texts" (1990, 1997). A good case in point is the critical discussion of Dunbabin's classic study, *The Western Greeks* (De Angelis 1998), or that of the intimate involvement of the French colonial authorities in the study and representation of the Roman Maghreb (Mattingly 1996), which both leave little doubt that there is good reason and ample scope for taking the postcolonial critique onboard in Mediterranean archaeology.

There is nevertheless no intrinsic reason why archaeologists should not be drawing on postcolonial theories in studies of past colonial situations. Anthropological practice demonstrates, in fact, that critical discussions of "partial texts" can very fruitfully be combined with ethnographic analysis of practice on the ground (Werbner and Ranger 1996). Although the literary bias of postcolonial studies might make it understandable that there is little archaeological exploration of postcolonial approaches to past colonial situations, its viability need not be doubted, as recent publications have now begun to demonstrate (Lyons and Papadopoulos, eds. 2002, this volume).

Postcolonial Histories

As a substantial number of historical and ethnographic case studies demonstrate (Pels 1997), the postcolonial insistence on the cultural dimension of colonial situations is indeed best supported by detailed and contextualized studies that unravel the intricate interconnections between cultural and political as well as symbolic and economic features in the reproduction of colonial situations. For both Foucault and Said, representation and discourse are, after all, intimately connected to the "real" economic and political situation on the ground. From this perspective, contextualization is indeed critical, since both discourse and representation are created in and are very much part of a specific colonial context. Cultural hegemony and economic exploitation are therefore not two different or even opposed interpretations of colonial power, but they should rather be seen as two sides of the same coin that are related to each other in intimate, but ever-varying ways. It is precisely these tensions between the various ways of exerting or, on the contrary, opposing colonial power that can provide valuable insights into the dynamics of colonial societies (see Stoler and Cooper 1997).

Historical contexts are particularly critical for the study of colonial situations, because it is the wider historical conditions created by colonialism that, to a large extent, structured local colonial situations—at the very least, they created them. As different colonized regions have usually given rise to quite different colonial contexts that were yet related to one another by precisely the same historical conditions, the obvious question is not only how these differences can be explained in relation to the same colonial influences. It also raises the perhaps even more important question of whether such different contexts can meaningfully be grouped together under one unifying label—as, for instance, British colonialism or Greek colonization?

Such sweeping labels are, in fact, at odds with the postcolonial view that colonial situations should not be understood in binary terms—that is, as basically structured by the "colonial divide" between colonizers and colonized (Pels 1999; van Dommelen 1997a, 2002). This view is based on a growing number of ethnographic studies that have shown that such "dualist" representations of colonial situations grossly simplify the complex realities of colonial societies by reducing them to a straightforward opposition between colonizers and colonized (Stoler 1989, 1997). By ignoring the much more nuanced and complicated social and economic divisions at the grassroots level, in which criteria such as gender, age, and class intersect with the colonial-indigenous distinction, dualist representations not only assert the dominant position of colonizers, but they also overlook much of the social dynamics of a colonial situation. It is, in fact, the contrast between the black-and-white opposition of people's dualist representations and the many shades of gray evident in people's actions, that offers intriguing insights into colonial communities and their strategies for making sense of their colonial context.

Hybridization as Cultural Practice

Since dualist perceptions of colonialism leave no room for groups of people other than the two sides of the divide, colonial situations are often depicted as lesser variations or, in more extreme cases, even as "aberrations" of the colonizers' home society. From a postcolonial perspective, however, colonial situations can alternatively be seen as made up by people of both indigenous and colonial descent who have together created distinctly new communities that are characterized by what the postcolonial theorist Bhabha has termed "hybrid" meanings and appearances (1992:173–83).

Cultural hybridity is a concept that has been propagated particularly by Bhabha as a means to capture the "in-betweenness" of people and their actions in colonial situations and to signal that it is often a mixture of differences and similarities that relates many people to both colonial and indigenous backgrounds without equating them entirely with either (Bhabha 1985). For Bhabha, cultural hybridity is "the effect of an ambivalence produced within the rules of recognition of dominating discourses as they articulate the signs of cultural difference" (1985:110). This means that by complying with colonial norms and standards and yet hanging onto certain indigenous perceptions, people develop new cultural norms of their own and effectively "invent" new traditions that are peculiar to each colonial situation (see Keesing 1994).

Hybridity is also a concept with a troubled background, however, as it is a nineteenth-century biological metaphor with heavy racist overtones: basically, it denoted a lack of (racial) purity (R. J. C. Young 1995:1–89). Although there is ground to accept the claim that recent postcolonial usage has superseded these racist connotations (Papastergiadis 1997:257–58), there is no such retort to the critique that the notion of cultural hybridity is based on "the presumption of the existence of once pure cultures" (Friedman 1995:73). Theoretically, this suggests that the term "cultural hybridity" is based on an outdated holistic and essentialist view of culture, as is shown by references to cultures "flowing" and "mixing" as if these were autonomous entities (Friedman 1995:80–85).

A convenient alternative to overcome this shortcoming may be found in the associated term "hybridization." This active form refers to the social actors who make up the colonial situation rather than to reified cultures, and yet it retains the notion of "mixture." Because it is through the social interaction of the inhabitants of colonial situations that new traditions are invented and that the colonial situation is eventually shaped, "hybridization" can be used to describe such processes of interaction and negotiation between various groups. In short, hybridization represents "the *practice* of mixed origins," and hybrid cultures can effectively be seen as the outcome of such practices (Friedman 1995:84; emphasis added).

Since material culture, and the archaeological record by extension, is inevitably implicated in these processes in a variety of ways, the meanings of objects must similarly be regarded as hybrid constructs of these particular contexts. It is therefore no coincidence that the few archaeological case studies that go beyond critical discussion of "partial texts" have focused on precisely the hybrid appearance of some material culture in both past and present colonial contexts (van Dommelen 1997a; J. Webster 1997).

Studying hybridization as a means to start writing the alternative histories advocated by postcolonial theory, however, includes sustained attention for the colonizers of a particular region, since resisting partial and dualist representations of colonialism should entail more than a shift in focus to the previously ignored indigenous inhabitants of the region: it should equally take a fresh look at the colonizers' involvement in the region (see Gasco this volume). Studying hybridization suggests a different perspective on the colonizers, emphasizing, on the one hand, the local roots and local interests of at least part of the colonial community, while, on the other hand, also acknowledging their extraregional involvement in a colonial network. It is precisely such a double-edged approach that I propose for understanding some of the colonial situations of the western Mediterranean in the seventh to fourth centuries B.C.E.

COLONIAL BEGINNINGS

The network of Phoenician "colonies" that spanned a large part of the western Mediterranean in the seventh and sixth centuries B.C.E. was rooted in the Phoenician exploits of these regions in the preceding centuries (fig. 4.1). The earliest firm archaeological evidence of a Phoenician presence in the central and western Mediterranean dates to the beginning of the eighth century B.C.E., and literary references to an earlier "precolonial" presence have so far remained unsubstantiated. Although there had already been extensive exchange contacts throughout the Mediterranean since the second millennium B.C.E., it was only from the eighth century onward that actual settlements were

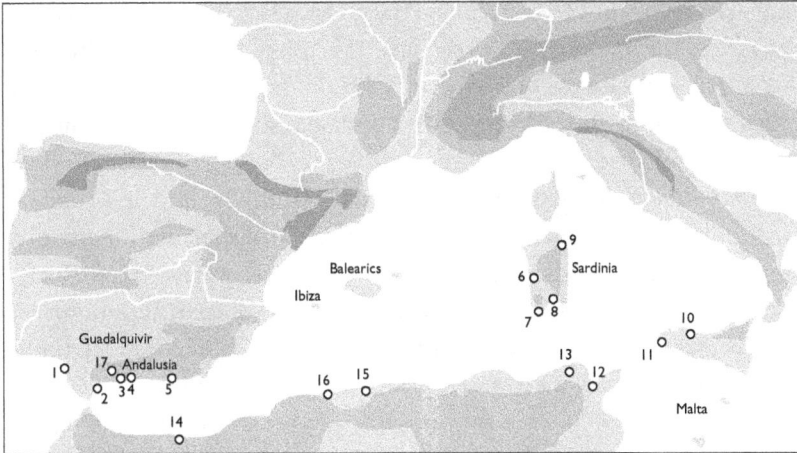

FIGURE 4.1

Phoenician settlement in the western Mediterranean: "colonized" regions and principal settlements. 1. Cádiz; 2. Cerro del Prado/Carteia; 3. Cerro del Villar; 4. Málaga; 5. Villaricos; 6. Tharros; 7. Sulcis; 8. Cagliari; 9. Olbia; 10. Palermo; 11. Motya; 12. Carthage; 13. Utica; 14. Rachgoun; 15. Tipasa; 16. Cherchel; 17. Acinipo.

established in the West. These settlements maintained intensive relationships with their Phoenician "home towns" or "mother cities" on the coast of modern Syria and Lebanon.

From the mid-sixth century onward, however, these connections were severed, and the central Mediterranean city of Carthage (near modern Tunis) became the focal point of the colonial network. Although many of the settlements of this network were based on preexisting Phoenician foundations, they are usually labeled "Punic" rather than "Phoenician" from this time forward, in reflection of the changed colonial configuration.[2] Because of the prominent role of Carthage in the Punic world, "Carthaginian" is used as a synonym for "Punic."

Phoenician Colonial Enterprises

Some of the earliest signs of Phoenician presence in the western Mediterranean consist of Phoenician and Greek imported objects in otherwise distinctively indigenous contexts, such as the village of Sant Imbenia in northwest Sardinia and the burials of Doña Blanca in southern Spain. The material culture of these find spots includes both Phoenician and Greek (usually Euboian) pottery and some occasional metal items, many of which can be traced back to Cyprus. In most cases, however, the Phoenician presence largely centered on exclusively "colonial" settlements that were established in previously uninhabited places. All of these settlements were situated in isolated places on off-shore islands and peninsulas, apparently preferring good anchorage and protection to easy access into the hinterland. The principal regions where the earliest colonial settlements were established in the early and middle decades of the eighth century (fig. 4.1) were central North Africa (Carthage and Utica), southern Sardinia (Sulcis), and southeast Spain (Toscanos and Almuñecar). According to a rich literary tradition, the region of the Guadalquivir estuary in south Spain (Cádiz) should be added to this list, even if reliably dated archaeological deposits are so far lacking. During the later part of the eighth century, similar colonial settlements were established at the western and northern shores of Sicily (Motya, Palermo) and on the island of Malta, while elsewhere the existing network expanded with the establishment of new settlements in the same regions of the western Mediterranean. Further settlements may have been established along the North African coast (Rachgoun), but reliable evidence is lacking.

Most of these colonial settlements have yielded evidence of Phoenician domestic pottery and of regularly laid-out courtyard houses built of mud brick that were quite different from contemporary indigenous ceramic and architectural traditions in those regions. As hardly any of the Phoenician settlements were established in places where Phoenician objects had already been circulating, it seems there was neither a structural relationship between the two types of early Phoenician presence nor a "colonial strategy" of "reconnaisance" preceding permanent settlement. One of the few exceptions to this rule, however, may have been the Guadalquivir estuary. Here, in the early eighth century, the indigenous inhabitants had already deposited Phoenician objects in the burial mounds at Doña Blanca; and, probably by the late eighth century, a Phoenician settlement was subsequently established at nearby Cádiz (Fernández Jurado 2000). On the whole, however, the Phoenician exploration of the central and western Mediterranean seems to have proceeded primarily with the foundation of new settlements (see C. Wagner 2000).

Phoenician expansion in the "far west" has usually been explained as a function of the Phoenician reputation, in the ancient literary sources, as skilled artisans and traders. Since Phoenicia itself does not offer many natural resources apart from the murex snails for the highly valued Phoenician purple dyes, trade has generally been seen as the necessary quest for raw materials needed for the production of silverware, furniture of precious wood and ivory inlay, and jewelry of precious metals and stones. The Phoenician presence in Cyprus, which led to the "colonial" establishment of Kition in the ninth century, and their explorations of the southern Anatolian coast around the same time are usually regarded as the natural prelude to the later western expansion (Niemeyer 1999). This view has especially been elaborated by Susan Frankenstein (1979, 1997), who singled out the quest for silver as particularly instrumental in the expansion and creation of a Phoenician "colonial" network. Taking the high demand for silver in the Levant of the Neo-Assyrian period as a starting point, she related the early Phoenician presence in southern Spain, as demonstrated by the finds in the Doña Blanca burials, to the silver ores of the Río Tinto (Frankenstein 1994). The establishment of other Phoenician settlements elsewhere and in later times, including Carthage, is usually explained as either a search for other raw materials or as staging posts for supplies and protection along the trans-Mediterranean sailing routes (Aubet 1993:155–66).

Given their alleged commercial role, it is not surprising that Phoenician settlements are regarded as quite different from the contemporary Greek establishments in Sicily and the south of peninsular Italy. Whereas the former have been defined as trading posts, the latter are seen as settler colonies where people set up a new life, literally "away from home" (*ap-oikia*). As the remark by Diodorus Siculus cited at the start of this chapter makes clear, this is a long-standing view that has recently been reasserted as a distinctively "non-Greek model for expansion" (Niemeyer 1990). As illustrated by the string of eighth- and seventh-century Phoenician settlements in southeast Spain, the settlements of this model are characterized by the lack of a formal territory (*chora*) and a generally less urban appearance than the Greek establishments. Carthage is the only settlement that seems to have defied this model and to have resembled the Greek one more closely. This anomaly is seen as particularly appropriate, given the exceptional development and expansion of this city in later times (Niemeyer 1990:487).

In order to emphasize the distinction between Phoenician and Greek settlements, in many cases colonial terminology has been abandoned as a label for the Phoenician establishments and substituted by such terms as "port of trade" and "emporium." Although the call for a "non-Greek model" of colonial expansion does signify a departure from the traditional Hellenistic focus in Mediterranean archaeology, it nevertheless still perpetuates the assumption that *all* Phoenician or Greek settlements must be understood in one single model that is equally applicable to all Phoenician or Greek foundations. The uncontested implication of this is that colonialism continues to be seen as a process in which the colonizers' contribution is ultimately determining and the colonized are assigned a subordinate part.

The Punic Expansion of Carthage

The uniform representation of the Phoenician colonial network is also undermined by developments in the seventh century and its collapse in the following century. In the seventh century, first of all, additional Phoenician settlements were established in the western Mediterranean, some in the immediate vicinity of existing ones—such as Othoca and Monte Sirai near Tharros, and Sulcis on Sardinia (see below)—and some in previously "uncolonized" regions such as the Balearics and the Algerian coast. These regions must nevertheless have been more or less familiar ground, as they are "en route" for Phoenician vessels crossing the western Mediterranean basin (Aubet 1993:160–64). The Spanish regions, however, do not seem to have participated in this intensification of colonial presence, as the densely spaced series of settlements on the Andalusian coast that had been established in the late eighth century did not see significant changes. Second, and perhaps even more significant, is the alleged demise of the Phoenician colonial network, which seems to have affected the Spanish settlements more than the other ones: the Andalusian ones, in particular, were almost all abandoned in the earlier decades of the sixth century, while a few surviving ones, such as those at Málaga and Villaricos, were substantially enlarged. Since Phoenician settlement continued to thrive elsewhere in the western and central Mediterranean, it seems likely that, contrary to Niemeyer's (1990) assertion, this particular group of settlements was the exception rather than the rule. This view is supported by the continued existence of Cádiz and the wider Huelva area, where Phoenician settlement had never been as dense as on the Andalusian coast. Instead of a unified "non-Greek model," there seem to have coexisted at least "Andalusian" and "central Mediterranean" models of Phoenician "colonial" settlement that remained relatively unaffected by the demise of the Phoenician colonial network—with Cádiz apparently adhering more closely to the latter than to the former (see Aubet 1993:280–84).

The middle decades of the sixth century nevertheless passed anything but unnoticed in the other Phoenician settlements of the western Mediterranean, as is suggested by the replacement of the dominant burial rite of cremation by inhumation: new cemeteries of rock-cut chamber tombs and trench graves were inaugurated in all "colonial" settlements around this time. The establishment of several new major settlements that expanded the "colonized" regions in Sardinia (Olbia and Cagliari), Sicily (Palermo), and North Africa (Tipasa and Cherchel) similarly signals a change in "colonial" strategies. The creation of several smaller settlements in the immediate vicinity of existing ones (such as Neapolis in Sardinia: see below) yet remained well in line with previous developments. In order to signal other minor changes in the material culture of the Phoenician settlements, such as the disappearance of certain characteristic Phoenician pottery types, the label "Punic" is usually preferred for referring to the period from the mid-sixth century onward (see above).

The Punic emergence is conventionally explained as Carthage taking over control of the western Mediterranean network after the conquest and destruction of the Levantine Phoenician cities, Tyre in particular. Although the relationships between developments in the eastern and western Mediterranean in the sixth century remain open to debate (C. Wagner 1989), the interventionist strategy of active occupation of the western "colonies" ascribed to Carthage is rather more doubtful. Not only is this view primarily based on very late and obscure literary sources (Justin), but the archaeological evidence to support straightforward military Carthaginian conquest of the Phoenician settlements is also lacking. Instead, a much more complex situation has been suggested in which the major Phoenician/Punic settlements, including Carthage, engaged in ever-shifting commercial and political alliances among themselves as well as with Greek and Etruscan settlements in the western Mediterranean, as is best exemplified by the confusing situation in Sicily. Although Carthage gradually did emerge as a dominant player on this scene (not unlike Syracuse in the Greek sphere of southern Italy), it did not gain direct territorial control of overseas territories until the late fifth or early fourth century (Barcelò 1989; Chapa Brunet 1997; van Dommelen 1998:118–25).

Unless "colonial" developments are regarded as the sole relevant elements of colonial situations, however, interaction with local indigenous inhabitants must be taken into account for understanding the developments of Phoenician and subsequent Punic settlement in the western Mediterranean. In order to do so, local colonial situations must be examined in considerable detail instead of speculating on alleged colonial ambitions.

LOCAL INTERACTIONS

The three different colonial situations selected for comparing Phoenician and Punic colonialism are those of the Andalusian coast of southeast Spain, west-central Sardinia, and the island of Ibiza (fig. 4.1). Together, these regions span the entire western Mediterranean and, perhaps more importantly, offer a relatively well-published record of archaeological work throughout the area: in both Sardinia and Ibiza, intensive archaeological surveys have been carried out that complement excavations undertaken in both colonial and indigenous settlements. In Andalusia, such survey evidence is largely lacking, but the numerous excavations in this area go some way toward making up for this lacuna. The chronological focus on the seventh to fourth centuries is purposefully at odds with the conventional break of the mid-sixth century between the Phoenician and Punic periods. The intention is to allow developments in this period to be seen in their own right, without being prejudged as either the final Phoenician or the initial Punic phase.

Andalusia

Phoenician settlements were established on small offshore islands and headlands along the coastline of southeastern Spain in the middle

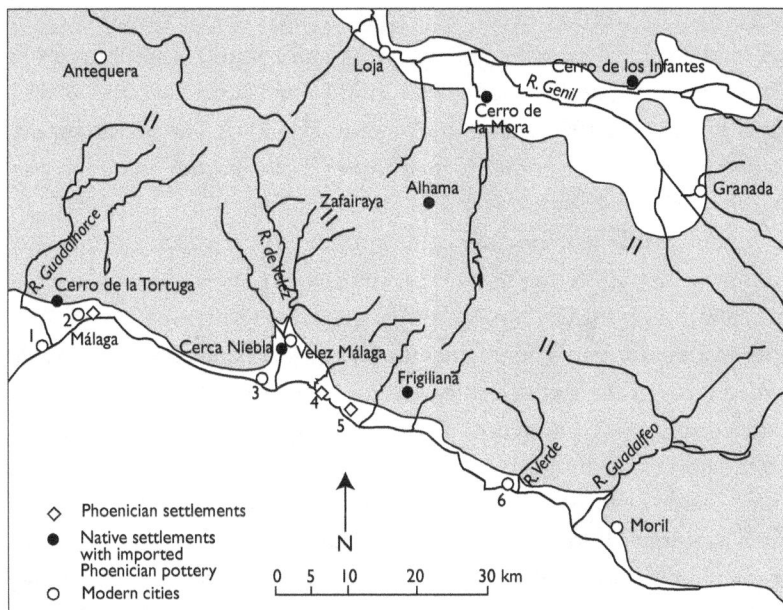

FIGURE 4.2

Phoenician settlement in Andalusia: 1. Cerro del Villar; 2. Málaga; 3. Toscanos; 4. Morro de Mezquitilla; 5. Chorreras; 6. Almuñecar.

decades of the eighth century (fig. 4.1). All these locations take advantage of the local topography: numerous parallel narrow valleys and small coastal plains that have been created by as many streams running from the Subbaetic mountain range into the sea. Phoenician settlement was particularly dense in the area around Málaga, where no less than six habitation sites and at least four associated cemeteries have been documented along no more than 30 kilometers of coastline (fig. 4.2). Despite the short distances separating the settlements, each occupied a stream valley of its own, with its cemetery often on the opposite riverbank. Toscanos and the cemetery of Cerro del Mar on the western and eastern banks of the Vélez River are typical in this respect (Schubart 1982; Aubet 1991). All of these settlements were quite small, usually covering not more than 2 to 3 hectares—with the exception of Toscanos, which by the later seventh century came to measure some 15 hectares. Although they were largely made up of carefully constructed houses that were regularly laid out along one or two streets, artisanal activities were quite prominently present, as is well demonstrated by the metallurgical workshops in Morro de Mezquitilla, the potteries of Cerro del Villar, and the large "warehouse" in Toscanos (Aubet 1997a, 1997b; Schubart 1998; compare Aubet et al. 1999). The abundant evidence of small-scale domestic activities such as weaving, livestock husbandry, and fishing suggests that these sites were inhabited by independent, self-supporting communities who actively exploited the opportunities offered by the direct hinterland of their homes (Aubet et al. 1999). As both the houses and cemeteries testify, they lived their lives in an eminently Phoenician way. For these people, however, the so-called crisis of the sixth century, whatever its precise nature, became a hard-hitting reality, as almost all of these settlements were abandoned in the course of the first half of that century. Only Málaga developed into a Punic town, alongside settlements farther up and down the coast such as Adra, Villaricos, and Cerro del Prado. As a result, the distances separating the colonial settlements multiplied from less than a kilometer to several dozens of kilometers (Martín Córdoba and Recio Ruiz 2002).

The Phoenician and Greek imports found at these sites show that the inhabitants actively engaged in the overseas Phoenician network. Their contribution presumably consisted of agricultural produce, metalwork, and perhaps dyed cloth, as murex shells suggest. After the crisis of the sixth century, the inhabitants of the few Punic settlements continued this involvement in the Mediterranean network, as is shown by Punic imports from Carthage and elsewhere. Throughout these periods, however, remarkably few indigenous finds have been encountered in the settlements and none in the cemeteries. Although this underscores the independence of the inhabitants of these settlements and their allegiance to their own customs, interaction with the indigenous inhabitants of southeast Spain is nevertheless demonstrated by occasional imported objects and minor changes in the indigenous settlements. Surface finds in the lower reaches of the stream valleys of coastal Andalusia suggest that the indigenous inhabitants of these areas were in frequent and relatively close contact with their new "colonial" neighbors (López Pardo and Suárez Padillo 2003). The higher reaches of the Andalusian coastal mountains and the regions of the upper Guadalquivir farther inland were, by contrast, characterized by a modest number of "orientalizing" burials with Phoenician imports. The persistence of existing Final Bronze Age settlement patterns of dispersed small-scale villages until the later seventh century similarly suggests that contacts with these areas farther afield were less intensive and perhaps restricted to certain groups within the indigenous communities. It was only from the end of the seventh century onward that a gradual process of centralization and fortification signaled profound social and economic changes (Aguayo, Carrilero, and Martinez 1991; Carrilero Millán 2000; Carrilero Millán et al. 2002). It was in this period and in these uplands that the so-called Iberian culture took shape, which despite its ostensibly Greek-style funerary sculpture and the large number of imported Attic pottery in the hill forts, represented a primarily local formation that maintained close ties with the Punic settlements on the coast (Ruiz Rodríguez 1997; Chapa Brunet 1997, 1998).

West-Central Sardinia

The central feature of this region is the wide bay of Oristano, the northern and eastern shores of which are bordered by the sandy soils of the Cabras and Arborèa wetlands that give way to the coarse sediments of the smaller Sìnis Plain to the north and the large Campidano Plain to the east and southeast (figs. 4.1 and 4.3). Phoenician settlement initially kept aloof from the access to the island interior offered by these plains and remained confined to the southern tip of the San Marco Peninsula on the northwestern shore of the bay of Oristano. As shown by the oldest deposits of the *tophet* sanctuary[3] situated to the north of the site and grave goods from the Torrevecchia cemetery farther down the peninsula, Tharros was established in the later decades of the eighth century B.C.E. and would remain continuously inhabited for the following 1,500 years. The settlement area was located on the leeward side of the Torre San Giovanni hill, but the Phoenician phase has as yet hardly been explored. The inauguration of a second cemetery at San Giovanni di Sìnis farther north in the course of the seventh century suggests that the settlement was thriving and expanding by that time. This impression is strengthened by the establishment of Othoca on a sandy knoll across the bay in the northern Arborèa, which was a small settlement with its own cemetery. It yet lacked a tophet, which underscores its dependency on Tharros (fig.4.3). As a subsidiary

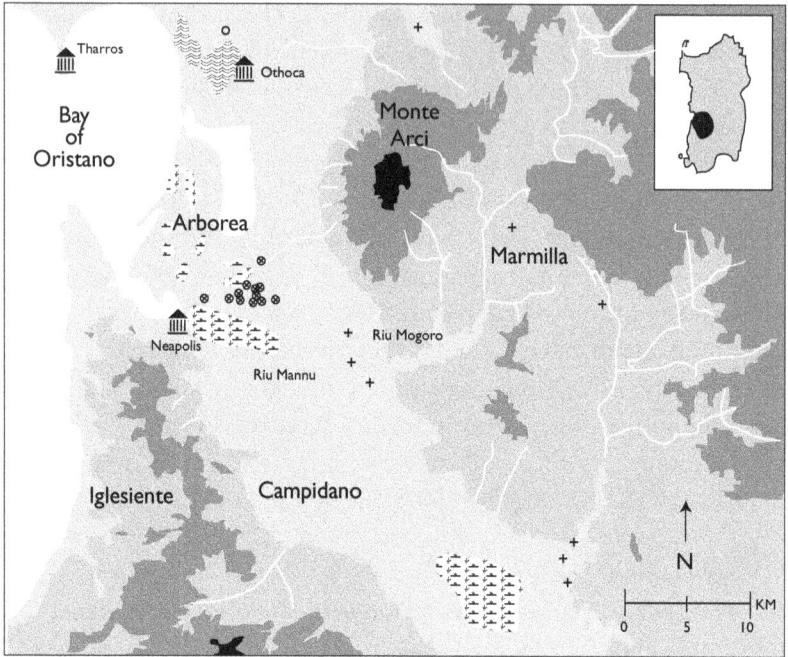

FIGURE 4.3
Phoenician and Punic settlement and fifth-century colonial imports in west-central Sardinia.

foundation of Tharros, the establishment of Othoca suggests that contacts with the interior of Sardinia were substantially intensifying in the later seventh century. It also marks a shift in interest, since such contacts do not seem to have played any role when Tharros was founded and the sheltered harbor and excellent maritime opportunities of Cape San Marco were preferred (Acquaro 1983, 1991).

The Punic period is well defined in the archaeological record of Tharros and Othoca, as rock-cut chamber tombs replaced the cremation burials in cemeteries and stelae made their appearance in the tophet sanctuary in Tharros. The layout of the settlement seems to have followed the local topography, but monumental public buildings were not constructed in Tharros before the fourth century, while none are known from Othoca. The establishment of Neapolis on the southern shore of the bay of Oristano in the mid-sixth century (fig. 4.3) was in itself hardly innovative, as it mirrored that of Othoca—as is reflected by

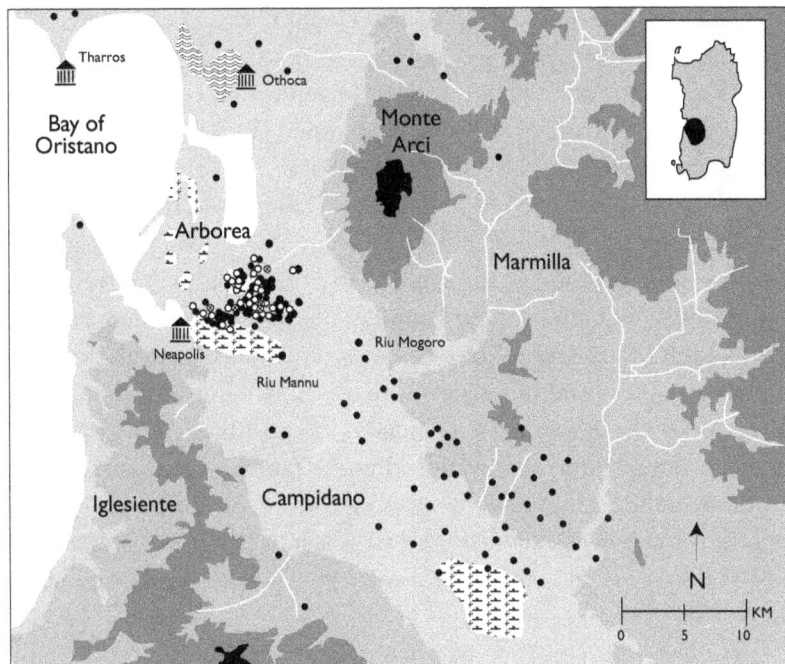

FIGURE 4.4

Punic settlement in west-central Sardinia from the fourth century onward.

the ancient names of the towns: "new town" versus "old town" (Zucca 1987, 1991). More significantly, however, it was accompanied by the foundation of a dozen or so small-scale rural sites, which represented small- to medium-sized single farmsteads of a markedly Punic nature. These sites signaled a significant shift in the colonial attitude toward the interior of Sardinia, as the contacts were intensified from an exchange-based approach to a territorial one. The consequences of this change turned out to be profound, as this handful of farms more than tripled in the course of the following century. By the beginning of the fourth century, their numbers exploded, with the appearance of another 60, resulting in a total of some 115 rural sites in a small area just north of Neapolis (fig. 4.4). The latter expansion was moreover matched by a spread of rural settlement inland, resulting in the appearance of Punic farms all over the Campidano Plain. Contemporary local production of transport amphorae suggests that export of agricultural produce was a major feature of the emerging rural economy (van Dommelen 1997b, 1998:130–44).

Throughout the eighth and seventh centuries, contacts between the indigenous Iron Age Nuragic inhabitants of Sardinia and the Phoenician settlers on the coasts had remained rather low-key, as they were effectively restricted to elite-level exchanges of precious objects, in particular metal wares. They were also largely channeled through so-called well sanctuaries, which functioned as regional politico-religious centers. Although the Nuragic communities of the island underwent a profound transformation from the ninth century onward, this development was basically an indigenous process, which was only marginally affected by the Phoenician presence on the island. This is nicely demonstrated by the observation that the famous *nuraghi*, the large dry-stone walled settlement towers of the Bronze Age, lost their habitation function but yet retained their significance in the local communities (Lilliu 1988:433–36; G. Webster 1996:179–94; van Dommelen 1997b; Blake 1998).

The low intensity of contacts in west-central Sardinia is reflected by the fact that all three colonial settlements were established in previously uninhabited places. Even the expansion of colonial settlement across the bay of Oristano, including the establishment of rural settlement in the sixth and fifth centuries, only occurred in a restricted zone devoid of indigenous settlement (van Dommelen 1998:146–57). At the same time, however, it is from the fifth century onward that colonial imports such as Attic finewares and Punic amphorae became more common finds in Nuragic settlements in inland west-central Sardinia, suggesting that interaction between the two communities was increasing as well as becoming more direct. The spreading of Punic rural settlement over the entire region suggests that these developments eventually culminated in the acculturation of the indigenous inhabitants of west-central Sardinia.

Ibiza

Of the four Balearic Islands, it was initially only Ibiza that saw the foundation of Phoenician and Punic settlement. In obvious contrast to the larger islands of Mallorca and Menorca, which had been inhabited by indigenous "Talayotic" people since at least the early Bronze Age, the so-called Pitiussae islands of Ibiza and its tiny adjunct Formentera

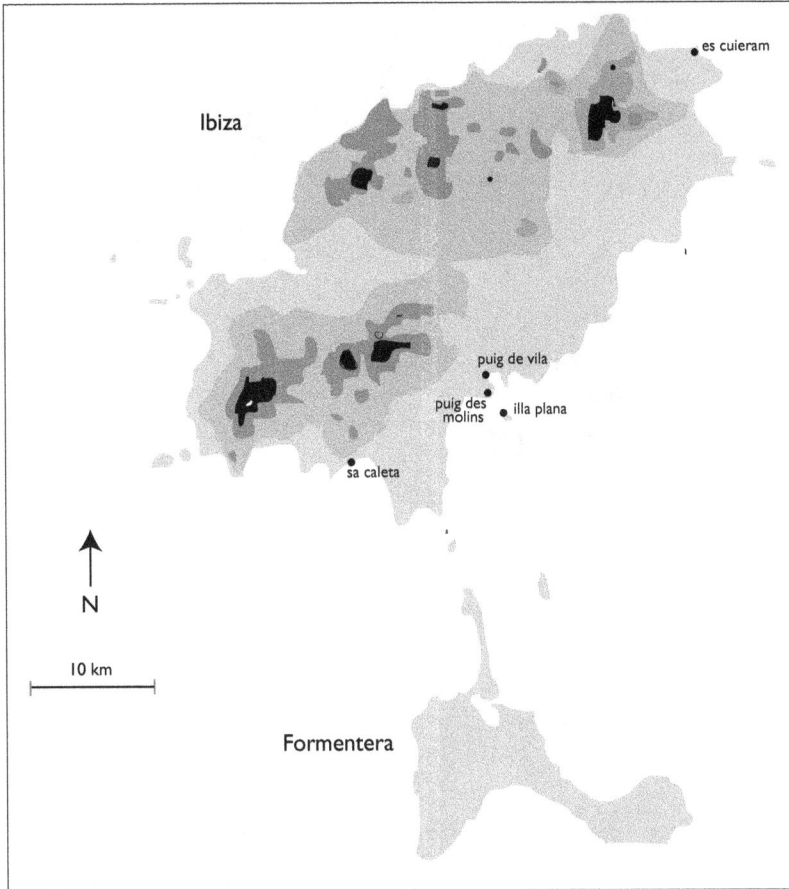

FIGURE 4.5

Principal Phoenician and Punic settlement on the Balearic Islands.

had been uninhabited for almost half a millennium when they were first explored by Phoenician seafarers (figs. 4.1 and 4.5; Guerrero 2000). The absence of any permanent colonial settlement on Formentera is no doubt largely due to the combination of a lack of reliable water sources and its proximity to Ibiza, from which the available resources of this tiny island could easily be exploited: this islet has indeed repeatedly remained uninhabited in more recent centuries (Gómez Bellard 1995a).

On Ibiza, the first Phoenician presence was established on the

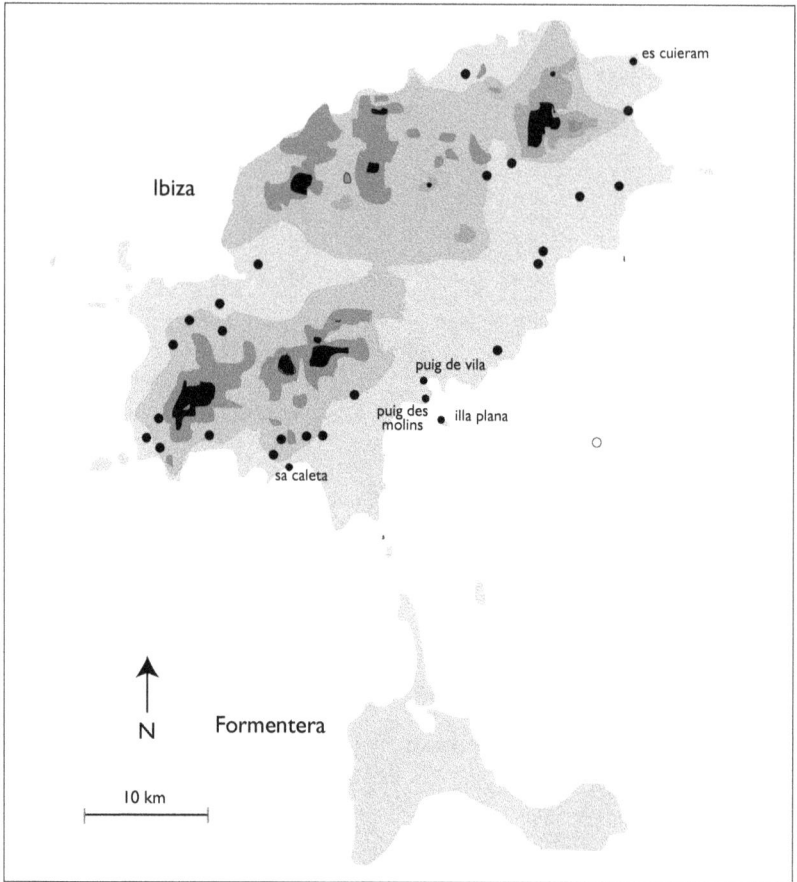

FIGURE 4.6

Punic rural settlement on Ibiza from the later fifth century onward.

small promontory of Sa Caleta shortly after the mid-seventh century (fig. 4.5). It seems to have been rather ephemeral and was probably related to Phoenician seafarers on their way to or from the Valencian or Andalusian coast. This site was abandoned only half a century later, in favor of the much larger and better-sheltered bay of Ibiza. Here a permanent settlement was established, with the habitation area and the cremation cemetery occupying the slopes of the Puig de Vila and the Puig des Molins, respectively (fig. 4.6; Costa and Fernández 2000). Not much later, in the second half of the sixth century, we can see a transition to the Punic phase in the appearance of rock-cut chamber tombs in the slopes of the Puig des Molins, the erection of stelae over the graves, and the establishment of a sanctuary on the Illa Plana Island in the bay of Ibiza with Carthaginian-type statuettes (Gómez Bellard 1991, 1995b). The subsequent appearance of small rural sites in other parts of the island from the later fifth century onward, followed by permanent settlement on Formentera, demonstrates that the nature of the Punic presence underwent a fundamental reorientation toward a territorial occupation and agricultural exploitation of the entire islands group (Gómez Bellard 2003). Large numbers of locally produced, distinct "Pitiussaean" types of amphorae found on the Spanish mainland suggest that much agricultural produce, such as olive oil, was destined for export. The early-fourth-century inauguration of a shrine in the cave of Es Cuieram in the far northeast of the island underscores that the Punic inhabitants were indeed putting down roots all across the island (Gómez Bellard 1986, 1996). The establishment of a small settlement on the islet of Na Guardis off Mallorca followed earlier infrequent contacts with the Balearic Islands proper and underscores the gradual Punic expansion on these islands, which slowly but inevitably led to increasing interaction with the indigenous inhabitants of Mallorca and Menorca (Guerrero Ayuso 1991; Fernández-Miranda 1997:67; Guerrero 2000).

COLONIAL SETTLEMENTS, INDIGENOUS INHABITANTS, AND HYBRID INTERACTIONS

Despite the somewhat cursory descriptions, it may be evident from the above that all three areas discussed present a number of characteristics that set each of them apart from the other two or that, on the contrary, group two of them together. At first sight, the impression therefore seems to be that these colonial situations do not share any obvious common denominator—apart from the cultural background of the colonizing communities, of course, who share common traditions of Phoenician and subsequently Punic customs and material culture. Although the transition from the Phoenician to the Punic period in the middle decades of the sixth century can be distinguished in each of the colonial situations, the transformation is never identical, even if certain features such as rock-cut chamber tombs occur more than once.

The most discriminating and interesting feature seems to be the level of interaction between the "colonizing" and indigenous inhabitants of these regions through time, because it is paradoxically precisely in the two regions where little or no interaction took place during the Phoenician phase (west-central Sardinia and Ibiza) that a colonial rural presence developed that would eventually spread over the entire region. In Andalusia, by contrast, a more intensive interaction between the Phoenician and indigenous communities resulted in what appears to have been a marginalization of the Punic settlements and a buoyant development of Iberian society.

Cultural Change and Structural Transformation

The key for understanding, or rather dissolving, this paradox lies in the west-central Sardinian colonial context. Although the similarities between Punic rural settlement on Sardinia and Ibiza are obvious, the social contexts of both regions cannot so easily be equated, as the Sardinian situation was inevitably affected by the simple reality that many of the rural inhabitants of the internal areas were of indigenous descent and had incorporated some of their Nuragic customs in the local Punic traditions. Although they clearly had adopted the Punic way of agrarian production and that of daily life more generally, including the use of the classical-style farms, black-glazed tablewares, and Punic transport amphorae, they resisted such intrusion in other dimensions of their lives. Punic farms in the interior were, for instance, preferably situated in the immediate vicinity of by-then abandoned nuraghi for reasons that must have had less to do with good farmland than with local perceptions of and long-standing ties with the landscape. Local roots are particularly evident in the ritual sphere, as is nicely demonstrated by the local reworking of the cult of Demeter at Genna Maria of Villanovaforru. Here, the mainstream Carthaginian rituals had been reworked into a typical local fertility cult that incorporated both foreign ("colonial") elements, such as the incense burners, and indigenous features, like the offering of oil lamps. Initially lamps continued to resemble Nuragic Iron Age types, but over time they were replaced by Classical and Hellenistic ones (van Dommelen 1997a:313–20, 1998:151–56). On Ibiza, by contrast, both the "urban" sanctuary at Illa Plana and the rural one at Es Cuieram adhered quite closely to

Carthaginian models, as is perhaps obvious, since there were no indigenous inhabitants with traditions of their own on Ibiza. It is interesting in this respect that the statuettes from Illa Plana have been compared with those of the Punic sanctuary of Bithia on the south coast of Sardinia, as these figurines stand out in the Sardinian context as remarkably mainstream Carthaginian-Hellenistic products (San Nicolas 2000). They are, in fact, substantially different from figurines found in other Punic sanctuaries in Sardinia, including the one near Neapolis in west-central Sardinia (Campus 1997).

In many respects, the west-central Sardinian colonial situation of the Punic period is much closer to the Andalusian one in Phoenician times, where the local inhabitants not only interacted actively with the Phoenician inhabitants of the region but also did so on their own terms. The Final Bronze Age (eighth century) hut at San Pablo, for instance—which was situated just across the Guadalmedina stream from the Phoenician settlement at the Alcazaba of Málaga—demonstrated that its inhabitants had opted to adhere to their indigenous architectural traditions but had at the same time also adopted wheel-thrown pottery at a large scale (Efrén Fernández et al. 1997). By contrast, in the contemporary hill fort of Acinipo—which is situated some 50 kilometers inland in the mountains (fig. 4.1)—the oval houses of the Final Bronze Age phase were eventually replaced in the seventh century by rectangular "colonial-style" houses (Aguayo, Carrilero, and Martinez 1991; Carrilero Millán et al. 2002). Despite such similarities, it remains quite difficult to assume any intrinsic connection such as a shared "colonial strategy" between eighth- and seventh-century Andalusia and fifth- and fourth-century Sardinia, because differences abound no less. One major difference, for instance, was that fifth- and fourth-century B.C. Sardinia had a substantial colonial presence, whereas the interior regions of Andalusia enjoyed much more intermittent and limited colonial contacts in the eighth and seventh centuries.

Much more closely connected, but perhaps less obviously so, were the colonial situations of west-central Sardinia and Andalusia in the Punic period, since it was in these centuries that the distinction between colonial and indigenous became blurred in both regions. At first sight, however, there seem to be few similarities, as the Sardinian region became entirely assimilated to the colonial Punic culture, and the indigenous communities of Andalusia incorporated, by contrast, only selected colonial features into their own newly invented Iberian cultural traditions. This opposition is more apparent than real, however, as the transformations are structurally analogous: as I argued above and elsewhere (van Dommelen 1997a:318–20), the adoption of Punic *material* culture does not imply that Punic meanings and values were embraced as well. This means that the construction of Punic farmsteads and the transport of agrarian produce in Punic amphorae do not warrant the conclusion that the indigenous inhabitants of Sardinia were "utterly deculturalized" (Lilliu 1988:472). This does not imply either, however, that these people somehow managed to preserve their Nuragic culture "in disguise." It leads rather to the recognition that a new cultural identity and a new set of values were forged in which local indigenous standards were matched to "colonial" objects and customs—which by that time had been around long enough to have become equally local. Herein lies the key for appreciating the processes at work in the Sardinian colonial context and for understanding the role of material culture in these developments (compare Rogers 1993b, this volume). The use of Punic- and Greek-style sculpture in sixth- and fifth-century Andalusia in "Iberian" religious and political practices similarly does not detract from the local significance of these practices, as is underscored by the observation that much of the Iberian monumental sculpture in the Córdoba area clustered along a local sociopolitical boundary (Chapa Brunet 1998).

Hybrid Practices in Context

The common underlying process at work in both colonial contexts can usefully be characterized as "hybridization" since this term emphasizes the construction of a new set of standards and values or cultural tradition out of a range of available traditions, materials, and perspectives. Since hybridization regards culture and identity as context-dependent social constructs, it does not distinguish between colonial and indigenous (material) culture and regards all available traditions and materials as potential building blocks for constructing a new cultural identity. It is indeed only when the constructed nature of the meaning of material culture and of the new cultural identity is recognized that the structural similarities between Iberian Andalusia and Punic west-central Sardinia become evident.

Hybridization particularly draws attention to the active involvement of people in these developments, because it is they who opted to continue living in oval huts in eighth-century Andalusia and to prefer Punic-style farmsteads in fifth-century west-central Sardinia. Instead of reducing colonial situations to abstract instances of "culture contact" and acculturation, hybridization centers on the colonial contexts as social encounters in which people made decisions that made sense from their own context-dependent point of view. In the Iberian situation, for instance, it was the political and social concerns of a local elite reaching for Punic and Greek sculpture as a means to assert their dominant position in their local community that led to the so-called Hellenization of eastern Spain, rather than any recognition of a superior artistic quality of classical sculpture. The Iberian case is also a fine example of the ways in which cultural elements can be mobilized to political ends, which underscores the claim that postcolonial analysis of colonial situations need not be ahistorical or ignorant of matters of power and domination.

There remains another interesting parallel between Ibiza and west-central Sardinia: in both regions, the earlier Phoenician situations of the seventh century were characterized by an absence of interaction between the Phoenician and indigenous communities. The remote location of Tharros is particularly significant in this respect. In both regions, too, colonial settlement subsequently developed in the Punic period a rural presence based on dispersed small- and medium-sized farmsteads of a well-established classical type throughout the region. A further parallel may be found in the probable influx of Punic migrants who in west-central Sardinia presumably did not venture much beyond the coastal area but who in Ibiza must have made up all of the rural population (van Dommelen 1998:157; Gómez Bellard 1986:187). In the light of the Ibizan evidence, it seems quite possible that the intentions of the Carthaginian colonial authorities were at least comparable, if not similar, but that in the Sardinian case the Nuragic inhabitants of the interior of west-central Sardinia rewrote the colonial policies—by adopting them in part and by adapting other elements of them. The sanctuary near Neapolis suggests, moreover, that the Punic settlers of the coastal area were at the same time equally responsive to the Nuragic inhabitants and the customs they encountered in the hybridization process.

CONCLUSIONS: POWER AND MATERIAL CULTURE IN COLONIAL CONTEXTS

Although the colonial terminology may well be too entrenched to be abandoned, the foregoing discussion suggests that it carries two major shortcomings. The first and principal one is that the labels "Phoenician" and "Punic" colonization gloss over the many differences between the colonial situations grouped together under this heading (compare Osborne 1998:267–68 on ancient Greek colonialism). Although the use of terms such as "emporium" and the proposal to single out an "Andalusian model" of Phoenician colonization (Aubet 1993:280–84) recognize the deficiencies of the current terminology, such changes remain superficial, as they fail to acknowledge the indigenous contribution to these differences. As subsequent refinements of Phoenician colonialism now distinguish as many colonial strategies as colonized regions, it is perhaps ironic that they fail to appreciate that these differences may be not so much consequences of different colonial intentions and policies as the outcomes of different regional situations encountered by the colonizers. Although I fully subscribe to the distinctions between Andalusian, Sardinian, southern Spanish, and Sicilian colonial situations, my basic argument is that these differences cannot be attributed to colonizers using different "models" in different contexts; instead, they must at least as much be ascribed to the reactions of the local inhabitants of the regions frequented by Phoenicians. It is the presumed but highly questionable similarities between colonial situations that share the same colonizers that must be abandoned in order to make meaningful comparisons between colonial situations.

The second shortcoming regards the very term "colony" itself, which is indiscriminately used for a very wide range of Phoenician settlements whose only shared feature is an identifiable foreign presence in indigenous contexts. Definitions of colonialism, however, usually insist on the existence of an uneven economic, political, or military relationship between the communities involved (van Dommelen 1997a:306; Rowlands 1998:327). From this perspective, the peripheral Phoenician presence in Sardinia can hardly qualify as colonial; and the Punic settlements in Andalusia similarly appear to have been too marginal to be labeled colonial. The absence of indigenous inhabitants on Ibiza would, moreover, set the Phoenician and Carthaginian presence on this island apart as an exceptional case. The advantage of at least recognizing the difference of these situations is that structural similarities and differences can be much more easily identified.

A postcolonial perspective on ancient colonialism is one way forward for undermining conventional "partial histories" and classifications, because the recognition that colonial situations are locally constructed contexts is a very efficient way of downsizing the significance of colonial imports and of underscoring the relative context-dependent meanings of material culture (compare Dietler 1995, this volume). Hybridization is an appropriate and powerful concept in this respect because it emphasizes that classificatory labels such as "colonial" or "Phoenician" "have no essence or [that] their essence was fabricated in a piecemeal fashion from alien forms" (Foucault 1971:142; cited in Dreyfus and Rabinow 1982:107).

A focus on the structural characteristics and underlying processes of colonial situations moreover paves the way for cross-cultural comparisons. Several aspects noted in Punic west-central Sardinia provide, for instance, a meaningful basis of comparison with other colonial situations of very different times and places without anachronistically or simplistically equating them. The large-scale import, imitation, and use of colonial material culture without a wholesale adoption of colonial norms and values in inland west-central Sardinia is, for instance, comparable with the adoption of Spanish and central Mexican pottery in sixteenth- and seventeenth-century colonial Soconusco. Despite the integration of this region in the Spanish colonial economy and administration, the indigenous Indian communities remained largely in control of their own daily lives, including the production of cacao (Gasco 1993, this volume). The hybrid rituals performed in Punic shrines across west-central Sardinia can likewise be compared with the much better-documented interactions between Spanish missionaries or Russian trappers and Native Americans in eighteenth-century California. The (hidden) performance of indigenous rituals and the use of indigenous customs of food preparation in the otherwise eminently colonial settings of the Californian missions show that hybridization is indeed a recurrent process in colonial situations (Lightfoot, Martinez, and Schiff 1998; Lightfoot this volume).

This comparison of the evolving colonial situations in Andalusia, west-central Sardinia, and Ibiza finally provides solid archaeological support for the viability of a postcolonial archaeology of colonialism. More specifically, I want to draw attention to the following three points. In the first place, I suggest that a postcolonial archaeology of colonialism must be based on regional contexts rather than on the colonizers' provenance, because colonial settlements must be examined in their regional context, which includes, of course, indigenous settlements. Such an approach would also be in keeping with the postcolonial tenet that colonial situations are not simply structured by the colonizers alone, but that they develop in the interaction between the "colonizing" and "colonized" inhabitants of the region involved. It follows from this, in the second place, that a postcolonial approach takes regional sociopolitical organization as its primary object of study, rather than the opposition between colonizers and the colonized. The third and final point concerns the recognition of the locally and chronologically situated nature of cultural identities and the meaning of material culture. As I hope to have demonstrated in my discussions of Phoenician and Punic Andalusia, west-central Sardinia, and Ibiza, such an approach will focus attention on the human dimension of colonial situations as encounters between communities sharing the same space and time.

Acknowledgments

This chapter has considerably benefited from the week of discussions in Santa Fe, which have me made think again about many issues. I also thank Carlos Gómez-Bellard for sharing his views on the Phoenician and Punic archaeology of Ibiza and Andalusia.

Notes

1. It has become customary to spell "postcolonial" without the hyphen when referring to the theoretical perspective and to retain it when the term is used in strictly chronological sense, indicating the period of decolonization.

2. The difference is one of historical convention, as the two words are two versions of the same term, Phoenician being derived from the Greek *Phoinix* and Punic from the Latin *Poenus*. It reflects the simple fact that most literary sources about the Phoenicians are in Greek and that Latin texts are the main sources for the Punic world, as Rome rose to prominence roughly in the same period as Carthage.

3. The *tophet* is an open-air sanctuary that is exclusively found at the largest Phoenician and Punic settlements of the central Mediterranean (Sardinia, Sicily, and central North Africa) and was usually situated at the northern perimeter of the built-up area. Its principal feature is myriad urns containing the ashes of cremated young children and animals, usually with some grave gifts. From the Punic period, stelae are common. Although there is hot debate whether these children were stillborn or had been sacrificed, the tophet clearly was an important focal point for the community of the cities and their territories in the central Mediterranean (Gras, Rouillard, and Teixidor 1991; Moscati 1992).

5

The Political Economy of Mesopotamian Colonial Encounters

Gil J. Stein

INTRODUCTION

This chapter examines the two main episodes of ancient Mesopotamian colonization and places them within the broader historical context of interregional exchange between Mesopotamia and its neighbors from 4000 to 323 B.C. Specifically, I compare the Uruk colonies of the fourth millennium B.C. with the Old Assyrian trading colonies of the early second millennium B.C. This comparison allows us to investigate the nature of colonization in the Mesopotamian world, while establishing a baseline to determine the potential degree of comparability to colonization in other ancient societies.

We can define a colony as an implanted settlement established by one society in either uninhabited territory or the territory of another society. The implanted settlement is established for long-term residence and is both spatially and socially distinguishable from the communities of a host society. The settlement at least starts off with a distinct formal corporate identity as a community with cultural/ritual, economic, military, or political ties to its homeland, but the homeland need not politically dominate the implanted settlement. The corporate nature of the foreign community, its formal organizational existence, and its formalized ties with its homeland (and with its host community) are important elements that provide a major point of distinction between colonies and episodes of migration by individuals or families. This definition has the advantage of encompassing the colonies of European expansion from the sixteenth to twentieth centuries while also allowing us to compare a wide variety of ancient, non-Western and/or precapitalist networks of colonies within a single general framework. The establishment of colonies appears to be unique to state-level societies (Algaze 1993a). Colonies exist in a formal relationship to the state societies of their homeland, but need not be fully controlled by them. At the same time, colonies do not necessarily control the regions in which they settled, or are allowed to settle (Stein 2002a, 2002b).

I suggest that the establishment of colonies was an extremely unusual economic strategy in Mesopotamian states before the Hellenistic period. The Uruk and Old Assyrian colonies are the only known cases where Mesopotamian states established networks of trading colonies in neighboring regions.[1] In all other periods, Mesopotamian polities obtained the resources they needed either through imperial tribute (Postgate 1979), diplomatic "gift" exchange between rulers (see, for example, Zaccagnini 1987), or most commonly, a combined system of (1) Mesopotamian entrepreneurs operating independently of the state (or state officers who in addition engage in business ventures "on the side"; see R. McC. Adams 1974), (2) foreign merchants residing in or visiting Mesopotamia (see, for example, De Graef 1999a, 1999b; Parpola, Parpola, and Brunswig 1977) and (3) ports of trade (Polanyi 1963) in regions immediately outside Mesopotamia proper. I suggest that Mesopotamian states rarely organized or sponsored colonial ventures because it was far easier, cheaper, and safer to have individuals and groups outside the palace sector assume the risks and costs of international exchange (even if the temples and palaces as institutions were among those who acted as investors backing these private ventures; see, for example, Oppenheim 1954).

A comparison of the two unusual cases when Mesopotamian states established colonial networks—the Uruk and Old Assyrian colonies—suggests that they were organized in similar ways. Although one system developed in a pristine/primary state (Uruk) and the other in a secondary state society (Assur), I suggest that both colonial networks reflect the constraints shared by relatively weak city-state centralized institutions operating in the fragmented, highly competitive political landscapes of their homelands. At the same time, both Assur and Uruk were trading with foreign polities whose preexisting social complexity and distance from Mesopotamia allowed them, depending on the local balance of power relations, to negotiate more or less favorable terms of exchange and political relationships with the colonies in their midst.

LONG-TERM PATTERNS IN MESOPOTAMIAN RESOURCE PROCUREMENT AND INTERREGIONAL INTERACTION

Natural Resource Distributions and the Development of Mesopotamian States

Mesopotamian civilization developed in the southern alluvial plain between the Tigris and the Euphrates Rivers. The extraordinarily rich yields of irrigation agriculture and pastoral products in this region produced the surpluses that formed the basis for the development of the world's earliest known urbanized state societies in the fourth millennium B.C. However, aside from soil, water, fish, and forage, southern Mesopotamia lacks virtually all the major natural resources that played key economic roles in ancient complex societies. Mesopotamians had to obtain virtually all their essential raw materials and high-status items such as obsidian (G. Wright 1969), copper (Muhly 1973; de Jesus 1980), tin (Stech and Pigott 1986), iron (Moorey 1994:278–83), gold (Maxwell-Hyslop 1977), silver (Yener 1983), chlorite (Kohl 1978), lapis lazuli (Herrmann 1968), chert (H. Wright 1972), and lumber (Rowton 1967) from neighboring and even more distant regions (fig. 5.1). The vast majority of these raw materials were to be found in the resource-rich neighboring highland zones of Anatolia (modern Turkey) to the north and the Zagros (modern Iran) to the east. Oman (ancient Magan) at the southern end of the Persian Gulf provided an additional important source of copper from the third millennium B.C. onward, while tin and lapis lazuli seem to have come to Mesopotamia from as far away as Afghanistan (Stech and Pigott 1986; Cleuziou and Berthoud 1982).

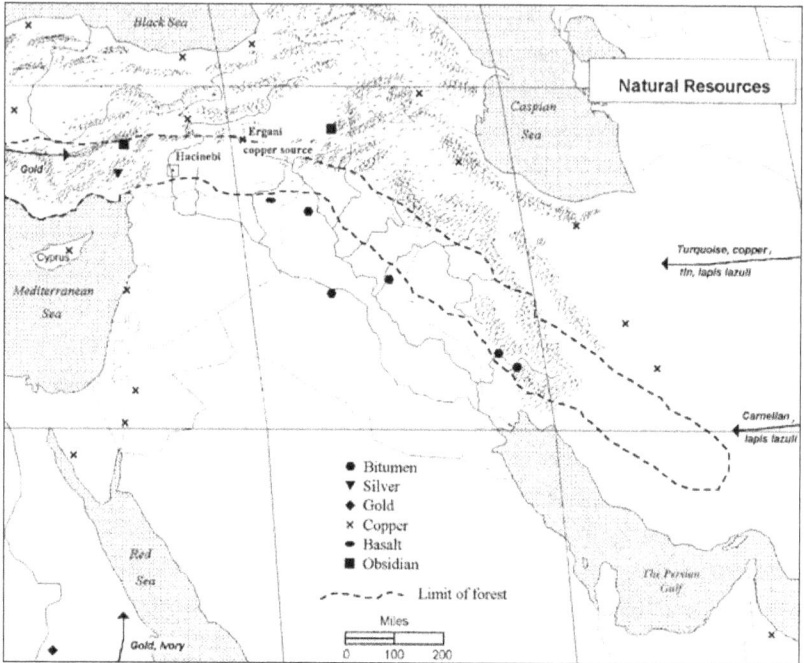

FIGURE 5.1

Resource map of the Near East.

As a result of this basic resource imbalance, Mesopotamian history from the eighth millennium B.C. onward shows repeated efforts to gain access to or control the resources of these neighboring regions through a variety of different strategies such as trade, colonization, gift exchange, raiding, or outright conquest (Algaze 1989; Kohl 1978; Marfoe 1987; Yener 1982; Yoffee 1981). These efforts were facilitated by the existence of three major routes of trade and communication: (1) north–south routes using the Euphrates and Tigris Rivers, allowing for downstream shipping of copper, lumber, and other bulk goods from their highland Anatolian sources; (2) the "Great Khorasan road"—an east–west trade route including a series of passes leading from north-central Mesopotamia into the Zagros Mountains; and (3) the Persian/Arabian Gulf, linking southern Mesopotamia with Oman and areas farther afield such as the Indus Valley. Inside Mesopotamia proper, a vast network of rivers (multiple branches of the Tigris and

Euphrates), canals, and towpaths allowed for the circulation of trade goods between different city-states.

Organizational Patterns in Mesopotamian Exchange

Large-scale, high-volume exchange networks connecting the southern alluvium with Anatolia and Iran seem to have emerged more or less concurrently with the origins of state-level polities in southern Mesopotamia during the Uruk period circa 3700 B.C. (Algaze 1993a, 1993b; Rothman 2001; Stein 1999b; Sürenhagen 1986). The Uruk period sees the establishment of the world's earliest-known colonial network, in which a series of outposts was established along trade and communications routes leading to the highland resource zones of Iran and Anatolia. This phenomenon is generally called the "Uruk Expansion" (see discussion below). Since writing was not invented until the end of the Uruk period, circa 3200 B.C., this colonial network is known only from archaeological evidence: the excavation of Uruk outposts at sites such as Habuba Kabira (Strommenger 1980; Sürenhagen 1986), Jebel Aruda (Van Driel 1977; Van Driel and Van Driel-Murray 1979, 1983), Hassek (Behm-Blancke 1981, 1992), Hacınebi (Stein 1999a), and Godin (Weiss and Young 1975; T. C. Young 1986). The Uruk colonial network seems to have been abandoned suddenly at the end of the fourth millennium B.C. It remains unclear whether this apparent collapse was due to social and political upheavals in Mesopotamia proper; resistance by the indigenous polities of Anatolia and Syria; incursions by tribal groups (mobile pastoralists known archaeologically through their use of "Karaz," "trans-Caucasian," or "Khirbet Kerak" wares; see, for example, Weiss and Young 1975); or some combination of these factors.

In the periods following the Uruk Expansion and collapse, interregional exchange appears to have continued under substantially different organizational forms. During the third millennium B.C., the political landscape of Mesopotamia underwent several major transformations, from a pattern of politically autonomous city-states in the Jemdet Nasr and Early Dynastic periods (fig. 5.2) through the emergence of short-lived imperial attempts of the Early Dynastic king Lugalzagesi and others, to the more successful imperial effort of the Akkadian Empire under Sargon and his successors (for overviews

FIGURE 5.2

City-states of third-millennium B.C. Mesopotamia.

see, for example, Kuhrt 1995:44–55; Liverani 1993; Postgate 1992). After a short period of collapse, imperial organization reemerged under the rule of the Ur III dynasty. Documentation in the form of Sumerian and Akkadian texts from palace, temple, and private archives becomes increasingly common throughout the third millennium.

Most third-millennium exchange on the southern alluvium seems to have taken place in the form of trade in bulk commodities (grain, fish, wool, animals, and the like) among the different Mesopotamian cities (see, for example, Crawford 1973). The palace, temple, and "private" sectors of Mesopotamian society all seem to have engaged in or invested in these exchange activities (R. McC. Adams 1974). Even at the height of centralized control under the Akkadian Empire, there is clear evidence that professional business agents (*dam-gar*) operated as both individual entrepreneurs and as operatives of the state (B. Foster 1977). Merchants from one Mesopotamian city-state residing in another city would often live as a community in an area called the *karum*. A karum (literally "quay" or "harbor") was the trading quarter of a Mesopotamian city, where merchants both lived and transacted their business. The term refers to both the physical neighborhood and to the community of traders residing there. The relationship between the state and these merchants appears to have fluctuated over the course of the third millennium. In periods of great centralization (such as the Ur III period at the end of the third millennium), the state regulated trade and traders closely. However, at other times, merchants had a much higher degree of autonomy (M. Larsen 1987:49).

The organization of interregional exchange is far more ambiguous. We know from both archaeological and textual evidence that third- and second-millennium Mesopotamian states imported a variety of commodities and preciosities such as tin, copper, gold, silver, carnelian, lapis lazuli, and shell from Anatolia, Iran, the Persian Gulf, and (indirectly) the Indus Valley (Edens 1992; M. Larsen 1987:51). Mythical accounts in Mesopotamian literature from the third-millennium Early Dynastic period suggest that there might have been some state involvement in long-distance exchange. In the myth of Enmerkar and the Lord of Aratta (Kramer 1952), Enmerkar, the king of Uruk, requires exotic raw materials to decorate the temple of the goddess Inanna; to obtain it, he attempts to trade Mesopotamian grain for gold and lapis lazuli from the kingdom of Aratta, thought to be in highland Iran (S. Cohen 1973; Kohl 1978; Moorey 1993:36; Potts 1994:90), However, the historicity of this myth is open to question.

Significantly, there is no archival evidence (such as economic texts, ration lists, and the like) that the palace sector or central state apparatus was actively engaged in *organizing or controlling* interregional exchange (B. Foster 1977:37), although temples did participate in trade indirectly as investors during the Ur III period at the end of the third millennium (Oppenheim 1954). Obviously, we have to be careful in arguing from absence, especially in the case of texts, since the lack of textual reference to a specific topic may reflect either sampling problems or else the fact that the topic in question simply was not relevant to the person or institution writing the document. However, we have neither textual nor archaeological evidence—in Mesopotamia or surrounding regions of Iran, Syria, Anatolia, and the Persian Gulf—to indicate that third-millennium Mesopotamian city-states or empires used a system of trade colonies to obtain these foreign goods (M. Larsen 1976:228). For the entire third millennium (and the second millennium as well in all of Mesopotamia except for Assyria; see below), Mesopotamian interregional exchange took place without colonies. The palace sector sponsored some merchants but not all. Nor did it control international trade (R. McC. Adams 1974; B. Foster 1977; M. Larsen 1976).

Instead, Mesopotamian states seem to have acquired foreign goods through three mechanisms. First, the Mesopotamian merchants involved in interregional exchange appear to have been entrepreneurs operating outside the purview of the state. For this reason, they do not appear on palace ration lists as "salaried" personnel receiving rations, nor do shipments of foreign goods appear in the accounts of Mesopotamian palace households (B. Foster 1977:37). Texts from the Akkadian period refer to the presence of merchants from the Mesopotamian city of Umma residing in Susa, the capital city of neighboring Elam (B. Foster 1977:39; 1993).

We know from trading contracts in the city of Ur that south Mesopotamian merchants of the later third and early second millennium B.C. were "private" entrepreneurs using short-term "venturing contracts" (*tappatum*) for each individual voyage, rather than long-term financial agreements (M. Larsen 1976:229). Although the merchants were subject to government taxes and duties (Oppenheim 1954), they were clearly acting in their own interests (as were the Old Assyrian merchants; see below). The Mesopotamian merchants traveled frequently to Dilmun (modern Bahrain) as the entrepôt where they obtained gold, lapis lazuli, and other luxury goods and did not venture farther than Magan (presumably Oman, at the southern end of the Persian Gulf).

The second mechanism by which third- and second-millennium

Mesopotamian states acquired foreign goods was through indirect exchange (Lamberg-Karlovsky 1972). This seems to have taken place at ports of trade in areas close to, but outside of, Mesopotamia proper. Thus, for example, trade with the Harappan civilization was largely a system of indirect exchange, where merchants from the Indus and from Mesopotamia met on neutral ground at places such as Dilmun, often with local merchants acting as intermediaries. The local middlemen can be identified through their use of distinctive "Persian Gulf seals"—round stamp seals whose designs evoke the iconography of Harappan seals (and occasionally employ the Indus script) but are typologically distinct from the actual square, carved stamp seals of the Indus Valley (Lamberg-Karlovsky 1972).

Finally, Mesopotamian state authorities facilitated interregional exchange by encouraging foreign merchants to come to Mesopotamia. The Akkadian king Sargon (circa 2350 B.C.) boasted that in his reign, ships from as far away as Magan (Oman) and Meluhha (the Indus Valley?) docked at the quay in the city of Agade (B. Foster 1977:39; M. Larsen 1976:228). We know from textual accounts that interpreters of the Meluhhan (Harappan) language were present (and presumably needed) in the Akkadian period (M. Larsen 1976:228). At the end of the third millennium, texts from the Ur III period refer to a "Meluhha village," presumably a neighborhood of people from the Indus Valley, located in the vicinity of the city of Lagash. This settlement seems to have started as a karum-like merchants' quarter but evolved over time into an ethnic enclave as its inhabitants intermarried with Mesopotamians and became acculturated to Sumerian society (Parpola, Parpola, and Brunswig 1977). Occasional finds of authentic Indus Valley seals in Mesopotamian urban centers such as Ur, Umma, and Kish also suggest the presence of individual Harappan traders (Lamberg-Karlovsky 1972).

These noncolonial strategies operating outside of centralized state institutions were extraordinarily effective in assuring a steady supply of foreign prestige goods and commodities into Mesopotamia throughout the third millennium. Imports of copper reached such high volumes that this metal underwent a "category shift" in Mesopotamian ideology from the status of a rare prestige good to that of an industrial commodity (Edens 1992). Similarly, the extraordinary abundance of gold, silver, carnelian, and lapis in the mid-third-millennium Royal Cemetery of Ur (Woolley 1934; Zettler and Horne 1998) show that these trade mechanisms were equally effective for the importation of prestige goods.

All three strategies for procuring foreign goods suggest that the centralized institutions of Mesopotamian states of the third millennium did not feel the need to monopolize access to and profits from trade in foreign commodities or preciosities. This is particularly striking in the case of prestige goods, because one might have expected centralized state authorities to have attempted to control access to these "politically charged commodities" (Brumfiel and Earle 1987). Yet this was clearly not the case; the palace sector seems to have been willing to allow others to bring these goods to Mesopotamia, even if they attempted to monopolize control over these preciosities once they were actually in Mesopotamia (see, for example, Stein and Blackman 1993). The absence of any evidence for colonization by third-millennium Mesopotamian states and empires is also consistent with this idea. The state authorities seem to have followed strategies that reaped the benefits of interregional trade, while devolving its risks and costs onto either private Mesopotamian entrepreneurs or onto foreigners.

Overall, Mesopotamian state institutions were, from their inception, very involved in interregional exchange, but only rarely through strategies of colonization. Over the course of three and a half millennia, from the first emergence of urbanized state societies in the mid-fourth millennium B.C. Uruk period down to the Hellenistic period (late fourth century B.C.), colonization seems to have been quite rare as a form of interregional interaction (table 5.1). As far as we can tell from the archaeological and textual evidence, the Old Assyrian trading colonies were very atypical, even within the context of nineteenth to eighteenth century B.C. Mesopotamia. At the same time as the Assyrians had a network of trading stations in Anatolia, the Mesopotamian city-states of the southern alluvium were obtaining foreign goods without recourse to colonization (M. Larsen 1976:228–29). In Mesopotamian history, whenever trade could be organized in other ways, then colonization appears to have been unnecessary and was not practiced. In most periods, economic interaction with neighboring regions took the form of exchange without colonization.

TABLE 5.1

Mesopotamian chronology: states, empires, and foreign interaction

Period	Dates	Colonies?
Hellenistic	330–143 B.C.	Military and civilian colonies throughout Near East
Median/Persian	539–330 B.C.	Imperial administration
Neo-Babylonian	625–539 B.C.	Imperial administration
Neo-Assyrian	911–612 B.C.	Military outposts, mass deportations/resettlements
Middle Assyrian	1363–1076 B.C.	Military outposts, provincial administrative centers
Middle Babylonian		
Kassite	1600–1154 B.C.	
Old Babylonian	1800–1600 B.C.	
Old Assyrian (North)	1880–1740 B.C.	Trading colonies in Anatolia
Isin Larsa (South)	2000–1800 B.C.	
Ur III Dynasty	2112–2004 B.C.	
Gutians, Gudea	2193–2100 B.C.	
Akkadian Empire	2350–2193 B.C.	Military outposts (e.g., Tell Brak)
Early Dynastic I–III	3000–2350 B.C.	
Jemdet Nasr	3200–3000 B.C.	
Uruk	4000–3200 B.C.	Trading colonies in Syria, Anatolia, Iran

Even in those periods when Mesopotamian states did establish colonies, the latter fall into two very different types: (1) trading colonies established by city-states in the territories of politically autonomous neighboring complex societies (Uruk and Old Assyrian colonies); and (2) imperial outposts—that is, forts and administrative centers established by empires as tools of military and administrative control over conquered territories. Such outposts are known from the Akkadian Empire (at Tell Brak; see Mallowan 1936), the Middle Assyrian Empire (see, for example, Akkermans and Rossmeisl 1990), and the Neo-Assyrian Empire (Tadmor 1975). Although interregional exchange may have taken place (and may even have flourished) in these periods of imperial expansion and military/administrative colonization, economic motivations do not appear to have been the main reason for the implantation of Mesopotamian settlements in areas outside the homeland. Although over time we can see a shift from trade colonies to imperial outposts from the mid-second millennium onward, the latter did not function as primarily commercial enclaves. One possible exception might be the presence of Neo-Assyrian colonies in the Levant during the ninth century B.C.; however, these settlements appear to have fulfilled a dual function as both military outposts and tribute collection points beyond the actual frontier of the Assyrian empire.[2] As a generalization, it seems fair to say that although Mesopotamian empires encouraged trade, commercial activity was not the driving force of expansion, since imperial revenues derived from tribute imposed on conquered states, rather than the profits of commercial ventures. Imperial outposts were the military and administrative consequences of expansionist, not mercantile ideologies (see, for example, Oded 1992).

In those cases when Mesopotamian states established colonies, the crucial factors underlying differences in colonial strategies may be best understood within the larger context of political economy (Roseberry 1988; Yoffee 1995:282). I focus here on the Old Assyrian period (circa 1880–1740 B.C.) and the Middle/Late Uruk period (circa 3700–3200 B.C.) as the only known cases in which Mesopotamian states established networks of trading colonies in the midst of indigenous polities in Anatolia, Syria, and Iran. Such a comparison must of necessity be fairly sketchy and speculative for two reasons.

First, the nature of the available evidence differs quite markedly for the two cases. The Old Assyrian colonial network is known from both excavations at the colony of Kanesh in central Anatolia (fig. 5.3) and from literally thousands of economic texts and letters documenting the activities of the Mesopotamian merchants. Although our understanding of the Old Assyrian system has evolved considerably, there is now general agreement among scholars about the organization of the colonies and their relations with the local polities of Anatolia (see, for example, Dercksen 1996; Garelli 1963; M. Larsen 1976; Orlin 1970; Veenhof 1972, 1995). By contrast, the Uruk colonies in Anatolia, Syria, and Iran predate the invention of writing and are thus known only from archaeological excavation. As a result, interpretations of this

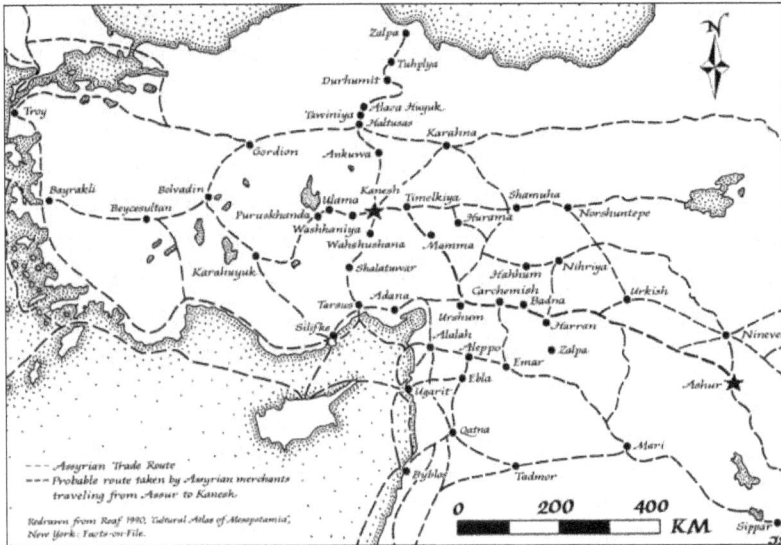

FIGURE 5.3

The Old Assyrian colonial network.

network vary widely (see, for example, Algaze 1993b; G. Johnson 1988–1989; Rothman 2001; G. Schwartz 1988; Stein 1999b; Sürenhagen 1986).

A second potential problem lies in the fact that Uruk Mesopotamia was a primary or pristine state, while the Old Assyrian polity was a secondary state society that developed after the collapse of the Ur III Empire. Algaze has argued that the colonial systems of pristine states would have benefited from immense power disparities in relations with their less complex neighbors, thereby allowing for economic dominance over the colonized areas (Algaze 1993a). By contrast, in later, secondary states, Algaze suggests that power relations with neighboring polities would have been much less unequal, with concomitant differences in colonial organization. Algaze's analysis points to a broader problem in social evolutionary theory: the fact that anthropological archaeologists have yet to develop a clear framework specifying the structural differences between primary and secondary states.

Bearing these two potential problems in mind, we can attempt a controlled comparison of the Uruk and Old Assyrian colonial networks in terms of several key aspects of political economy: (1) the scale and form of political organization of the Mesopotamian homeland, in particular the strength and degree of centralization in the state apparatus; (2) the degree of social complexity and political independence of the indigenous host communities within which the Mesopotamians established their colonies; (3) the organization of the colonies and the colonial network, including spatial variation in each network; (4) power relations between the homeland and the colonies; (5) power relations between the colonies and the host communities; and (6) the degree to which exchange between the colony and the host community was symmetric or asymmetric. This comparison suggests that the Old Assyrian case may be a surprisingly good analogy for the operation of the Uruk system (Steinkeller 1993), while also highlighting some important structural characteristics of trade colonies as a strategy for interregional resource procurement.

THE OLD ASSYRIAN COLONIES

After the collapse of the Ur III Empire at the end of the third millennium B.C., the city-states of Mesopotamia regained their independence and resumed their traditional patterns of intense economic, military, and political rivalry. In the rolling steppes of northern Mesopotamia, the city-state of Assur took advantage of its freedom and borderland location to develop a far-reaching trade network based on a series of trading colonies in Anatolia during the early second millennium B.C.

The Old Assyrian trading colonies are best known from the site of Kültepe in central Turkey (fig. 5.3), where excavations have exposed the indigenous early-second-millennium B.C. Anatolian city-state of Kanesh and the Old Assyrian karum or merchants' quarter on its outskirts (Özgüç 1963, 1986). The houses of the karum yielded some seventy separate archives of different Assyrian (and even some local) merchants—a total of approximately 20,000 texts, comprising business letters, legal documents, promissory notes, loan contracts, judicial records, and commercial inventories (Garelli 1963; M. Larsen 1976; Orlin 1970; Veenhof 1972). The discovery of both the physical colony and its written records have allowed researchers to reconstruct the workings of this ancient colonial network with a high degree of detail

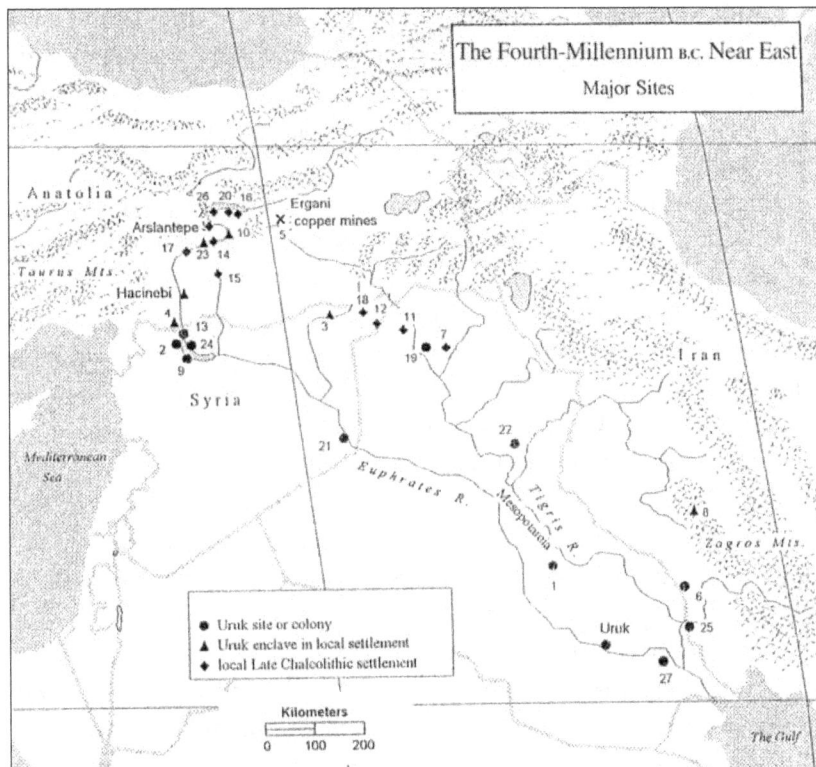

FIGURE 5.4

The Uruk Expansion, its outposts and indigenous communities, in the fourth millennium
B.C. Near East, showing Hacınebi, Arslantepe, Uruk, and other main sites. 1. Abu Salabikh;
2. Aruda; 3. Brak; 4. Carchemish; 5. Ergani copper mines; 6. Farukhabad; 7. Gawra;
8. Godin; 9. Habuba Kabira; 10. Hassek; 11. Hawa; 12. Hamoukar; 13. Jerablus
Tahtani; 14. Karatut Mevkii; 15. Kazane; 16. Korucutepe; 17. Kurban; 18. Leilan;
19. Nineveh; 20. Norsuntepe; 21. Qraya; 22. Rubeidheh; 23. Samsat; 24. Sheikh Hassan;
25. Susa; 26. Tepecik; 27. Ur.

over the course of its main period of activity (*Karum* II: circa 1880–1810
B.C.) and decline (*Karum* Ib: circa 1810–1740 B.C.).

The Assyrian presence at Kanesh took the form of individual family
"firms," probably 500 to 700 foreigners (Veenhof 1977:109) concentrated in an area of about 4 hectares (Veenhof 1995:861). Although
each family-based trading enterprise pursued its own commercial
ventures and profits, the merchants acted together as a corporate

administrative body in their dealings both with the kings of the local Anatolian city states and with their metropole, the city-state of Assur (M. Larsen 1974:470).

The Assyrians acted as middlemen in an extremely far-reaching and highly profitable overland trade network. They traded tin from Afghanistan and woolen textiles from Mesopotamia in return for silver (and some gold) from Anatolia (M. Larsen 1976:86–89). Tin was an essential and largely unavailable commodity in central Anatolia[3], where it was needed for the production of bronze. The Assyrians also transshipped large amounts of copper within Anatolia from source areas on the Black Sea (and possibly Ergani in the eastern Taurus Mountains) to metallurgical production centers located in the various indigenous central Anatolian city-states (Dercksen 1996). The volume of goods transported was enormous. In the fifty-year period covered by the karum II texts, the Mesopotamians brought an estimated 800 tons of tin and 100,000 woolen textiles by donkey caravan to Anatolia (M. Larsen 1976:90).

To conduct this overland trade efficiently, the Assyrians established a network of thirty commercial enclaves (M. Larsen 1976:864). These were of two types: larger colonies (*karu*, pl. of *karum*) and smaller outposts or way stations (*wabaratum*) along the main transportation routes from northern Mesopotamia to central Anatolia, and in the capitals of the main city-states of the latter region (fig. 5.3). Karum Kanesh was the most important Assyrian colony and seems to have been administratively superior to all the other enclaves in the network.

The Political Context of the Metropole

The city-state of Assur was a poorly centralized polity existing in a landscape of multiple competing polities in Mesopotamia and north Syria (M. Larsen 1987:49). Due to its marginal environment, it could not generate great amounts of wealth from agriculture (M. Larsen 1976:27) and was almost entirely dependent on trade as a source of state revenue. Economic competition with rival Mesopotamian city-states was intense. Assur went to great efforts to exclude competitors from its commercial sphere and even concluded trade agreements with local Anatolian rulers that required the arrest and execution of merchants from rival Mesopotamian polities: "You will not allow Akkadians to come up to your country; if they go overland to your country you will surely hand them over to us and we will surely kill them" (text Kt n/k 794; quoted in Dercksen 1996:162).

Although Assur had a titular king in the early second millennium, his powers seem to have been limited and constrained in a delicate equilibrium with other individuals and groups such as the city assembly, an official called the "eponym," and the powerful merchant families of the city (M. Larsen 1974:471, 1976:220). The king's powers seem to have been limited. He was the chief priest of the city, the head of the royal lineage, and the chief magistrate. One of his main roles was as a mediator among the different powerful kin groups in the city. Thus a kin-based trading elite, and not the palace sector, was the true power in Assur:

> ...Old Assyrian society (w)as dominated by the great families
> of Assur, and the existence of these powerful families and
> the pattern they created could well constitute another factor
> which explains why the Old Assyrian trade was organized as
> it was. We may in this light view the colonial system as a tech-
> nical device which served to facilitate the trade of compa-
> nies in Assur and diminish the risks" (M. Larsen 1976:230).

In short, early-second-millennium Assur was a poorly centralized city-state dominated by private commercial interests in a political landscape characterized by intense economic and military competition with neighboring Mesopotamian polities.

The Indigenous Host Communities of Anatolia

The Assyrians were trading with a complex, state-level society in early-second-millennium central Anatolia. The local polities were orga-nized as a mosaic of city-states that varied considerably in size; some, like Purushhadum (Acemhöyük), were quite large and wealthy, with powerful kings. The central Anatolian city-states were undergoing a process of expansion, conquest, and consolidation (M. Larsen 1974:472), culminating in the emergence of the Hittite Empire. To ensure their own survival and the security of their caravans, the Old Assyrian colonies negotiated a series of commercial treaties with the local rulers. The Assyrians agreed to pay stiff taxes (*nishatum*) on every donkey-load of textiles or tin that they imported to an Anatolian city. The Anatolian rulers had the right to buy at discounted prices up to 10 percent of all incoming textiles. Finally, the local palace retained a monopoly in the trade of certain prestige goods such as semiprecious stones and meteoric iron. The Assyrians also had to pay a road tax (*datum*) equal to 10 percent of the value of the shipment to the local authorities through whose territories the caravans passed. The Assyrians had to formally recognize the right of the local Anatolian rulers to arrest and punish any smuggler attempting to evade these requirements. In return, the Anatolian city-states guaranteed residence and trading rights to the Assyrians, and a limited form of extraterritoriality, so that "the colonies were in a political and judicial sense extensions of the government of Assur" (M. Larsen 1976:245). The local polities also guaranteed the security of Assyrian caravans against banditry while passing through their territories. The Assyrians adjusted to the shifting power relations within central Anatolia, conceding more in their treaties with powerful local states like Purushhadum, while extracting more favorable terms in their dealings with the smaller polities such as Tumana (M. Larsen 1974:473).

Colonial Organization and Assyrian-Anatolian Interaction

Karum Kanesh was a multiethnic community in which Assyrian, Anatolian, and even Syrian merchants lived side by side. We know of numerous cases of intermarriage between Assyrian men and Anatolian women (Veenhof 1982), possibly as a way to cement trade relations with local commercial and political elites. The Assyrians did not dominate the people of their host community, and in fact experienced clear limits in their legal relationships with Anatolians (Orlin 1970:175). For example, Assyrians did not or could not own Anatolian slaves (Veenhof 1977).

Although they were well integrated within Anatolian society, the Assyrians still maintained close contact with the mother city of Assur through the constant stream of arriving and departing caravans. Communication by letters was frequent and surprisingly rapid. Although they were long-term residents of the karum, Assyrian merchants nonetheless returned frequently to Assur for economic, familial, or ritual reasons. These factors are all important in explaining the fact that the Assyrians at Kanesh, despite their minority status and close contact with the host community, were still able to maintain a distinct social and cultural identity. They retained their language and their status as a corporate community of foreigners (Veenhof 1977). At the same time, the Assyrians at Kanesh may have attempted to minimize potential conflict by adopting local styles of architecture, ceramics, and other forms of material culture. In fact, the excavators of Kanesh state that, were it not for the presence of Mesopotamian cylinder seals (Porada 1980) and thousands of texts identifying the owners of the houses (Emberling and Yoffee 1999), they would not have been able to distinguish the Assyrians as a foreign community at the site (Özgüç 1963). However, we should note that many of the markers of this trade diaspora's social identity might have been in the realms of language (both spoken and written) and perishable items of material culture such as textiles and food remains. It is especially regrettable that no analyses have ever compared faunal and macrobotanical remains between the Assyrian karum and the indigenous Anatolian neighborhoods of the city of Kanesh, since these might reveal significant differences in food preferences and preparation procedures between the two groups.

Everything we know about the Old Assyrian colonies in Anatolia suggests that, although the situation varied depending on local circumstances, there was often a balance or symmetry in political, economic, and social relations between the foreigners and their host communities. The Assyrians did not dominate the Anatolians militarily (Orlin 1970:171); if anything, the colonists were at the mercy of their hosts. The colonies cannot be interpreted as imperial outposts designed to control and exploit an indigenous population. At the same time, the terms of the commercial treaties show that there was a symmetric set of power relations in which "Anatolian military and administrative power was balanced by the economic strength and commercial skills of the Assyrians, who had made themselves fairly indispensaible as importers,...customers,...and traders" (Veenhof 1982:148).

THE URUK COLONIES

In contrast with the textually documented Old Assyrian commercial enclaves, we have only archaeological data as the basis for our interpretations of the earliest-known colonial network: the outposts established by Mesopotamia during the "Uruk Expansion" of the fourth millennium B.C. Urban-centered state societies developed in southern Mesopotamia during the Uruk period in the mid-fourth millennium B.C. (R. McC. Adams 1981; G. Johnson 1973; Wright and Johnson 1975). Almost immediately, the economic sphere of Uruk city-states expanded to form extensive exchange relations with the less urbanized polities in the neighboring highlands. Several sites in the latter areas have been identified as Uruk trading colonies, apparently established to control trade and communication routes while extracting metals, lumber, or other commodities from the resource-rich highland zones, in what several researchers consider the world's earliest-known colonial system (fig. 5.4). Sites identified as Uruk colonies or enclaves were established in the key routes through the Iranian Zagros (Weiss and Young 1975), on the Tigris River in northern Mesopotamia (Algaze 1986), across the Habur headwaters region (Oates 1993; Oates and Oates 1997), on the Euphrates River in Syria (Sürenhagen 1986), and up into the Taurus highlands (Behm-Blancke 1992; Frangipane and Palmieri 1987:297; Stein 1999a). This network of settlements was first established on a small scale in the Middle Uruk period (circa 3700–3400 B.C.), and expanded substantially in the Late Uruk (circa 3400–3200 B.C.).

The Uruk enclaves are quite distinctive as alien settlements, established in the midst of local Iranian, Syrian, and southeast Anatolian cultures. Several different forms of Uruk material culture—notably ceramics, architecture, and administrative technology—occurring in combination serve to identify the Mesopotamian implanted settlements while distinguishing them from contemporaneous local settlements (Sürenhagen 1986:9–13). Sites identified as "colonies" have the full repertoire of Uruk ceramics while generally lacking local ceramics. These sites also have distinctive Mesopotamian styles of architecture, such as the tripartite "middle hall" house, wall cone mosaic decoration, and niched facade temples. A third distinctive feature of the Uruk enclaves is the presence of south Mesopotamian administrative technology such as cylinder seals, bullae, tokens, and clay tablets with numerical inscriptions used to monitor the mobilization, transportation, storage, and disbursement of goods (Nissen 1985).

The purpose of the Uruk enclaves remains the subject of continued debate (see, for example, chapters in Rothman 2001). Schwartz proposes that some Uruk settlements (for example, Hassek) were emporia or trading outposts, while particularly large sites such as Habuba Kabira—south, Hamoukar, and possibly Brak were colonies that combined commercial functions with the settlement of excess Mesopotamian population on easily available agricultural land (G. Schwartz 1988). Other researchers have suggested that the Uruk settlements are actually indicators of an Uruk collapse, rather than a commercial expansion (G. Johnson 1988–1989). However, the predominant view sees the Uruk enclaves as trading colonies or way stations whose main purpose was to insure south Mesopotamian access to Anatolian and Iranian resources such as copper and perhaps lumber (Algaze 1993b; Frangipane and Palmieri 1989; Stein 1999b; Sürenhagen 1986).

We do not know what goods the Mesopotamians traded in return for these items. The economics of upstream transport over the 1,200 kilometers from the city of Uruk in southern Mesopotamia to the copper sources in eastern Anatolia would almost certainly have limited Uruk exports to prestige items or other goods with a high ratio of value to weight (or bulk). Based on analogies with the textual record of Mesopotamian exchange and colonial networks in the third and second millennia B.C., researchers have suggested that these items may have been high-quality wool textiles or some other distinctively Mesopotamian prestige good (see, for example, Algaze 1993b:74–75).

The Political Context of the Metropole

Analyses of the iconography of sculptures and stone vessels found at the site of Warka/Uruk confirm that temples were powerful institutions in the Uruk state, probably connected in some way with the newly emergent institution of kingship. Kinglike figures also appear on sculptured reliefs and a number of Uruk cylinder seals (Brandes 1979). The administrative technology of cylinder seals, hollow clay balls, and tokens that developed in this period seems to have stemmed from the need to record the mobilization, storage, and disbursement of food and other commodities by the cities from the rural hinterlands of these early states (Nissen 1985; Nissen, Damerow, and Englund 1993).

Although we can see the unmistakable emergence of cities and state institutions in the Uruk period, it remains unclear how centralized these states actually were. In particular, although we have iconographic evidence for the emergence of kingship, we can say very little about the power of Uruk kings. For example, although some buildings in the Eanna precinct of Uruk/Warka may have been administrative rather than ritual in function, there are no clearly identifiable royal palaces in Mesopotamia until after the Uruk period, when they appear at sites such as Kish (Moorey 1978) and Jemdet Nasr (Moorey 1976). Instead, the largest structures in the urban core of the city of Uruk are temples; and the earliest-known written records are economic texts associated with these religious institutions. There is thus good reason to believe that, although while kings may have played an important role as war leaders, they functioned as part of a multicentric or incompletely centralized political economy in which temples were powerful competing institutions as well. This was almost certainly a fundamental characteristic of Mesopotamian political economy down into the first millennium B.C.

Survey and excavation work in the countryside around Uruk/ Warka and Susa show the emergence during the Uruk period of a four-tiered settlement hierarchy consisting of large centers, small centers, towns, and villages, with approximately half the population living in "urban" settlements larger than 10 hectares (R. McC. Adams 1981:75). The replication of urban-centered, clustered settlement hierarchies in several parts of both southern Mesopotamia and southwestern Iran (see, for example, R. McC. Adams 1981:64–81; G. Johnson 1973; 1980a,1980b) strongly suggests that Uruk society was composed of multiple, probably competing, complex polities, rather than forming a single unified state (Algaze 1993b:115–17; Baines and Yoffee 1998: 216). Iconographic evidence from seals and sealings shows scenes of warfare and the subjugation of prisoners (see examples in Brandes 1979); although we cannot confirm the identities of the combatants, it is fairly safe to assume that we are dealing here with warfare between neighboring rival Uruk polities, rather than invasions of foreign regions. In short, the political landscape of Mesopotamia in the Uruk period was probably characterized by competing city-states, in which the processes of state centralization and the emergence of kingship was counterbalanced by rich and powerful ritual institutions.

The Indigenous Host Communities of Anatolia

The limited available data suggest a high degree of variability in the indigenous economic and political systems of southeast Anatolia during the time of the Uruk Expansion. The most complex of these local polities may have been located in the steppe zone of north Syria and north Mesopotamia. Site-size data suggest that Local Late Chalcolithic centers of the north Syrian/north Iraqi steppe zone such as Hammam et Turkman (15 hectares?), Leilan (15 hectares?), Tell Barri (20 hectares), Hamoukar (about 14 hectares), Tell el Hawa (30–50 hectares), and Brak (43-plus hectares) were significantly larger than the average size of local centers (2–4 hectares) in the piedmont and highland zone of southeast Anatolia (Algaze 1993b:92–95).

Some of our best evidence for local Anatolian sociopolitical organization in this period derives from the site of Arslantepe/Malatya in southeastern Turkey (Frangipane 1993:135). During the period of trade contact with Uruk Mesopotamia, Arslantepe VI-A shows evidence for a centralized bureaucracy using both Anatolian and Mesopotamian styles of administrative technology to monitor the collection, storage, and disbursement of goods. Many of the products moving in and out of the palace and temple storerooms were locally exchanged agricultural and pastoral goods (Frangipane 1994, 1997).

Local Late Chalcolithic societies appear to share several key characteristics, among them two-level site-size hierarchies, regional centers with internal functional differentiation, monumental architecture, exotic raw materials obtained through long-distance exchange, advanced copper and silver metallurgy, mortuary evidence for hereditary elites, and complex administrative systems based on stamp seals whose broadly similar wild animal motifs suggest some kind of shared elite ideology across the Syro-Anatolian borderlands (Stein et al. 1998). Taken together, the available evidence suggests that these Local Late Chalcolithic polities were complex societies that for the sake of convenience and cross-cultural comparison we can call "chiefdoms" (while fully recognizing the need for caution due to the problematic nature of this concept; see, for example, Yoffee 1993).

Thus there were clear developmental disparities between the populous urbanized states of southern Mesopotamia and the smaller-scale, but still complex chiefdoms of Anatolia in the fourth millennium B.C. However, the organizational and demographic advantages of the Uruk states were mitigated by a number of factors—notably the parity in technology between the two zones, and especially the leveling effects of distance. The highland resource zones were 1,200 kilometers upstream from Uruk along the Euphrates River trade route. As a result, the Mesopotamians were never able to bring to bear their demographic or military advantages in their dealings with the local polities of Anatolia.

Colonial Organization and Mesopotamian-Anatolian Interaction

The Uruk expansion formed a heterogeneous network of interaction with the local polities of Syria, the Zagros, and the Anatolian highlands. Mesopotamian settlements and material culture cluster along historically known routes of trade and communication. Interaction between Mesopotamians and local polities within this network almost certainly took three different and often overlapping forms: exchange, emulation, and the establishment of actual Uruk settlements in the territories of local polities.

Throughout the Uruk Expansion—that is, in both the Middle and Late Uruk periods—we can see considerable spatial variation in the organization of the Uruk colonial network. The organization of the Uruk settlements and the ways they interacted with their local neighbors varied markedly, depending on the distance from Mesopotamia, the size of the local population, and the degree of preexisting social complexity in the indigenous polities. A comparison of (1) the city of Uruk itself, (2) fortified, completely Mesopotamian colonies such as Habuba Kabira, and (3) small, distant outposts such as Hacınebi shows a marked degree of variation in the social and economic organization of this earliest colonial network as one moves outward from the urbanized Uruk heartland to the distant regions with which it traded. In the south Mesopotamian alluvium, cities such as Uruk and Susa controlled their rural hinterlands, exacting taxes and sending out administrators to control the most basic activities such as planting, harvesting, and collecting crop surpluses (Wright, Miller, and Redding 1980; Wright, Redding, and Pollock 1989). In the areas of Syria closest to Mesopotamia proper, Uruk colonies, such as Tell Sheikh Hassan (in the Middle Uruk period) and Habuba Kabira (in the Late Uruk period), were fortified settlements that seem to have been powerful enough to use coercive economic influence over the sparsely populated local Syrian communities around them (Boese 1996; Strommenger 1980; Sürenhagen 1986). In more distant regions, Middle and Late Uruk settlements such as Hacınebi in southeast Turkey (Stein 1999a) and Godin V in highland Iran (Weiss and Young 1975; T. C. Young 1986) took the form of small "outposts" located inside the preexisting towns of local polities. In contrast with the apparent social isolation of the colonies at Habuba Kabira/Qannas and Jebel Aruda, the large amounts of local material culture in the more distant Uruk outposts such as Godin and Hacınebi suggest that the latter interacted very closely with their host communities. We have no evidence to suggest that these outposts dominated local economies through asymmetric exchange or coercion (Stein 1998, 2002). Instead, the small numbers and vulnerable position of the Mesopotamians at Godin and other outposts meant that they could only survive by remaining on good terms with their more powerful indigenous neighbors. These differences suggest that the organization of these settlements and the ways they interacted with their local neighbors varied markedly, depending on local conditions in the area where a specific colony or outpost was located.

Analyses of economic and administrative activities at the site of Hacınebi (where an Uruk outpost was located inside a preexisting Anatolian town; see fig. 5.4) suggest that the foreign traders did not dominate the exchange system. Instead, the Mesopotamians and their Anatolian host community maintained parallel, autonomous economic systems, with relatively low levels of exchange between the two. Both groups traded for copper and worked it on site. Each group farmed its own land, herded its own animals, and manufactured its own crafts, maintaining its own food preferences and technological styles as critical aspects of social identity (Stein 1999b). There is no evidence for core control over an asymmetric/unequal exchange system at Hacınebi. Instead, the evidence suggests that local groups retained their access to the preexisting trade network and allowed Uruk merchants to participate as an autonomous group focused on extending the trade routes to supply southern Mesopotamia as well. The Mesopotamians did not (and were probably unable to) extract tribute or taxes from the local populations in the highland resource zones of Anatolia.

Overall, the colonies formed in the Uruk Expansion seem to have been founded by a metropole that was divided into competing, partially centralized city-states. The colonies themselves were located at such a great distance from the metropole that the urbanized states of Mesopotamia were not able to dominate their Anatolian host communities. The colonists were a small minority, far from home, in the midst of populous complex polities. As a result, the Uruk colonies at the outer limits of the exchange network had no choice but to deal with their Anatolian host communities as equals in a system of symmetric exchange.

CONCLUSIONS: MESOPOTAMIAN COLONIES IN COMPARATIVE PERSPECTIVE

A comparison between the prehistoric Uruk Expansion and the historically documented Old Assyrian trading colony system must remain somewhat speculative for both methodological and empirical reasons. Certainly texts and archaeological data provide different kinds of (often complementary and sometimes contradictory) evidence. We know from treaties, contracts, and private letters what kinds of political arrangements existed between the traders of Assur and the local Anatolian city-states of the early second millennium B.C. Similarly, we know the terms of trade, the prices of the trade goods, and even (to some extent) the actual volume of the Old Assyrian trade. By contrast, for the fourth millennium B.C. Uruk Expansion into Anatolia, we can only make educated guesses based on detailed analyses of material culture and its patterning. The Uruk "pristine" or "first generation" city-states were interacting with less complex, nonurbanized societies; by contrast, the Old Assyrian polity, a "secondary state," was establishing colonies in the territories of what were, by and large, urbanized polities at a comparable state of social complexity.

However, although the textually documented Old Assyrian system is better understood than the late prehistoric Uruk network, I suggest that the two were organizationally similar in a number of important ways, and that these commonalities outweigh the superficial differences. The Old Assyrian and Uruk societies both functioned in a fragmented social landscape of competing city-states. In both cases, we are dealing with polities where the central authority of kings was not that powerful. In the Assyrian case, kingship was counterbalanced by powerful mercantile families, while in Uruk, the newly emergent institution of kingship coexisted with powerful and autonomous temple institutions. Uruk kings do not appear to have been nearly as powerful in Uruk society as they were in later periods—for example, in the Early Dynastic, Akkadian, Ur III, or Old Babylonian periods.

Due to the leveling effects of distance (see, for example, Bairoch 1988; Stein 1999) pristine states (such as Uruk) may not have enjoyed any more of an advantage over their trading partners than did secondary states such as Assur. The indigenous polities of central and southeast Anatolia were stratified, internally specialized, populous, technologically advanced, and, most of all, distant enough from Mesopotamia that there was an essential parity in power relations between the two pairs of trading partners. We can see this in the fact that neither the Assyrian nor Uruk colonies were able to bring military pressure on their host communities. There is no evidence for warfare associated with either the Old Assyrian or Uruk trading systems in Anatolia. Instead, both colonial networks maintained peaceful relations with local communities in the source areas and appear to have relied on strategies of alliance rather than either outright political control or indirect economic domination. It is especially noteworthy that the Uruk Expansion lasted for at least 500 years, an accomplishment that would not have been possible if colonial control of an area 1,200 kilometers away from the metropole were maintained by the application or threat of armed force. In both cases, the colonies only survived at the sufferance of the local rulers. Both the Assyrian and Uruk colonies seem to have traded with the local polities on equal terms when circumstances such as the local balance of power dictated. Overall, then, the Uruk and Old Assyrian colonies appear to have been surprisingly similar in several key aspects of interaction systems, despite the enormous gulf of time between the fourth and second millennia in Mesopotamia.

These results suggest that there may be recurring patterns in the political economies that give rise to Mesopotamian trade colonies and in the ways that these colonies were organized. Trade colonies undoubtedly have some advantages for the states that sponsor them: (1) they guarantee access to strategic resources without reliance on foreign powers; (2) they can provide a vertical monopoly from the source areas; and (3) they allow the state to restrict access to prestige goods. Despite these advantages, Mesopotamian states seem to have eschewed trade colonization for most of their history. When Mesopotamian states were strong with powerful centralized rulers, they appear to have devolved the risk and expense of resource procurement on entrepreneurs outside the direct purview of the state, and seem to have been willing to let non-Mesopotamian foreigners play an active role, either in ports of trade outside of Mesopotamia or as resident alien traders inside Mesopotamia. In the majority of historically documented periods, Mesopotamian states did not control the regions from which the texts indicate they obtained their most important raw materials and prestige goods ((Lamberg-Karlovsky 1996:88). Unless they were able to actually conquer the areas with which they traded, powerful states may have avoided the use of colonies as a strategy of resource procurement due to their high costs, the necessity for the state to assume an inordinate amount of risk in maintaining the colonies, and the fact that colonies are very vulnerable to political fluctuations in the host community. This raises the intriguing and counterintuitive possibility that trade colonization might actually be a sign of political weakness, rather than strength, in early state societies.

Acknowledgments

I wish to thank the School of American Research, especially Douglas Schwartz and Nancy Owen Lewis, for providing us with the opportunity, facilities, and support to conduct the advanced seminar on the archaeology of colonization.

The Hacınebi excavations were conducted with the permission of the Turkish Ministry of Culture, General Directorate of Monuments and Museums. Thanks are due to the staff of the Sanlıurfa Provincial Museum and its directors—the late Adnan Mısır and his successor Eyüp Bucak—for their administrative assistance. The project was funded with support from the National Science Foundation (grant number SBR-9511329), the National Endowment for the Humanities (grant numbers RO-22448, RK-20133-94 and RZ-20120), The National Geographic Society (grant numbers 4853-92, 5057-93, 5295-94, and 5892-97), the Wenner-Gren Foundation for Anthropological Research (grant number 6309), the Kress Foundation, the American Research Institute in Turkey (ARIT), the de

Groot Fund of the Metropolitan Museum of Art, Faculty Research Grants from Northwestern University, and the generosity of private donors.

I wish to thank the participants in the SAR seminar for their valuable insights and constructive criticisms of this chapter. I am especially grateful to Guillermo Algaze, Christopher Edens, Theo van den Hout, Piotr Steinkeller, Christopher Woods, Norman Yoffee, and the two anonymous reviewers for the SAR Press for their careful reading and detailed comments on earlier drafts of this paper. I have attempted to address their concerns in this revision. Any remaining errors of fact or interpretation are my own.

Notes

1. Although technically speaking the Old Assyrian colonies were not founded by the king or palace sector of Assur, the close formal relationship between the systems of *karu* (colonies) and the state religious, political, and legal structures meant that the operation of the colonial system was completely imbricated in the structure and operation of the Old Assyrian state.

2. I am grateful to Guillermo Algaze (University of California San Diego) for bringing this article to my attention, and to David Schloen (University of Chicago) for discussing this interpretation of Neo-Assyrian colonization with me.

3. Recent excavations by Aslihan Yener and her colleagues at Kestel have located a source of tin in the Bolkardag region of the Taurus Mountains of southern Turkey (Yener et al. 1989; Yener et al. 1996; Yener 2000). This source was utilized in the Early Bronze Age (third millennium A.D.) but does not appear to have been used by those central Anatolian city-states that traded with the Assyrians. Either the city of Kanesh was outside the area of distribution for Kestel tin, or else the source had been mostly exhausted by the early second millennium B.C.

6

A Zapotec Diaspora Network
in Classic-Period Central Mexico

Michael W. Spence

ECONOMY AND POLITY

World-systems theory and related core-periphery models enjoyed a
brief vogue in Mesoamerican studies (Pailes and Whitecotton 1979;
Weigand 1982; Blanton and Feinman 1984; Whitecotton and Pailes
1986; B. Price 1986; Santley and Alexander 1992). The movement of
exotic goods across broad regions was taken as evidence for the economic articulation of major Mesoamerican polities with regions well
beyond their borders. This articulation was often believed to result in
some degree of political subordination to the center. Shortly, however,
Mesoamericanists started to express some concerns about the applicability of these models. These reservations focused particularly on the
more ambitious variants that attempted to link Mesoamerica with the
Southwestern US, or the civilizations of central Mexico with the societies of west Mexico or the Maya region (McGuire 1986; Stark 1986;
Spence 1996a, 2000; Feinman, Nicholas, and Upham 1996; Santley and
Alexander 1996; Nelson 1997). Given their scale, these models left little
room for fine-grained analysis.

Stein (1998, 1999b) has pointed out the major weaknesses of core-
periphery models. Prominent among these are the assumptions that

the economic relationships between core and periphery are, as implied by the terms, unequal, and that these relationships have a profound effect on the political structures. This perspective is tempered somewhat in analyses of Aztec society, where a rich body of historic data is available. The role of marketplace exchange is undeniable, and the professional merchants, although often state sponsored, clearly had a rather ambiguous relationship with the Aztec nobility. However, we lack these archival restraints for earlier periods. The political landscape of Classic-period central Mexico was quite unlike the crowded and contested territories of the Late Postclassic. It was dominated by a limited number of large, often primate, centers ruling over dispersed rural populations. The proportion of public to residential architecture in these centers was far greater than in the Late Postclassic cities. This impression of a bloated state apparatus has led to a conflation of political and economic institutions by archaeologists working with Classic-period societies. Even when they are trying to avoid the exaggerations of core-periphery models, they still view economic structures as inextricably linked to political institutions. The peer polity and network strategy models currently favored by archaeologists working with Epiclassic societies make no assumptions of political asymmetry and are a considerable improvement over the core-periphery models that they have supplanted, but they still view the circulation of nonlocal goods as tied to the political ambitions of regional elites (Jiménez and Darling 2000; Blanton et al. 1996).

We must remain open, however, to the possibility that some economic institutions in the ancient world may have played important roles within or between societies while remaining largely independent of their political structures. These institutions may have been involved in major economic transactions, perhaps with the consent or even encouragement of the state, which could then avoid the expense and risk associated with extraterritorial ventures while still benefiting through a tax-in-kind on the incoming goods (Stein this volume). Systems of production and exchange of this sort may have paralleled or even complemented state-based procurement systems like tribute, colonization, or royally sponsored merchants. The trade diaspora is a likely candidate for such a system (A. Cohen 1969, 1971; Curtin 1984; Stein 1999b).

DIASPORA NETWORKS

As it has been defined, the trade diaspora consists of a number of spatially separated communities that rely on their shared ethnic identity to structure their interactions, both among themselves and with "outsiders," and to secure their economic advantage (Curtin 1984). Although trade diasporas may be closely linked to governments, they may also function quite independently of them (Stein 1999b:49). Depending on the number and distribution of the consumers that they serve and on the materials that circulate in the network, they can play a major economic role yet have no direct impact on the political structures of the larger societies in which they are embedded.

However, care should be taken not to privilege the economic functions of these ethnic networks. Rather than viewing their economic role as the fundamental motivation for the cultural distinctiveness of diaspora communities, perhaps we should be thinking of it as an inextricable part of their identity. In this view, trade is not a vehicle for amassing wealth and power so much as an ethnic role and a medium for interaction. The economic niche is not necessarily the driving force behind the zealously maintained ethnic identity. That identity can play a number of other roles in the community, some of which may be considered equal in importance to economic benefit: allowing access to culturally appropriate spouses, differentiating the diaspora "citizens" from a large and perhaps domineering indigenous society, creating a widespread network of support, ensuring the favor of the ancestors, and so on. It may be appropriate, then, to remove the adjective "trade" and simply refer to these phenomena as diaspora networks.

The concept of a diaspora network also allows us to examine interregional interaction at a finer scale, to explore the roles of individuals and groups that are often obscured in the grander core-periphery models. Practice theory becomes a potent approach, particularly in view of the intensive intercultural interaction experienced between diaspora communities and the host societies into which they have inserted themselves (Lightfoot, Martinez, and Schiff 1998:201–2). Agency comes into focus, as individuals are presented with a range of opportunities along the fault lines between the systems.

Diaspora communities are not always readily identifiable in the archaeological record. To some degree they will have adopted the material culture of the indigenous society, perhaps living in local dwellings and relying on local craft specialists and marketplaces for their material needs (Spence 1996b). However, to the extent that they presented their identity materially, they should be archaeologically visible. In fact, it is unlikely that they could have effectively sustained their identity over time without some material expression of their distinctiveness and unity. Elsewhere I have suggested a set of criteria that can be used in the identification of ethnic enclaves, distinguishing them from other phenomena that might be confused with them, such as the presence of a few foreign residents rather than a functioning community, or the use of exotic materials by members of the local society (Spence 1996b:335–36; see also Santley, Yarborough, and Hall 1987; Stein this volume). Salient criteria would include the following:

1. The distinctive characteristics of the group should be widespread in the area, rather than just confined to one or two residences. They may also be concentrated in a public area or structure, reflecting broad participation by the residents in communal events focused on their ethnic identity.

2. There may be quantities of goods in foreign styles. Although the enclave inhabitants may have adopted much of the material culture of the host society, some artifact categories may have been preferred in the homeland style (for example, Stein 1999b:138–39, fig. 7.10). The selection of which categories of material culture to retain in homeland style and which to abandon in favor of local analogues can be particularly informative (Spence 1992). It is also important to determine whether the items in homeland style were imported from there or were manufactured locally (for example, Rattray 1987).

3. Architecture, or certain architectural elements, may be in the homeland style. Domestic structures in homeland style will have a rather different significance than would civic-ceremonial architecture.

   In the case of Teotihuacan, this criterion is complicated to some extent by the urban renewal program undertaken there in the third and fourth centuries A.D., when existing residences were razed and replaced with the standardized multifamily apartment compounds typical of Teotihuacan (Millon 1976).

4. Mortuary practices are more likely to follow homeland than local canons but may be a mixture of both. Given the social and ideological sensitivity of mortuary programs (Carr 1995), the choices made by immigrants can be especially revealing.

5. The osteological characteristics of the enclave population may distinguish it from the larger host population, particularly if the enclave inhabitants practice endogamy (Goldstein 2000:190–91). Extensive intermarriage with the host community would generally lead to the rapid erosion of the enclave's distinctive cultural identity, so some degree of endogamy (or marriage with people from other diaspora settlements or the homeland) is a frequent feature of enclaves. However, in a large multiethnic city, it may be difficult to define a clear osteological profile for the host community that could then be compared to the enclave (Spence 1994:411).

Beyond these, there are still other factors that must be considered. One is the audience for which any particular expression of ethnic identity is intended. It may have been oriented toward the host community at large (or some specific segment of it), the homeland, the residents of other communities in the diaspora network, the residents of the enclave itself, or even the members of the household (M. Wobst 1977; Spence 1992, 1996b). The items used as a medium for the expression and their contexts offer clues to the intended audience. For example, public architecture may be seen by a very wide audience, including members of the host community, while domestic service wares are likely to be viewed only by members of the household. Although most of a community may participate in a burial ritual, especially of an elite person, it is unlikely that outsiders will attend it, suggesting that the social effects of a distinctive mortuary practice will be played out within the enclave.

Another factor to be considered is the demography of the enclave (White et al. 2003). The number of residents in the community, the balance between the sexes, the birthrate, and the level of subadult mortality are particularly important. If numbers were low, the community may not have been demographically self-sufficient over the long term. If exogamy occurred, it is important to know its frequency, gender structure, and the source of the external spouses (Lightfoot this volume). Intermarriage with members of the host community would have had a more corrosive effect on enclave culture than marriage with the residents of sister diaspora communities or the homeland. The postmarital residence practices of the enclave will also be crucial; whether the incoming spouses were males or females could have had a profound effect on the enculturation of the young, and so ultimately on the cultural survival of the enclave (Spence 1992).

Of course, the identification of an ethnic enclave does not necessarily mean that it was linked with a functioning diaspora network. It could have been an ambassadorial community, a refugee settlement, or any number of other things. To be sure that the site was part of a diaspora network, it is necessary to link it to a wider set of similar communities. A. Cohen (1971:269–70) has said that this wider network must be studied, rather than focusing exclusively on one site within it. He notes the difficulty of doing this with ethnographic data; it is that much more difficult with only archaeological evidence.

In the following pages I will examine a particular ethnic enclave in Teotihuacan and some related sites elsewhere in central Mexico. Teotihuacan, in the northeast corner of the Valley of Mexico, dates from approximately 150 B.C. to A.D. 650. At its peak the population was about 150,000 (Millon 1973, 1981, 1988). Like any major city, it was multiethnic (Rattray 1987). However, the ethnic identities of some immigrants were surely obscured by their reliance on the specialized workshops and marketplaces of Teotihuacan for their material needs and by their residence in the standardized Teotihuacan apartment compounds (Rattray 1987; Spence 1996b). Others, among them a number of Zapotec immigrants from the Valley of Oaxaca, were nevertheless able to maintain a distinctive cultural identity over some centuries of life in Teotihuacan.

Tlailotlacan

Tlailotlacan, an area near the west edge of Teotihuacan, was settled by these Zapotec immigrants at about A.D. 200, the start of the Early Tlamimilolpa phase (Spence 1998). Their homeland, a state that occupied the Valley of Oaxaca with Monte Albán as its capital, was some 400

FIGURE 6.1

Tlailotlacan

kilometers to the southeast of Teotihuacan (fig. 6.1). Tlailotlacan includes about fifteen structures, most of them apartment compounds, although two (TL5 and 34:N1W6) may have had public functions (Spence 1992, 2002; Rattray 1993). The apartment compounds are clustered together, set off somewhat from the rest of the city by open land. The estimated population is approximately 700 people.

Some 850 meters to the northeast is another culturally similar area, consisting of at least one apartment compound and some adjacent areas. This smaller zone, which I will refer to as the N2W5 area, probably included about fifty to one hundred additional people. The land between the N2W5 area and Tlailotlacan proper is largely open, with only a few structures intervening between the two areas. A ten-minute walk would get a person from one to the other.

We might, then, estimate a total population for Tlailotlacan of about 800 people. This is probably above the threshold necessary for the survival of the community, but not comfortably so (Goldstein 2000:190). We should not assume that this number was stable. The original immigrants may have numbered either more or fewer when they first arrived. Also, a Oaxacan-style tomb and architectural facades have been found in an apartment compound (19:N1W5) about 150 meters beyond the east edge of the enclave, suggesting that in the earlier part of its existence the enclave may have been somewhat larger. Interestingly, this same apartment compound has revealed evidence of occupation by immigrants from the Michoacán region, some 250 kilometers to the west, raising the possibility of some sort of cooperation between the two ethnic groups (Gómez 1998).

The N2W5 area has not yet been excavated. However, several apartment compounds in Tlailotlacan proper have been partially excavated: TL1 (Gamboa 1995; Ortega and Palomares 2003), TL5 (Michelle Croissier, personal communication, 2003), TL6 (Spence 1989, 1992, 1998), TL7 (Millon 1973:41–42; Spence 1976; Rattray 1987, 1993), TL20N (Gamboa 1995), and TL69 (Quintanilla 1982, 1993). These reports and a few broader syntheses (Spence and Gamboa 1999; Spence 2002) provide the data for the following analysis.

One overriding concern seems to have driven the Tlailotlacanos, shaping their practices and institutions: survival, in both demographic and cultural terms (Spence 1992). With a relatively small population, which probably regularly suffered the loss of disaffected members to the larger Teotihuacan society, the physical reproduction of the community would have been a constant source of concern. If birthrates were too low to ensure replacement, new members would have needed to be recruited from outside the community.

Even if the enclave could maintain its numbers, it would have been in constant danger of cultural assimilation. This risk would have been enhanced if new members recruited into the community came from the host society, and even more so if they were the principal agents in the enculturation of the young. In any case, there would inevitably have been some erosion of the enclave's original culture. When the immigrants arrived in Teotihuacan from the Valley of Oaxaca, they would have carried with them a fully Zapotec culture. That probably did not last beyond a generation or two. In a new cultural environment and with limited contact with the homeland, some traditional practices would have been discarded or lost while others would have been adopted from the host community. This selection would not have been random, but rather would have been guided by the fundamental imperative of the enclave residents—the survival of their community. Thus, although the enclave culture has been referred to as Zapotec, it was in fact something rather different, a construct responsive to the pressures and opportunities of the new environment (Spence 1992; Stein 1999b:49; van Dommelen this volume; Alcock this volume).

Architecture

The earliest architecture uncovered in Tlailotlacan is a small courtyard altar in TL6 with some associated subadult burials, dating to the Early Tlamimilolpa phase (circa A.D. 200–300). Unfortunately, these early levels have been disturbed by later construction. The altar was preserved because it had been later covered by a larger platform of adobe blocks. The altar had an orientation of 2 degrees east of astronomic north, although the standard Teotihuacan orientation (followed by the overlying adobe structure) is 15 degrees 25' east of north.

By the Late Tlamimilolpa phase (circa A.D. 300–450), the enclave residences were all standard Teotihuacan-style apartment compounds, following the Teotihuacan orientation. These multifamily residences were built throughout Teotihuacan in an urban renewal program, a massive building project that started about A.D. 250–300 and eventually resulted in the complete destruction of all the earlier residences in the city and their replacement by apartment compounds. Virtually all of the city's population, from the poorest to the most powerful, lived in these structures. A project on this scale could only have been carried out on the initiative (probably including some threat of force) of the state. In some respects—for example, their orientation—the state may have set general standards for their construction.

Most Mesoamerican residences, both before and after Teotihuacan, consisted of two or three single-family houses grouped around a central patio, the whole complex probably housing an extended family (Manzanilla, ed. 1986). This was the case in the Valley of Oaxaca (Winter 1986) and would have been the residential template that the immigrants carried with them to Teotihuacan. The apartment compound seems, to some extent, to offer a compatible residential format, with interior complexes of rooms around patios that could have accommodated extended family units (Millon 1976). There is, however, one significant difference from the earlier households. Several such extended families were grouped together in the apartment compound, forming a larger and well-integrated social unit of some thirty to one hundred people.

The Teotihuacan apartment compound was unique in Mesoamerica. It seems well suited to life in a crowded city, offering the residents privacy, security, and easy access to light and air through the patios scattered throughout each structure (Millon 1976). Despite this, nothing like it was characteristic of earlier, later, or even contemporaneous Mesoamerican societies (although some elite residences were similar; Hirth 1993). It would seem, then, that this format was not a comfortable one for most Mesoamerican peoples. It created a social environment that did not entirely suit them (Spence 2002).

Nevertheless, the people of Tlailotlacan accepted this format, although their previous residential format must have been the extended family compound. It is possible that they were given little choice in this; the scale of the urban renewal program implies an element of coercion. Still, the people of the Merchants' Barrio were able to build their circular structures (Rattray 1990b), so there must have been some flexibility on the part of the state.

In any event, whether through choice or through force, the Tlailotlacanos lived in Teotihuacan apartment compounds. Since the built environment has the capacity to transform the relationships of the people who live in it, the organization of the Tlailotlacanos must have changed in some respects. In particular, a level above that of the extended family would have been created or, if present before, made more prominent. This apartment-compound social unit would have become a fundamental structure in the lives of the people. In that respect, then, the Tlailotlacanos became Teotihuacanos.

However, this may not have been an entirely unwelcome transformation. Beyond its general suitability for urban life, the apartment compound may have been the appropriate structure to accommodate the new pressures in the lives of the Tlailotlacanos. Matters that had formerly been the domain of the nuclear or extended family, such as birth, marriage, and death, had now become vital concerns of the community at large in its new social environment. They bore directly on the survival of the enclave. The apartment compound may thus have created the appropriate social vehicle for dealing with these newly elevated concerns, a closely knit kin group above the level of the family (Spence 2002).

There is less evidence on the structure of the enclave as a whole. Quite apart from its distinctive culture, the clustering of the apartment compounds and their separation from the others in that part of the city indicate a well-defined group. There may have been one or even two public structures in the enclave providing focal points for the community. One is TL34 (site 34:N1W6), interpreted as a platform of some sort rather than a residence. The only data we have on TL34 is from a surface collection there, so any interpretation of its function is highly speculative. It stands a little beyond the neighboring residences at the south edge of the enclave, near West Avenue, the main street into the city from the west. It could have monitored access to the enclave from the avenue.

The other possible public structure is TL5, at the east edge of the enclave. The open space between it and TL6, its immediate neighbor to the west, is larger than usual and is crossed by a freestanding north-south wall. Recent excavations in TL5 by Michelle Croissier (personal communication, 2003) have revealed platforms with architectural facades that appear more Zapotec than Teotihuacan.

Ceramics

The chipped and ground stone artifacts from Tlailotlacan, as well as the stone and shell ornamental goods, are of Teotihuacan forms. However, about 5 percent of the ceramic materials are of Zapotec styles (Rattray 1987, 1993; Spence 1989, 1992; Winter 1998:155; Gibbs 2001; see also Caso, Bernal, and Acosta 1967). Most of the ceramics recovered in the excavations come from construction fill. Although I believe that most of these were originally used in the enclave (though not necessarily in the structures in which they were found), the lack of more specific context limits the inferences that can be drawn from them. Some, however, are from particular contexts—burials, for the most part—and are more informative.

Neutron activation analysis of an extensive sample has shown that nearly all of the Zapotec-style pottery was produced from local clays (Abascal, Harbottle, and Sayre 1974; G. Harbottle, personal communication, 1991). Only a few specimens are actually of Valley of Oaxaca clays. The gray color of many of the Zapotec-style items indicates firing in a reducing atmosphere with a kiln, a technology brought by the Tlailotlacanos from the Valley of Oaxaca (and, interestingly, not adopted more widely in Teotihuacan, where open-air firing continued to be the preferred method).

The Zapotec-style ceramics cover a wide range, including both domestic and ritual items. The majority are household vessels, perhaps reflecting the continued preparation and consumption of favored Zapotec foods. The most common form is a conical bowl with a scraped exterior and burnished interior, suitable for a variety of domestic tasks (Spence 1992:68–71). It is identified as Type G35 in the Valley of Oaxaca sequence (Caso, Bernal, and Acosta 1967; Winter 1998:155). There are also two kinds of fine service bowls, one with a grooved interior rim (Valley of Oaxaca Type G12) and one with zoomorphic elements. Among the ritual items are urns, braziers, handled censers, and figurines (some of which were probably really toys). Of course, a variety of other forms and wares in use in the Valley of Oaxaca do not appear in the Tlailotlacan assemblage, raising the question of why certain ones were selected and others rejected. It might be that the retained forms were the standard types, the ones most common in the homeland repertoire and most central to Zapotec life. However, although this may be true of the ritual types, it is not an entirely satisfactory explanation for the continued manufacture of supposedly utilitarian types like the conical bowls, for which adequate Teotihuacan analogues were available.

Most of the Zapotec-style ceramics made and used in Tlailotlacan were part of the domestic inventory. It is thus unlikely that they would have been seen by people outside the apartment compound, or even outside the extended family. The question arises, then, as to why these vessels were consistently produced in Zapotec styles. M. Wobst (1977:323–27) considers materials confined to such restricted social contexts to be ineffective as media for social expression; they would simply be repeating what was already well understood by their limited audience. Nevertheless, the fact remains that these vessels were made in Zapotec styles. Furthermore, those styles were maintained over a considerable time without any major changes. The association of these vessels with Xolalpan-period ceramics indicates that their manufacture continued for at least three centuries after the founding of the enclave (Gibbs 2001).

Bourdieu's (1977) concept of *habitus* is relevant here. The habitus grows out of the material and social environment and consists of a set of "dispositions" that guides behavior in all aspects of life, including and perhaps even particularly in the domestic sphere (Dietler and Herbich 1998:246–48; S. Jones 1997:87–100). The habitus can change as agents reinterpret and reapply practice, but these changes will be constrained by the social weight that it has acquired. Furthermore, the habitus acts on both the producers and the consumers of goods (Dietler and Herbich 1998). Thus, in the case of Tlailotlacan, the habitus would have had its effect on the artisans who produced the ceramics for local use and on the consumers who brought the vessels into their households, thereby conforming to and reproducing the habitus. These ceramics were not simply passive props in the household. They entered into a variety of daily activities (food preparation and consumption, washing, ritual, and the like), reinforcing the dispositions already in place. It is in this context that enculturation took place, the new generation incorporating the habitus of their predecessors (Spence 1992:78).

The habitus is not immune to change. In fact, modest changes that remain in fundamental accord with the basic dispositions can be expected as individual agency intervenes in practice, and over time these can result in significant shifts. The marked conservatism of the Zapotec-style ceramics in Tlailotlacan, then, requires some further explanation. Bourdieu (1977:168–69) states that, for the most part, the dispositions of the habitus are implicit and assumed, not so much beyond as beneath question—his state of *doxa*. At times, however, a challenge arises. At that point, what was implicit becomes explicit, accessible to analysis and discussion—his condition of *heterodoxy*. This may result in changes to practice or in its affirmation and reinforcement (*orthodoxy*; Bourdieu 1977:169–71). In Tlailotlacan, heterodoxy was probably a regularly occurring condition, the challenge to the enclave's dispositions raised constantly by the encompassing presence of Teotihuacan and the plethora of alternatives to practice that it offered. In some instances, these conflicts were resolved by the changing or abandonment of the traditional pattern and the adoption of the Teotihuacan analogue, while in others the enclave practice remained strong—indeed, perhaps stronger but with less flexibility (Bourdieu's orthodoxy)—as a result of its exposure to critical inspection and its explicit affirmation. In the enclave's situation, this conscious affirmation and rationalization would probably have involved reference to the enclave's ethnic identity, effectively enlisting these forms in the enclave's struggle for cultural survival. That would have had the effect of freezing them, insulating them somewhat from the normal drift created by agency. In an enclave, a community essentially in a constant state of cultural siege, many elements of the habitus would acquire a force and an inflexibility that they would escape in more relaxed circumstances. In effect, these less flexible and more explicit dispositions would form the core of the community's identity, the cultural face that it would present to those both within and outside the enclave.

Ritual

Ceramic items used in rituals included both Teotihuacan and Zapotec forms, the former being more common. Some items were made specifically for ritual, like the various censer forms, while others were ordinary household items enlisted for use in ritual events.

There were undoubtedly rituals at the enclave level, involving wide community participation, but without excavating public structures little can be said about them. That leaves rituals at the level of the apartment compound and below to be examined. These can be dichotomized into public and private categories, based on their locations in the structures (Spence 2002). Events that took place in the principal courtyard or temple of the apartment compound would have involved the participation of most of the residents, and so are treated here as public. Those that occurred in the residential sectors are considered private, involving only the nuclear or, at most, extended family. Of particular interest in Tlailotlacan is the apparent conflation of the two levels, where rituals that normally were the concern of the immediate family now fell in the domain of the larger apartment-compound social group (Spence 2002). The concern of the enclave with its physical and cultural reproduction trumped family interest, so events that touched on that concern, together with the rituals that accompanied them, now drew the attention of a much wider segment of the community.

The two major ritual events for which evidence is available are birth and death. Birth is represented by the nineteen enigmatic "ritual deposits" of TL6 (Spence 2002). These usually consist of two bowls, the upper one placed upside-down on top of the lower one. Ritual deposits are common in the principal courtyards of Tlailotlacan but are rare elsewhere in the city of Teotihuacan. Parsons (1936:76) describes the early-twentieth-century practice of Oaxacan Zapotecs burying the afterbirth of a newborn in a covered ceramic jar in the family patio. I believe, by analogy, that the ritual deposits reflect this same custom. Their presence in the main courtyards of Tlailotlacan indicates the importance assigned to birth in the enclave.

This broad concern with the reproduction of the community is also reflected in the mortuary practices associated with subadults, who were nearly always (twenty-six of twenty-eight cases in Tlailotlacan) buried in a public space, often in or beside the courtyard altars. They frequently had good offerings in their graves (Spence and Gamboa 1999). In the larger Teotihuacan community and in the Zapotec homeland, their status was not as high and their burial was more often in family residential space or outside the household complex.

In terms of a variety of measures, women in Tlailotlacan seem to have enjoyed a status equal to that of men (Spence and Gamboa 1999). They were as likely to be buried in a public space and in the tombs, and to have offerings. These offering were as likely as those of men to include goods that indicated wealth (marine shell, greenstone items), access to the supernatural world (censers), and the celebration of ethnic heritage (Zapotec-style ceramic goods). The high status of women may, like the treatment of subadult burials, reflect the community's concern with its renewal. Women were not only the bearers of future

generations, but they were probably also the primary agents of enculturation. Their roles were thus crucial in both the physical and cultural
reproduction of the community. Beyond this, isotopic data suggest that
women also played an important part in the maintenance of the wider
diaspora network (see below).

The Tlailotlacan mortuary program was more Zapotec than
Teotihuacan (Spence and Gamboa 1999). Prominent elements in it
were burial in stone tombs; burial in individual, smaller stone-walled
graves; and burial in the extended position, none of which occurred
anywhere else in Teotihuacan. The tombs and stone-walled graves,
which follow Zapotec structural canons, were among the very few
Zapotec features in the enclave's architecture. Each apartment compound had only one tomb at any given time, and it was used over
some generations for the burial of the senior couple of the residential
group. Nonmetric skeletal and dental data from the TL7 tomb indicate
that the tomb occupants, especially the men, were closely related, so
leadership positions may have been inherited in the male line (Spence
1976, 1994:364). Tomb mortuary rituals continued over some time, as
later entries into the tomb were the occasion for rituals that also
included prior (and by then ancestral) burials (Spence 1994:359–61).
In contrast, senior Teotihuacan individuals were buried in simple
earthen pits.

This implies that there may have been somewhat more social distance between senior and junior kinsmen in Tlailotlacan, perhaps
because of the need for a cohesive and orderly internal structure in
expatriate communities (Stein 1999b:47–48; Spence and Gamboa
1999:195). Still, as Urcid (1983) has pointed out with respect to the
Valley of Oaxaca, those in tombs did not form a separate elite class; they
were simply the senior members of the apartment-compound social
unit, linked to everybody else by the duties and obligations of kinship.
Their position did not entail the sort of privilege that would have
resulted in riches or superior health. Levels of dental enamel hypopla-
sia, a good indicator of childhood health, were the same in tomb as in
non-tomb burials (Spence and Gamboa 1999).

The ritual paraphernalia of the enclave, those items produced
specifically for ritual, were largely censers of one sort or another. There
were urns, Zapotec braziers, and handled censers, all of Zapotec style,

and Teotihuacan biconical (theater) censers and candeleros (Spence 2002). Their contexts in the enclave are variable and difficult to interpret. The handled censers seem to have served as personal ritual equipment in Tlailotlacan, much as they did in the Zapotec homeland. The one Teotihuacan candelero found in context had been used in a public ritual, although elsewhere in the city candeleros were generally personal items. The Teotihuacan biconical censers were found in varying degrees of completeness and in both public and private contexts, while the Zapotec braziers seem to have been used in public rituals. The urns, or iconographic elements from them, also occurred in both private and public contexts, although in the Valley of Oaxaca they have generally been found in tombs.

As with some other aspects of Tlailotlacan life, there seems to have been a conflation of the public and private realms in the use of some categories of ritual paraphernalia, in particular the urns and biconical censers. This suggests again that the Tlailotlacan social units were tightly integrated, with private and familial concerns elevated to the level of the apartment compound as a whole. It is also interesting to note that both Zapotec and Teotihuacan ceremonial items were used, although not interchangeably (Spence 2002). The urns, Zapotec braziers, and Teotihuacan biconical censers all bear culturally specific iconography, the potency of which was apparently recognized and respected. Isolated fragments of these items, with iconography on them, were buried with people or placed in other special contexts.

Postmarital Residence and Oxygen Isotope Ratios

The postmarital residential practices of the enclave would have been crucial in the maintenance of its identity. A high level of intermarriage with the larger Teotihuacan society would have led to a rapid cultural erosion of the community, even though it may have sustained it demographically. Presumably, then, it was preferable to find spouses within the enclave or in culturally related groups elsewhere, in the Valley of Oaxaca homeland or in sister diaspora communities.

Analysis of stable oxygen isotopes indicates a high level of movement and relocation among the enclave occupants (White et al. 2003). The ratio of stable oxygen isotopes in the skeletal and dental phosphate of an individual is determined by their ratio in the groundwater of the region where that individual lives. This latter ratio varies from one region to another in response to a variety of geographic and climatic factors such as altitude, temperature, and distance from the ocean. In essence, then, the individual's isotopic ratio forms a sort of geographic signature, a marker of his or her geographic location at the time that particular tissue was forming (White et al. 1998).

Furthermore, this ratio can be used to track the individual's movements. The deciduous and permanent teeth develop sequentially over a considerable time, from the fetal period to about the fifteenth year. As each tooth develops, it takes on the isotopic ratio of the region where the individual is living at that time. That ratio is then locked in, since dental tissue does not change after tooth formation. Bone, in contrast, continues to turn over throughout life, so earlier isotopic ratios are continuously revised (or re-created, if no relocation occurs). The skeletal isotopic ratio of a burial will thus reflect that individual's residence in the years immediately preceding death. Stable strontium isotope ratios offer similar evidence (Price, Manzanilla, and Middleton 2000).

Earlier isotopic analyses of Tlailotlacan burials suggested a possible bias toward virilocal postmarital residence (White et al. 1998; Price, Manzanilla, and Middleton 2000). However, a more extensive recent analysis has changed that perception (White et al. 2003). Of five adults for whom we have third molar values, indicating their location at the age of 13 to 15 years, three (two women and one man) had relocated to Tlailotlacan from foreign regions after their third molar formation, perhaps coming to the enclave as spouses. The other two, both women, had apparently resided in the enclave since at least their later childhood. This suggests that there was no fixed gender preference for postmarital residence, allowing a flexibility that would have facilitated the location and circulation of culturally appropriate spouses of both genders (White et al. 2003).

In fact, the scale of movement among enclave residents may have been even greater than the isotopic data indicate. Some of the other diaspora communities are not far removed from the Valley of Mexico and may have isotopic ratios that overlap those of Teotihuacan (White et al. 2003). Until we have tested samples from those regions, we cannot be entirely confident that some of the isotopic values that we have assumed to represent Teotihuacan, or Tlailotlacan, may not in fact represent one of these other communities.

Political Identity

There is abundant evidence to show that the Tlailotlacanos zealously maintained a distinct ethnic identity. Their political identity is a different matter. Did they view themselves as citizens of the Teotihuacan state, or did they believe that they were somehow politically independent of it?

When they first came to the area, at the start of the Early Tlamimilolpa phase (circa A.D. 200), they settled on irrigated farmland. Their structures were built over the canals. Water-rolled sherds in the fill of the canals date from the earlier Tzacualli (0–A.D. 150) and Miccaotli (A.D. 150–200) phases. It seems unlikely that the occupants of good, irrigated land would have surrendered it willingly to foreign newcomers, so the Teotihuacan state may have intervened in support of their settlement there, viewing them in a sense as a desirable resource (Nichols, Spence, and Borland 1991; Stein 1999b:49).

The architectural facades on the structures around the TL6 entry courtyard, where people first entered the building, were in the *talud-tablero* style. The location of these facades inside TL6 suggests that whatever message they carried was meant for enclave residents, rather than for people beyond the enclave. The TL6 talud-tableros have been largely destroyed, but a few remnants indicate that they were in the Valley of Oaxaca style, differing from the Teotihuacan variant in that the recessed tablero face is framed by a projecting border only on its top and sides, not on the bottom; the Teotihuacan variant is fully enclosed. A few structures elsewhere in Teotihuacan have this Oaxacan variant (Cabrera 1998:60–63). Site 19:N1W5, just 150 meters east of the enclave, had a Zapotec tomb and the Oaxacan talud-tablero on its platforms; it might once have been part of the enclave (Gómez 1998). On the other hand, the main temple in TL7, the immediate neighbor of TL6 to the west, had a typical Teotihuacan talud-tablero with a projecting lower border (Millon 1973:41–42, personal communication, 2001). It thus seems that both variants were in use in the enclave, the Teotihuacan variant perhaps replacing the Oaxacan variant over time (the TL7 temple is later than the TL6 and 19:N1W5 examples).

Another piece of evidence was found with the burial of a child in TL6. The offering with the child includes a fine cylindrical vase of Valley of Oaxaca clay and two figurines. The figurines were clutched in the child's left hand. They are of Teotihuacan style and are identical, made from the same mold. They represent a standing man wearing cotton armor, a Teotihuacan soldier (Séjourné 1966:107–10; Warren Barbour, personal communication, 1991). Although some figurines may have ritual significance, in this case I believe that they were simply favored toys. This implies that the child, or whoever was responsible for burying the child, viewed Teotihuacan soldiers favorably and probably identified with them.

The evidence is ambiguous, but over their centuries of occupation in Teotihuacan, the Tlailotlacanos must have developed some sort of relatively stable understanding with the rulers of the city. If not initially, they probably came eventually to view themselves as Teotihuacanos in political terms. The presence of Oaxacan-style talud-tablero facades in the enclave need not be a contradiction; they may represent a statement of ethnic, not political, affiliation. As will be discussed below, the Zapotec state centered on Monte Albán in the Valley of Oaxaca apparently conducted its relationships with the Teotihuacan state without reference to Tlailotlacan, suggesting that the enclave was not part of the Zapotec state's political apparatus.

Social Memory

An expatriate community usually encounters particular difficulties with its social memory, the collective myths, beliefs, and stories that underlie its identity and provide its charter (Alcock 2001, this volume; Van Dyke and Alcock 2003). To the degree that social memory is embedded in the landscape, movement to a new region could create significant disruption and weaken the community's cohesion. Their initial response might be an attempt to transfer their social memory to the new environment, reinterpreting the new landscape in familiar terms.

This is perhaps what Peeler and Winter (1993) are suggesting when they say that the location of Tlailotlacan and even the basic orientation of Teotihuacan itself were fixed by solar events celebrated in the Valley of Oaxaca. According to their interpretation, the enclave lies at the intersection of two lines, one passing over the Pyramid of the Moon from the rising sun's location on the horizon on the day of zenith, and the other passing over the Temple of Quetzalcoatl from the sunrise point on the morning after the nadir. However, the dates of zenith and nadir are those of the Valley of Oaxaca, not those of Teotihuacan; zenith and nadir in Teotihuacan are eleven days different from those solar events in the Valley of Oaxaca (Peeler and Winter 1993:8). If this hypothesis is accepted, it would appear that the Tlailotlacanos had attempted to transplant important calendrical dates from their home-land to their new environment, in the process reinterpreting local monuments and ignoring local solar events. Peeler and Winter (1993:9–10) further claim that the orientation of the Street of the Dead, the basic north–south orientation of the city, was also determined by those zenith and nadir lines.

This hypothesis has met with some reservations (Cabrera 1998:66). For one, the orientation of Teotihuacan can be adequately explained with reference to locally visible solar events (Šprajc 2000). Also, it seems unlikely that a small group of newcomers could have effectively imposed their own interpretations on a sacred landscape made up of such immense natural and man-made features as Cerro Gordo and the pyramids, features that would already have been playing well-established central roles in the local social memory.

THE ZAPOTEC DIASPORA

Tlailotlacan needs to be considered as part of a much wider network (Hirth and Swezey 1976:15–16; Crespo and Mastache 1981; Rattray 1987:256–58). However, we do not have the sort of data for these other components that we do for Tlailotlacan. Their identification as terminals in a widespread network based on a constructed Zapotec ethnic identity depends on the criteria that we use to define that network. This requires not only determining what those criteria are, but also how they functioned in the network—as trade goods, symbols of ethnic identity, elements of a terminal's internal social structure, and the like.

The salient characteristics of these possible diaspora terminals are Zapotec tombs, Monte Albán (Zapotec)–style gray wares, Teotihuacan ceramics, and Thin Orange ware. The latter is a very fine service ware manufactured near Tepexi in the state of Puebla (Rattray 1990a, 1998).

Although this area is some 150 kilometers southeast of Teotihuacan, the production of Thin Orange there was apparently under Teotihuacan control, and large amounts of it were imported annually by the city (Rattray 1998:87–92). From Teotihuacan it was distributed throughout Mesoamerica, where it is usually seen as a hallmark of Teotihuacan contact.

Some suggested components of the diaspora are briefly described below (see fig. 6.1).

Tehuacan

Noguera (1940, 1945) reports two Zapotec tombs in the city of Tehuacan, Puebla (Hirth and Swezey 1976:15). The material in them included Zapotec- and Teotihuacan-style ceramics, among them a number of Thin Orange vessels. What Noguera (1940:308) refers to as "the purest Zapotec style of black or grey ware," MacNeish, Peterson, and Flannery (1970:251) suggest may be El Riego Gray, a local Tehuacan ware. Robert Drennan (personal communication, 2000) agrees that the gray ware ceramics are probably local and suggests that the site may not be unusual for the region. Without further investigation, its status as a diaspora site remains uncertain.

Los Teteles

Los Teteles, near Manzanilla in Puebla, was an important site in the Middle Classic period (Plunket and Uruñuela 1998:105–6, 112). Three Zapotec tombs have been located near the main plaza of the site (Hirth and Swezey 1976; Noyola 1993:23; Patricia Plunket, personal communication, 2000). Their contents include Thin Orange vessels, Teotihuacan black ware, and gray ware (Plunket and Uruñuela 1998:106, fig. 3). The gray ware from the site and from some of the tombs includes local copies of Monte Albán G35 conical bowls (Hirth and Swezey 1976). The G35 type is also well represented in local copies at Tlailotlacan (Winter 1998:155).

Cerro del Venado

Muller (1948:35–37, 46–47, figs. 4–6, 9) examined looted tombs at the Cerro del Venado site in the state of Morelos. Some of the tomb ceramics were gray ware vessels similar to Monte Albán II types. Unfortunately, the earlier looting makes it impossible to say much about the external relationships of the site. Some elements of the tombs, such as the false arch opening of Tomb 1, are not Zapotec features. Like the Tehuacan case, the relationship of this site to the diaspora remains unclear.

Chingú

Chingú, a large Classic-period site with some public architecture 60 kilometers northwest of Teotihuacan, may have been a regional capital under Teotihuacan (Díaz 1980, 1981). The estimated population was 6,500 people during the peak of its occupation (Díaz 1980:61–62). The site has been extensively surface collected, but no excavations have been done. It is thus not possible to say whether or not Zapotec tombs are present.

The surface ceramics include some local wares but are largely Teotihuacan types. Thin Orange ware is well represented. Zapotec-style ceramics form about 7 percent of the Tlamimilolpa phase total but consist mostly of bowls with a double groove around the interior rim—the Monte Albán G12 type. Although this type is also common in Tlailotlacan, the main Tlailotlacan type is the conical bowl (G35), which is not mentioned for Chingú. The Zapotec ceramics of Chingú were probably manufactured in a local workshop (Díaz 1980:67). Zapotec ceramics are also concentrated in the area of obsidian workshop activity, suggesting that the people who claimed a Zapotec ethnic identity may have played a role in the regional distribution of obsidian artifacts.

Acoculco

Acoculco is a smaller site 15 kilometers southwest of Chingú. In contrast to the situation in Chingú, 54 percent of the ceramics are of Zapotec style, and these include a wider range of types (Crespo and Mastache 1981). Conical bowls (G35) and G12 bowls are present, although no Zapotec ritual items have yet appeared there. No excavation has been conducted.

El Tesoro

El Tesoro is 2 kilometers southwest of Acoculco. It is also a small site, but 63 percent of the surface-collected ceramics are of Zapotec types, again including a variety of forms but no ritual items (Crespo and Mastache 1981). However, a Zapotec tomb has recently been found there (Hernández 1994). Its contents included two G12 bowls and two Zapotec-style handled censers. Also, local inhabitants have collected fragments of Zapotec urns in the vicinity, suggesting that their absence in the earlier collections (and possibly also in those of Acoculco and Chingú) was just due to sampling. Another tomb, unfortunately looted, was on an adjacent hill (Hernández 1994:129). The presence of tombs in El Tesoro indicates that the residents were not there simply on a temporary basis. They were part of a stable, transgenerational community.

Monte Albán

As the capital of the Zapotec state in the Valley of Oaxaca and apparently a place with some sort of special relationship with Teotihuacan, one might expect Monte Albán to have some link with the diaspora network. Identifying it, however, is a difficult task. The principal criteria used to identify the other communities—Zapotec tombs and ceramics—are, of course, ubiquitous at Monte Albán.

Winter (1998:161–70) has identified an area on the North Platform of Monte Albán that may have been occupied by Teotihuacanos, or elite Zapotecs with close ties to Teotihuacan. It was involved in the processing and exchange of sheet mica, a material much valued in Teotihuacan. However, as Winter (1998:169–70) points out, there are some important differences between Tlailotlacan and this area that make it unlikely that the two are linked (such as the absence of tombs in the North Platform area and its very high status).

To date, there are no other strong candidates for a network terminal in the region. Goods certainly moved between Monte Albán and Teotihuacan: Thin Orange and other Teotihuacan ceramics, Oaxacan gray wares, mica, obsidian, and probably more. The apparently amicable relationship between the two states would have facilitated a high level of exchange (Millon 1973:42; Marcus 1983). Nevertheless, it is not entirely clear how the movement of goods was managed. The location of mica-processing debris together with Teotihuacan materials in a very high-status area on Monte Albán's North Platform, and of mica stores in the Viking Group on Teotihuacan's Street of the Dead, indicate that mica at least was exchanged through direct elite contacts at the highest level. Mica is not particularly common in Tlailotlacan, suggesting that the enclave played no major role in its movement.

Ceramics imported from Oaxaca are distributed widely in Teotihuacan (Rattray 1987:253–56, figs. 4–5; 1993:54–68, figs. 1, 15–16, pls. VII–XII). However, they are not very common in Tlailotlacan, nor do they cluster along the Street of the Dead or in other public/elite areas. Their distribution suggests no particular point of entry, and indeed they may have arrived in Teotihuacan through a variety of contacts.

The Economic Roles of the Terminals

El Tesoro, Acoculco, and probably at least some segments of Chingú were evidently linked to Tlailotlacan (Crespo and Mastache 1981; Rattray 1987). The area has extensive limestone deposits, and Colonial-period Mexico City relied on this general region for much of its supply of lime for making plaster. Crespo and Mastache (1981:100, 103) suggest that these northern communities were processing limestone and sending the lime to Tlailotlacan, which then distributed it to the rest of Teotihuacan. Plaster was in use in the Valley of Oaxaca well before it was used in Teotihuacan, but from A.D. 200 on, Teotihuacan had an enormous appetite for lime—literally speaking, since it was used in the preparation of tortillas as well as in construction (Barba and Córdova 1999). It seems plausible that the immigrants of Tlailotlacan brought with them from Oaxaca the knowledge of lime processing and the manufacture of plaster, and used this advantage (and their ethnic identity) to dominate the production and supply of lime to Teotihuacan. Given the Teotihuacan urban renewal program that saw several hundred apartment compounds built throughout the city at this time, the state would have welcomed the bearers of this knowledge, perhaps even acquiring land from Teotihuacanos for their settlement (Nichols, Spence, and Borland 1991).

There is some evidence that Tlailotlacan was involved in the procurement and importation of lime. No storage facilities containing it have yet been located there. However, one of the earliest burials in TL6 included in its offering a ball of stucco with lime, one of the principal ingredients in Teotihuacan wall and floor surfaces. The interior of a bowl used in a later ritual event was caked with plaster, apparently from its prior use as a container for plaster. Also, Burial 381, an adult male, had an offering of a plaster smoother and two polishing stones, indicating that he was a mason. Although there is evidence for the preparation and application of plaster at several Teotihuacan apartment compounds beyond the enclave (Manzanilla 2004:135), the Tlailotlacanos were probably responsible for bringing the raw materials into the city and, at least in the enclave's early years, providing many of the masons working in Teotihuacan.

The northern sites require more intensive investigation. For one thing, Chingú, Acoculco, and El Tesoro seem to differ significantly from one another in terms of their ceramic assemblages—for instance, in the proportions of Zapotec-style wares in the collections, the Zapotec types represented, and their colors. It is not clear whether this variation is due to different collection strategies, to analysis by different archaeologists, to different site functions in the network, or to the founding of the sites at different times (Crespo and Mastache 1981:101–3). Some of the differences may well disappear with excavation and larger samples. If they do prove to be real, these ceramic variations carry implications for the social functions of the Zapotec types. However, given the changes in our understanding of the region brought about by the accidental discovery of one tomb, our first priority should be to determine whether these differences actually exist.

The northern sites had their primary link to Tlailotlacan and in fact may have been colonies of Tlailotlacan (Rattray 1987:258). Some of the other sites in the network, however, may have been interacting with Tlailotlacan in a different way. It is not clear what goods were moving through these links, but Thin Orange ware is one likely item (Spence 1992:80; Rattray 1993:70). Charlton (1977, 1987) has examined a trade route from Teotihuacan that led ultimately to Puebla and Oaxaca and found Zapotec gray wares associated with quantities of Thin Orange at several rest areas and camps along the route.

Another possible good is the high-quality green obsidian from the Pachuca source. The only place in Teotihuacan where there are appreciable quantities of locally made Zapotec-style conical bowls, besides Tlailotlacan and the N2W5 area, is in five sites near West Avenue, just west of the Great Compound (Rattray 1987:253). Four of these sites have obsidian working debris from the manufacture of cores and blades of Pachuca obsidian. At Chingú, obsidian working and Zapotec-style ceramics appear to have been spatially associated (Díaz 1980).

Sojourning

The diaspora network must also have had a number of social functions (A. Cohen 1971). The most important of these would have been oriented toward the perpetuation of the network components and their continued articulation. Although some might see this as secondary to the economic functions, with the network serving primarily as a vehicle for the ongoing exchange of goods and protection of resources, I am more inclined to take the opposite view. In this perspective, the principal concern of the network citizenry was the survival of the wider ethnic community that the network created, with the associated trade providing economic support and perhaps even a certain measure of prosperity.

The links created by exchange would not in themselves have been sufficient to counteract the considerable centrifugal forces acting on the network communities. Their social memories, incorporating different migration stories and imprinted on different landscapes, would have diverged. Different experiences with different host societies would have altered the habitus of each community, reducing the stock of mutually held dispositions and practices that might form the basis for a broader common identity. Some strong integrative devices would have been needed to offset these pressures. One of these, suggested by the oxygen isotope data, was the circulation of spouses, of both genders, among the network communities.

The isotopic values also suggest another integrative practice (White et al. 2003). Most subadults in Tlailotlacan seem to have relocated during their first year of life. Their deciduous medial incisors, which develop in the fetal stage, identify the geographic location of the pregnant mother. However, the deciduous second molars, forming in the first year after birth, have markedly different values, indicating the infant's movement to a different region at that time. These sojourns apparently lasted for a year or so, after which the infant returned to the natal community.

The range of foreign isotope values is large and probably represents at least three different regions, one of which was the Valley of

Oaxaca. The other regions cannot yet be identified with confidence. It is possible that some of the diaspora components closer to Teotihuacan are also represented in the values but overlap too much with the city to be distinguished.

These sojourns may have been intended to establish the diaspora "citizenship" of the infants, possibly by linking them with the natal community of one of the parents. More important, however, is the fact that these nursing infants must have been accompanied in their sojourns by their mothers. The infants themselves were far too young to have played any active role in the integration of the diaspora components, but their mothers would have been well placed to harmonize social memory and articulate practice between their marital community and the child's sojourn community (which may, in fact, have been the mother's natal community). The high status of women, then, may have been due to this broader integrative role, as well as to the vital part they played in the demographic and cultural reproduction of their particular communities.

The isotopic evidence also suggests that sojourning was not restricted to infancy. Some dental values show relocation even through the development of the second molar, at about 6 to 8 years of age. A few individuals appear to have lived in three different regions during their infancy and childhood.

CONCLUSIONS

Tlailotlacan, Acoculco, El Tesoro, and probably parts of Chingú were components in a network based on a constructed "Zapotec" ethnic identity and probably focused in part on the exploitation and processing of lime for Teotihuacan. Although their ethnic identity played a major role in their control of this economic resource, their knowledge from the Valley of Oaxaca of lime processing and plaster manufacture would have been instrumental in the early consolidation of their monopoly. However, the network may have been wider than this, involving still other communities to the east and south and circulating other goods, such as Thin Orange pottery, artifacts of Pachuca obsidian, and cotton (Rattray 1987, 1998; Spence 1992). More information is needed on these other components. Los Teteles in Puebla seems to be a particularly good candidate for a diaspora site, but it has to be linked more directly to Tlailotlacan. A detailed analysis of the Zapotec-style ceramics from the site should shed further light on this.

At least the Tlailotlacanos, and probably also the residents of the offshoot communities to the north, had formed a working relationship with the Teotihuacan state. The evidence from Tlailotlacan suggests that they may have identified politically with Teotihuacan even while differentiating themselves culturally. On the other hand, it seems unlikely that they were acting as agents or factors of the state government, their trade returns being appropriated by the state. The enclave is located on the west edge of the city, about as far as it can get from the city's core and its major public structures while still being in the city. There is no evidence of elite status in the enclave. Mural art is absent, there are no very rich offerings or human sacrifices, and the quality of the construction materials is what would be expected in a middle- or lower-class structure. Nor, as noted above, does Tlailotlacan seem to have played a role in the political and economic relationships between the Monte Albán and Teotihuacan states (Winter 1998:169–70).

This diaspora network is comparable to the Andean archipelago. In some expressions of the archipelago, Andean communities created long-term colonies in distant areas in order to exploit their resources, developing a procurement network that functioned outside the central political institutions of the metropole (D'Altroy this volume; Schreiber this volume; Goldstein 2000). The relationship between Tlailotlacan and the smaller northern sites, El Tesoro and Acoculco, was probably very similar. The ceramics from El Tesoro and Acoculco indicate that they were directly tied to Tlailotlacan and, in fact, may have been colonies created by Tlailotlacan. The relative paucity of Teotihuacan ceramics in these two northern sites shows their reliance on Tlailotlacan and their relatively limited access to the markets and goods of Teotihuacan proper.

Also, the tombs at El Tesoro indicate that the communities were intended to be permanent, with little or no expectation of return to Tlailotlacan by the residents. Rather, they fully expected to live out their lives there, maintaining and ultimately reproducing their social groups and their distinctive ethnic identity. The emphasis on Zapotec-style ceramics would have been an integral part of this effort. This seems very similar to the Uruk colonies in the Near East, where Uruk material culture was maintained and local analogues largely rejected (Stein 1999b, this volume). In contrast, the Assyrian residents of the *karum* in Kanesh adopted the indigenous material culture and residential architecture (Stein this volume). Their apparent lack of interest in reproducing the habitus of the metropole is somewhat puzzling. It suggests that, despite long periods of residence in the karum, the Assyrian merchants very deliberately did not consider it "home" and had no intention of raising families (that is, Assyrian families) there.

It is also important to note that El Tesoro and Acoculco were established in a region considered to be within the borders of the Teotihuacan state and administered locally for Teotihuacan through Chingú. This is one major point of difference with at least some of the archipelago networks (D'Altroy this volume), and at odds with some definitions of colonies (see Stein this volume). The wider network, however, did extend into foreign territories. Los Teteles was probably beyond the Teotihuacan state, and if there were related settlements in Tehuacan, Morelos, and the Valley of Oaxaca, they would definitely have been extraterritorial. However, this is not to say that these were colonies sponsored originally by Monte Albán or by some particular institution within the Zapotec metropole. Tlailotlacan shows no evidence of an ongoing close or formal relationship with the Valley of Oaxaca, although there was probably some exchange and intermarriage between the two (Price, Manzanilla, and Middleton 2000; White et al. 2003). It is possible that the diaspora network was based on ties that were developed after the various groups had left the Valley of Oaxaca. Indeed, it might even be that it was Tlailotlacan (or Los Teteles), not Monte Albán, that developed the network.

Some of the major goods moving into Teotihuacan through Tlailotlacan were widely disseminated in the city. Lime, used in the preparation of plaster to coat surfaces in both residential and public structures (as well as to make tortillas and to provide a surface for painting fine ceramics), must have been imported in very large quantities (Barba and Córdova 1999). It was used everywhere in the city. A number of burials in different apartment compounds have plaster smoothers with them, suggesting that the masons who prepared and applied the plaster lived in many areas besides just TL6 (Manzanilla 2004:135). In the case of the Oztoyahualco apartment compound, which has no state ties, this work appears to have been a minor specialty of the residents (Lizárroga and Ortiz 1993). There is thus no evidence to suggest that the state dominated the distribution of lime or plaster within Teotihuacan, or the mason's craft.

Thin Orange ware was also widely distributed in Teotihuacan, appearing even in the poorest areas of the city. However, distributional analysis shows that it was not closely associated with elite residences and was not especially well represented in the central core of the city, where the major state structures were located (Cowgill, Altschul, and Sload 1984:163–65). Again, then, it does not seem likely that state institutions controlled the importation and distribution of Thin Orange.

The diaspora network may thus have played an important economic role in Teotihuacan, bringing in large quantities of materials that were in wide demand in the city. Although the rulers of Teotihuacan supported their endeavors, they apparently did not play a direct role in these exchanges and received no more benefit from them than perhaps a tax-in-kind. For example, the lime (and possibly even some of the masons) used to plaster the public structures in the city's heart may have been obtained by the state through taxes on the Tlailotlacanos.

However, the Zapotec diaspora may not have been the only network with a terminal in Teotihuacan. The Merchants' Barrio, at the east edge of the city, was occupied by people with ties to the Gulf Coast and Maya regions (Rattray 1987, 1990b, 1992:40–52, 76, 204–21; Spence 1996b). They are thought to have traded a variety of goods: Thin Orange ware, cotton, rubber, cacao, and salt, among others. Oxygen isotope analysis indicates that the occupants of the enclave included both locally and foreign born individuals, the latter deriving from at least three different regions (White et al. 2000).

A Gulf Coast site, Matacapan, is said to have been a Teotihuacan colony (Santley, Yarborough, and Hall 1987). However, there is some uncertainty about whether Matacapan was really a colony of Teotihuacan, and whether it had any sort of formal relationship with the Merchants' Barrio (Yarborough 1992; Spence 1996b:344–45; Cowgill 1997:135; Daneels 2002). Its architecture, mortuary programs, and ceramics are quite different from those of the Merchants' Barrio, although some Matacapan sherds have been found in the barrio. There are circular structures, large secondary burials, and imported Gulf

Coast (including some Matacapan) and Maya ceramics in the Merchants' Barrio, in contrast to rectangular structures, primary burials, and locally made versions of some Teotihuacan wares at Matacapan. It seems unlikely that two such culturally different groups could have been participating together in a network supposedly built on a shared and constructed ethnic identity, a trade diaspora (Curtin 1984), although they may still have been trading with each other simply as groups with a mutual economic interest and, perhaps, some familial links among their residents.

In any event, the Merchants' Barrio was a culturally distinct enclave within Teotihuacan. As with Tlailotlacan, there is nothing to indicate that it was affiliated with state institutions. The Merchants' Barrio may have been part of a different diaspora, although we have not yet identified any of its sister communities. Given the fact that its inhabitants come from at least three regions beyond Teotihuacan, it may more properly be viewed as a multiethnic ward devoted to long-distance trade with a variety of regions—a Mesoamerican equivalent of the Assyrian karum (Stein this volume). In either event, it may have been competing to some degree with Tlailotlacan, particularly if both enclaves were importing Thin Orange ware and exporting Pachuca obsidian artifacts (and perhaps overlapping in other goods, too).

It would appear, then, that large amounts of material goods that were consumed widely across the social spectrum entered Teotihuacan through institutions that were essentially independent of the state. This is not to say that the state did not have its own procurement system. That system, however, may have been based on state-sponsored merchants who focused on goods in more limited demand, like items for elite display or ostentatious consumption in state events, such as jade and colored feathers. The state system may have complemented rather than competed with the other networks, whose products in any case would have been available to the state through taxes.

This separation seems to have been comfortably accepted by all parties. It persisted for some four or five centuries, until the collapse of Teotihuacan. There is no indication that the state ever tried to intrude directly on the enclaves. It probably preferred to have its political institutions safely buffered from them, while it siphoned off a share of the goods through taxation. A closer political affiliation could have been destabilizing, since the enclaves' access to trade wealth and arcane knowledge would have given them considerable potential political power.

Acknowledgments

My work in Tlailotlacan has been supported by grants from the Social Sciences and Humanities Research Council of Canada and the University of Western Ontario. I would like to thank Rubén Cabrera, Sergio Gómez, George Cowgill, Rene Millon, Evelyn Rattray, and Marc Winter for their help with many aspects of my research. This paper has been greatly enriched by comments and suggestions from the other seminar participants over the week of intense discussion at the School of American Research. Indeed, it is a very different paper from the one that I brought to the seminar. I am grateful to them, and to the School of American Research, for this opportunity. I also thank the anonymous reviewers, whose comments have led to several changes. Most particularly, though, I must thank my colleague Christine D. White, whose isotopic analysis and interpretation provided a depth of understanding that would not otherwise have been possible.

7

The Archaeology of Colonization

California in Cross-Cultural Perspective

Kent G. Lightfoot

How useful or advisable is it to compare the colonial practices of
ancient states or empires with those that unfolded during European
colonialism from the sixteenth through early twentieth centuries? This
question elicited considerable debate among this book's authors participating in the SAR seminar on the archaeology of colonization.
These scholars are ideally suited to address this question, given their
expertise on colonial programs associated with ancient Mesopotamia
polities, Phoenicia, Greece, and Rome in the Old World; the prehistoric Teotihuacan, Wari, Tiwanaku, and Inka states or empires in
Mesoamerica and South America; and historic European expansion
into Mesoamerica and North America. The seminar discussion was very
instructive about the current status of cross-cultural comparisons in the
archaeology of colonization. On one hand, there was a general recognition that cross-cultural comparisons may provide important insights
for understanding similarities and differences in colonial ideologies,
dominance structures, political strategies, interethnic relationships,
and native agency in a diverse range of historical settings. On the other
hand, there was a strong reaction from some scholars working in non-
Western and noncapitalistic contexts that the application of models

and concepts from European colonialism may be inappropriate, and that the historical contingencies of ancient states and their colonies may be so different that little can gained by such a comparative analysis.

The purpose of this paper is to explore the issue of cross-cultural comparisons of colonization and to offer one perspective for undertaking such an approach. My chapter is divided into three parts. The first discusses a common concern raised by seminar participants about the uncritical use of concepts derived from the colonial systems of early capitalist Europe to interpret colonial relations in non-Western and noncapitalistic settings. This problem has clearly dampened enthusiasm for the development of a broader cross-cultural perspective among some of my colleagues. In the second part, I suggest that the underlying conundrum may have more to do with current models employed in colonization studies than with the potential for undertaking cross-cultural comparisons per se. My participation in the seminar opened my eyes to some striking commonalities (as well as differences) in several dimensions of colonialism that crosscut space and time. For example, seminar participants described colonial practices of ancient states that were relevant to my study of mercantile and mission colonies in California, including the political motivations of homeland polities, resettlement of native peoples, interethnic marriages, and various kinds of native and colonist entanglements. One approach for undertaking cross-cultural comparisons is to consider those dimensions of colonial domination, demography, and time that may provide common variables for examining the nature and outcome of native and colonist interactions in divergent historical contexts. In the third part, I employ five dimensions (enculturation programs, native relocation programs, interethnic unions, demographic parameters, and chronology of colonial encounters) to compare colonizer-native interactions for two different colonial institutions (missionary and mercantile) deployed in California by Spain and Russia in the late 1700s and early 1800s.

THE SAR SEMINAR: PERSPECTIVES ON EUROPEAN COLONIALISM

A common point made by most seminar participants, and reiterated in this book, is that the current models of colonization tend to be shaped and colored by European colonial experiences in the Americas,

Africa, South Asia, and Southeast Asia beginning with the Age of Discovery and continuing through the early part of the twentieth century. As summarized by Gil Stein in his prospectus for the seminar, these models make a number of explicit (as well as implicit) assumptions concerning the power relations of homelands and colonists. The technological superiority of colonists is typically assumed, a factor that is seen to promote their economic, political, and military control over indigenous peoples. By presuming asymmetrical power relations from the very outset, European-based colonial models often impose hierarchical structural relationships between homelands, colonies, and indigenous populations that very much influence the kinds of analyses and interpretations that take place. The papers written by Gil Stein on Uruk and Old Assyrian trading colonies, by Michael Spence on the Zapotec trade diaspora in Mesoamerica, and by Katharina Schreiber on the colonial strategies of Wari and Inka expansion in the Sondondo Valley and Nasca region are excellent illustrations of why power relations between colonists and host communities cannot be assumed a priori. Several contributing authors note in chapters and previous writings (for example, Dietler 1998a; Stein 1998, 1999b) that the inappropriate use of the world-systems model to analyze ancient states and their colonies exemplifies some of the problems of using a European-based model to interpret colonial practices in non-Western, noncapitalistic settings.

Several contributing authors also emphasize that there is an unfortunate tendency to conflate European colonialism itself into a single mode or model. Janine Gasco, Dan Rogers, and I stress the tremendous variation that embodied European colonial practices, power relations, and colonist and native entanglements in the Americas. Gasco highlights this diversity in her seminar chapter on the establishment of Spanish colonies in Mesoamerica by considering how colonial policies and practices varied depending on the objectives of the colonizers, the specific purposes of the colonies, the kinds of native societies encountered, and to what degree the colonists and natives shared similar kinds of political systems, gender roles, and ideological constructs. The critical point made by Gasco and others in the seminar is that European colonialism in the Americas cannot be viewed as a monolithic entity, but rather represents a series of separate colonial encounters in which very different kinds of dominance structures and native and colonist interactions unfolded over time. We need to keep in mind that each European homeland (for example, France, Britain, Russia, and Spain) had its own distinctive economic and political agenda for establishing colonies in the Americas, and that the colonial policies and practices of individual homelands varied greatly across time and space. Furthermore, the European colonial programs recruited a diverse assortment of colonists from many backgrounds and homelands to represent their interests in the Americas. Finally, these colonists became entangled with a diverse array of native peoples who were characterized by highly variable sociopolitical organizations, levels of tribal integrations, and unique cultural value systems (see also Champagne 1994:209–14; Gasco 1993:163; Rogers 1993b:75–77; Schortman and Urban 1998:114; Simmons 1988).

DIMENSIONS OF COLONIAL ENCOUNTERS

After participating in the SAR seminar, my own thinking on cross-cultural comparisons in the archaeology of colonization was transformed in three ways. First, I feel that any comparative approach must take into account the great range of variation evident in the colonial programs associated with both ancient states/empires and historic European nations. One cannot assume a priori in any of these colonial settings that specific kinds of asymmetrical power relations or native and colonist interactions will be found. For example, when one considers the colonial programs of the Spanish, Russian, French, and British in the Americas, and how they changed over time, it is clear that considerable variation characterized the degree to which colonial agents actually dominated native peoples and exerted power in the exploitation of resources, goods, and labor (for example, Crowell 1997; Weber 1992; R. White 1991; Wolf 1982).

Second, given the tremendous range of variation in colonial programs, I believe it is futile to rely on a few models to understand the processes and mechanisms of colonialism. Furthermore, we do great injustice to the study of cross-cultural variation by attempting to pigeonhole our case studies into a few discrete colonial types. Peter van Dommelen noted in his chapter the difficulties of using one overarching model to describe all Phoenician and Greek settlements. And it is clear that the world-systems model is only applicable to a limited number of historical cases (Stein 1999b:42–43). Rather than subsuming colonial practices into a few models or characteristic types, I think we must examine the variation that embodied colonial and indigenous interactions in non-Western and noncapitalistic settings, as well as in cases involving European colonialism. For cross-cultural comparisons to be of much use, they must provide an approach that can enhance our understanding of the historical variation that underlies colonial practices and processes.

Third, I think it is a mistake to view European colonial expansion as separate and distinct from other practices of colonialism. Although admittedly the world-systems model does not work very well for understanding many non-Western colonial programs, it should not serve as the litmus test for turning our backs on cross-cultural comparisons. It is not clear to me how well this model works in understanding the full range of European colonialism. In reading the seminar papers and talking to fellow participants, I was struck by some common practices of colonialism in non-Western settings when compared with my own work in colonial California. These include the creation of multiethnic communities, the establishment of commercial and imperial colonies, resettlement of native peoples as part of colonial policies, intermarriage between colonial agents and indigenous peoples, and differences in the timing of colonial encounters. Some significant differences were also emphasized, the most blatant relating to demographic parameters, specifically the massive depopulation of Native Americans who were exposed to Euro-Asiatic pathogens. This monumental population decline may have little analogy for most cases of ancient colonization in the New and Old Worlds. But here again there is considerable variation in European colonialism, as the endemic diseases of West Africa limited European expansion into the interior for several centuries (Stein 1999b:56).

Based on my own research on colonial California, my reading of relevant literature on European colonialism in North America, and my participating in the SAR seminar, I offer an alternative approach for undertaking cross-cultural comparisons that focuses on dimensions of colonial encounters situated along the axes of domination, demography, and time. These dimensions are viewed as key variables in considering similarities and differences in the mechanisms and processes of colonialism. I have selected those dimensions that I feel may be important for understanding the outcomes of colonial entanglements in historically contingent situations. This kind of approach allows the researcher to examine different processes of colonialism by considering a full continuum of potential power relations between colonists and natives, very different kinds of demographic relationships between foreign and indigenous populations, and divergent chronologies of colonial encounters.

The key to this approach is examining how a particular dimension of colonial domination, demography, or time may play out very differently in specific historical contexts, and how the combined effects of the different dimensions may be important for understanding the outcomes of colonial encounters. For example, a common dimension of many colonial experiences is interethnic unions between colonists (typically men) and natives (often women), which may be characterized by very different power relations, gender ideologies, and cultural perspectives. Examining how interethnic unions are constituted in varied case studies and how they are affected by other dimensions of colonization may prove to be important for understanding how colonist and native interactions are transformed under different colonial contexts.

Specifically, I describe five dimensions of colonial encounters that consider variation in (1) enculturation programs, (2) native relocation programs, (3) interethnic unions, (4) demographic parameters, and (5) chronology. I selected these dimensions based primarily on my reading of colonizer-native interactions in European colonies in North America, but I also note below how they are applicable to non-Western case studies presented in the seminar and in this book.

1. Enculturation Programs. Colonial agents commonly employed enculturation programs to transform the social, economic, political, and religious practices of indigenous peoples residing in colonies. Enculturation programs represent an important dimension of colonial encounters that varied greatly along an axis of "directed" culture change. As first articulated in acculturation studies in the 1930s and 1940s, "directed" contact involved encounters in which one society clearly dominated another and forced its values, lifeways, and worldviews on the subservient one (see Linton 1940). A cross-cultural perspective that considers variation in enculturation programs along an axis of directed culture change may provide important insights into why some colonial contexts cultivated significant cultural transformations among individuals and groups, and why some natives engaged in strategies of resistance and violence when cultural innovations were forced on them (see Cusick 1998:6).

At one end of the axis are the directed enculturation programs of missionaries and plantation owners in North America who explicitly tried to alter the basic cultural values and ideological structures of subordinate workers, using a suite of coercive, and often brutal, methods, such as spying, corporal punishment, curtailment of freedom, and the like (Jackson and Castillo 1995:31–39; Singleton 1998:179–81). The purpose of these enculturation programs was to create a reliable, subservient labor class who would imitate, to some degree, the cultural practices (language, clothing, diet, work ethics) of the dominant order. At the other end of this axis were colonial enterprises that minimized the implementation of enculturation programs and strategies of directed culture change. These colonial enterprises would probably characterize most examples of colonization associated with ancient states and empires discussed in the book, especially those involving trading or merchant colonies (for example, seminar chapters by Dietler, Spence, Stein, and van Dommelen). It would also characterize many of the colonial agents who participated in the European fur trade in North America. Oppressive methods were sometimes employed to obtain furs, goods, and labor from native peoples, but force and coercion were rarely used to change native diets, dress, language, tools, and house types. In some cases, natives who participated in these colonial enterprises were allowed to follow their traditional lifeways and ritual practices, so long as they did not adversely affect the profitability of the mercantile colonies (for example, Crowell 1997; Lightfoot, Wake, and Schiff 1991:11–28; M. J. Wagner 1998; Whelan 1993).

2. Native Relocation Programs. The establishment of new colonies often involved the removal of native peoples to the periphery of the advancing frontier or resettlement in newly created colonial settlements, including missions, plantations, mines, and barrios. As discussed by Terence D'Altroy, one of the most massive resettlement programs of indigenous peoples in the Americas may have been undertaken by the Inka, who relocated hundreds of thousands of people to new settlements. Native relocation programs varied greatly in how indigenous populations were persuaded to move (from force to economic incentives), in how far they were moved, and in what kinds of social and physical environments they were resettled. A cross-cultural perspective that considers variations along this dimension of native resettlement may be important for understanding the construction and transformation of native identities in colonial settings. In his seminal book, *Cycles of Conquest*, Spicer (1962:576–77) concluded that one of the most critical factors in the continuation of native identities in the American Southwest was the maintenance of residence patterns within traditional tribal territories. The sacred relationship between land and ancestors appears to have been significant in symbolizing the continuity of group identities. Kicza (1997:15) also observed that consistency in the placement of rural indigenous communities in colonial Spanish America facilitated the maintenance of traditional identities, political organizations, and ritual systems over time.

The most directed and disruptive native relocation programs in North America tended to take place on Indian reservations, plantations, and missions. Missionary orders, such as the Jesuits and Franciscans, employed native relocation programs to facilitate the settlement of native converts at mission complexes, although the specific practices varied in time and space (for example, Jackson 1994:13–54; Milanich 1995:167–83; Spicer 1962:570–71). In places where traditional native settlement patterns were dispersed and/or residentially mobile, missionaries implemented a policy of *reducción* to remove natives from settlements in the hinterland and to relocate them in centrally placed missions.

The least directed relocation programs tended to be associated with mercantile colonies, such as fur trade outposts, where colonial agents typically gave local natives a wider latitude in where they could live. However, the spatial organization of these settlements usually reflected the underlying social and status hierarchies of the colonizers and typically involved the spatial segregation of managerial elites, non-Indian workers, and Indians (Crowell 1997:227; Lightfoot 1997:4–5). Economic incentives were often used to induce some natives to live near colonial settlements and to participate as local laborers. This stimulated a process of population aggregation around many trade outposts where "post" or "Home Guard" Indians resided (Swagerty 1988:370).

3. Interethnic Unions. There is a growing body of culture-contact research that explores how members of interethnic unions or marriages often played important roles as cultural brokers and intermediaries in pluralistic colonial contexts. Cohabitation between colonial agents and tribal members promoted political alliances (especially between administrators and elite native families), facilitated trade relations, produced polyglot translators and interpreters, and provided sex partners (Deagan 1995a; Swagerty 1988; M. J. Wagner 1998; Whelan 1993). Colonial and native partners could also serve as conduits for introducing each other's cultural values and material objects into the daily practices of pluralistic families on colonial frontiers. More importantly, the offspring of interethnic unions produced mixed-blood or mestizo populations who were often at the forefront of creating innovative, often synergistic, cultural practices that were neither purely "native" or "colonial," but something new. Some mixed-blood populations constructed their own group identities in colonial settings through the process of ethnogenesis (Deagan 1998).

Several chapters discuss interethnic unions in non-Western settings. Susan Alcock examines intermarriage in Roman colonies in Greece and Anatolia, Michael Spence considers intermarriage with the host community in his Zapotec trade diaspora, Gil Stein notes the frequent intermarriage in Old Assyrian colonies, while Peter van Dommelen explores the concept of "hybridity" in Phoenician and Carthaginian settlements in the Mediterranean. The frequency of interethnic unions varied greatly across space and time in European colonies in North America. The occurrence was tied to such factors as the population size and sex ratios of colonial and local populations, and changing cultural perspectives on mixed marriages among the colonizers and natives. Some colonial powers, such as Spain, Russia, and France, favored and even encouraged interethnic marriages in diverse colonial contexts as strategies for populating distant frontiers with political allies and colonial workers, whereas other colonial homelands, such as Britain, tended to frown upon or actively discourage this practice (Deagan 1995a:452; Fedorova 1973:206; Hoffman 1997:28; Wade 1988:24). Tribal groups also varied greatly in how they perceived sexual relations with strangers (Ronda 1984:62–63, 208, 232), and their views about interethnic unions often changed over time depending on their experiences with colonizers (for example, Aginsky 1949:290). Interethnic unions in North American colonies were greatly influenced by gender politics and cultural proscriptions, since the majority involved colonial men and native women. Several studies have noted the power and influence that non-European women wielded in colonial societies through interethnic unions (Deagan 1990:240; Martinez 1998; McEwan 1995:228).

   4. Demographic Parameters of Colonial and Native Populations. This dimension has probably received the most attention by researchers in North America, primarily because of the ongoing debate concerning the introduction of Euro-Asian pathogens to Native Americans, and the devastating impact the epidemics had on local populations (for example, Crosby 1986; Dobyns 1983; Ramenofsky 1987). Native depopulation is viewed by some scholars as a critical factor in the transformation of colonizer-native interactions. It is argued that native population collapse resulted in the extinction of native languages; contributed to the loss of traditional knowledge, material culture, and rituals as entire cohorts of elders were eliminated; produced refugee communities in which survivors amalgamated into fewer and fewer settlements; and fostered the development of "creole" communities and cultures as the frequency of interethnic and intertribal marriages increased. There is no question that early European exploration and later colonization had grave effects on the health and cultural survival of native groups; the real question revolves around the specific timing and spread of epidemics and the magnitude of native population loss (see Baker and Kealhofer 1996; Deagan 1998:28–29; Dobyns 1991; C. S. Larsen 1994; Rogers 1990:53–54, 80–84).

   Cross-cultural comparisons of colonization among European colonies in the Americas need to consider the effects of native population decline and how this may have created different processes of colonial interactions than those found among the colonies of ancient states and empires. In considering colonizer-native interactions over time, it is important to examine the changing relation between native demography and colonizer population parameters (numbers, sex ratios, ratios of individuals/families). Changing population ratios of colonizers to natives can have important ramifications for the kinds of encounters that took place. A relatively small number of single men who rotated in and out of a colony's workforce during the initial period of colonization would have very different implications for colonizer-native interactions compared with historical settings in which hordes of settlers are unleashed into an area suffering from severe native depopulation.

5. *Chronology of Colonial Encounters.* The temporal dimension of colonial encounters is very important to consider. Contributing authors discuss colonial programs that lasted for more than a half millennium (Roman colonization in some areas of the Mediterranean) to only a few decades (Colony Ross). Recent studies stress the very different kinds of colonizer-native interactions that take place across this temporal dimension. Much attention has focused on "first contacts," including early European explorations and the establishment of new colonies. Several recent papers stress the importance of examining later post-contact interactions in well-developed colonial settings, where dominance patterns and cycles of violence become established over successive generations (Hill 1998; Ruhl and Hoffman 1997). Consequently, an important component of this dimension is considering how colonizer-native interactions were transformed over time. This is especially germane in comparing the encounters of first-generation colonizers and native peoples, with those of second-, third-, and fourth-generation persons who were born and raised in the colonies. For example, Kicza (1997:13–14) suggests that it takes about three generations for creole populations to become distinct ethnic entities in colonial settlements.

COMPARING MISSION AND MERCANTILE COLONIAL INSTITUTIONS IN CALIFORNIA

Colonial California affords an ideal setting to examine the above five dimensions from a cross-cultural perspective. Its history of colonialism involves both mission and mercantile colonies—probably the most common socioeconomic institutions employed by European powers in North America to integrate local indigenous peoples into colonial infrastructures. Spain relied primarily on Franciscan priests to subjugate and civilize Native Californians along its northernmost frontier of New Spain, whereas Russian agents recruited local natives into the workforce of its mercantile colony of Fort Ross. The comparison of the five dimensions of colonial encounters in mission and mercantile social settings is particularly germane to California for the following three reasons.

1. Time and Space. The Spanish missions and Russian mercantile colony of Fort Ross were relatively contemporaneous and separated by little more than 110 kilometers (fig. 7.1). Spain founded twenty-one Franciscan missions, four military presidios, and three civilian pueblos that extended from San Diego Harbor to the greater San Francisco Bay during the period of 1769 to 1823 (although the last mission, San Francisco Solano, was technically inaugurated after Mexican independence). The Franciscan missions were designed from the outset as the focal point of native and Hispanic interactions in Alta California. Fort Ross was established in 1812 by the Russian-American Company, a mercantile monopoly that represented Russia's interests in the lucrative North Pacific fur trade. Situated on the rugged northern California coastline, it was the administrative and mercantile center of the Ross colonial district (or counter). Colony Ross served as a California base for harvesting sea otter and fur seal pelts, for raising crops and livestock, and for producing manufactured goods, many of which were traded to Franciscan missions for wheat and barley. Colony Ross remained in operation for only twenty-nine years, as declining profits forced the Russian-American Company to sell its California holdings in 1841.

2. Coastal Hunter-Gatherers. California provides the opportunity to compare and contrast the long-term effects of two very different colonial programs on relatively similar coastal hunter-gatherer populations. Although the native communities that once blanketed the coastal zone of southern and central California varied greatly in their languages, tribal affiliations, populations, and settlement patterns, they had much in common in their material culture, broader worldviews (religious practices, dances, ceremonies), trade networks, and subsistence pursuits oriented to both the sea and land. The Franciscan priests initially focused their evangelic efforts on hunter-gatherer peoples from hundreds of coastal communities who resided near the mission complexes. Most coastal groups were organized into small polities that are defined by anthropologists as "tribelets," "village communities," or "tiny nations"

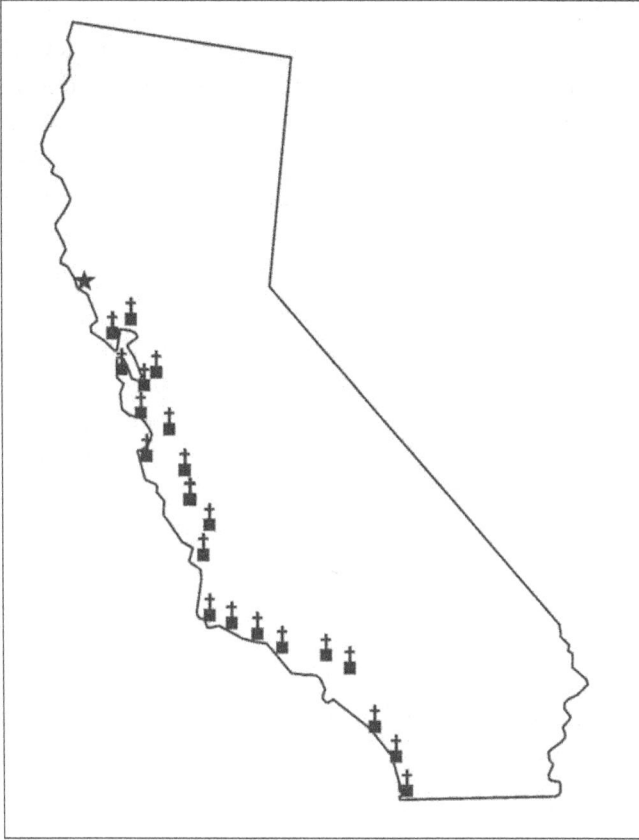

FIGURE 7.1

Colonial California, with Franciscan missions marked with crosses and Colony Ross by a star.

that often numbered between 200 and 500 people and may have extended no more than 13 to 19 kilometers across (Kroeber 1966; Milliken 1995:21–24; Simmons 1997:56–60). These small-scale polities represented the largest political units in most of coastal California, with the possible exception of the Santa Barbara Channel region, in which groups were self-governing and landowning.

Anthropologists have defined much larger ethnolinguistic units based on the languages or families of languages that were spoken by groups of related polities. These language groups are sometimes referred to as "tribes" in California anthropology (Simmons 1997:56).

The language groups that were initially incorporated into the missions include the Coast Miwok, Ohlone (Costanoan), Esselen, Salinan, Chumash, Gabrielino, Luiseño, and Kumeyaay (Diegueño). In the later decades of the missions, people speaking Yokuts, Cahuilla, and Interior Miwok languages from the interior were enlisted into the missions. The Russian-American Company concentrated its recruitment of native laborers from native peoples speaking Coast Miwok, Kashaya Pomo, and Southern Pomo languages who lived in the hinterland of Fort Ross.

It is important to distinguish between individual Californian Indian polities and the broader "ethnolinguistic units" in which they have been classified. The former represent a cluster of related villages and hamlets that were identified from a native perspective with a particular sociopolitical entity or "tribal" group. By contrast, the latter are anthropological constructs that never really functioned on the ground as tribal entities with unified political leadership or well-defined territories that native peoples would have recognized (Simmons 1997:56). The one notable exception to this observation is the Kashaya Pomo who represent one of the few language groups that have a name for themselves as a whole (McLendon and Oswalt 1978:277). In defining "tribal" identities in this chapter, I refer to the smaller polities as opposed to the broader language groups, unless otherwise noted.

3. Outcomes of Colonizer-Native Interactions. The consequences of colonial encounters in the Franciscan missions and Colony Ross differed among Native Californian groups. Ohlone, Esselen, and Salinan speakers incorporated into the northernmost missions underwent a process of cultural transformation that resulted in the disintegration of small-scale tribal entities and the dispersal of surviving descendants into disjointed remnant groups. In fact, until very recently most scholars argued that the descendants of the northern missions (Mission San Antonio, Mission Santa Cruz, and Mission San Francisco de Asís) had become largely extinct, both culturally and genetically. Alfred Kroeber (1925:275, 544, 550–51, 621) observed that most of these coastal hunter-gatherers had either become "extinct" or had "melted away" to a very few survivors. Subsequent anthropologists and historians who have undertaken research on the California mission Indians have largely echoed this interpretation (for example, Garr 1972:306; Kelsey

1985:508, 511; Mason 1984:140; Monroy 1990:8). Although the descendent groups who trace their genetic and cultural heritage back to the northern mission Indians have emerged as political players in contemporary California, they continually confront skepticism about their identity as "real" Indians, and they remain unacknowledged by the United States government.

A different history unfolded for the Luiseño and Kumeyaay Indians associated with the two southernmost missions, Mission San Luis Rey and Mission San Diego. Although significant cultural changes took place with the adoption of new agricultural practices, architectural innovations, and the incorporation of Catholic symbolism into native rituals, local Indian communities appear to have perpetuated some aspects of their traditional political structures, economic practices, and ceremonial cycles. In contrast to the northern mission Indians who were mostly ignored by Kroeber and other early anthropologists from the University of California, a number of scholars worked among the Luiseño and Kumeyaay Indians. Today, more than thirty native groups once associated with Mission San Luis Rey and Mission San Diego are recognized as official Indian entities by the federal government (Bureau of Indian Affairs 2002; Kammeyer, Emberson, and Singleton 2002).

The Kashaya Pomo—the principal Native Californian polities associated with Colony Ross—have maintained their "Indian" identity and close connection with their ancestral past. In contrast to the contested identities of the northern mission Indians, the Kashaya Pomo are a federally recognized tribe whose members reside in a BIA-administered reservation north of Fort Ross. Most of the elders can still speak the Kashaya language, and they maintain a seasonal schedule of dances, feasts, and ceremonies. Prominent in much of their ritual and social life is the consumption of native foods and the practice of Kashaya values and worldviews.

The different outcomes of colonizer-native interactions in the mission and mercantile settlements of California provide an excellent test case for developing a cross-cultural perspective on colonization. Can the five dimensions of colonial encounters provide insights as to why cultural reorganization takes place in some historical contexts and tribal coherence and vigor are maintained in others?

FIVE DIMENSIONS OF FRANCISCAN MISSIONS AND COLONY ROSS

Enculturation Programs

Franciscan Missions. The cornerstone of the missionary enterprise in Alta California was a directed enculturation program designed to transform the population of pagan Native Californians into a peasant class of devout Catholics who were loyal to imperial Spain. The new Christian converts or neophytes would provide the labor to build the mission and presidio infrastructure, support an impressive agricultural enterprise, and assist in protecting the northern frontier of New Spain from foreign invasion (namely, Russians and British). Neophytes were indoctrinated into the Catholic faith, taught European crafts and trades, and forced to alter their traditional work habits, subsistence practices, dress, and menu. Recruitment of Indian converts to the missions involved a wide range of inducements including food, clothing, gifts, protection from enemy tribes, and contact with powerful spiritual forces (Jackson and Castillo 1995:107–8; J. R. Johnson 1989:367; Phillips 1975:22, 24). As articulated by Milliken (1995:222–24), many natives probably had little choice but to move to missions, as their traditional economic practices deteriorated, diseases took their terrible toll, and traditional village communities disintegrated as people died or moved away.

Once Indians were baptized, they were no longer free to leave the mission complex without permission from the priests. The neophytes were then subjected to a rigid schedule of prayers, meals, work, and more prayers that were announced by the tolling of the mission bells (Geiger and Meighan 1976:81–85; Monroy 1990:53, 65–66). Infractions of the work schedule and moral code were punished through a variety of coercive measures, including solitary confinement, whippings, stocks, and leg chains. Neophytes who attempted to escape into the bush were pursued and either persuaded to return through negotiation or brought back by force (Milliken 1995:96–97). Six soldiers stationed at each mission, as well as nearby presidio soldiers, were employed to protect the missions from foreigners and native rebellions, and to insure that the mission indoctrination program was followed by all neophytes.

Colony Ross. The commercial agenda of the Russian-American Company's colony in California involved no concerted efforts to enculturate local natives in Russian values, meanings, or lifeways. Although the colonists at Fort Ross were members of the extensive Sitka (Alaska) Parish, no Russian Orthodox priest was ever permanently stationed in the California colony (Osborn 1997). There is little evidence of proselytizing activity among the local Miwok and Pomo workers, although some native women who married Native Alaskan and Russian men were listed as Russian Orthodox in the censuses of 1836 and 1838 (Osborn 1997:199). Success at Colony Ross was not measured by the number of baptisms performed, but rather by the profits generated by the outpost. Company managers allowed the local Indian groups to continue their traditional cultural practices, as long as they did not adversely affect the daily schedule of mercantile operations (Lightfoot, Wake, and Schiff 1991). The critical policy governing Russian relations with local natives was that they remain peaceful and a reliable source of labor for company projects. It must be stressed, however, that Colony Ross was no utopia for Indians, as the Russian managers could be very brutal about coercing local natives to work for them when extra hands were needed, such as at harvest time (for example, Wrangell 1969:10–11).

Native Relocation Programs

Franciscan Missions. In Alta California, where coastal hunter-gatherers resided in dispersed rancherias or villages, new converts were induced as part of the reducción policy to move to centrally located mission complexes. This process of native aggregation was the centerpiece of Franciscan proselytization across much of the Spanish borderland in North America (Guest 1978; Jackson 1994:13). Franciscan priests argued that the concentration of local native populations into central mission settlements facilitated their conversion to Catholicism and training as Spanish neophytes. Population agglomeration also allowed the priests to keep a close surveillance on natives, as they attempted to control their interactions with gentile (nonbaptized) relatives and friends who still resided in the countryside. Furthermore, this program of population reduction allowed the priests to segregate the neophytes from the immoral and undisciplined influence of other Hispanic colonists moving into Alta California (Guest 1978:106–7, 113).

Native residences at missions consisted of separate dormitories for unmarried girls and women, housing for married families, and often separate quarters for unmarried boys and men.

The reducción policy was not implemented evenly across the Alta California missions. Although the majority of Ohlone, Esselen, and Salinan neophytes in the northern missions were required to reside in mission settlements, this was not the case for Mission San Diego and Mission San Luis Rey. A modified resettlement program was instituted at the two southernmost missions, where only some categories of neophytes (those training for baptism or specialized jobs, orphans, unmarried girls, widows, the sick, and elderly) had to live in the missions. The remainder of the Luiseño and Kumeyaay Indians remained in native villages in the hinterland, and they only had to report to the missions during festivals, for training, religious services, or to fulfill communal labor tasks (see Lightfoot, n.d.).

Colony Ross. The Russian-American Company did not implement a formalized native relocation program at Fort Ross. The major consideration for the company was that native laborers would be available when needed. Archival and archaeological research indicates that Colony Ross was divided into four distinct ethnic neighborhoods that separately housed elite Russian managers, lower-class Russian and Creole (people of mixed native and Russian ancestry) personnel, Native Alaskan (primarily Alutiiq and Unangan) hunters and artisans, and Native Californian workers (Lightfoot, Wake, and Schiff 1991:22–24). The Native Californian neighborhood was located to the north of the Ross stockade, where it appears that considerable latitude was given by the company in terms of how and where native workers lived in this area. Native aggregation did take place with the construction of Fort Ross, as some Kashaya Pomo who lived in outlying ridge-top settlements moved to the north side of the stockade and established several villages.

Interethnic Unions

Franciscan Missions. Although the Franciscan priests attempted to shield their flock from other Hispanic colonists, they were theoretically not adverse to interethnic marriages between colonists and native neophytes. In the first years of the missions, marriages between single male soldiers and female neophytes did take place. However, deteriorating relations between the soldiers and priests, and the fact that most married soldiers wanted to live away from the missions, put a damper on these marriage practices. Interethnic marriages between Hispanic men and Indian women continued throughout the mission period in California, but they never occurred in great numbers (Hurtado 1988:25, 170; Kelsey 1985:507, 510; Monroy 1990:107, 148).

Another form of interethnic marriage that took place in the missions was the union of neophytes from different polities and language groups. Although one may question whether these should be considered "interethnic" marriages, members of different native polities probably recognized ethnic distinctions, especially if they spoke unintelligible languages. However, to distinguish these different kinds of marriage patterns, in the remainder of the chapter I define interethnic unions as those taking place between colonists and Native Californians, and *intertribal* unions as those taking place between members of different Native California polities.

Colony Ross. Interethnic unions or marriages were common at Colony Ross. The earliest census data available for Fort Ross (Kuskov censuses of 1820 and 1821) show that interethnic households were among the most common residences in the colony that contained two or more people (Istomin 1992). The vast majority of these interethnic households consisted of Kashaya Pomo and Coast Miwok women who lived with Russian, Creole, or Native Alaskan men. The most common unions were between Native Californian women and Native Alaskan men, and these couples resided primarily in the Native Alaskan neighborhood, situated south of the Ross stockade (see Lightfoot, Schiff, and Wake 1997). The Veniaminov censuses of 1836 and 1838 indicate that interethnic unions were still common at Fort Ross, but that the number of native marriages with Native Alaskan men decreased significantly, while the number of unions with Russian and Creole men increased (Osborn 1997).

Demographic Parameters of Colonizer and Native Populations

Franciscan Missions. The initial colonization of Alta California was undertaken by relatively few colonists, primarily priests and soldiers. Hispanic numbers remained relatively low in relation to Indian neophytes until after the missions were secularized in the mid-1830s and the vast mission holdings were broken up into numerous private ranchos (see Silliman 2000 for overview). The demographic profile of local native populations was inversely related to Hispanic population trends in the coastal zone; the latter increased as the former plummeted in number. Native population densities in 1769 were among the highest in native North America, but the founding of the missions began a drastic decline in native numbers that continued well into the early twentieth century.

Much has been written about the high mortality rate, especially among children and women, and low birthrate in California missions. Epidemics of smallpox and measles did take their toll on mission Indians, but diseases tended to hit missions erratically, and mortality rates varied considerably from mission to mission (see Walker and Johnson 1992, 1994). In contrast to the situation in Baja California and northwest Mexico, the epidemics were relatively few and the most severe ones hit late at the end of the mission period (Jackson 1994; Kealhofer 1996:68). A recent overview by Jackson and Castillo (1995:41–50) suggests that the primary culprits in the high mortality rate were chronic diseases, such as syphilis, respiratory ailments, dysentery, and a miserable quality of life that involved overcrowding, inadequate ventilation in mission dormitories, poor sanitation, polluted communal water sources, and overwork in some instances. A diet of reduced variability and questionable nutritional balance may also have been a contributing factor (Hoover 1989:399–400). The alarming death rate had a significant consequence by the first and second decades of the 1800s: in order to maintain the mission infrastructure, the Franciscans were forced to recruit new neophytes located in the interior at increasingly greater distances from the missions.

Demographic decline hit the Indians living in large neophyte villages in the northern missions the hardest. Population loss was somewhat less for the Luiseño and Kumeyaay Indians of the southernmost missions. Not only did neophytes residing in small, homeland villages experience lower mortality rates than those living in the dense, overly congested settlements of the northern missions, but the southern mission Indians maintained some aspects of their traditional hunter-gatherer economy, in addition to Franciscan agricultural production, and this provided a greater diversity of nutritious foods (see Shipek 1977:65–73; Lightfoot, n.d.).

Colony Ross. During the occupation of Fort Ross, the Russian-American Company maintained a relatively modest-sized population of Russians, Creoles, and Native Alaskans at the outpost. Although fluctuations in the size of the workforce took place over time, there were usually only between 100 to 200 foreigners stationed at Ross at any one time (Lightfoot, Wake, and Schiff 1991:22). Similar to the coastal hunter-gatherer populations to the south, the local Kashaya Pomo underwent population decline over time. However, the exact rate and magnitude of this decline are not known. Unlike the Franciscans who recorded religiously the number of baptisms, marriages, and deaths that occurred at the different missions, few detailed records were kept on the Kashaya.

Chronology of Colonial Encounters

Franciscan Missions. The missions were employed as an instrument of colonization in Alta California for about a seventy-year period (1769 to roughly the early 1840s). Although the founding dates of the missions ranged from 1769 to 1823, the majority (n= 18) were in operation before 1800. This implies that several generations of neophytes may have been born and raised within the social and cultural environment of the missions. Franciscan padres reported much greater success in teaching neophytes who grew up in the missions how to speak and read Spanish, and how to conduct themselves properly, in contrast to older men and women who were raised in gentile villages and converted late in life (see Geiger and Meighan 1976:36–39). Some padres were convinced that the older generation of neophytes misled the younger ones by maintaining old superstitions and tribal traditions in the missions (Geiger and Meighan 1976:57).

Colony Ross. A notable characteristic of the Ross colonization was the relatively short chronology of colonizer-native interactions. The Russian colony was active for about twenty-nine years (1812–1841), about half the time of the Franciscan colonial program. The shorter time interval may be important in that only one and a half generations of people could possibly have been raised in this mercantile colonial environment.

DISCUSSION

These five dimensions provide a framework for understanding why coastal hunter-gatherer encounters with Franciscan padres and Russian merchants may have produced such divergent outcomes. I discuss three points below in considering why new kinds of native identities, social forms, and tribal relationships emerged among the northern mission Indians (Ohlone, Esselen, and Salinan) in comparison with the southernmost mission Indians (Luiseño and Kumeyaay) and the Kashaya Pomo.

1. Interethnic Unions. Interethnic unions between colonists and natives do not appear to have been a very significant factor in the cultural transformation of mission Indians. Interethnic marriages with Hispanic soldiers and settlers did provide an avenue for native women and their children to create mestizo or Hispanic identities (Monroy 1990:107; Weber 1992:307). Indian women who married Hispanic men could alter their residence pattern by moving with their husbands outside the missions. Children from interethnic marriages would usually take the name of the Hispanic man, which provided them with the opportunity to take on his family's identity as well. However, during the mission period it appears that the construction of Hispanic identities in this manner was relatively rare, as comparatively few interethnic marriages were recorded for the missions (see above).

A similar pattern is found at Colony Ross, where interethnic marriages provided Kashaya Pomo women with the potential to metamorphose their ethnic identities. Interethnic marriages were common at Fort Ross, but they appear to have had little lasting impact on the Kashaya people. Most of the marriages were quite fragile and unstable, and many unions appear to have lasted only a short time, with native women returning to their villages in the Kashaya homeland (Lightfoot and Martinez 1997:4–5). In cases where interethnic unions lasted for more than a few years, Native Californian women may have adopted new colonial identities that separated them from local Indians. Some native women did accompany their spouses when they were reassigned to other Russian-American Company colonies in the North Pacific. And some may have even made it to Russia (Lightfoot and Martinez 1997:5). But like neophytes who married Hispanic colonists, the women typically resettled outside the native homeland and were no longer active members of the Kashaya community.

2. The Enculturation Program. The enculturation program of the Franciscans did have a significant influence on the mission Indians, but not in the manner that the padres intended. The Franciscans did make significant transformations in the daily lives of neophytes, not the least of which were obligating hunter-gatherer peoples to become full-time agriculturalists, teaching new crafts, enforcing a strict daily routine, and introducing new foods and material culture. But they were largely unsuccessful in converting coastal hunter-gatherers into devout Catholics who readily adopted Hispanic values and lifeways (see Guest 1966:209; Hurtado 1988:25; Jackson and Castillo 1995:34–37). Some natives did incorporate elements of Hispanic culture and Catholicism into their lives, but those elements that were chosen conformed largely to extant native values and worldviews (for example, Farnsworth 1987:98–102; Haas 1995:28–29; Jackson and Castillo 1995:36–37). Four decades into the colonial enterprise, some Franciscans were quite candid about their failure to convert neophytes into good Christians. Some priests noted that many pagan practices were still employed in the missions, that Catholicism had only been superficially adopted, that native curers and "sucking doctors" still attended the sick, and that Indian shamans organized dances and ceremonies among the neophytes in secret locations (Geiger and Meighan 1976:47–51, 71–80).

Archaeological research provides the best evidence for how resilient native cultural practices were in California missions. The degree of "acculturation" as evidenced in assemblages excavated from native contexts varied from mission to mission and across time (Costello and Hornbeck 1989; Farnsworth 1989). Furthermore, the composition of the archaeological assemblages was greatly influenced by the timing of massive recruitment efforts when waves of gentiles were relocated to some missions (Farnsworth 1987:602–17). Nevertheless, it is remarkable how much the material culture of the mission Indians was grounded in traditional technology. Although Hispanic influences were certainly present in some elements of technology and food remains, neophytes continued to use native artifact forms and manufacture techniques that were clearly linked to the past. This is especially evident in the chipped-stone tools, ground-stone tools, shell fishhooks, shell and bone beads, bone tools, and bird-bone whistles and rock crystals (probably used in native rituals). Excavations of neophyte quarters indicate that European-introduced foods (cattle, sheep, wheat, and corn) were being cooked alongside native foods, such as deer, sea mammals, geese, ducks, rockfish, shellfish, hazelnuts, and possibly even seaweed (Allen 1998:55–62; Hoover and Costello 1985). Farris (1991:40) notes that some of these new foods, such as wheat and barley, were prepared and cooked according to traditional native practices. This point is supported by the presence of fire-cracked rock recovered from neophytes' quarters (Allen 1998:63, 88). These are probably the residue from cooking food in watertight baskets, hearths, and earthen ovens. Excavations indicate a significant underground economy in some neophyte quarters, involving the manufacture of native tools and ornaments, the cooking and consumption of native foods, and the practice of native ceremonies that went on behind closed doors (Allen 1998:68, 73, 82).

In comparing the archaeological assemblages from native contexts in the missions with those from Colony Ross, I am struck by the overall similarities. Allen's (1998:53) recent analysis of the Mission Santa Cruz neophyte quarters indicates that although natives were forced to reside in a built environment that was completely alien to them, the organization of space within adobe barracks was based on native dictates and practices. A similar pattern has been detected at Colony Ross, where excavations of the domestic refuse from interethnic households indicates that Kashaya women retained their own organization of space within and immediately around residential structures (Lightfoot, Martinez, and Schiff 1998). A comparison of the artifact assemblages from native contexts in the missions and at Colony Ross also highlights many concordances in the kinds of materials represented (stone, bone, and shell artifacts, glass beads), the diversity of native food remains recovered (deer, sea mammal, fish, shellfish), and the employment of traditional native practices to prepare and cook meals (for example, Ballard 1997; Martinez 1997, 1998; Wake 1995, 1997). The chipped-stone tool assemblages from Mission Santa Cruz and Fort Ross are both characterized by a paucity of formal tool types but large numbers of expediently manufactured flakes that could be used for various kinds of tasks. Another striking similarity is how European objects, such as glass bottles and ceramic containers, were used as sources of raw material for the manufacture of native artifact forms. The remains of glass and ceramic containers recovered from archaeological deposits in the

Santa Cruz neophyte barracks and native villages at Colony Ross are very fragmentary and highly disorganized, with hardly any reconstructable vessels (Allen 1998:67; Farris 1997). This pattern suggests that native peoples were scavenging and recycling usable foreign objects in both colonies. But instead of using them in the European fashion as ceramic and glass tablewares, they were probably obtaining them primarily for use as sources of raw material for making "Indian" objects.

3. Cultural Transformations. The combined effects of the native relocation program, changing intertribal marriage patterns, and high mortality rates were instrumental in creating new kinds of tribal relationships in the northern missions. One effect of removing Ohlone, Esselen, and Salinan people from their homeland villages and relocating them at missions was the creation of distinctive and novel social arenas at each mission. Natives were forced to interact closely with members of other tribal groups (polities) while at work, during communal meals, in religious services, and in dormitories. The debilitating death rate contributed to the restructuring of native social relations and marriage networks in missions, as exemplified by the large number of intertribal marriages that apparently took place. As many marriage partners died, especially women of childbearing age, the Franciscans applied continuous pressure for widows (and widowers) to remarry. As a consequence, new marriage unions were created that linked men and women from different polities and language groups. For example, after 1810 new neophytes (often women) recruited from distant native communities in the interior were typically wed very quickly to surviving coastal hunter-gatherers who had been raised or had resided in the missions for many years (Geiger and Meighan 1976:61).

I think this unprecedented pattern of intertribal interactions in the northern missions began to transform the cultural practices of neophytes, breaking down traditional tribal polities and affiliations as new social forms and identities began to emerge. Over the course of several generations in which Ohlone, Esselen, and Salinan peoples were born, raised, and died in the missions, most probably did not lose their "Indian" identity, as indicated by the continuity in native cultural practices in the archaeological record. Rather, what was constructed out of this colonial entanglement was a more generalized sense of native identity that was not tied to any particular tribal polity. For example, Allen's (1998:41, 97) investigation of two different neophyte dorms at Mission Santa Cruz, each probably associated with different tribal polities and language groups, indicates that individual tribal identities were probably merging into a more generalized "Indian" expression.

A significant factor in the development of novel social forms and relations in the northern missions was the creation of new kinds of factional groups. The Franciscan enculturation program incited considerable resistance, including violence and revolts in some cases, among almost all the mission Indians (Castillo 1989; Jackson and Castillo 1995:73–80; Phillips 1990). Significantly, by the 1820s and 1830s, armed raiders composed of escaped neophytes and interior Indians were raiding missions and private ranchos throughout central and southern California. Some of the most famous resistance leaders and raiders were ex-neophytes who had grown up in the missions. They proved to be very formidable adversaries because they understood the military tactics and weaknesses of the Spanish and later Mexican colonists. Factionalism within the northern missions centered around those neophytes in the northern missions who were loyal to the padres versus those who were not. A potential fracture in many mission communities revolved around those who participated in the missionary hierarchy of native alcaldes, as chosen by the priests, and those who adhered to traditional native power structures, as represented by headmen and shamans (Hoover 1989:397; Sandos 1997:211).

The picture is quite different for the Luiseño and Kumeyaay Indians of Mission San Luis Rey and Mission San Diego. Significantly, they were able to maintain homeland villages where they continued to practice some aspects of their hunter and gatherer economy and to re-create more traditional forms of political structures and small-scale native polities. In contrast with the northern missions, the padres in the south allowed traditional Luiseño and Kumeyaay leaders to retain their power and authority in return for their cooperation (Shipek 1977:152–77). Marriage patterns no doubt changed, but with the less draconian population losses, they probably did not involve the traumatic restructuring of marriage networks as in the northern missions. Although significant cultural transformations took place, rather than adopting a more generalized "pan-mission" identity, most of the

Luiseño and Kumeyaay maintained close ties with the polities and the villages of their ancestors—an outcome that facilitated, as I argue elsewhere (Lightfoot, n.d.), their recognition as "real" Indians by anthropologists and the federal government.

The construction of a distinctive Kashaya Pomo identity was also facilitated by the maintenance of native villages in tribal homelands. Interethnic unions took place with the colonists, but, as noted above, most of these unions did not last and the women returned to their native villages. Some intertribal marriages undoubtedly took place with the Coast Miwok and Southern Pomo, but they were probably not as common as intertribal unions in the northern missions. There is also less evidence of native resistance and violence at Colony Ross than at most of the Franciscan missions. The main problem experienced by the Russian-American Company was the occasional poaching of their free-range livestock (Parkman 1996–1997). There is no indication that any armed raid or uprising ever took place at Fort Ross. One factor that certainly contributed to the "peaceful" history at Colony Ross was the presence of a well-armed militia. However, a more important consideration was the ability of discontented native workers to vote with their feet. When the Company attempted to intensify agricultural production in the 1830s, some Russian managers were quite barbaric about recruiting native laborers. But as the chief manager of the company, F. Von Wrangell (1969:210–11), remarked after his visit to Ross in 1833, most native peoples simply disappeared into the bush, and the company needed to increase the pay and quality of food to recruit them to work.

CONCLUSION

The purpose of this chapter is to consider an alternative approach for undertaking cross-cultural comparisons in the archaeology of colonization. The approach highlights the great variation in colonial practices and recognizes both the similarities and differences in the dimensions of colonial programs. By examining specific dimensions of colonial encounters (enculturation, relocation, interethnic, demographic, and chronological), we can evaluate how the interplay of a particular dimension plays out in different historical contexts, and how the combined effects of the dimensions may be critical for understanding divergent processes and outcomes.

The approach proved useful in understanding the divergent outcomes of colonizer-native interactions in the Franciscan missions and Russian mercantile colony of Fort Ross in California. I found that the combined effects of the native relocation program, intertribal marriages, and very high mortality rates were crucial for understanding the cultural reconfiguration of the northern mission Indians. Archaeological findings indicate that although Indian cultural practices continued to be pursued behind closed doors, the Ohlone, Esselen, and Salinan people constructed new kinds of social relations and social forms in neophyte villages. More generalized "Indian" identities were created that were an amalgamation of many distinct tribal polities. Further cultural transformations took place among the northern mission Indians after the secularization of the missions in the 1830s and the annexation of California in 1846 by the United States. The transformed native practices led some early anthropologists to claim these groups had become extinct, and the United States government has yet to recognize them as official tribal entities (see Lightfoot, n.d.).

A divergent outcome unfolded among the Luiseño and Kumeyaay Indians of Mission San Luis Rey and Mission San Diego. The crucial dimensions for understanding this historical path are the native relocation program and demographic parameters. The modified reducción program provided the opportunity for neophytes to maintain homeland villages, to sustain lower mortality rates, and to maintain traditional native power structures. The upshot was the re-creation of more traditional-looking lifeways (mixed agriculture/hunter-gatherer economy, small-scale native polities, and native ceremonies) that resonated among early anthropologists and contributed to the recognition of these tribal groups by the federal government.

The critical dimensions in the survival of the Kashaya Pomo as a cohesive cultural group were the relocation program (that is, the lack of a "directed" program), native and colonial demographic parameters, and the chronology of colonial encounters. The absence of a formal relocation program allowed the Kashaya to remain in their own communities within their tribal homeland. Spicer (1962) recognizes this factor as important in the maintenance of traditional tribal identities in the American Southwest. By maintaining their own distinct communities, the Kashaya were able to retain many of their cultural practices and to adopt selectively new innovations (such as in dress, foods, and tools) that were modified and incorporated into a dynamic construction of Kashaya identity. Demographic parameters were also important as the Kashaya, despite unknown but probably high mortality rates, remained a reproductively viable population in Russian and post-Russian times. There are currently about 300 members of the Kashaya tribe living on or near their Stewarts Point Rancheria (Kammeyer, Emberson, and Singleton 2002:147). Finally, the short time span of colonization implied that no more than one generation, and possibly part of another, were raised in the Russian colony. Consequently, one does not see very much Russian influence (language, religion, foods) among the Kashaya today (see Kennedy 1955; Oswalt 1957).

In conclusion, I think an approach that examines different dimensions of colonial encounters may be useful for undertaking comparisons of colonial systems associated with ancient states and empires and later capitalistic European powers. By considering how different dimensions of colonial domination, demography, and time were constituted and how they related to one another in specific case studies, we may begin to learn more about mechanisms and processes that transformed native and colonizer interactions under very different historical conditions.

Acknowledgments

I am indebted to the SAR seminar participants for their thoughtful comments concerning the potential of undertaking cross-cultural comparisons in the archaeology of colonization. The paper was written while I was working at the School of American Research on a longer, book-length manuscript on the mission and mercantile colonies of California (Lightfoot, n.d.). I am thankful for the generous support provided by the School of American Research Weatherhead Resident Fellowship, the University of California President's Research Fellowship in the Humanities, and the University of California, Berkeley, Humanities Research Fellowship.

8

Imperial Agendas and Local Agency
Wari Colonial Strategies

Katharina Schreiber

Archaeological research into expanding states and empires has typically made two critical errors. First, the state is often treated as a single, monolithic entity, rather than as a complex entity with multiple, and even competing, agendas. Second, indigenous groups conquered or otherwise consolidated within the state enterprise often have been treated as being unreactive and passive, simply receiving and accepting the control of the so-called dominant society.

This chapter seeks to disentangle these issues and to provide evidence for multiple imperial agendas and the ways in which they varied both spatially and temporally. Archaeological data can provide evidence of multiple agendas, even within a single region, as well as different agendas that motivated the actions of the expanding state in different cultural and geographic settings. This chapter also considers the indigenous societies as active participants in the process, contributing materially to a negotiated outcome.

This discussion will be oriented around three axes, as defined by Gil Stein (this volume). The first axis is termed the "metropole" and refers to the expanding society. The second axis is the host polity, the indigenous society into which the metropole expands. The third axis is the colony, the point of contact between the metropole and the host society. The study of colonies is an appropriate venue for archaeological investigation, in part because colonies are material entities; they can be identified, studied, and interpreted using the techniques of archaeological inquiry.

The most useful theoretical paradigms can contribute to the furthering of our knowledge, in this case our knowledge and understanding of the past, in two important ways. In the first place, they enable us to look at the past through new lenses; our focus is sharpened on things we overlooked, or paid scant attention to, even though they were evident the whole time. Data do not exist in a vacuum; they are inextricably linked with the models we consciously or unconsciously use to structure knowledge. Models do not exist without data, and data are not interpreted in the absence of models. New interpretive models allow new interpretations of our data. By the same token, the very best and most useful paradigms sow the seeds of their own demise. As the models mature, we move beyond our initial elation at arriving at new interpretations, and we begin to see where the models fail, where they also overlook or ignore factors newly seen to be crucial to further interpretation. Useful models thus provide the necessary catalyst for the development of newer and better models.

World-systems theory is one such useful theoretical paradigm. As originally envisioned by Wallerstein (1974, 1980, 1989), this model explains the rise of modern capitalist societies within a global-scale analytical unit, beginning in the sixteenth century A.D. (see also Braudel 1992). Competing polities exist worldwide, and each expands to include cores, peripheries, and semi-peripheries; differential levels of economic integration and exploitation characterize each type of region. European archaeologists have sought to push their interpretation of world systems back to the Bronze Age (Frank 1993; Gills and Frank 1991). Algaze has found the paradigm useful in understanding the expansion of Mesopotamian Uruk society (Algaze 1993b), and Blanton and Feinman (1984) have used it to enhance interpretations of prehispanic Mesoamerican society. Others have found the core-periphery distinction provided by the model to be a useful point of departure for archaeological inquiry, and one not limited to capitalist or precapitalist societies (Rowlands, Mogens, and Kristiansen 1987; Santley and Alexander 1992).

But as useful as these new views of the past were, seeds of doubt began to grow, and the limitations of the model became increasingly apparent, especially when investigators turned to the study of culture contact between cores and peripheries (Stein 1998). As Dietler writes, "In general, the effect of world systems models in archaeology has been less heuristic than hallucinogenic: they have caused otherwise sensible scholars to see things that are not there and to ignore crucial developments in some areas in an effort to impose structures that, in their uniformity, deny the fundamental historicity of colonialism" (Dietler 1998:297). World-systems models tend to overemphasize the role of the core in controlling or structuring events in the periphery and tend to gloss cultures of the periphery as simply "traditional society" (Dietler 1998:296–98; Stein 1998:246–47). Core/periphery relations are characterized variously as active/passive, giving/receiving, and dominant/dependent. Part of the problem lies in the nature of the source material used by scholars. In the case of world-systems models, social historians rely on written texts, the source of which is typically the metropole, expressed in terms of a rhetoric of dominance. The voices of the host polities are rarely heard. However, as Lightfoot has noted, "Archaeology is the field of choice for examining lifeways and interaction of poorly documented peoples in the past" (1995:201), and the limitations of the models should be quickly apparent when applied to any archaeological investigation of culture contact or the colonial situation. Unfortunately, applications of the models, especially in core-periphery studies, have suffered from the same inadequate treatment of the societies of the peripheries (Dietler 1998:290). For example, in their identification of three structures of core-periphery systems, Santley and Alexander (1992) continue to take a top-down approach, privileging the core as the active player in core-periphery interactions. Moreover, following Hassig (1985) and Luttwak (1976), they draw a distinction between hegemonic and territorial empires, qualitatively distinguishing processes that actually represent two ends of a continuum, and obscuring the myriad of strategies that were actively used by particular empires (see D'Altroy 1992; Schreiber 1992).

It is unlikely that any host society welcomes control by a foreign metropole, but its willingness to cooperate or ability to resist varies from place to place, or even within different segments of a single society. Local individuals may find it to their political and economic advantage to cooperate with the colonists or, at the other extreme, may be in a position to mount overt resistance. The less empowered may find their options limited to more subtle forms of resistance that in some cases may give the appearance of cooperation. Local agency may be difficult to discern archaeologically, but explanations of changes in local society during colonial encounters should consider the active role of the host society. The final result of the expansion of control of the metropole and the establishment of colonies in host societies is a negotiated result, the interdigitation of multiple imperial agendas with multiple local agendas.

Finally, as Dietler warns us, we must beware of anachronistic interpretations of colonial encounters; both imperial agendas and local agency may vary through time, and to describe the entire encounter by its final denouement may obscure crucial aspects of the initial incursion and early phases of interaction between colonists and the host polity. "[I]t is a serious analytical error to assume that asymmetrical relations or structures of power that ultimately appeared in later periods were necessarily a feature of the first stages of the encounter rather than a product of a subsequent complex history of interaction and entanglement" (Dietler 1998:298).

ARCHAEOLOGICAL APPROACHES

Archaeological research in areas in which complex states and empires arose is still often aimed exclusively at large sites, public monuments, and elite tombs, thus ignoring or denying the voices of the majority of the people. More recent efforts in the area of domestic archaeology (for example, Bawden 1982; Bermann 1994; Schwartz and Falconer 1994) have begun to provide a more balanced perspective, but the two extremes are rarely considered together, to flesh out a more complex and dynamic view of prehistoric society, considering people of varying ranks and statuses. Another promising avenue of archaeological inquiry is intensive, systematic regional survey, with (as nearly as possible) 100 percent coverage (see Fish and Kowalewski 1990; Billman and Feinman 1999). By focusing on the region as the unit of analysis, rather than on the single site, one considers the entire cross section of site types, from the small indigenous village to the imperial colonies. Regional surveys also provide data that inform us on changing ecological adaptations, including intensified exploitation of certain resources or resource zones, and they also reveal terrain that was unoccupied and resources that were underutilized. Being able to see the regional distribution of material remains of both the host polity and the colonizing metropole enables us to identify point of contact and levels of interface. Perhaps most importantly for the purposes of this argument, identifying changes in the host society and its exploitation of local resources, correlated with incursion and occupation by foreign colonies, can in turn allow us to reconstruct some of the multiple agendas of the metropole and their variations through time.

This chapter takes a regional approach to the study of colonial encounters in the Middle Horizon Wari[1] Empire of prehispanic Peru (circa A.D. 750–1000; table 8.1), comparing data from the Nasca region of the Peruvian south coast with that from the Sondondo Valley of the central highlands. The empire takes its name from the modern name of the site presumed to be its capital; we do not know what its people called themselves, their capital, or their colonies. There are no documentary sources to help (or hinder) the reconstruction of this early empire (see Schreiber 2001), so we rely purely on archaeological evidence to tease out the multiple agendas of the metropole and to identify elements of resistance and agency among the host polities.

The domain of the Wari Empire is thought to have included most of the Andean highlands of what is today Peru, as well as the central and south coastal regions (fig. 8.1). Wari colonies are located throughout this area, identified by their distinctive architectural style: great rectangular enclosures, subdivided into cells with central open patios and peripheral galleries (Schreiber 1978; Spickard 1983). In a typical top-down fashion, Wari colonial encounters usually have been approached archaeologically through investigation of the imperial colonies, with little attention paid to the host polities (for example, Isbell and McEwan 1991). Thus, Wari has been seen as a singular, monolithic entity, extending its architecture and material culture (and presumably political control) across the landscape; much of Wari research has been aimed at describing Wari sites and material culture. Indeed, the empire

TABLE 8.1

General Andean chronological phases, with details pertaining to the Nasca and Sondondo valleys.

Radiocarbon Years	General Peruvian Periods	South Coast (Nasca)	Sondondo Valley	Approximate start date in calendar years
A.D. 1533	LATE HORIZON	Inka conquest of local LIP Nasca culture	Inka conquest of Andamarca Lucana ethnic group	A.D. 1533
A.D. 1476				A.D. 1476
	LATE INTER-MEDIATE PERIOD	Regional cultural development	Emergence of Andamarca Lucana culture	
A.D. 1000				A.D. 1150
	4 3	Period of conflict and reorganization	Period of conflict and reorganization	A.D. 1000
	MIDDLE HORIZON			
	2 1	Wari conquest and occupation	Wari conquest and occupation	
A.D. 600				A.D. 750
	7 6	Late Nasca		A.D. 550
	EARLY INTER-MEDIATE PERIOD	5	Middle Nasca	Kancha phase	A.D. 450
		4 3	Early Nasca		A.D. 100
100 B.C.		2 1	Proto-Nasca		A.D. 1
	EARLY HORIZON	Chavin influence	Sacrahua phase	
800 B.C.				
	INITIAL PERIOD	No evidence of occupation	Accanta phase	
1800 B.C.				
2500 B.C.	COTTON PRECERAMIC	No evidence of occupation	Mobile hunter-gatherers	

was only recognized as such in the 1950s, and for the next several decades Wari studies were still in their infancy; there is still a long way to go, and certainly dozens of colonies remain to be discovered. We

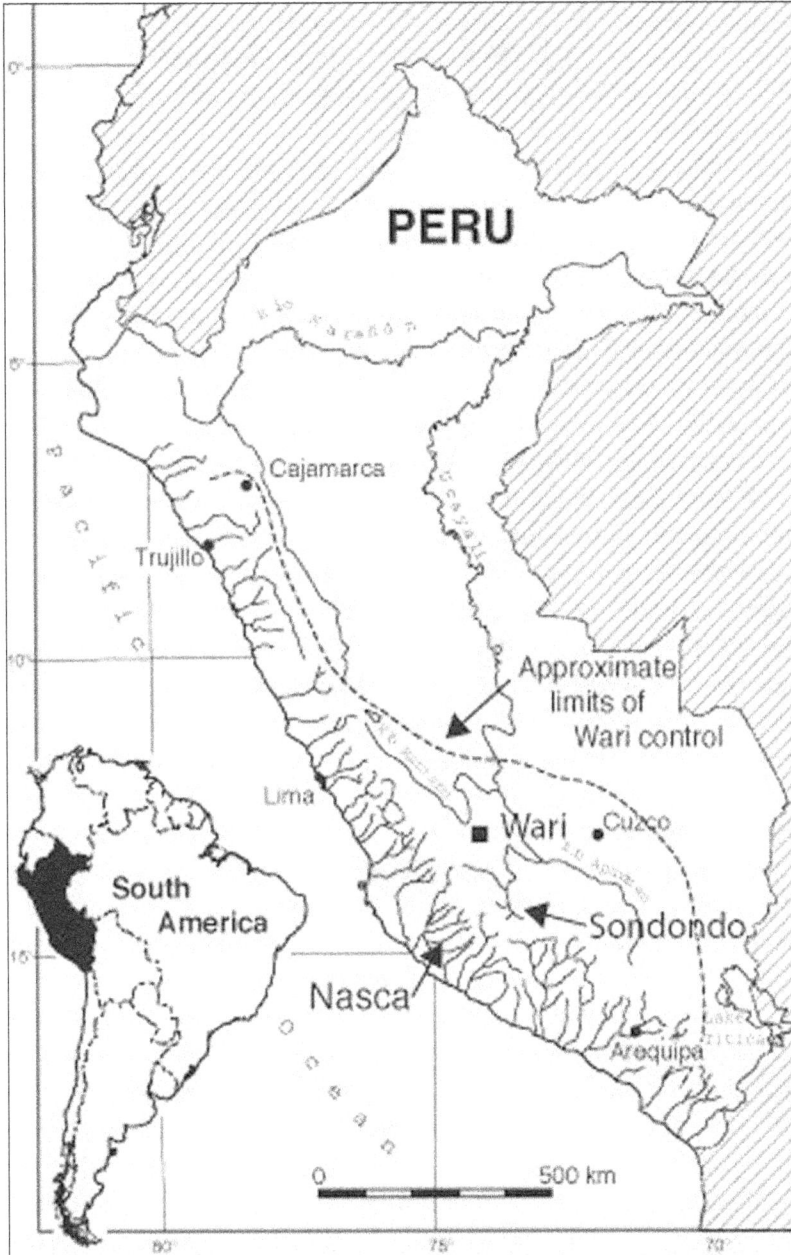

FIGURE 8.1

Map of Peru showing the locations of Wari, Nasca, and Sondondo, along with major modern cities. The dotted line represents the approximate limits of the distribution of Wari colonies.

have now reached the point, however, that data do exist that will enable us to move into new spheres of analysis and to reveal aspects of the polymorphous nature of Wari and the complexity of its interactions with its host polities.

Most prior work on Wari, including my own, has neglected to consider several crucial elements of the colonizing process. That prior work stressed primarily the political agenda, which I define as establishing control over people, as seen through the imposition or modification of hierarchies of control. I have argued, and hopefully demonstrated, that both the Wari and the later Inka used different strategies in different regions, and that these were conditioned by a number of factors, especially the degree of sociopolitical complexity of the conquered polity (Schreiber 1987, 1992, 1993). This work did not, to any appreciable degree, explicitly attempt to address multiple imperial agendas or to clarify temporal changes in Wari agendas within a single region (although see Schreiber 1999). And it stopped short of considering local agency and the active roles played by the indigenous polities in the negotiated outcomes. I propose to begin addressing some of those issues here. A more balanced consideration of all three axes of the colonial process—metropole, colony, and host polity—allows, indeed demands, consideration of these hitherto neglected areas of inquiry.

THE WARI METROPOLE

The imperial capital, Wari, is located in the Mantaro drainage of the central highlands of Peru near the modern town of Huamanga (Ayacucho). It is located on the eastern flank of a broad intermontane basin, rich in agricultural resources although semiarid in climate. The city core covers about 2 square kilometers, and the distribution of surface artifacts around the core covers another 3 or 4 square kilometers. Excavations at the site have been undertaken on several occasions, especially in the 1930s by Tello, in the 1960s by MacNeish's Ayacucho Archaeological-Botanical Project, and in the late 1970s by Isbell and his students, but few results of those excavations have ever been published (A. G. Cook 1994; Isbell, Brewster-Wray, and Spickard 1991). Only recently have excavations resumed at the site, after more than a decade of terrorist activity in the region (for example, González Carré et al. 1996; Pérez Calderón 1999).

The architectural core of the site includes large sectors of typical enclosure-style architecture; identifying this architecture as the same as that found at certain provincial sites was a major key to discerning the existence of this empire (see Rowe, Collier, and Willey 1950). Also present at Wari is a sector of stone slab chambers, probably tombs, looted long ago (Benavides 1991), near a sector with numerous stone-lined underground galleries. Religious architecture at the site includes the Templo Mayor, a large D-shaped structure, as well as smaller D-shaped temples located throughout the site (González Carré et al. 1996; A. G. Cook 2001).

The regional context of the capital is still poorly understood. Reconnaissance of portions of the basin in the 1960s (Benavides 1978; see also Isbell and Schreiber 1978; Schreiber 1992) suggests that the pre–Middle Horizon Huarpa phase was characterized by numerous small villages and towns, but no political centers. Middle Horizon Phase 1 saw the city of Wari emerge as both a local capital and the center of the expanding state. Middle Horizon Phase 2 saw a general depopulation of the countryside and explosive growth of the capital. The connection of the metropole to the colonies is seen in current research through their sharing of architectural forms and ceramic styles. Although the influence and direct effect of the metropole on the provinces is clear, elucidating the effects of the provinces on the capital is an area for future research.

THE WARI COLONIAL EXPERIENCE IN NASCA

Colonies do not simply appear on an undifferentiated and uncomplicated cultural landscape, but rather are located among people and cultures with an ongoing, dynamic historic trajectory. The pre-Wari history of Nasca was especially dynamic, as it was home to the well-known Nasca culture (circa A.D. 100–750). In its early phases, Nasca people lived in small villages without obvious centralized political control, but they all shared a vibrant tradition of ceramic and textile art. They also shared the large ceremonial center of Cahuachi, to which they made pilgrimages (Silverman 1993), and around which they buried their dead. In about the sixth century A.D., this culture underwent substantial change, perhaps occasioned by serious droughts in the adjacent highlands—rainfall from which was the only source of water available

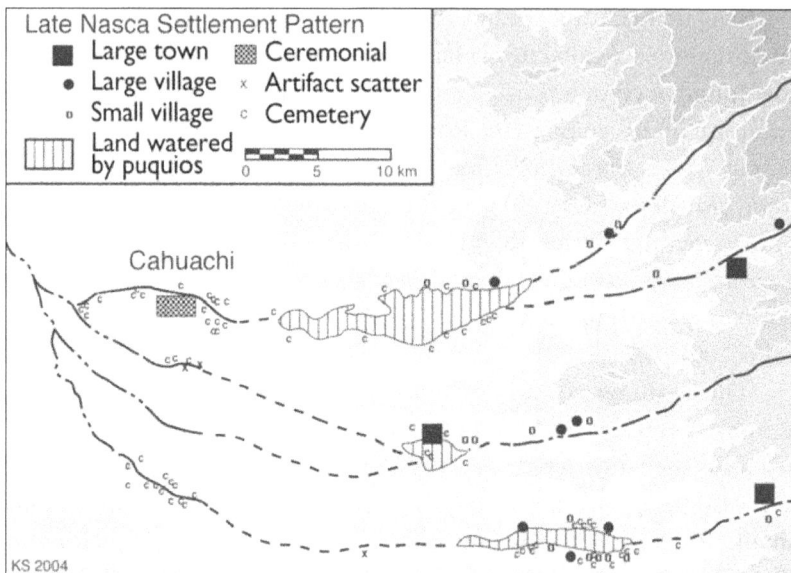

FIGURE 8.2

Settlement pattern of the southern tributaries of the Nasca drainage, showing sites pertaining to the Late Nasca phase, just prior to the Wari expansion. Contour interval = 500 meters.

to the rivers and people of Nasca. By the seventh and eighth centuries, the northern tributaries of the Nasca drainage were virtually abandoned (Reindel and Isla 1998). In the southern valleys, Nasca people were living in large towns, some of them in defensible locations (fig. 8.2); construction had long ceased at Cahuachi; and underground aqueducts, *puquios*, supplied water for agricultural and domestic purposes (Schreiber and Lancho 1995, 2003). It was into this situation that the Wari arrived and established first one, and then a second, colony.

Why did the Wari want or need a colony in Nasca? The answer is yet unclear, but it seems that a relationship existed between the pre-Wari Huarpa culture of Ayacucho and that of Nasca. Huarpa ceramic styles exhibit clear Nasca influence in their final phases (Knobloch 1976). The nature of this "influence" is not known. It may simply have been that certain Huarpa potters were copying designs they liked; it may have been the result of increased interregional interaction in the years just before the expansion of Wari. One also wonders what happened to

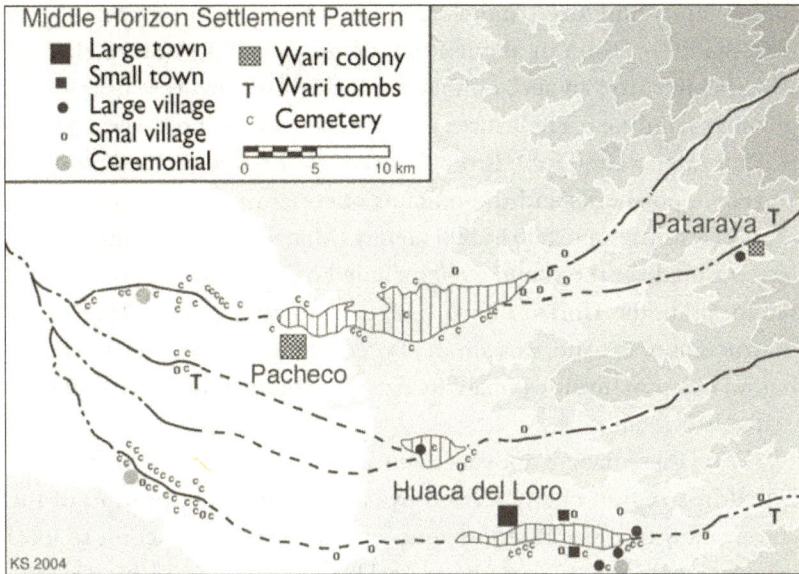

FIGURE 8.3

Settlement pattern of the southern tributaries of the Nasca drainage, showing sites pertaining to Middle Horizon Phases 1 and 2, including local sites and Wari colonies.

all the people who left the northern Nasca valleys in the century or two before the Wari expansion. There is no evidence of an influx of people into coastal valleys north or south; if the people moved up into highlands, they may have relocated near Huarpa peoples. Regardless of which, if any, of these scenarios occurred, the ceramic evidence indicates a pre–Middle Horizon relationship between Wari and Nasca.

Pacheco: A Wari Colony

A large Wari colony, Pacheco, was establish in the lower-middle Nasca Valley in Middle Horizon Phase 1, far from the locations of any of the local towns, all of which were located farther upstream (fig. 8.3). This site is known for a major "offering deposit" excavated by Julio C. Tello in 1927; the remains of hundreds of very fancy, and reconstructible, smashed ceramic vessels were found in a series of subterranean chambers made of adobe. Unfortunately, the attention of the archaeologists was given over to the fabulous finds of the so-called offering, and little attention was paid to the rest of the site. The site was subsequently bulldozed and cleared for cultivation. A minimal sketch plan made by Olson in about 1930 suggests possible Wari enclosure-style architecture; an aerial photograph taken in 1944 reveals traces of possible rectilinear enclosures covering 8 or more hectares. In 1958 Dorothy Menzel and John Rowe visited the bulldozed site and observed Wari-style potsherds and the remains of structures extending over an area measuring some 300 by 300 meters (Menzel 1964:23). Surface collections made at the site in 1990 include both Wari imperial styles and the local Middle Horizon Loro (also called Nasca 8) style. Due to the destruction of the site, we cannot at present measure its precise extent, but we can tentatively estimate its size as close to 10 hectares based on available evidence.

From these data, it appears that Pacheco was a sizable colony established in a region characterized by large towns. The location of the colony away from local settlements may have been a reaction to local intraregional warfare, or perhaps local hostility toward the empire. The establishment of such a colony also created a single political capital, the point of contact between the metropole and the host polity, and provides us evidence of a Wari political agenda in their initial incursion into the region. The presence of local ceramic styles at the site also suggests that its residents included both Wari and Nasca people.

Local Resistance

When we compare the Late Nasca period to the beginning of the Middle Horizon, changes in local settlement patterns are quite striking and provide strong evidence for local resistance to the Wari presence. Immediately prior to the arrival of the Wari, local sites were widely spaced, but spread throughout all four valleys (see fig. 8.2). In the Middle Horizon, most of those towns were abandoned and new settlements were established in the southernmost valley (see fig. 8.3). I suggest that the movement of people out of the valley in which the colony was established, and into the valley farthest away, is a clear indication of their lack of willingness to cooperate with Wari.

This change also occasioned a change in local political complexity. Whereas the pre-Wari society may be best described as a series of small regional polities, the new Middle Horizon polity had characteristics of a small state: a single primate center (Huaca del Loro), secondary and tertiary centers spread through the region, and very small villages at the lowest level. The emergence of this small, but well-centralized "statelet" can also be seen as a response to the colonial encounter.

Pataraya: A Second Colony, and a Second Agenda

In Middle Horizon Phase 2, Pacheco may or may not have been abandoned. Although I have suggested in the past that the site was probably abandoned in Middle Horizon 2 (Schreiber 2001), it has become increasingly apparent to me that our chronological control is yet insufficient, and our extant ceramic collections from the site are too small (apart from the offering ceramics) to say this with any certainty. Indeed, currently ongoing investigations suggest that some styles thought to date to Middle Horizon 1 may in fact date to Middle Horizon 2. Thus I leave open the question of whether Pacheco was abandoned early or remained extant until the collapse of the empire.

What is clear, however, is that a second Wari colony was established in Middle Horizon 2, in the upper drainage, at Pataraya. The sector of land in which it is located takes its name (which means "high place of lines") from its hillsides, which are covered with lines of stones. These stones form low terraces and create arable fields designed to catch limited rainfall. These fields lie at elevations ranging from 1,200 to 1,600 meters above sea level (henceforth meters asl); this corresponds to the range of elevations at which coca will grow in this region. There are several earlier Nasca sites associated with the fields, indicating a pre–Middle Horizon date for their construction. However, in the Middle Horizon, all of the local sites were abandoned, and a Wari colony was established at the lower end of the sector of lined hills.

This colony is quite small, comprising a Wari-style enclosure of only four or six cells, plus some sixteen round houses. These houses and their associated ceramics indicate the multiethnic nature of the colony. However, in contrast to Pacheco with its local Nasca styles, the architecture and ceramics at Pataraya indicate that the residents were highlanders. The location of this site in a limited ecological niche suitable for coca production indicates a second imperial agenda: the exploitation of specialized resources—an economic agenda. The fact that no local Nasca people lived in this portion of the valley in the Middle Horizon, and that people from the highlands lived side by side with the Wari, suggests perhaps a lack of cooperation between Wari and Nasca people.

The Pacheco "Offering": Resistance after the Fact?

I close this discussion of the colonial encounter between Wari and Nasca with a consideration of an alternative interpretation of the so-called offering at Pacheco. This offering included hundreds of pots found in a series of adjoining subterranean chambers made of adobe. The vessels are reconstructible—all the pieces are there—and there is no trash mixed in with the deposit. To date, this offering, along with two deposits of ceramics at Conchopata near Wari, have been considered evidence of religious practices: the breaking and offering of highly valued ceramics to the gods (Menzel 1964:24–28). Wari iconography, the symbols of its power, was most vividly displayed in two media: textiles and ceramics. The Pacheco deposit includes a number of oversized urns on which depictions of the Wari staff god were painted. These vessels were destroyed by blows aimed at the face or chest of the deity.

Although it is certainly reasonable to think that this deposit represents the remains of a religious practice, one wonders if there might be some alternate interpretation of the deposit. Data presented here suggest that the people of Nasca were none too pleased with the presence of Wari colonies and that local resistance reached significant levels. When the empire collapsed and the colonists finally left, they left behind their deserted colony, along with numerous material representations of their former power in the form of fancy decorated ceramics. I suggest that the people of Nasca may have acted to intentionally destroy those old images of Wari power, smashing the vessels, depositing them in underground chambers, and interring them. I offer this scenario as a possible example of Nasca resistance after the fact.

If this interpretation is reasonable, then we must also reconsider the two deposits of broken ceramics found at Conchopata. This is an important Wari site, only about 10 kilometers from the capital, located on a prominent ridge top. Although the function of the site is still a matter of debate, it clearly included Wari-style architecture, D-shaped Wari temples, and elaborate Wari ceramics. The first deposit, excavated by Tello in 1942, contained numerous oversized urns, with depictions of the staff god and also winged profile attendants. The second deposit, excavated by Isbell in 1977, contained oversized face-neck jars painted with the images of men (perhaps rulers) in elaborate costumes (A. G. Cook 1994). As at Pacheco, these vessels were intentionally smashed with blows to the faces or chests of the depicted icons. Although these deposits may indeed represent some sort of religious ritual, I suggest they may also be interpreted as the result of the intentional destruction of Wari symbols of power at the time of the collapse of the empire.

THE WARI COLONIAL EXPERIENCE IN SONDONDO

The Sondondo Valley[2] is located in the south-central highlands of Peru, south of Wari and northeast of Nasca. It is a small, deep inter-montane valley with very steep sides, whose flanks support the cultivation of maize and tubers. It is located with easy, direct access to broad expanses of high elevation plateau (*puna*) suitable for supporting large numbers of native camelids. It has a very long history of human habitation, beginning at least 10,000 years ago, when hunter-gatherer groups exploited its abundance of resources. Sedentary villages were established as early as 2000 B.C., and population grew and new villages were established as the centuries went by.

At the end of the Kancha phase (circa A.D. 1–750; fig. 8.4), people lived in villages ranging up to 1 hectare in size, scattered throughout the valley at elevations of 3,300 to 3,800 meters asl. Such elevations were devoted to tuber cultivation and are located immediately adjacent to the puna grazing lands, suggesting a mixed agropastoral economy. No village is distinguished from any other in terms of size or internal complexity, and there is no evidence of local political centralization. One site, Piruruyoq, was a local shrine with a very long history of use; it will be discussed at more length later.

The decision to establish a Wari colony in this small valley may have been based on its strategic location halfway between Wari and Nasca. To journey on foot from Wari to Nasca, one has two obvious choices: (1) to go west across the continental divide, down to the Pacific coast, and south through the desert to Nasca; or (2) to head south through the highlands to the Sondondo Valley, then turn southwest, cross the continental divide, and descend directly to Nasca. One could argue that highlanders, being both more familiar with the highland landscape and also physically adapted to life at high elevations, may have

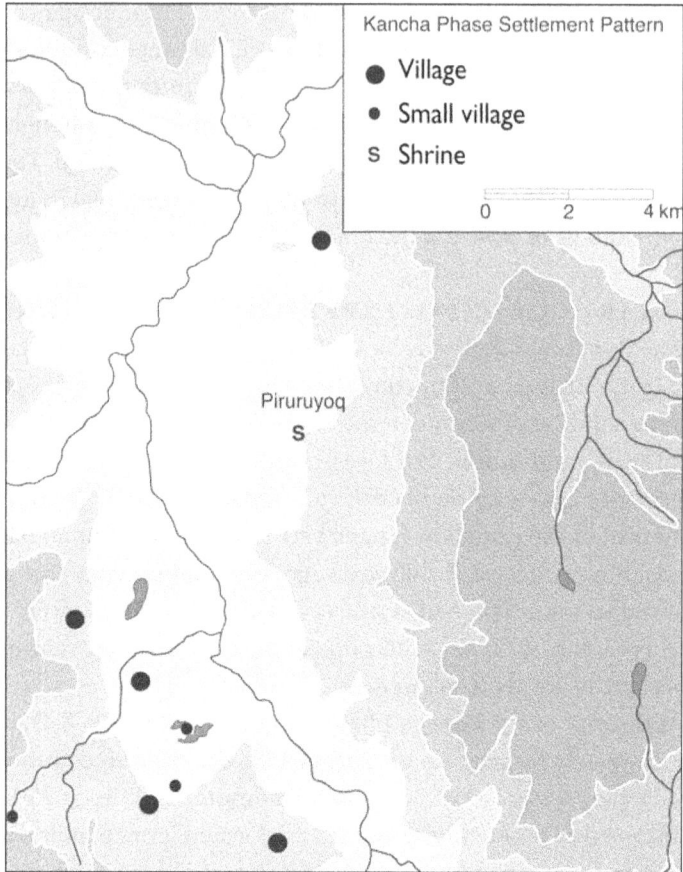

FIGURE 8.4

Settlement pattern of the Sondondo Valley, showing sites pertaining to the Kancha phase, just prior to the Wari expansion. Contour interval = 400 meters.

preferred a route that stayed mostly in the Andes. Material evidence that the highland route was preferred is provided by an ancient road that connected Sondondo and Nasca and that was incorporated by the Inkas into their system of royal roads. Wari sites (Jincamocco and Pataraya) lie at either terminus of this road, suggesting that its use dates back at least to the Middle Horizon. There is a second ancient road that enters the Sondondo Valley from the north; a Wari site (Mamachacorral) lies adjacent to this road as it enters the valley, suggesting that this road, too, was in use in the Middle Horizon. If the spacing of Inka way stations along its

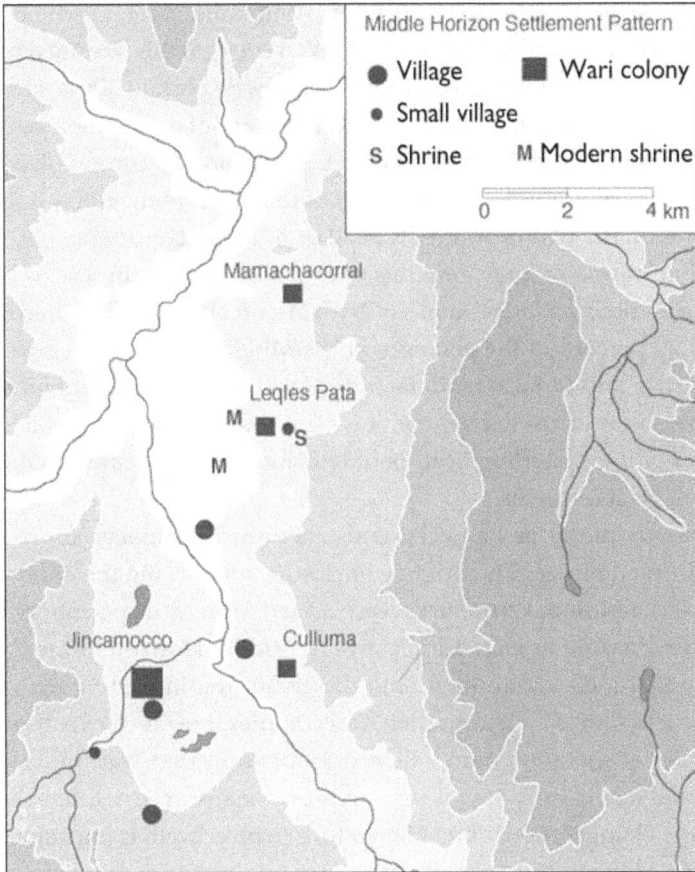

FIGURE 8.5

Settlement pattern of the Sondondo Valley, showing sites pertaining to Middle Horizon Phases 1 and 2, including local sites and Wari colonies. Modern shrines in the area of Leqles Pata are also shown.

roads is a measure of distance traveled in a day, then the Sondondo Valley lay four-days' walking distance from both Wari and Nasca.

Jincamocco: A Wari Colony

In Middle Horizon Phase 1 (fig. 8.5), a Wari colony, Jincamocco, was established on the west flank of the valley, in a setting with exceptionally good views to the east and north. The original construction at the site was a typical Wari enclosure, measuring 128 by 256 meters, one half of which was divided into twenty-four cells, some of which were further divided into smaller cells. As Wari sites go, this was not a particularly large colony at the beginning. But it was substantially larger than any local settlement, and it provided the point of articulation between the metropole and the host polity. The creation of a central place provided a local administrative capital, and thus evidence of a political agenda on the part of Wari—its need or desire to control people.

Excavation of large amounts of redeposited trash in several patios at Jincamocco provides details of both architecture and other artifacts. Fully 90 percent of the ceramics in the Middle Horizon levels were of local style and of local manufacture. If we can associate ceramics with people, even to a small degree, it is clear that Jincamocco was a multi-ethic colony, including both people from Wari and substantial numbers of local residents.

Sometime after its initial construction, Jincamocco more than quadrupled in size. The original enclosure still formed the core of the site, but additional structures were added around its periphery until the site covered at least 15 hectares in Middle Horizon Phase 2. The additional walls are abutted onto the enclosure, indicating their relatively later date. Few if any other Wari colonies show such expansion. In the case of the Sondondo Valley, it is apparent that Wari initiated its colonial occupation based on one set of needs or ideas, but that its agenda changed over time. Many more people lived at Jincamocco in Middle Horizon 2 than in the beginning. Whether these were permanent or temporary residents cannot be known, but additional evidence suggests that large numbers of laborers—probably numbering at least in the hundreds—were brought into the region to build agricultural terraces, and Jincamocco may have been expanded to house them.

Culluma: A Second Colony and Another Agenda

Several lines of evidence suggest that large tracts of the valley were terraced in the Middle Horizon; this includes the movement of nearly all local people from higher settlements above 3,300 meters to the zones newly terraced below 3,300 meters. At the high altitudes of the Sondondo Valley, it is impossible to grow maize in the absence of stone-faced bench terraces; terracing covers most of the valley sides up to an elevation of 3,300 meters above sea level, the approximate upper limit of maize cultivation in this valley. Adjacent to one especially large tract of terracing is another Wari colony, Culluma, built in Middle Horizon Phase 2. This site comprises a probable Wari enclosure roughly 80 by 100 meters, located on a windy exposed ridge directly across the valley from Jincamocco and within sight of it. Little architecture remains to be seen on the surface because the enclosure was dismantled by the Inkas; they used its stones to build a double row of forty-six small, round storehouses at the same location. The location of the Wari site adjacent to agricultural terraces, and the suitability of that setting for cool, dry storage of perishables, suggests a probable function as a store-house. Associated ceramics indicate a small resident population as well, probably including both Wari and local people.

Taken together, the construction of terraces and the construction of a storehouse indicates another aspect of the Wari agenda—the economic exploitation of the region.

Mamachacorral: A Third Colony

Yet another Wari colony, Mamachacorral,[3] was located at the northern end of the valley, adjacent to the ancient road that enters the valley from the north, from the direction of Wari. This site, measuring about 80 by 100 meters, occupies a unique position in that it has a clear view of Jincamocco, although it is some 9 kilometers away. This site probably served two aspects of the Wari agenda: political control and economic exploitation. In the first place, this site controlled access into and out of the north end of the valley: given the severe terrain, one cannot avoid passing immediately adjacent to the site. It was therefore ideally situated as a lookout, enabling colonists to observe the movement of people and, possibly, to signal Jincamocco in the event of trouble.

In the second place, the site is located adjacent to a small obsidian source, Jampatilla (Burger et al. 1998). Obsidian from this source has been identified at Jincamocco, indicating its exploitation by Wari colonists. Thus Mamachacorral also contributed to the economic agenda of the Wari colonists in the exploitation of this small, circumscribed resource. Jampatilla obsidian, although used extensively in the Sondondo Valley, was not used as a raw material at Wari or any other Wari sites, based on current data. This suggests that the exploitation of the source was for local purposes only, and not for the support of the capital.

Leqles Pata: Yet Another Colony and Another Agenda

A fourth Wari colony, Leqles Pata,[4] was also established in the northern portion of the valley on the east flank, and both its location and internal configuration distinguish it as a very different sort of colony than the three already discussed. The site is located on a ridge separating two of the basins on the east side of the valley. It has an excellent view of the valley, and it lies within Jincamocco's view shed. The date of the site's construction is unclear; until recently I dated it to Middle Horizon 2 (Schreiber 1992:154), but based on a recent restudy of the site I now entertain the possibility that it was built earlier in the Middle Horizon. Just up the ridge from Leqles Pata is the most important local shrine identified archaeologically in the region. This site, Piruruyoq, mentioned above, is a circular mound that may be a modified natural feature. Ceramic artifacts associated with the shrine indicate it was used from at least the earliest ceramic periods and continued in use up to the Late Horizon and perhaps later (Ccencho Huamaní 1991). Down the ridge from Leqles Pata is a modern shrine, a unique rock formation, revered today by residents of the town of Huaycahuacho. Directly below the ridge on which the site sits, and clearly visible from it, is a tract of distinctive terrain that today holds cosmological significance to the local population; within the tract is a large boulder and a small pond that are also locally revered shrines. This tract of land was said to be the result of an enormous landslide that took place in the distant past, burying a great city. There is no archaeological evidence of such a buried city, but the landslide sheered off the mountainside immediately below the Wari colony. In sum, the location of Leqles Pata places it in close proximity to a prehistoric local shrine and on a ridge that continues to have sacred connotations to the present.

Like the other Wari colonies, Leqles Pata includes a rectangular compound of characteristic Wari style; but this compound is by far the smallest, measuring only 30 by 35 meters. Unique to this site, however, is the presence of at least one, and possibly as many as four, D-shaped structures. Such structures are thought to be Wari temples (A. G. Cook 2001). The Templo Mayor at Wari itself is the largest and most elaborate example of this form (González Carré et al. 1996). Also unique to this site, within the Sondondo Valley, is the presence of large cut-stone slab tombs, of a form similar to what were probably royal tombs at Wari (see Benavides 1991).

Unique attributes of the site, coupled with its location on a landform with sacred connotations, point to another aspect the Wari metropole's agenda, beyond political control and economic exploitation. I suggest that this site represents the co-option of a local sacred landscape by Wari.

Movement of Local Settlements—Whose Agenda?

Analysis of settlement patterns indicates quite clearly that most people of the local host polity moved to locations at lower elevations during the Middle Horizon. Prior to the arrival of Wari colonists, sites were located at elevations ranging from 3,300 to 3,800 meters asl. By the end of the Wari occupation, nearly all local sites were situated below 3,300 meters asl. We cannot precisely date these relocations within the Middle Horizon, as our dating of these sites is based only on limited surface collections of artifacts; we can only say that they did take place during the period of Wari colonization. Was the movement of the local populace to new village sites motivated by the agendas of the Wari colonists, by local agendas, or some combination of the two? In the past I have assumed that the movement of local people to new settlements was the result of Wari force, but here I open up the possibility that local motivations may have played a role.

In one case we can be confident that the move was a forced one: a local village was situated where Wari colonists chose to build Jincamocco. A local site newly occupied in the Middle Horizon on the low hill just southwest of Jincamocco may be the place to which they were moved.

The construction of tracts of terraced fields at elevations generally below 3,300 meters asl may be directly implicated in the movement of the people. For the first time, large tracts of land were suitable for maize agriculture, and people moved, or were moved, to have more direct access to this land. Perhaps, too, local individuals or groups were motivated to move in order to situate themselves close to the colonists—that is, to gain whatever political and economic advantages might accrue from cooperating and associating with them. The site that was moved when Jincamocco was built did not move very far. Local ceramics found at each of the four Wari colonies may indicate that local people were actually living in these settlements. And one local site was established adjacent to the Wari colonial site of Leqles Pata.

Local Resistance

Evidence of local resistance in Sondondo is rather elusory, and certainly we do not see it as clearly as, for example, in Nasca. However, evidence from Jincamocco suggests that although local resistance may have been very subtle, it was probably there nonetheless. The fact that Jincamocco was built on the location of a local village provides us with a unique opportunity to compare local ceramics made prior to the arrival of Wari with those made during the Wari occupation. As mentioned above, some 90 percent of the ceramic assemblage of the Middle Horizon levels comprised local styles; we recovered substantial quantities of immediately pre–Middle Horizon ceramics in deep excavations intended to reveal the foundations of the Wari architecture. A detailed analysis was undertaken of each diagnostic sherd, including attributes of firing, temper, surface finish, design, execution, and painting, among many others. In the case of local ceramics (plainware, incised bowls, serpentine jars, and vessels with other forms of tactile decoration), the earlier, pre-Wari vessels were more evenly fired, the temper was finer and better sorted, surfaces were more carefully smoothed, incisions and applique designs were more carefully executed, and post-fire paints were more common (see Schreiber 1992: ch. 7). A cursory inspection of the vessels made by the casual observer would see little difference in terms of shape, color, and general decoration; to the makers of the pots, the differences would have been obvious. These several lines of evidence demonstrate that more time and care was devoted to ceramic production prior to the colonial encounter. One simple explanation for this deterioration in quality might be that the potters had less time for their craft under the colonial regime. However, as I have suggested elsewhere (Schreiber 1992:251–52), it is also plausible that, when making pots for use in the Wari colony, local potters did not invest the time or care they had in the past when they were making the vessels for their own use. These very subtle alterations in ceramic production may reflect one way in which the local people resisted the Wari presence.

Excavations at Jincamocco also revealed one unit, a raised platform with fine plaster finish, upon which were found in situ a large face-neck jar smashed in the center of the platform and about a dozen smaller vessels found broken at the base of one wall. The breaking of these vessels represents an event that took place at or shortly after the use of this platform was terminated. The sherds do not form any sort of dedicatory offering, as they are not embedded in walls or buried under floors like other such offerings. And had the platform still been in use after the breaking of the pots, the sherds would have been swept up or else scattered about. The large face-neck jar was modeled and painted with the image of a human male in an elaborate costume and headdress; the smaller vessels were mostly very fancy Wari styles. As in the case of the Pacheco offering, I suggest that this may represent resistance after the fact: the smashing of the old Wari symbols of power, once the empire collapsed and the colonists abandoned the colony and the region (Schreiber 1992:246).

CONCLUSIONS

From this short summary of data from two regions within the Wari domain, we can discern a variety of agendas on the part of the metropole, as well as changes in some aspects of those agendas over time. These agendas were multidimensional, stressing different forms of control at different times and in different places. Changes in Wari agendas may have been the result of a variety of factors, including local resistance from the host polities, modification of implementation strategies as relations with local polities evolved, and policy shifts within the metropole. The initial Wari incursions into Nasca and Sondondo were undertaken for different reasons perhaps, but in both cases political aspects of the agenda seem to have been paramount, imposing control over people and their local political hierarchies by establishing a new political capital in each region. In the case of Nasca, the colony was set apart from local settlements, whereas in Sondondo it was centrally located, suggesting different levels of interaction with the host polities, and perhaps different levels of resistance, or the ability to resist, on the part of those host polities.

In both regions as well, economic aspects of the imperial agenda seem to have increased in importance over time, with efforts aimed at exploiting particular resource zones. In Nasca, a second, much smaller colony was established adjacent to a tract of agricultural fields suitable for the growing of coca. A small group of highlanders lived side by side with the colonists from Wari; at the same time, that sector of the valley was abandoned by local Nasca inhabitants. In Sondondo, large portions of the valley sides were terraced, making them suitable for maize cultivation, and a small obsidian source was exploited for local use by the colonists. Additional colonies were established adjacent to these resource zones, and the bulk of the local population moved down from higher elevations to new sites in or adjacent to the new maize fields.

In Sondondo, we see as well an ideological aspect to the imperial agenda in the co-option of a sacred landscape, and the establishment of yet another small colony in sacred space. This is the only colony in the region with temples and tombs of Wari style. Such an agenda is less clear in Nasca.

Beyond the multidimensional aspects of the imperial agenda, it is useful to emphasize temporal change in the priorities given to the different aspects of imperial control. Whereas the political agenda conditioned initial efforts in each region, the economic aspects of the agenda came to play a greater role in the later years of the colonial encounter. And although we don't have a clear relative date of Leqles Pata's establishment in Sondondo, ideological aspects of the agenda probably surfaced rather early in the sequence. Were we to simply consider all the Wari colonies, their material associations, and the shift in local settlement locations as reflecting a single event, we would be struck with the monolithic nature of this empire and its ability to profoundly alter all that lay in its path. On the contrary, however, when we consider the colonial encounter as a series of events, spread over several centuries, we must acknowledge the complexity of the encounter and the changing agendas of the metropole, even within a single region. When we compare regions, we find that the Wari encounter differed greatly from place to place, but that the initial emphasis on political control of the people, and later on the exploitation of economic resources, is roughly similar—at least in the cases of Nasca and Sondondo.

This reconstruction of Wari colonial encounters in Nasca and Sondondo begins to consider local agency and the evidence of local resistance or cooperation. In Nasca, the host polity was apparently resistant to the Wari presence, as seen through the movement of nearly all settlements to the most distant valley. In Sondondo, quite the opposite occurred: the people moved to locations somewhat nearer the Wari colonies. I have argued that the so-called offering deposit at Pacheco may be an example of resistance after the fact, the destruction of the old symbols of Wari power. In both Nasca and Sondondo, local people were certainly living in the multiethnic colonies, alongside the Wari colonists, although the degree to which those people were coerced to do so cannot be known at present. In the case of Sondondo, we find possible evidence of subtle forms of resistance on the part of the host polity, seen in the lower quality of local-style ceramics produced for the colony at Jincamocco. And I have suggested that the smashing of fine ceramic vessels at Jincamocco may be evidence of vandalism at the site, another example of resistance after the fact.

Unlike most previous investigations of Wari provincial occupations, including my own, this paper has sought to disentangle the various agendas of the Wari metropole and understand the diverse aspects colonial encounter. In the case of Wari, we have necessarily relied strictly on archaeological data, as no written documents exist to guide us in our endeavors, and these data have indeed provided evidence for multidimensional agendas motivating the actions of the expanding metropole in its diverse cultural and geographic settings. Finally, the local people have been given a voice, and they can now be seen as active participants in this process, contributing materially to a negotiated outcome.

Acknowledgments

Funding for archaeological research in the Sondondo Valley, 1976–1981, was provided by two grants from the National Science Foundation; current research is supported by the National Geographic Society. I offer special thanks to José Cencho for his collaboration in our continued work there. Funds supporting survey and excavations in Nasca, 1984–1996, were provided by two grants from the National Geographic Society, plus grants from University Research Expeditions, the Kaplan Fund, and the Academic Senate of the University of California at Santa Barbara. I thank Johny Isla and Josué Lancho for their collaboration in the Nasca field projects, along with the many American and Peruvian students who participated in those projects.

I am most grateful to Gil Stein for organizing the advanced seminar at the School of American Research in Santa Fe and inviting me to participate. It was one of the most intellectually stimulating experiences of my career and led me to think in entirely new directions about expanding states and their complex inter-actions with those they conquered. Thanks also to the participants, without whose stimulating comments this paper would never have come as far as it did. And thanks are due to the capable staff of the School of American Research for providing a setting in which all this could take place. David Lawson of the Anthropology Graphics Laboratory at UCSB drew most of figure 8.1 and gener-ously shared his expertise in producing the remaining figures. I also thank two anonymous reviewers for their comments, which helped me to sharpen my prose and clarify my arguments.

Notes

1. Also spelled Huari.

2. I referred to this region by the name Carhuarazo Valley in some earlier publications (Schreiber 1987, 1992, 1993). In the mid-1990s, the valley was given an official name, Sondondo, by the Peruvian government.

3. Formerly referred to as Willkaya (Schreiber 1992:155–57).

4. Formerly referred to as Anta (Schreiber 1992:154–55).

9

Remaking the Social Landscape

Colonization in the Inka Empire

Terence N. D'Altroy

When the Spaniards invaded the Andes in 1532, they entered a social landscape that had been transfigured by a century of Inka rule. Although western South America had seen other empires with grand designs, none remotely approached Tawantinsuyu ("The Four Parts Together") in its impact on the scores of ethnically distinct peoples in the region (fig. 9.1). Beginning with the Spanish chroniclers, the Inka government has often been portrayed as an absolute monarchy whose sovereign relied on standardized policies and a uniform bureaucracy to rule his subjects. There is truth in that description, but it would be more to the point to say that the political system consisted of a veneer of ethnic Inka officials who supervised the leaders of diverse subject societies. In practice, Inka politics drew on coercion, ceremonial hospitality, and patronage to motivate their subjects to carry out state mandates, while the local subjects practiced self-reliance and paid regular labor duties to the Inkas (C. Morris 1998). In the central part of the empire, the local elites, who ranged from petty village chiefs to hereditary aristocrats, were often incorporated into a decimal hierarchy of officials.[1] Elsewhere, along the populous north coast of Peru and in the

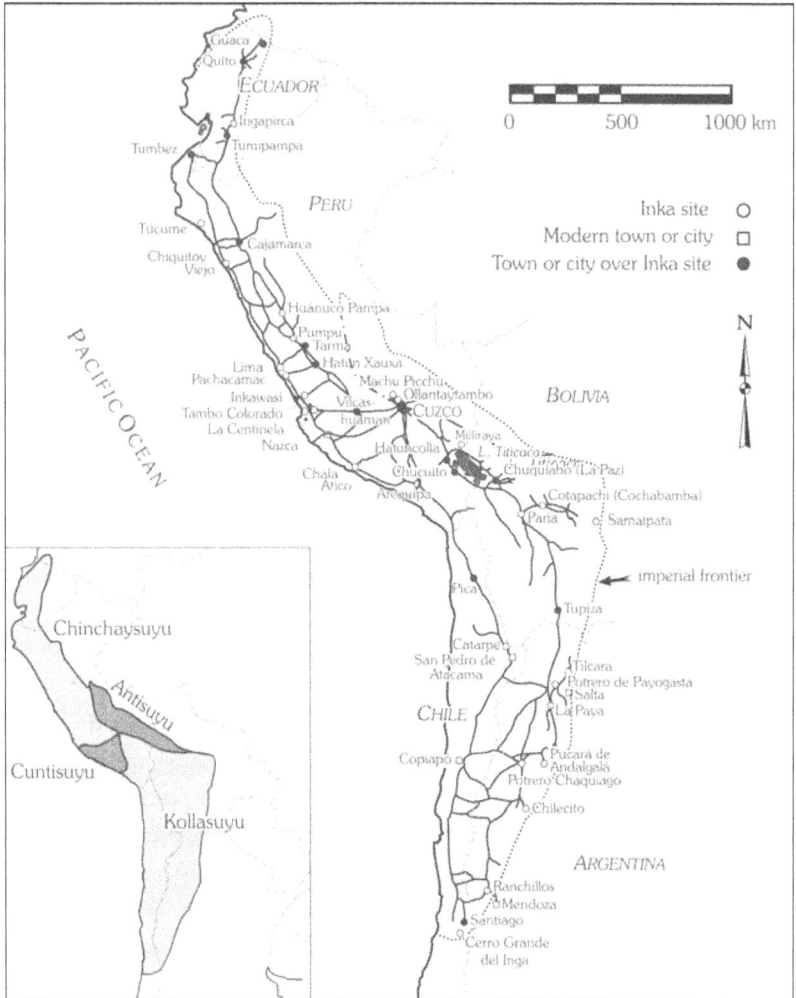

FIGURE 9.1

The Inka empire—Tawantinsuyu—at the time of the Spanish invasion of 1532 (after Hyslop 1984: frontispiece). The inset map shows the four parts of the empire.

far north and south, Inka rule was more indirect, as ethnic lords served more as intermediaries than as managers in an elaborate hierarchy. In order to mobilize labor and cultivate bonds of allegiance, the Inkas exploited long-standing relations between the local elites and their own people, representing the imperial obligations as little more than traditional mutuality written on a grand scale (Murra 1958).

Within this framework of standardized rule built on diversity, no policy transformed the Andes more than resettlement. In only three or four generations, the Inkas atomized and recombined an ethnic geography that was already unusually complicated. Many of the pre-imperial ethnic groups, called *etnías,* consisted of two or more named parts (for example, upper and lower) and contained several independent polities. The etnías typically provided the base for Inka provinces or internal divisions, but peoples were also divided, aggregated, and moved about for administrative convenience. Altogether, about three to five million people out of a total of ten to twelve million resettled in new locales. Some moves conformed to a classic conception of colonization—the settlement of peoples in foreign regions, who still identified and maintained contact with their homeland (see Stein this volume). Most resettlement, however, moved subjects about within territory already controlled by the Inkas, similar in some ways to Roman centuriation (see Alcock, this volume). Local practices complemented state resettlement, as communities and their lords sent off small groups to exploit isolated resources.

The resultant ethnic mosaic makes the study of Tawantinsuyu's social geography an exercise in fractal geometry—that is, the land looks different depending on the focus of our lens (figs. 9.2 and 9.3). A single one of the eighty-odd provinces, named after a particular ethnic group, could contain members of dozens of other etnías. Except for the highest provincial lords, witnesses describing their social identities in Spanish inspections typically named a local kin group or community rather than their etnía, which was more important for the Inka and Spanish rulers than for the peasantry. If subjects had been moved to a new location as colonists, however, ethnic identity apparently took on a greater weight. To further complicate matters, in areas such as the populous Lake Titicaca basin, linguistic patterns crosscut ethnic geography, so that languages could be shared across etnías and members of the same etnía could speak several different languages. Identity thus depended to a great degree on the referent context and the position of the individual demanding or providing the information.

In this article, I would like to examine the remodeled social landscape of Tawantinsuyu by placing case studies of colonization into a broader comparative framework. The analysis is complicated by evidentiary differences between the historical and archaeological

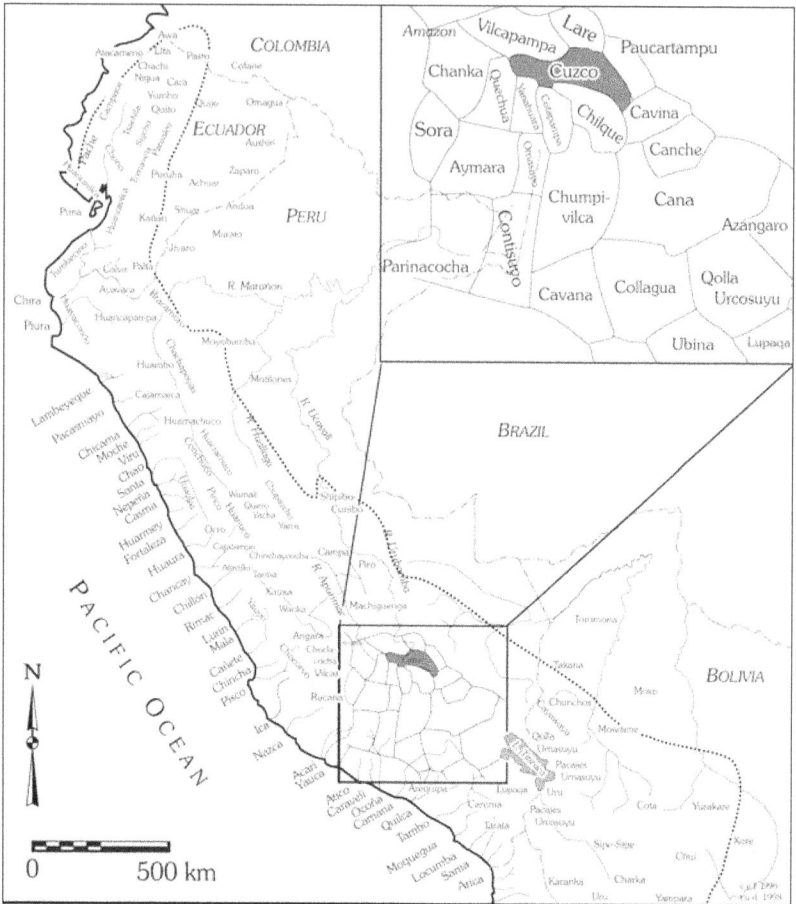

FIGURE 9.2

Distribution of major ethnic groups in the empire from the Bolivian altiplano north.
(Source: Maps in Rowe 1946; Saignes 1985; Fresco, personal communication, 1998)

records, but it is my hope that the cases will illustrate the variety of situations that existed.

COLONIZATION IN OUTLINE

We are on unsettled terrain in trying to sort out the trajectory of colonization in Tawantinsuyu, largely because the lack of indigenous writing and the political uses of the past make it difficult to reconstruct the empire's history. Conventionally, the empire was founded by a

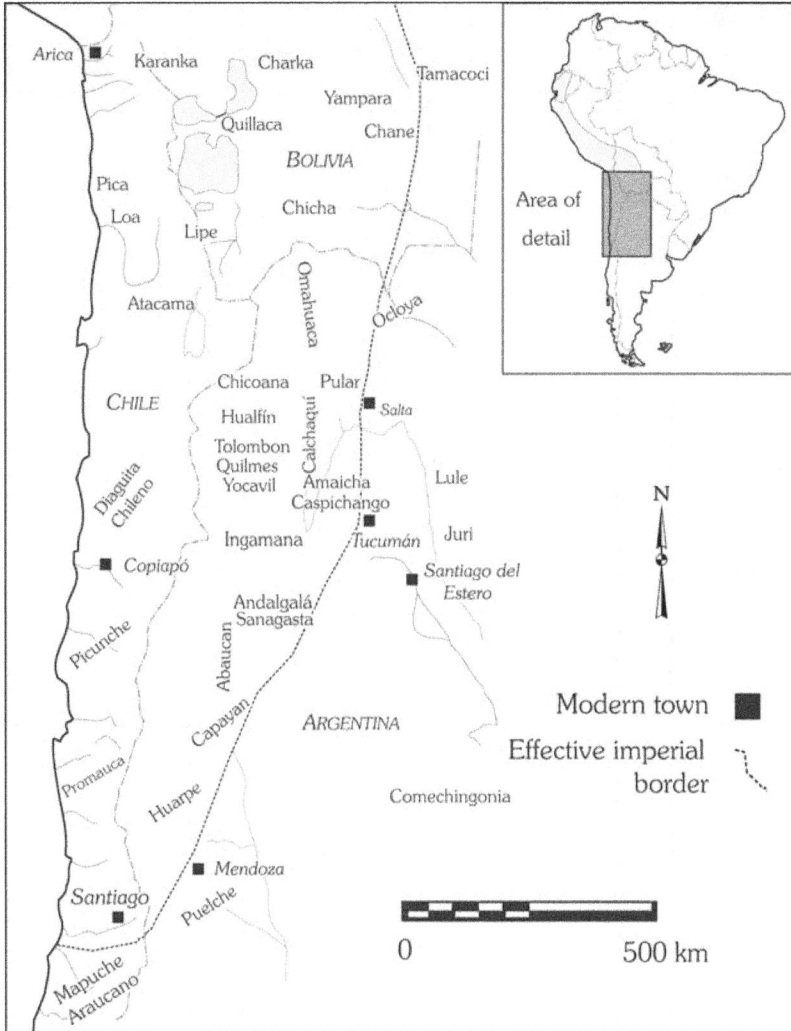

FIGURE 9.3

Distribution of major ethnic groups in the empire from the Bolivian altiplano south.
(Source: Maps in Raffino 1983, 1990; Berberián and Raffino 1986; A. M. Lorandi, personal communication)

prince, known to history as Pachakuti, who usurped the throne in the face of an attack by a neighbor early in the fifteenth century A.D. (table 1).[2] Pachakuti initiated the imperial era through military and

TABLE 9.1

The conventional list of Inka kings of the prehispanic era.

Lower Cuzco	Upper Cuzco
1. Manqo Qhapaq	6. Inka Roq'a
2. Zinchi Roqóa	7. Yawar Waqaq
3. Lloqé Yupanki	8. Wiraqocha Inka
4. Mayta Qhapaq	9. Pachakuti Inka Yupanki
5. Qhapaq Yupanki	10. Thupa Inka Yupanki
	11. Wayna Qhapaq
	12. Waskhar Inka
	13. Atawallpa

diplomatic ventures that expanded the domain into the altiplano and the central Peruvian highlands. Both Inka oral histories and Colonial interviews with ethnic lords reported that Pachakuti installed garrison colonies in newly annexed lands and began resettling subjects near Cuzco. Although the scale of movement may have been innovative, his actions extended long-standing Andean practices, as Schreiber (this volume) describes. Both the Wari and Tiwanaku states of the Middle Horizon sponsored colonies in distant locales to procure environmentally localized resources, a practice apparently duplicated on a smaller scale by local communities. In colonization, as in other policies, the Inkas consequently drew from existing statecraft and local practice (Murra 1972).

Pachakuti's successor, Thupa Inka Yupanki, is credited with having greatly enlarged the empire either as general of his father's armies or after his ascent to the throne, but the specifics of his colonization policy are still sketchy. The third emperor, Wayna Qhapaq, campaigned vigorously in the north, where twenty years of action only marginally extended the realm. Even so, Wayna Qhapaq notably elaborated the colonization programs both internally and at the edges of Inka control. His death in 1528, from a smallpox epidemic that foreshadowed the Spanish arrival, was followed by a dynastic war between two of his sons that ended just as Pizarro ascended the Andes. Even at that point, extensive resettlement was envisioned, as the victorious Prince Atawallpa had 15,000 Kañari from Ecuador in his camp intended for relocation.

In the empire's final years, the Inkas judged that they had incorporated virtually the whole world that was either civilized or worth the effort. Stymied as much by geography and logistics as by fierce resistance, they did not have the capacity to extend their reach into the far northern or southern Andes, nor into the eastern lowlands, territory they consequently dismissed as home to naked cannibals and other raffish folk. The imperial border itself was not fixed, since political, cultural, economic, and military relations varied in their reach (Dillehay and Netherly 1988). External affairs consisted largely of maintaining relations with small-scale societies whose waters and lands yielded desirable resources, such as gold, *Spondylus princeps* (thorny oyster) shell, wood, feathers, and other forest products. Only along the northern and southeastern frontiers did the Inkas establish a hardened perimeter. Even there, however, they encouraged cultural and economic exchanges with the peoples beyond, establishing farms, mining settlements, and other outposts well below the high garrisons (for example, Salomon 1986; Lorandi 1988; Mulvany and Soria 1998; Alconini 2001).

The most renowned resettlement program vacated entire provinces or moved towns of colonists, called *mitmaqkuna*, as much as 2,000 kilometers from their homelands. The seventeenth-century Jesuit chronicler Bernabé Cobo (1979:189) wrote that the Inkas usually extracted and resettled six or seven thousand families from each new province that they incorporated. That overly generalized figure, although broadly accurate, implies that about a quarter to a third of the population was relocated; in individual provinces, the resettled fraction may have run from 10 to 80 percent of the populace (Rowe 1982:107). Cobo (1979:190) added that the Inkas sometimes moved people to ecologically similar lands, presumably to ease the adjustment, and that groups from two locations were occasionally exchanged with one another.

Waldemar Espinoza Soriano (for example, 1970, 1973, 1975, 1987), the foremost modern scholar on mitmaqkuna, has published numerous documents that detail how and why particular groups of people were relocated. A principal reason for resettlement was to disperse societies whose members posed threats to state security, sometimes using the same people to garrison other hot spots. Pachakuti is usually credited with initiating that policy, but rulers practiced it right up to the moment of the Spanish invasion. The frontier, especially in northern Ecuador and along the southeastern sector, was dotted with at least one hundred redoubts, which could include *orejones* (nobles) from Cuzco, but the largest garrisons lay well within imperial territories. Espinoza has shown that a second major purpose for resettlement was to create groups of economic specialists whose products were destined explicitly for state use. Among the economic mitmaqkuna were artisans, such as weavers, potters, and metalsmiths; farmers, especially for maize, coca, and peppers; and herders, masons, and miners. Although creating production enclaves may have been Inka policy for several generations, Wayna Qhapaq was cited by native witnesses as the founder of the largest farms and artisan communities.

The rulers also reinforced the doctrine that Cuzco was the sacred center of the world by settling ethnic enclaves in neighborhoods around the elite core that replicated their geographic position in the realm. In addition, the royalty used transplanted communities (as well as lifelong servants) to staff their estates, tend their herds, and farm their crops. One of the largest estate colonies was Thupa Inka Yupanki's mining operation east of Samaipata, Bolivia, which reportedly included 1,000 miners and 5,000 support households (Pärssinen 1992:130–31). Under the mantle of state favor, ethnic lords likewise created multiethnic colonies to exploit coca lands, guano fields, salt springs, and other resources in distant locales (Murra 1972). In a complementary pattern, many villagers resettled locally to take advantage of farmlands, pastures, and other resources that had been off limits before the enforced peace put an end to the hostilities of the late pre-Inka era.

The Inkas went to some lengths to make sure that the colonists owed their identities to their homelands but their allegiance to the state. They were maintained on the census rolls of their points of origin, but were administratively subject to the governor of their new provinces. Colonists had to wear their traditional clothing and to speak their own languages, and interaction with the local societies was restricted. We may surmise that at least some colonists returned home after their useful work lives were over or after their death. This last practice is reflected at the formal state installations, which lack cemeteries befitting the scale of their populations (C. Morris 1972).

Mitmaqkuna received state support for only a couple of years, until they could sustain themselves, after which they had to support themselves on resources they were granted, even if they had not been farmers beforehand.

Relations among mitmaqkuna, their neighbors, and the state present intriguing problems for political and economic analysis, since the colonies were shaped by conflicting pressures. As (often unwilling) agents of the state, the mitmaqkuna may have seen their distinctiveness reduced by the Inkas' efforts to make them beholden to imperial institutions. The practice of settling members of multiple ethnic groups in the same enclave may have also contributed to some loss of distinctive identity. Within colonist communities, autonomy would have been fostered by the highland ethic and explicit state policy of economic self-sufficiency, reinforced by the widely recorded conflicts with displaced neighbors over resources. Since the colonists' resources were often alienated from existing communities, the fall of Inka power spawned a host of lawsuits in the early Colonial period, as communities tried to reclaim lost lands.

Even so, there is no tangible reason to believe that mitmaqkuna were completely self-sufficient and some reason to believe otherwise. On an everyday basis, colonists may have needed resources that were unavailable in the lands they had been granted; some documents indicate that they sometimes traded or forged social links with their neighbors. The well-informed magistrate of Cuzco, Lic. Polo (1916:68), stated flatly that mitmaqkuna owned no community herds, although there is some evidence to the contrary (see below on artisans). If he was broadly on the mark, then the colonists were at an extraordinary disadvantage in getting the culturally essential wool and meat, unless they were supplied directly from state herds, a source that was also apparently proscribed. Obtaining salt, ceramic clay or finished pottery, coca, maize, pepper, lime, metals, or lithic materials that were spatially concentrated may have also been a vexing problem for new settlers. Even if the settlers brought their own tools and household goods, those materials would have required replacement over time. One solution would have been to trade with neighbors in a low-level barter system that fell under the radar of state interest (see, for example, Ortiz de Zúñiga 1967, 1972). Alternatively, the colonists could have been given the right to form their own mini-colonist settlements where key resources could be exploited, or the right to work the sources temporarily, a practice that was recorded for some altiplano colonies. Nevertheless, it seems improbable that state officials actively ensured that each community had extraction rights to every kind of resource needed for daily life. Whatever the particulars, because the material conditions of life had changed, the detritus of the colonists' everyday life could not be expected to duplicate that of the homeland.

HISTORICAL ACCOUNTS VERSUS ARCHAEOLOGICAL SIGNATURES FOR COLONISTS

Considering the documentary reports, we might think that colonies would be easy to recognize in the archaeological record. Locally intrusive portable artifact styles, house forms, mortuary remains, and other physical manifestations of ethnic intermixing should be readily visible. But there's the rub—mitmaqkuna have gone virtually unnoticed archaeologically. Assuming that the written record on the scale of movement is reliable— and hundreds of references attest to relocation throughout the empire—we must assume either that archaeologists have paid little attention to the matter or that we need to rethink how to study colonization archaeologically. As to the first possibility, an intensive review of the published literature indicates that archaeologists have not been much concerned with recognizing *mitmaq* settlements (although see Céspedes Paz 1982; Lorandi 1984; Spurling 1992; V. I. Williams 1996; Alconini 2001). With rare exception, the provincial archaeology of the Inka era has been the archaeology of the Inkas, not their subjects, mostly because imperial affairs are infinitely more fascinating than the humdrum lives of ten million peasants (although see Earle et al. 1987; Schjellerup 1997; Parsons, Hastings, and Matos 2000; D'Altroy, Hastorf, and Associates 2001). But it is also true that it is easy to recognize most Inka sites because of their distinctive architecture and ceramics, whereas assigning subject villages to the era is difficult without intensive local work. Even where scholars have paid attention to the matter, clear signatures for colonization are rare.

The contrasting images of colonization in the historical and archaeological records suggest that it might be profitable to think about a joint historiography of the two forms of evidence. It would be particularly useful to know if the concepts involved in representing identity or power in Colonial documents are analogous to those that created the archaeological record, or if distinct media filter ideas through distinct lenses because the contexts and intentions differ.[3] Other authors in this volume have laid out significant problems facing the archaeology of colonization stemming from uncritical use of partial (written) texts, among them an overreliance on literary theory, outlooks of the colonial powers, and elite sources of information. The problems are especially well defined for the Mediterranean, where reimagined visions of antiquity helped to shape modern European imperialism/colonialism, which then acted back on interpretations of Greece and Rome (see Alcock, Dietler, and van Dommelen, this volume). Paradoxically, however, much of the discussion that redresses colonialist biases is still reflective of European contact in that the redefinition of colonial contexts is often framed as a response to the imposition of European history, philosophies, and cultural viewpoints (for example, Said 1978). The placement of Tawantinsuyu in Latin America and its constituent nation-states, for example, is new in historical terms and inappropriate with respect to past societies that inhabited the land. Although reinvented identity is already a matter of concern in postcolonial theory (for example, Dirks, ed. 1992), there is a particular danger when we apply newly formulated models anachronistically to archaeological contexts. It is just this problem that concerns many of the authors in this book.

A more subtle bias also pervades the study of ancient colonies—namely, the deference paid to intellectual traditions whose motivations and practices are expressed through documents. Written sources are of immeasurable value, but we need to be wary of systematically interpreting past colonization through Rome-colored glasses. As Alcock points out here, the term "colony" and its initial conception derive from the Roman experience, but there is no reason that linguistic or other precedence should confer the status of a model against which to compare all other situations. Neither should we expect the relationships among the various media that express identity, power, and history to translate neatly from one colonial situation to another. It seems especially problematic to transpose Classical models to colonial encounters where intellectual life was maintained orally or represented visually in ways other than documents, as was the Andean case. Comparisons are essential, but not at the expense of privileging one historical context over another.

The modern Andean reaction to European (Spanish) colonization, colonial policies, and intellectual dominance has taken its own path. Explicitly postcolonial theory has made few inroads into the analysis of pre- and early Colonial power relationships. Instead, the dominant interpretive viewpoints remain marxist or derive from a self-contained concept termed *el mundo andino* (the Andean world). From the latter perspective, Andean societies were so distinctive in prehispanic times that external comparisons are either superficial or misleading. Although I do not share that view (otherwise I would not be writing this paper), the Andean situation does admit some unusual circumstances. Most importantly, the Inkas did not have a writing system that we have been able to decipher, nor did anyone who knew an independent Tawantinsuyu ever put a Spanish quill to paper. The Inkas instead kept precise registers on knotted cords called *khipu* and also used tapestries, painted panels, and decorated poles as visual mnemonics. Together, these media provided information for historical narratives, census records, astronomical observations, tax records, and other ends. Although recent work is gaining insight into some of the codes (for example, Ascher and Ascher 1981; Salomon 2001; Quilter and Urton 2002; Urton 2003), the khipu undoubtedly contained more information than we can currently interpret. Their complexities acknowledged, these instruments were apparently still tools used to add specifics to memorized accounts. In Cuzco, the royal histories were kept as oral traditions by court savants called *amautas* and knot-record masters called *khipu kamayuq*, who recited chronicles tailored to the interests of the audience (Rostworowski 1999:vii–ix). There may have been several different genres of Inka narrative, such as genealogies and life histories (Julien 2000), which were not well distinguished by the Spanish chroniclers. Crucially, the narratives that were passed on to the Spaniards seem to have followed structures of power and space as much as temporal sequence.

The early Spanish authors who put accounts of Tawantinsuyu to paper thus had to sort through competing native versions, their own interpretations, and differing notions of the uses of the past, not to mention translators and scribes. Since credibility and power were inexorably linked in the intellectual climate of the time, it is not surprising that information from the eldest Inka aristocrats was valued most highly, whereas conflicting reports by lesser witnesses were dismissed. We also need to remember that the histories and logic of imperial policy that are available now were initially intended for an audience of the powerful, either Inka (oral) or Spanish (written). The idealized portraits of the Inka past were designed to persuade a narrow audience of the legitimacy of a particular cause, whether a royal family's claim to the throne (for example, Callapiña et al. 1974; Betanzos 1996) or Spanish righteousness in replacing a misbegotten tyranny (for example, Sarmiento 1960).

We therefore need to cast a wary eye on Cuzco's claims to controlling all aspects of subject life, even in state-sponsored colonies. The historians' resourceful response to this situation has been an emphasis on the study of provincial documents, especially court claims for resources sought by colonists, indigenes, and descendants of deportees. The picture of colonization that has been built up is still piecemeal, as it depends on the fortuitous preservation, discovery, and publication of particular documents. Nonetheless, the sources reinforce the view that the Inkas combined strategic resettlement in trouble spots and along the frontiers with tactical relocations in locales that yielded specific resources or were of cultural import.

Archaeologists, by and large, have been less compelling in asking questions about the partiality of messages embedded in the Andean material record than historians have been about documents. Even so, encouraging signs can be found in studies of mortuary remains and iconography (for example, Alva and Donnan 1994; Donnan and McClelland 1999) and the built landscape (Bauer 1998), which are providing insights into constructions of social identity as well as claims to power and history. In the built environment, the Inkas expressed their power mostly through infrastructure and practice, not through propaganda-laden statuary or reliefs, inscriptions extolling grand deeds, or monuments celebrating individual rulers. The scarcity of human representation in Inka material culture stands in marked contrast to the oral histories, which unabashedly attributed the realm's very existence and nature to heroic and ingenious rulers. In Tawantinsuyu, the massive plazas, ceremonial platforms, modular architecture, and ashlar masonry of provincial centers, along with the road system itself, speak to a concern for conveying messages of power to a polyglot, illiterate populace (Gasparini and Margolies 1980; Hyslop 1984, 1990). Access to the colorful Inka textiles, polychrome pottery, and other portable media conferred parallel messages of hierarchy and status within it (C. Morris 1991, 1995). Altogether, the built environment, the practice of power, and the narrative representations of Inka rule complemented one another, rather than repeating precisely the same message.

Concerning colonies specifically, we may ask which elements of the material record were a consequence of the deliberate or incidental imprint of which sociopolitical group. How did the built environment and material culture reproduce native ethnic styles (colonist or indigene) or impart messages of state jurisdiction? The documentary sources provide hints of both imperial and subject practice at work. The chronicler Cieza (1967:74), for instance, wrote that colonists were granted gold and silver bracelets, woolen and feathered clothing, women, and various other privileges, perhaps to help alleviate the pain of relocation. We also read that the colonists took their own tools and household goods to their new villages. Cobo (1979:196) added that each "nation" was required by the Inkas to wear its own distinctive garb; headgear was the most identifying feature. If he is correct—and textiles were the material medium in which messages were most obviously embedded—then much of the evidence that we could use to recognize identity and hierarchy is lost to us.

Despite the loss of many organics, an approach that emphasizes everyday residues (see Deagan 1995b; Stein 1999b, this volume) holds great promise for the future study of Andean colonies. Unfortunately, we rarely have the baseline information on dietary preferences, butchering practices, house design or masonry, tool design, and other elements of daily life needed to allow us to associate origin points with transplanted communities. Instead, we must rely on markers such as ceramic types that are culturally out of place but not simply trade pieces (Lorandi 1984; Spurling 1992; V. I. Williams 1996; D'Altroy and Williams 1998), or head deformation practices (I. Baffi, personal communication 1999). The relative lack of distinguishing ceramic evidence for mitmaq settlements is in itself an intriguing piece of negative evidence, since it suggests that most colonists did not enjoy a special privilege of hosting state-supported feasts (see below). In any event, we are a long way from clearly defining the archaeological markers of state colonies. The following case studies will illustrate our current state of knowledge and, I hope, provide some directions into investigating colonization in the future.

CASE STUDIES OF COLONIZATION
State Farms

One of the tenets of Inka rule was that the resources that sustained the state and temple economy were separate from those of their subjects. In order to ensure a steady supply of food, beer (*chicha*), cloth, and other supplies, officials set aside lands for state farms and pastures in every province where it was feasible. Most farms were located near provincial centers, but some also lay in favorable locales for particular crops, especially maize and coca leaf (fig. 9.4). The lands dedicated to supporting state and Sun (religion) activities often lay near one another, but their products were stored and administered separately. The farms were cultivated by both *corvée* workers as part of their rotating labor duties and multitudes of colonists.

The farms at Cochabamba, Bolivia, were among the most extensive in the empire. During a tour of the realm after his coronation, Wayna Qhapaq ordered the western part of the valley vacated. Witnesses reported to the Lic. Polo that 14,000 workers came in to cultivate the fields, mostly from the adjacent altiplano (fig. 9.5). Among them were Quillacas, Chilques, Chiles, Collas from Azángaro, Uros and Soras from Paria, and Caracaras, Chichas, Charkas, and Yamparaes from the southern altiplano. Other documents mention the Condes from Condesuyo and Icas from the Peruvian south coast (Wachtel 1982; Espinoza 1993). Polo's witnesses said that both permanent colonists and seasonal laborers were present but did not explain how many people lived there year-round. The farms were divided into seventy-seven narrow strips that transected the valley's ecozones. Workers were assigned specific strips whose margins they cultivated for their own use, supplementing the produce of separate plots. Polo was told that the farms were used to grow maize (more likely a full crop complex) for the Inkas' armies. Archaeological evidence for an intensive Inka occupation is found

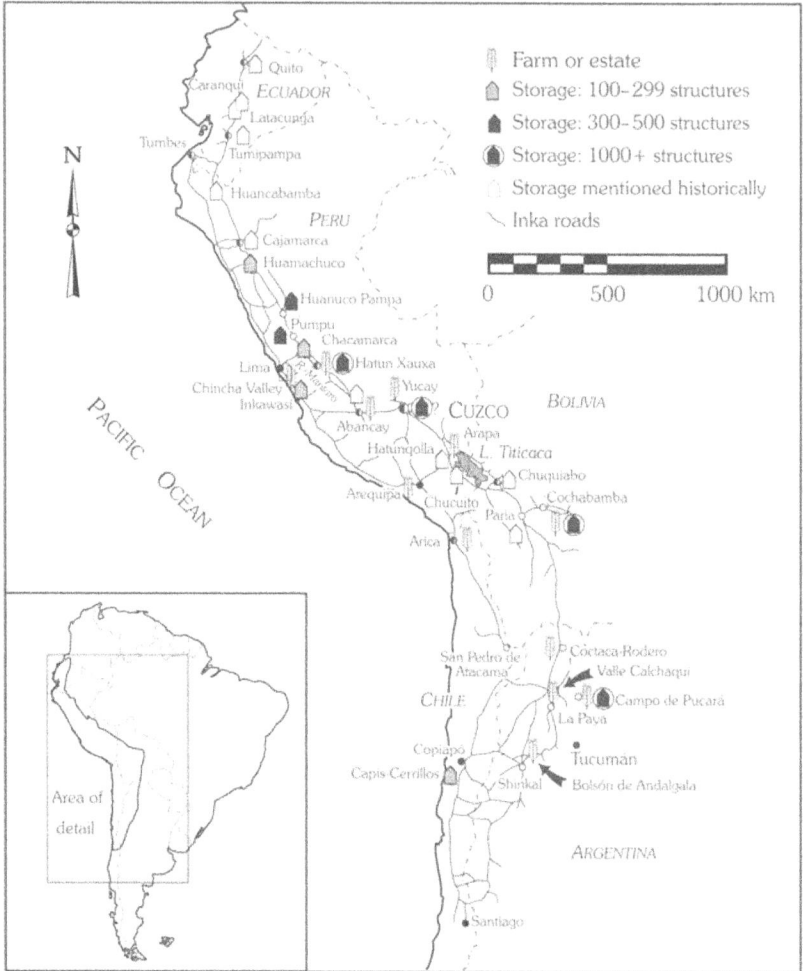

FIGURE 9.4

Distribution of major state, state church, and estate farms, and major storage complexes identified archaeologically or mentioned in early documents.

throughout the valley (Céspedes Paz 1982; Gyarmati and Varga 1999). In addition to more than a hundred known Inka-era sites, the Inkas built 2,400 storehouses at Cotapachi, where the produce was stored before being shipped to Paria, Cuzco, and elsewhere. The colonists were responsible for maintaining the storehouses on top of their agricultural duties. Despite the scale of the farm and the complete

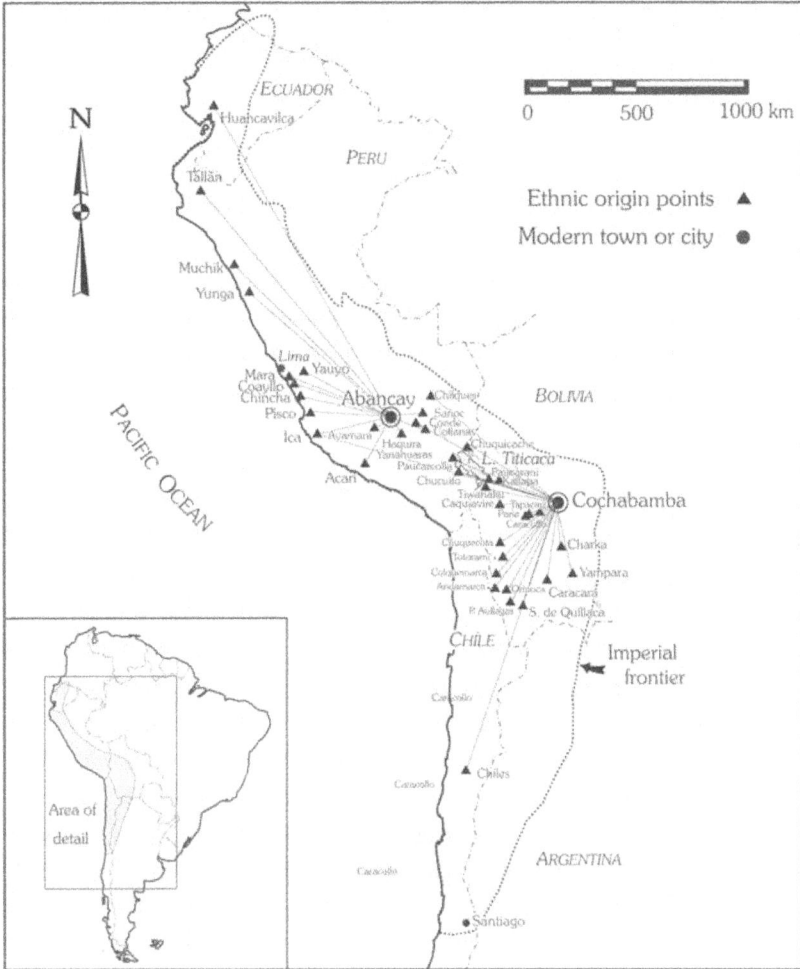

FIGURE 9.5

Movements of ethnic groups to staff major state farms at Abancay and Cochabamba,
founded by Wayna Qhapaq to provision his military efforts.

makeover of the valley's ethnic composition, the material evidence that
has been identified as part the enterprise is marked by architecture and
ceramics in the Inka, not subject, style.

Other farms were also dedicated to military uses, including some at
Arica (RGI 1965 [1557–1586]: v. 183, p. 338), Arequipa (La Lone and La
Lone 1987), and Abancay (Espinoza 1973). Like those in Cochabamba,

the farms in the warm western Abancay Valley were founded by Wayna Qhapaq to support his wars in the north. Rather than maize, the Abancay farms were dedicated to coca, cotton, pepper, and fruits. The Inkas claimed the best bottomlands for themselves and made hillslope fields available to the colonists brought in to work them. Members of at least thirteen different ethnic groups were brought in to staff the Abancay farms permanently (fig. 9.5). If a family died out, another was brought in to keep the number of households at a total of one thousand (Espinoza 1973; Lorandi and Rodríguez n.d.).

Extensive Inka farms have also been identified archaeologically in the Upper Mantaro Valley, Peru, and in northwest Argentina. In the Upper Mantaro, the prime farmlands within about 5 kilometers of the provincial center at Hatun Xauxa, and within 15 kilometers down valley, are virtually bereft of villages. The Inka-era sites that are present contain many farming tools but little evidence of other kinds of production, in sharp contrast to communities farther afield. In this same area lie thirty-three storage facilities—the largest known concentration in the empire. We know that several colonist groups were brought into the general region (for example, Yauyos, Tarama, Huamachucos, Chachapoyas, Collaguas), whose ceramic styles are easily distinguished from the local Wanka styles, and more than 125 sites belonging to the Inka era have been recorded. Nonetheless, at least three intensive surface surveys have failed to positively identify a single mitmaq settlement (Browman 1970; Parsons, Matos, and Hastings, field notes 1976–77; Earle et al. 1987; D'Altroy 1992).

At Coctaca-Rodero, Argentina, a massive, unfinished terraced field system covers about 6 square kilometers on the piedmont (3,700 meters) just below the altiplano (Albeck and Scattolin 1991; Albeck 1992–1993). Large tracts may have also been farmed at the Campo de Pucará, in the Lerma Valley of the eastern piedmont (Boman 1908; Fock 1961; González 1983). The positioning of the Lerma farms is revealing, since they lie well below the string of Inka military sites in the mountains. Their location suggests that the lower valleys were considered peaceful enough that they could be farmed with little danger from the mobile bands who lived on the eastern plains. These lowland farms fit the notion of a frontier colonization strategy better than most situations, but their creation is probably better seen as part of a larger picture in which ethnic groups were moved about to develop resources wherever they could be exploited. Unfortunately, we do not yet have good evidence for the ethnic composition of the farmworkers in each of those areas, but it is noteworthy that the only settlements in the midst of the Coctaca field system are marked by Inka polychrome ceramics, not other styles (Nielsen 1996).

In each of these cases, there is substantial evidence for an intensive imperial investment of labor in land improvements, provincial installations, or storage facilities. Even so, what has yet to be documented in any of these locales—to the best of my knowledge—is an archaeological signature for any of the ethnic groups who were resettled there. Instead, Inka-era occupations are identified on the basis of Inka ceramics and architecture, not ethnic material culture that appears out of place.

Islands of Artisans: Weavers, Smiths, and Potters

To meet an insatiable demand for craft goods, the Inkas set entire communities of colonists to work, making their products for state disposition (fig. 9.6). Many artisans were drawn from locales with a reputation for particular skills—metalsmiths from the coast, woodworkers from the eastern slopes, and weavers and masons from the altiplano. For close to two millennia, the coastal metalsmiths were the most accomplished in the Andes. Recognizing their skills, the Inkas transferred artisans en masse from Chimor and Pachacamac to Cuzco to fashion sumptuary items for aristocrats and temples. Regrettably, most of those objects met a fate in the Spanish forges as part of Atawallpa's ransom or during the sack of Cuzco in 1533. The scant documentary evidence that has been preserved suggests that the Inkas treated the smiths much as they treated any of their highland colonists. That is, they gave them lands upon which to support themselves and put them to work using materials from state supplies. That the smiths had been craft specialists and not farmers seems to have had no effect on state policy—the Inkas provided resources, not sustenance, to their colonists (Espinoza 1983).

Among the newly founded artisan colonies were weaving and potting towns that contained as many as 1,000 households. The etnías of highland Peru contributed many weavers. In a petition to Viceroy

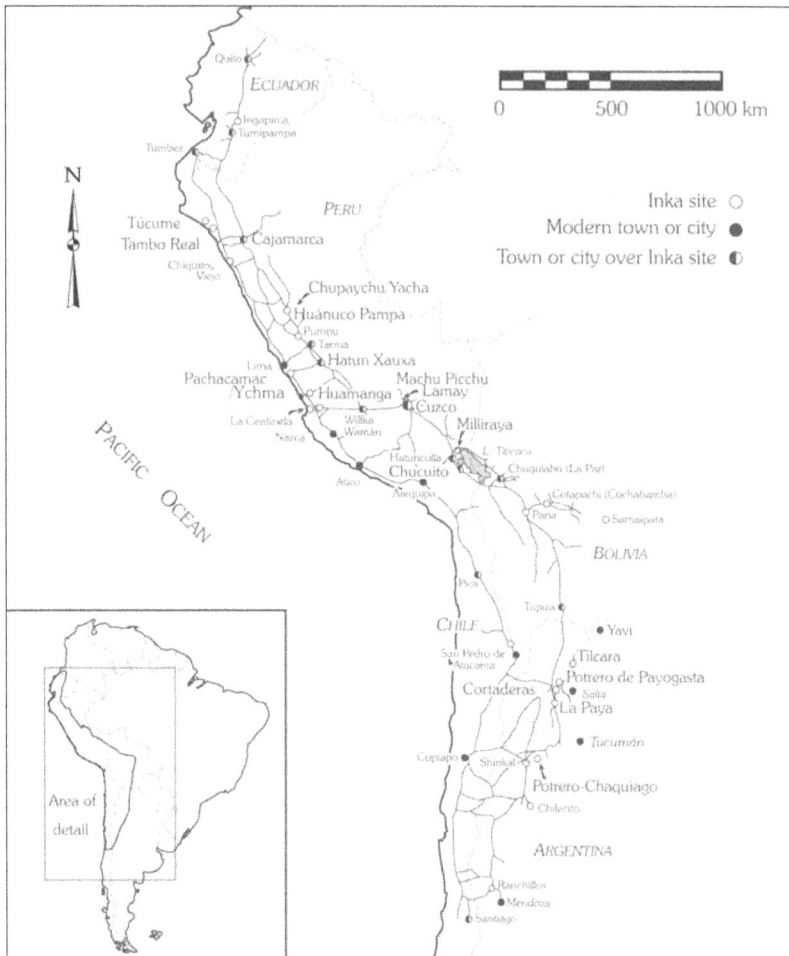

Figure 9.6

Distribution of major colonies of artisans named in early documents, resettled by the Inkas to produce ceramics, textiles, metals, and other objects.

Toledo for aristocratic privileges, for example, one Wanka lord claimed that an ancestor had supervised 500 weavers just north of Cuzco, where Wayna Qhapaq had an estate (Toledo 1940:71). In 1549, Chupachu lords from Huánuco also testified that 400 of their 4,108 enumerated households had been assigned to work as tapestry cloth weavers. The best-known artisan colony, called Milliraya, lay just northeast of Lake

Titicaca, but other weaving towns were founded elsewhere on the altiplano, because of the region's textile traditions and great herds (fig. 9.7; Diez de San Miguel 1964:106; Julien 1988, 1993; Spurling 1992:234–36).[4] The Milliraya enclave contained two neighboring settlements, one with either 100 or 300 potters and the other with 1,000 tapestry cloth weavers (Espinoza 1987; Murra 1978). By founding the enclave along the border between two political divisions while taking lands from only one, the Inkas nourished local tensions with an eye to stifling an alliance that had threatened their rule a few decades earlier (Spurling 1992). The artisans were drawn from the nearby Qolla, an etnía that resisted Inka rule, but were supervised by a Lupaqa governor, an early Inka ally. As Spurling (1992) observes, this provided one way in which particular groups could be rewarded or punished for their history of relations with Cuzco. Each town received irrigated fields, pastures, lakeshore lands, and lowland maize fields to support themselves. The weavers were installed to help outfit Wayna Qhapaq's northern campaigns, but the potters said they distributed their products around the north end of the lake. Spurling's archaeological studies show that the potters made vessels in a variety of styles, both Inka polychromes and local Qolla types.

An alternative approach was used for the enclave in Cajamarca, Peru, populated by ceramists from towns on Peru's north coast (Espinoza 1970; see D'Altroy, Lorandi, and Williams 1998). The potters were organized into a census unit of 100 households called Yanayaco, a word that implies that they had lost their affiliation with their original kin groups. Placed under the jurisdiction of an Inka lord by Thupa Inka Yupanki, they received lands for their own sustenance, on which they constructed canals and excavated sunken fields to cultivate *totora* for roofing material and for fuel. When Inka rule collapsed, most of the potters returned to their homelands, but some stayed put in an effort to retain the lands that the state had granted them. The local lord contested their claim and tried to integrate the artisans into his domain. A series of conflicts ensued, with the result that the indigenous populace forcibly settled the potters near their own towns, claiming that only the colonists knew how to make pottery. The quarrel was ended through negotiations that interlocked the groups through successive marriages.

A colony of potters in Catamarca province, Argentina, provides our

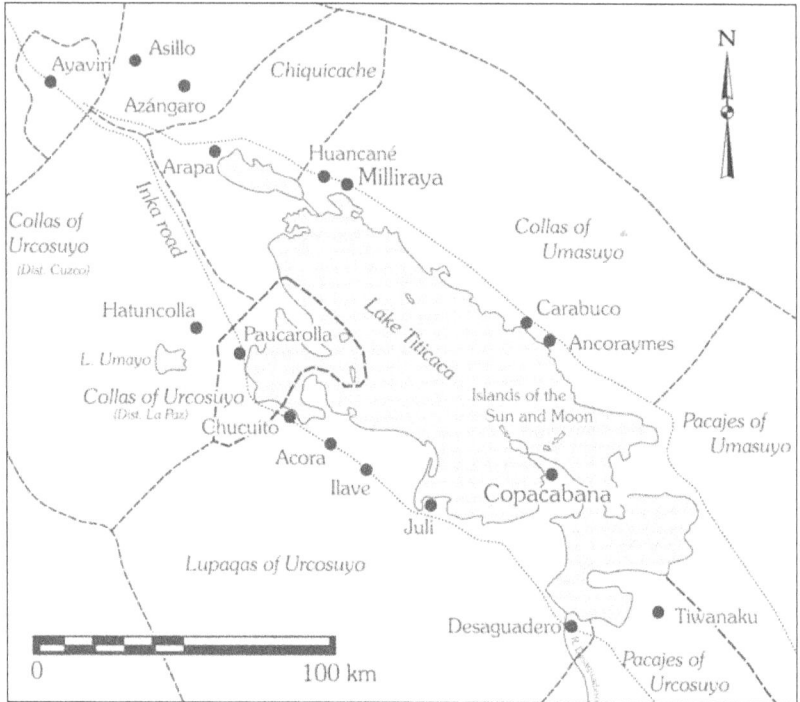

FIGURE 9.7

The Lake Titicaca basin as organized into provinces under Inka rule, showing the craft center at Milliraya and the sanctuary at Copacabana. (Adapted from Julien 1983)

best archaeological evidence for transplantation of artisans for state ends. The key site in this case is Potrero-Chaquiago, a small Inka installation that probably lay at an administrative level below the provincial capital called Shinkal. Its five sectors are distributed over only 4.3 hectares, but it has yielded considerable evidence for production of textiles and ceramics (Williams and Lorandi 1986; V. I. Williams 1996). Like many of the sites in the south, Potrero-Chaquiago was apparently designed to be agriculturally self-sustaining, to judge by the new terraces and canals that watered fields near the settlement. In an initial study, Lorandi (1984) used XRF analysis to show that two ceramic styles (Famabalasto Black on Red, Averías) that appeared to be from the eastern lowlands, hundreds of kilometers away, were actually manufactured using clays from Potrero-Chaquiago. She inferred that the pots had been made by lowland potters transplanted to the highlands, where they made pottery both in the Inka polychrome style and in the styles of their homelands, just as the Qolla did.[5] The archaeological evidence was paralleled by documentary sources, which said that the residents of the Tucumán region of the eastern lowlands appealed to the Inkas for protection from their marauding neighbors, the Lule. The Inka struck an alliance with the Tucumanos, dispersing them among various locales in the southern Andes and granting them a privileged status (Lorandi 1988).

Frontier Colonies

The Inkas created scores of loyal garrisons by founding military installations along the frontier and well inside it (Espinoza 1975, 1980). Even though some garrisons (for example, at Cajamarca, Peru, and Pocona, Bolivia) were founded by Pachakuti, both documents and archaeology suggest that permanent forts were generally a late phenomenon, most highly developed under Wayna Qhapaq's rule. Polo's (1916:98–99) list of the regions where the Inkas conducted warfare corresponds neatly to both the locations of known forts and Wayna Qhapaq's campaigns. In broad strokes, those areas include the frontier north of Quito, Ecuador, and the perimeter running southward from Inkallajta, Bolivia, all the way to Cerro Grande del Inga, south of Santiago, Chile. The northern campaigns were sustained by a great variety of ethnic groups, among them 5,000 Qolla (out of a total population of 20,000) who never returned home. Several groups were professionalized, most prominently the Chachapoyas and Kañaris, longtime Inka foes in the northern Andes who were finally subdued in the early sixteenth century. As much as half of their populace was dispersed throughout the empire as permanent military personnel (Espinoza 1980; Murra 1986; Schjellerup 1997). The Charkas, Karakaras, Chuis, and Chichas of the Bolivian altiplano also claimed that their service to the state lay exclusively in their military capacities, although those claims may have been exaggerated to escape obligations that the Spaniards sought to transfer from the Inkas to themselves (Wachtel 1982; Murra 1986:53–54).

Despite the garrisons' importance, Tawantinsuyu did not have a fixed border defended by a hard line of military posts in 1532. The forts often lay at high-elevation, retrenched positions, well behind farms, mines, and other outposts in the lowlands. C. Morris (1988) points out that most areas lay at or near a frontier at some point and that incorporation was an irregular process (see Dillehay and Netherly 1988). The forts in northern Chile and Argentina's northern Calchaquí Valley, for example, were probably front lines at one point that eventually lay 1,000 kilometers behind the empire's southern limits. Most frontier fortresses were neither large enough nor manned with personnel adequate to preclude all potential incursions by outside forces. Instead, they seem to have been designed to deter or control traffic through key natural points of transit, especially mountain passes. Pambamarca (Ecuador), Incallajta (Bolivia), Cortaderas and Pucará de Andalgalá (Argentina), and Cerro del Inga (Chile) were all situated in such locations. The complex of fourteen fortified hilltops at Pambamarca, 32 kilometers northeast of Quito, was by far the most concentrated array of strongholds in one region (Plaza Schuller 1976; 1980; Hyslop 1990:165–73). Salomon (1986:163) suggests that the site was likely the historical settlement of El Quinche, where the Inkas installed colonists from half a dozen Peruvian and Ecuadorian societies, including the Angaráes, Kañari, Wanka, Ichingui, Tacuri, and Yauyos. Among the most important fortified sites east of the altiplano were Incallajta, Pocona, Batanes, and Incahuasi. Pucará de Andalgalá and Pucará de las Pavas are impressive Inka citadels in the Bolsón de Andalgalá, and numerous other forts were also built or coopted (Raffino 1983, 1993). The Chilean forts at Cerro del Inga, Chena, and Angostura stand out as local sites at the southern margins of the empire that were taken over by the state (Planella and Stehberg 1994).

Like other state-sponsored settlements manned by colonists, the fortified garrisons generally bear the markings of Inka material culture, rather than those of subject groups. Permanent Inka forts usually consisted of walled enclosures with broad open areas and spare architecture, set on hilltops or at the crest of steep slopes. Many had several concentric walls, moats, and revetments. The largest forts each encompassed no more than about 10 hectares, which limited the number of people who could seek refuge, but kept the perimeters relatively short. The most important internal architecture consisted of a limited number of residential structures and the ever-present ceremonial platform.

Recent work by Alconini (2001) illustrates that intensive survey and close work at the forts are likely to yield useful insights, however. She has been able to show that inner forts along the eastern Bolivian border were designed in the Inka style, but contained ceramics in the Pacajes style from the altiplano south of Lake Titicaca, a region from which colonists were reportedly dispatched to the forts. Farther out toward the lowlands lay a zone of acculturation, in which the Inkas established a presence but apparently employed a lighter touch. This outer fringe seems to have been intended to both provide a degree of security and reach out to mobile plains societies, broadly known as Guaraníes. Alconini found that the forts and material culture of this zone show more evidence of subject styles from the borderlands, including the vessels used for hospitality that fueled political relations. This evidence parallels that recorded historically for Tucumán (Lorandi 1988), reported above, suggesting that particular ethnic groups who struck favorable bargains with the Inkas were only lightly supervised.

Huánuco: A Province Partially Converted to a Royal Estate

The Huánuco region of central Peru provides an exceptional opportunity to study Inka relations with subject etnías, because of its remarkable archaeological and documentary records. The provincial center, called Huánuco Pampa, is the grandest provincial center in Tawantinsuyu (Morris and Thompson 1985). It was one of six sites called "New Cuzcos," built in the conceptual image of the capital (see below). The city's great central plaza measured 550 by 350 meters and contained an ashlar platform (32 by 48 meters at its base) from which officials could preside over state ceremonies. The imperial highway entered the plaza on its southeast corner and exited to the northwest, mimicking the layout of Cuzco. Although the city could have housed about 15,000 residents at one time, Morris and Thompson suggest that only a fraction of that was present at any moment, including administrators, permanent service personnel, the maidens' order (*aqllakuna*), and workers serving out their rotating labor duties.

By a stroke of luck, two Spanish inspections of the area have been preserved, dating to 1549 and 1562. They provide detailed information on the societies and resources of the warm lands east of the center, showing that at least five different ethnic groups had lived in the province before the advent of imperial rule (Ortiz de Zúñiga 1967, 1972; see Murra 1972; Hyslop 1984:68–71; Grosboll 1993; Julien 1993). The Inkas undertook a resettlement and administrative reform that restructured the social landscape, while leaving local lords in charge of decimal units of 1,000 or fewer households. Julien (1993:210) summarizes the data: "First of all, 1,110 of the 4,108 Chupachos [sic] households were in Cuzco. Another 580 resided out of the province on a full-time basis. Another 918 were out of the province on at least a temporary basis, including the 500 assigned to army service. Those who remained, except perhaps the 500 assigned to do agricultural service, were permanently relocated to specialized communities within Chupachos territory." Two hundred Inkas from Cuzco were also resettled in the eastern sector of the province, to ensure security and gain access to gold and other forest products. Shortly before 1532, the emperor Waskhar claimed the Chupachu populace as a personal estate, exemplifying how human and other resources ostensibly belonging to the state could be alienated for the emperor's personnel benefit.

Despite its impact, there is little material imprint of Inka rule away from Huánuco Pampa and smaller facilities along the highway. Grosboll's (1993) field studies show that the Inkas invested most heavily in the northeastern area, where the Cuzqueñan mitmaqkuna were settled. This area, well suited to growing the prestige crops of maize and coca, contains the region's most elaborate canal and terrace systems. Thompson's studies of local villages found only one (Ichu) that yielded much architecture imitative of Inka canons or other material culture in the Inka style, probably because it was the home of Paucar Guaman, the paramount lord in the early Colonial era. Elsewhere, the Inka material presence at the village level is limited to a few structures and ceramics (Thompson 1967; Morris and Thompson 1985).

The Ideological Imprint

In addition to their economic and military purposes, the Inkas used colonies as a way of making an ideological claim to an animate landscape that housed oracular gods, ethnic ancestors, and spirits in mountain peaks, springs, and stones. The heart of Cuzco, Tawantinsuyu's sacred capital, accommodated the empire's royalty, aristocracy, religious institutions, and their retainers in ashlar palaces and temples. Surrounding the city's core were a dozen suburban neighborhoods that housed members of ethnic groups arranged to mimic provincial geography, to the end of creating an ethnic microcosm of the realm. Cayoache, for example, a neighborhood on the south side of the city, held the kin groups who had migrated northward with the Inkas in a legendary journey from the Inkas' origin cave at Pacariqtambo. Similarly, the Chachapoyas and Kañari, who hailed from northern Peru and Ecuador, were installed on the northwest side of the city. Regrettably, we do not have a complete list of Cuzco's ethnic composition at hand, nor a systematic archaeological study that would allow us to identify the ethnic groups' quarters (see Rowe 1967).

Just as they brought the empire to the capital, the Inkas exported Cuzco to the provinces. In addition to naming mountains elsewhere after the peaks overlooking Cuzco, the Inkas founded at least half a dozen other settlements called "New Cuzcos" that conceptually replicated the capital and its major shrines. Among them were Huánuco Pampa (see above), Inkawasi (Peru's coastal Cañete Valley), Hatunqolla (Bolivia), Charkas (Sucre, Bolivia), and Tumipampa, the empire's second capital in southern Ecuador (Salomon 1986:172–86; Idrovo 1988). Not only did Tumipampa share toponyms with the imperial capital (Arriaga 1968:24), but the heart of each site was laid out between two rivers that flowed northwest to southeast; one watercourse was named Huatanay in each city. Over time, the Inkas transformed a military occupation into an island of Inka culture through social engineering. The resettlement program of the central-southern Ecuadorian highlands was intensive, as the ethnic composition was altered as much as any part of the empire. The native Kañari, who had first vigorously resisted the Inka occupation and then sided with Waskhar's losing side in the final dynastic war, were ravaged by the victorious Atawallpa. During his visit some twenty years later, Cieza reported that the Kañari male populace had been almost totally erased by relocation or liquidation, so that there were fifteen times as many women as men in their land. The documents suggest that even before then, the area around Tumipampa had been reformed through installation of colonists from the south (Truhan 1998). Thousands of warrior-colonists had been settled in the area—perhaps as many as 5,000 Qolla alone (Murra 1986).

In political terms, what is most interesting about the colonies is that the decimal administrative hierarchy was found primarily among mit-maqkuna colonies, not among the native societies (Salomon 1986). This practice highlights one way in which the colonists could play a special role as political agents of the state.

Although the region has not been studied as intensively as other parts of the empire, the known archaeological remains in highland Ecuador again appear to be inconsistent with the intensity and character of Inka rule described in the sources (for example, Idrovo 1988; Hyslop 1990). The known sites associated with the Inka presence were dedicated to military activities (for example, the Pambamarca forts), transportation and communication (roads), ceremony (Ingapirca), and royal residence (Tumipampa). What has yet to be recorded are the sites we would expect to see from a radical reformation of the landscape through ethnic resettlement, especially agricultural and craft production sites, or military colonies with clear ethnic makers. Even residential sites dominated by Cuzco Inka polychromes are scarce.

For a final example of a colony that served as an ideological statement, we may turn to Copacabana, a peninsula of land projecting into Lake Titicaca, and the adjacent Islands of the Sun and the Moon. In Inka origin myths, the islands and the lake itself were a site of incomparable sanctity. According to one common account, the Creator God Wiraqocha caused the Sun, Moon, and stars to arise out of the lake (Molina 1988:52), whereas another legend said that the first Inka ancestor, Manqo Qhapaq, traveled underground from the lake to his origin place (Pacariqtambo, or "Inn of Dawn"; see above). In the imperial era, the Inkas vastly elaborated the local tradition of sun worship at the Island of the Sun (Bandelier 1910; Hyslop 1990; Bauer and Stanish 2001). They erected a ceremonial complex on the peninsula and islands that included a ritual pathway guarded by various gates and a series of facilities on the mainland and the islands. The most sacred location lay at a large sandstone bedrock (Titikala) on the Island of the Sun, where the sun rose.

In 1621, the cleric Ramos Gavilán (1988:93–95) wrote that the Inkas had created a colony at Copacabana populated by members of forty-two different ethnic groups from around the empire, among whose duties were maintaining the shrines on the islands (fig. 9.8).

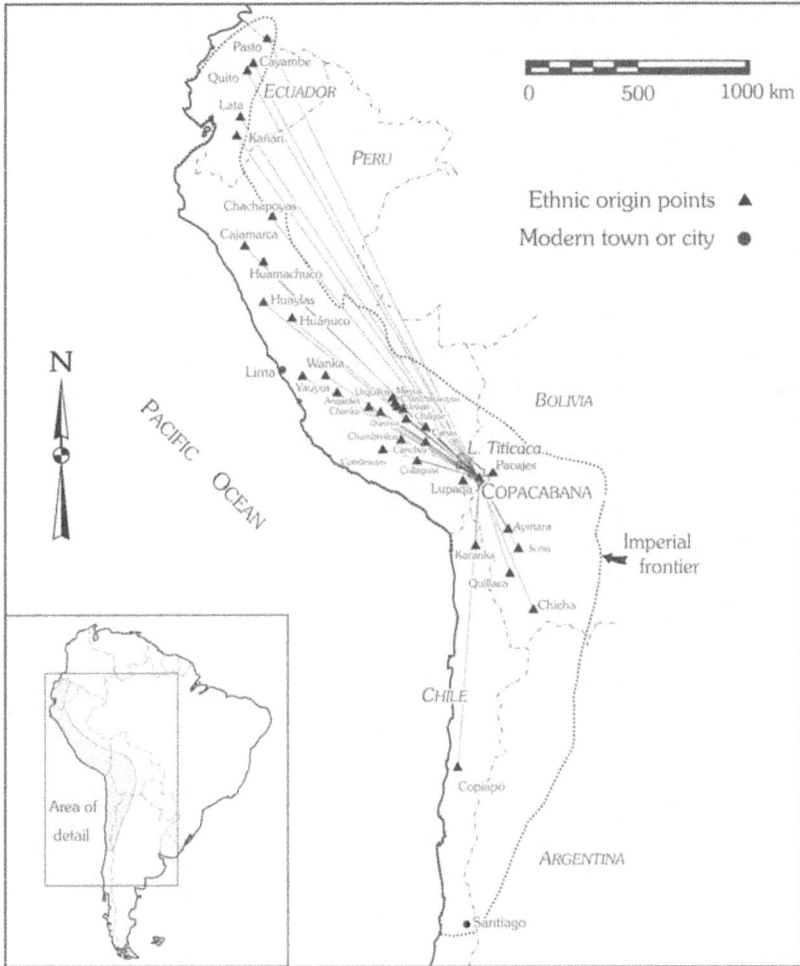

FIGURE 9.8

Identifiable locations from which colonists were drawn to settle the Inka sanctuary at Copacabana.

Many came from the central part of the empire, but some were transported from the farthest margins. The Pasto, for example, resided originally in the highlands that now form the border between Ecuador and Colombia. Their inclusion as part of the sanctuary's resident colony shows that the Inkas were tinkering with its composition in the last decade or so before the Spanish invasion. Other documents suggest that there may have been as many as 2,000 mitmaqkuna living at Copacabana in the time of the Inka. They served on a rotating basis for two years at a time, accompanied by a contingent of the women's holiest order, the *mamakuna* (Bauer and Stanish 2001:236–40).

To judge from more than a century's archaeology, the material evidence for Inka-era occupations at the sanctuary and on the islands is primarily, although not exclusively, the regional variant of imperial Inka. There are numerous ashlar structures and terraces on the islands, along with several cemeteries that were looted long ago but have still yielded a variety of Inka-style metal and ceramic objects. Studying the issue of multiethnicity at Copacabana and the islands is complicated by the modern town that overlies most of the Inka settlement. Even so, a full survey of the islands recently conducted by Bauer and Stanish (2001) sheds some light on the Inka-era occupation. They have been able to show, for instance, that the islands' occupants were removed by the Inkas, while the density of occupation was markedly increased. The site called Pilco Kayma built on the Island of the Sun during the Inka occupation mixes Inka and local ethnic architectonic elements. They suggest that the hybridization is a consequence of the use of local colonist labor on a state-sponsored project, whereas the extensive presence of Lupaqa-style ceramics was a consequence of the resettlement of members of this favored ethnic group on the island (Bauer and Stanish 2001:155, 173). Despite their extensive field research, the ethnic complexity of the sanctuary would have been well-nigh impossible to recognize from known archaeological remains.

CONCLUDING COMMENTS

Colonization in the Inka empire had many layers, as it was practiced by the state, the official religion, Inka aristocrats, ethnic lords, and local communities alike. Establishment of the colonies accomplished military, political, economic, social, and ideological goals. Despite the considerable attention that has been paid to the practice from a historical viewpoint on a case-by-case basis, no comprehensive study of colonization has yet been undertaken. As one who has wrestled with the problem intermittently for years, I can understand why. There is simultaneously too much and too little information. The documentary information is often piecemeal, and there is a remarkable lack of concordance between the historical and archaeological evidence. At present, we cannot be sure how much of that is attributable to incompatibility between expressed and actual practices, lack of systematic research, or failure to recognize the material fingerprints of colonization on the landscape.

The main advances into the subject have been made through analysis of Spanish inspections and native lawsuits before the Spanish courts and, more modestly, through archaeology. Depending on the institutional genesis of the colonies, the scale and goals of colonization varied appreciably. Broadly speaking, it seems safe to infer that rationales for colonization were initially weighted toward economic and offensive military reasons and became increasingly complicated by political, ideological, and defensive military concerns as the empire developed. The situation at Copacabana underscores a pattern that we have seen emerging from the other cases and that is most apparent in the final case discussed above. That is, the more important the colony was to state or state church activities—or to put it another way, the more directly integrated personnel were into the state institutions—the less likely it is that we may be able to recognize their ethnic signatures in the material record. In those cases where colonists served state interests but were left largely on their own for sustenance and maintained strong links with their homelands, such as along the Bolivian frontier, the more likely it seems that we will be able to recognize archaeological evidence for their places of origins. In addition, the more heavily involved the colonists were in making the goods that form the archaeological record—especially pottery—the more likely it is that we will recognize their presence.

The limitations of the current evidence notwithstanding, there is still hope for making some real advances into colonization archaeologically, if we are thoughtful about the genesis of the material record and meticulous in our methods. The Inkas thought it desirable to emphasize the identity of individuals according to their places of origin for political and symbolic ends, and thus we can see them both historically and in the material detritus of their lives. The best archaeological examples may be seen in the burials at the royal estate of Machu Picchu and at two coastal sites: Pachacamac, an oracular center of supreme importance for two millennia before and under Inka rule; and

Puruchuco, a burial ground just outside Lima. At Pachacamac, the Inkas built five complexes, including a house of the holy women (mamakuna) and a shrine on the pyramid of the Sun (Uhle 1903). At select locations within the sacred areas, such as at the gate to the main plaza, the Inkas interred young women apparently in sacrifice with clear markers of ethnic identity, most obviously ceramics (Cornejo 2000). Similar ethnically distinctive pottery and cranial treatments have also been recovered from tombs at Machu Picchu (Verano 2003; Burger and Salazar 2004). At Puruchuco, a newly discovered site with well over one thousand Inka-era burials, natural preservation has conserved the ethnically diagnostic headgear of many individuals, along with the head deformations created by many Andean societies (Cock 2002; Haun 2004). These practices may provide some of our best avenues to recognize the diversity of ethnic relocation, although the scale and rationales would need to be confirmed through complementary sources of information. Application of bioarchaeological methods, such as morphometric measurements (Haun 2004), DNA analysis, and bone chemistry, also look to pay dividends, but considerable work needs to be done before we can associate mortuary remains from colonies with points of origin to any great extent. Overall, we do not yet have an ethnic map of Andean material culture or biological markers that would allow us to move much farther forward on this issue, but the detailed work that is being done on several fronts holds considerable promise for the future, an encouraging note on which to close.

Acknowledgements

This paper is a distillation and extension of materials I have discussed elsewhere (see D'Altroy 2001). I thank Gil Stein and the School of American Research for the opportunity to participate in the conference that produced this volume. I am especially grateful to the other conference participants for their insightful comments, which helped me to focus my thoughts on the issues that this paper covers. I also thank Ana María Lorandi for her generous sharing of information and for the idea of graphing colonist movements that I use here.

Notes

1. This is a hierarchy in which taxpaying units were organized into a pyramid so that officials of ascending ranks administered 10, 50, 100, 500, 1,000, 5,000, and 10,000 households.

2. There is considerable debate among scholars as to the degree to which we can place faith in Inka accounts of their past, since different royal kin groups told different, often conflicting, stories that favored their own ancestors (for example, Rowe 1946; Zuidema 1983; Rostworowski 1999). For simplicity's sake in this paper, I am accepting the conventional account of three rulers in the imperial era, followed by a five-year dynastic war that ended with the Spanish invasion, but readers need to be aware that each succession seems to have been disputed both physically at the time and historically in later accounts (see D'Altroy 2001).

3. The distinction lies not between the documents and the material remains (that is, the physical consequences of practice), but between the processes of representing identity, creating memory, and reinforcing relationships of power (1) through the practice of writing or (2) through the practices of oral narrative and performance, supplemented by mnemonic devices. The different kinds of intentionality, message content, and practice result in different products with different kinds of information potentially preserved. Since documents and archaeological remains are also affected by different factors of preservation, the issue of partial messages concerns what ideas people are choosing to represent, how they choose to do so, and how the physical processes of preservation affect what we have to work with today. For my point here, the differences are crucial.

4. Qompikamayuq (tapestry cloth weavers) were mentioned for Conima, Capachica, and in the Lupaqa area, for example.

5. A neutron activation analysis of the Argentine and other related ceramics, as yet unpublished, by Verónica Williams, Michael Glascock, Hector Neff, and this author has reached the same conclusion.

10

Roman Colonies in the Eastern Empire

A Tale of Four Cities

Susan E. Alcock

When it comes to the analysis of colonies, we have the Romans to thank for the term. Yet Roman *coloniae* do not provide a single exemplary definition or unitary model against which to measure other, cross-cultural formations. Over the course of Rome's imperial expansion and maintenance—with an empire generally agreed to have endured for half a millennium or more—being a colony (*colonia*) could mean many things. In the years of Roman expansion within Italy itself (fourth to mid-second centuries B.C.), coloniae tended to be emplacements at strategic military points, with colonists drawn from the poorer elements of Roman society. With the stresses of territorial growth and accompanying social dislocation (very marked in the first century B.C.), settlements for army veterans, often dispossessed by their service to the state, became more common (Hopkins 1978; Salmon 1969; Wilson 1966). Julius Caesar (d. 44 B.C.) and Augustus, the first formal Roman emperor (d. A.D. 14), similarly sought to accommodate discharged veterans, as well as the "overflow" indigent population of Italy. These rulers were also concerned, at a time of increasing provincial institutionalization, about the development of regional economic and administrative infrastructures. Under the High Empire (first to fourth centuries A.D.), *colonia* would more and more become an honorary degree awarded to existing, imperially favored cities: a title carrying with it certain rights and something to be announced proudly, but having little to do with actual origins (A. H. M. Jones 1940:64, 133; Millar 1981:84-85, 1990).

This irregularity extends to colonial locations and foundation dates. Colonies were far from uniformly placed across the expanse of empire. Republican colonies (down to the end of the first century B.C.) were overwhelmingly located in Italy. Julius Caesar and Augustus were the first to embark on a widespread policy of "overseas" colonization, with Caesar founding some 30, and Augustus some 75, provincial settlements. These cluster along the western littoral of North Africa, in southern Spain, in Sicily, along the east coast of the Balkan Peninsula, around the sea of Marmara, and in south-central Anatolia (modern-day Turkey). A coastal orientation is common, but not universal. Nor were colonies created steadily, appearing instead in periodic bursts, with foundations becoming much less common after the first-century B.C./first-century A.D. efforts of Caesar and Augustus. The only pattern that seems to emerge is a basic one: that Roman coloniae follow the agenda, or the whims, of the central founding authority.

Most historical scholarship on Roman colonization is quite comfortable with that center-driven orientation. Based on textual information (such as Augustus's *Res Gestae*, his written testimonial of *Things Accomplished*, in which he enumerates where and how many colonies he established), or on epigraphic and numismatic data, scholars have identified colonies, dotted them on the map, discussed the origin and nature of the new settlers (when known), and hazarded hypotheses about the motivations behind foundation. The political status of the colonists—which granted Roman citizenship with the privileges and protection that entailed—has been examined, as have the rights granted to various colonies, including (at least initially) independence from provincial governors and possibly certain forms of tax exemption. The practice of *centuriation*—the division of agricultural land into regular allotments provided for each and every colonist—has also been the focus of much technical study.

With a reliance on such sources and addressing such issues, it is perhaps not surprising that much less has been made of the local-level impact of these creations, or of internal transformations in colonies over time. The decision to found, and the act of foundation, have been judged the most salient aspects of these affairs, from the central point of view. Such a reading of colonial activity—largely textually based and with its emphasis on one side of the story, that is, on "partial texts" (van Dommelen 1998:18)—is a familiar background element to many of the other papers in this volume.

Archaeology, as this volume also demonstrates, obviously offers the chance to counter that perspective. Yet it could be argued that Roman archaeology has been more interested in colonialism (writ large) than in colonies: that is, more interested in the wider phenomenon of domination and control than in more specific processes at work within particular colonial settlements and their immediate hinterlands. Nor have Roman archaeologists been entirely free of imperial bias, of the notion that colonies are "good things," just little slices of heaven. For example, one influential study of an early Italian coastal colony at Cosa, founded in 273 B.C., presented the new settlers as joyous pioneers in search of a better life, trundling in oxcarts to the "promised land" where they would build a town designed to look (in miniature) much like the model city of Rome (Brown 1980).

These implicit overtones of westward expansion in the United States, or of yearning waves of European immigration to its shores, can be detected in other, quite cheerful readings of the colonial process. Recent re-excavation of the type site at Cosa, however, has exploded arguments for any close correspondence between the colony's urban design and that of Rome (Fentress 2000), and Brown's image of the colonists as happy campers strikes a jarring note today. Yet Roman archaeologists must do more than merely wince at such interpretations, instead working toward analyses that consider long-term interactions between colonists, indigenous populations, and the founding authority of Rome. In this, of course, they are in much the same position as other archaeologists, investigating other colonies.

A TALE OF FOUR CITIES

Out of the spectrum of Roman colonial foundations, this paper will focus on examples drawn from a subset defined in space and time. The temporal range for their creation encompasses the late Republic/early Principate (first century B.C./first century A.D.), specifically the reigns of Julius Caesar and Augustus. Their geographic range is the eastern half of the empire, specifically the provinces located in modern-day Greece and Turkey. The point behind this type of controlled comparison is to assess just how similar these colonies were—in the reasons for their foundation, their structure, their settlers, their subsequent development—and where differences emerge and why. If the goal is to seek broad cross-cultural correspondences in colonial situations, it might seem a curious choice to focus on roughly contemporary, geographically proximate colonies of the same imperial system. Yet such a comparison might provide a more refined test of just what is common to being a colony, or of just how far a quest for regularity may be an *ignis fatuus.*

What will follow is a quick review of four eastern colonies—two in the province of Achaia (Corinth, Patras), a province more or less coterminus with the modern nation-state of Greece, and two in the province of Galatia (Pisidian Antioch, Cremna) in south-central Anatolia, what is today southern Turkey (fig. 10.1). Although both provinces are described as being part of the "Greek east," the two regions are, in important ways, quite different. Achaia was what would come to be called "Old Greece," home of the core values and traditions of Hellenism, which remained an intensely proud local heritage. Rome had a long and ambivalent relationship with Hellenic culture: a deep admiration for the Greek past, often marked by benefits to old and revered cities or sanctuaries, mixed with a deep disdain for the *Graeculi,* the Greeks of the Roman present (Dubuisson 1991; Swain 1996). Southern Anatolia, by contrast, had itself been "Hellenized" only following the conquests of Alexander the Great (d. 323 B.C.), and the region was far more of a plural linguistic and cultural mix, embracing as it did the indigenous tribal peoples of Pisidia, Lycia, and Pamphylia as well as intrusive Greek settlers.

The difference made by these preexisting cultural matrices to the historical understanding of these colonies is a significant point to bear in mind. Certainly the presence of Roman colonies in the Greek heartland of Achaia seems almost an embarrassment to later scholars who, although admitting Greece's political subordination, preferred to

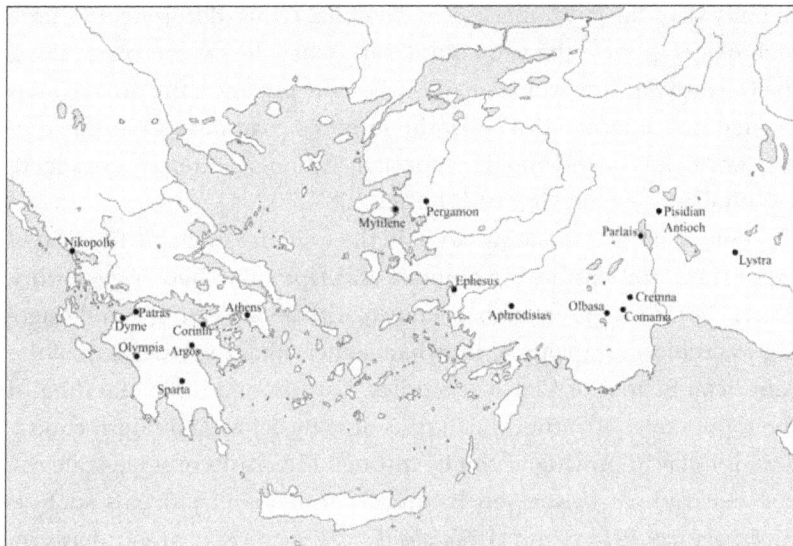

FIGURE 10.1

Location of principal sites mentioned in the text.

envision the province as an untouched, rarefied cultural museum. Roman interventions disturbed such an image, and evidence that at least one of these imperial colonies ultimately "went Greek" has been seized upon gladly as yet further proof that "Greece, the captive, took her savage victor captive..." (*Graecia capta ferum victorem cepit...*; Horace, *Epistles* 2.1.156). By contrast, the Anatolian colonies have been seen both as similarly giving way to their predominantly Hellenic setting and as providing enduring bastions of Romanitas in the wilderness. The validity of all these conclusions, and the assumptions on which they are based, require reassessment.

Security or military concerns also serve to differentiate the two sets of our case study. Achaia, in the middle of the imperial Mediterranean Sea, was an unarmed province (*provincia inermis*); the southern Anatolian provinces, by contrast, bore the reputation of a brawling, unstable area, with belligerently rebellious inhabitants (Shaw 1990; compare Lenski 1999). Although this characterization must be treated cautiously, as an ancient stereotype too quickly seized upon by modern scholars, there can be no doubt that issues of regional security and stability were far more marked in Anatolia. Other differences to note include geography: the two colonies in Achaia lie on the coast, along the Corinthian Gulf, which nearly bisects the province; the two colonies in Anatolia, although linked by the imperial road network to the outside world, are inland and lie (especially Cremna) in relatively rugged, mountainous terrain (fig. 10.1; Levick 1967:38).

Finally, there is much variation in the evidence available for each of these sites, not least in the amount and type of archaeological work done. Corinth is by far the best known, with a long-running and ongoing excavation campaign in its urban center, under the auspices of the American School of Classical Studies. Our limited understanding of the topography of Patras, which rests directly below its modern equivalent, is today improving, if chiefly through the results of small-scale rescue excavations (witnessed by annual updates in journals such as *Archaeological Reports* and *Archaiologikon Deltion*). Recent emphasis on regional archaeology in Greece has led to exploration within the hinterlands of both colonies (Petropoulos and Rizakis 1994; J. Wright et al. 1990; and see preliminary reports on the Eastern Korinthia Archaeological Survey, for example, *Archaeological Reports* 49 [2002–2003]:18–19). By contrast, work at the Anatolian sites has been restricted largely to urban surface reconnaissance and architectural mapping, together with some early, poorly recorded excavation (S. Mitchell 1995:9–26; Mitchell and Waelkens 1998:19–35). Lacking in all cases, unfortunately, are detailed, quantitative studies of residential or commercial quarters, zones where others have sought the impact of a colonial presence (for example, Gasco 1993; Lightfoot, Martinez, and Schiff 1998; Spence 1992, 1996b). Conversely, thanks to the predilections of classical archaeology, urban centers and monumental spaces are more clearly understood (see Schreiber 1998 on a similar affection for "temples-and-tombs"). To adopt the terminology of Lightfoot and his collaborators, this analysis willy-nilly must work primarily at a macro level, rather than at the microscale of daily practice—with all the implications that carries with it:

> ...Microscale studies of domestic activities in household contexts may be best suited for observing individual responses to colonial settings and encounters with others, while the layout of space at the broader community or

regional scale may provide many insights on the overarching political hierarchy and organizational policies of colonizers (1998:202–3; see also Deagan 1983, 1995b).

At this juncture, not much can be done to balance this investigation, beyond awareness of the likely interpretive bias thus placed on our understanding.

Each colonia will be briefly reviewed in turn. As far as possible, certain key themes will be touched on in each "colonial biography": the reasons for its creation, the nature of its settlers, the provincial situation into which it was inserted, the impact on indigenous regional dynamics, and the urban form the settlement took. As far as possible (and this is difficult), the colonies will be treated diachronically, echoing recent arguments that they should be seen as "works in progress," as changing over time (Gasco 1993:169; Dietler 1998:289). Even if on particular topics more can be said in some cases than in others, the sample will bring out both resonances and dissonances in Roman colonial activities.

Corinth: Colonia Laus Iulia Corinthiensis

Located at a highly strategic point, at the base of a narrow isthmus linking central Greece and the peninsula of the Peloponnese to the south, Corinth was one of the major poleis (city-states) of preconquest Greece (fig. 10.1). Following the Achaean War, an unsuccessful struggle against increasing Roman interference in Greek internal affairs, Corinth was destroyed in 146 B.C. Literary sources make the sack sound quite devastating, while dwelling chiefly on the Roman response to looted Corinthian artistic treasures. Although archaeological evidence suggests some level of ongoing "squatter" habitation at the site, a definite caesura in Corinthian civic identity and traditions must be accepted. This includes both disruptions in ancient religious rituals (Pausanias 2.3.7) and the conversion of civic territory to *ager publicus* (Roman public land).

In 44 B.C., the year of his assassination, Julius Caesar established Colonia Laus Iulia Corinthiensis at this site (Broneer 1941). His motivation is assumed to have been fairly obvious, given the significance of the Greek isthmus in Mediterranean systems of east–west communications. The dangers of leaving disorganized such a militarily and commercially strategic point must have been perceived, and the status of the land as ager publicus may have made this a "cheap" and relatively simple territory to redivide and give away (Rizakis 1997:18; C. K. Williams 1993:31). The colonists were primarily drawn from Rome's freedmen (freed slave) class, together with members of Rome's urban poor and a few Caesarian veterans; some of the freedmen were themselves Graeculi, originally of Greek origin (Strabo 8.6.23; Engels 1990:67; A. H. M. Jones 1940:63; Spawforth 1996). The exact number of colonists (*coloni*, with Roman citizenship) is not known (probably somewhere in the range of 3,000 people), but the new colony seems quickly to have grown in size, surpassing its preconquest state—in part, no doubt, thanks to inmigration from other, less successful cities of the province. Unless they achieved citizenship, such new residents would assume the status of *incolae* (resident aliens, literally "inhabitants"), being thus disbarred from participation in the colony's governance. Although reliable estimates of city sizes are difficult, when compared with other Greek cities in Roman times, Corinth emerges as abnormally large, achieving a kind of primate, "super city" status in the province and indeed in the eastern Mediterranean at large (Alcock 1993:158–62, fig. 56; Engels 1990:79–84; Woolf 1997).

In his *Metamorphoses* (10.18), Apuleius refers to Corinth as the *caput* (head) of the province of Achaia. It is usually agreed that the city served as capital of that province—which was actually created only after the foundation of Corinth (following an Augustan administrative reorganization of the empire around 27 B.C.). The institutional impact of this designation should not be overestimated, as provincial administration was to a very great extent decentralized into individual civic units and their own local elites, and as governors traveled widely to review affairs and conduct business. Nonetheless, any provincial capital would house the governor, his officials, and the military guard and would become a focus for the imperial cult and for displays of loyalty to Rome.

Oddly enough, given all this evidence, there seemed for a long time a certain modern hesitation about accepting Corinth (one of the principal cities of the preconquest *Greek* world) as a "real" colony and about seeking the normal Roman accoutrements of that status. This emerges as part of a general avoidance of the Roman period in Greece, or indeed of the archaeology of any period in which Greece was not

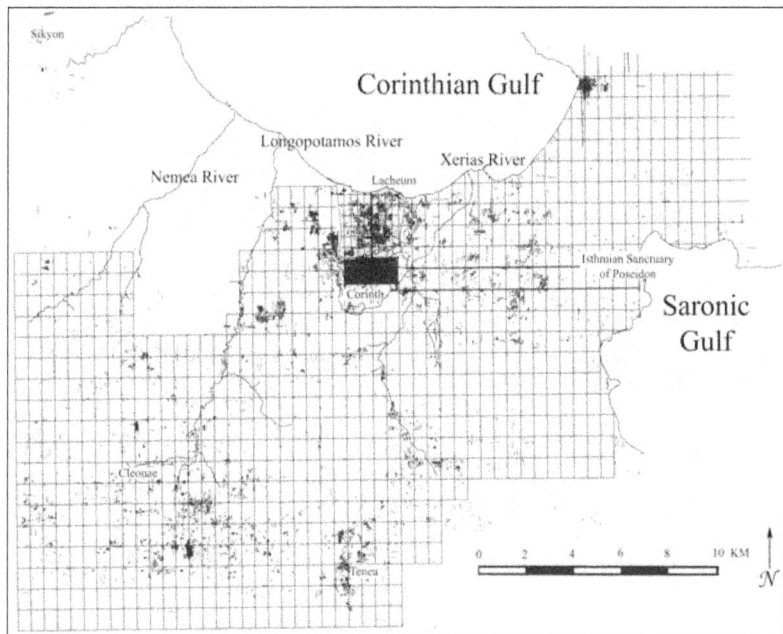

FIGURE 10.2

Plan of the proposed system of centuriation at Corinth, 44 B.C. (Source: Romano 2000; courtesy David Romano and the Journal of Roman Archaeology)

"free" but part of a wider imperial system—a condition that essentially lasted from the time of Augustus until the Greek Revolution of the early nineteenth century A.D. As one remarkable result, only in the past decade or so has an extensive and multistage system of centuriation (systematic land division) been fully recognized in the vicinity of the ancient city (fig. 10.2). Although its dating and extent are still under debate, the principal investigator, David Romano, links one major reorganization of the territory to the original colonial *deductio* of 44 B.C. These centuriated patterns speak to redivision and reallocation of land on a significant scale, extending far beyond the limits of the city walls (Romano 1993, 2000; Romano and Schoenbrun 1994; Rizakis 1997:26; compare Wiseman 1978). Just how far this reallocation uprooted pre-existing rural settlement and landholding patterns, or how far the area remained in flux from the 146 B.C. destruction, remains a question, but it seems unlikely that centuriation would not have been a severe shock

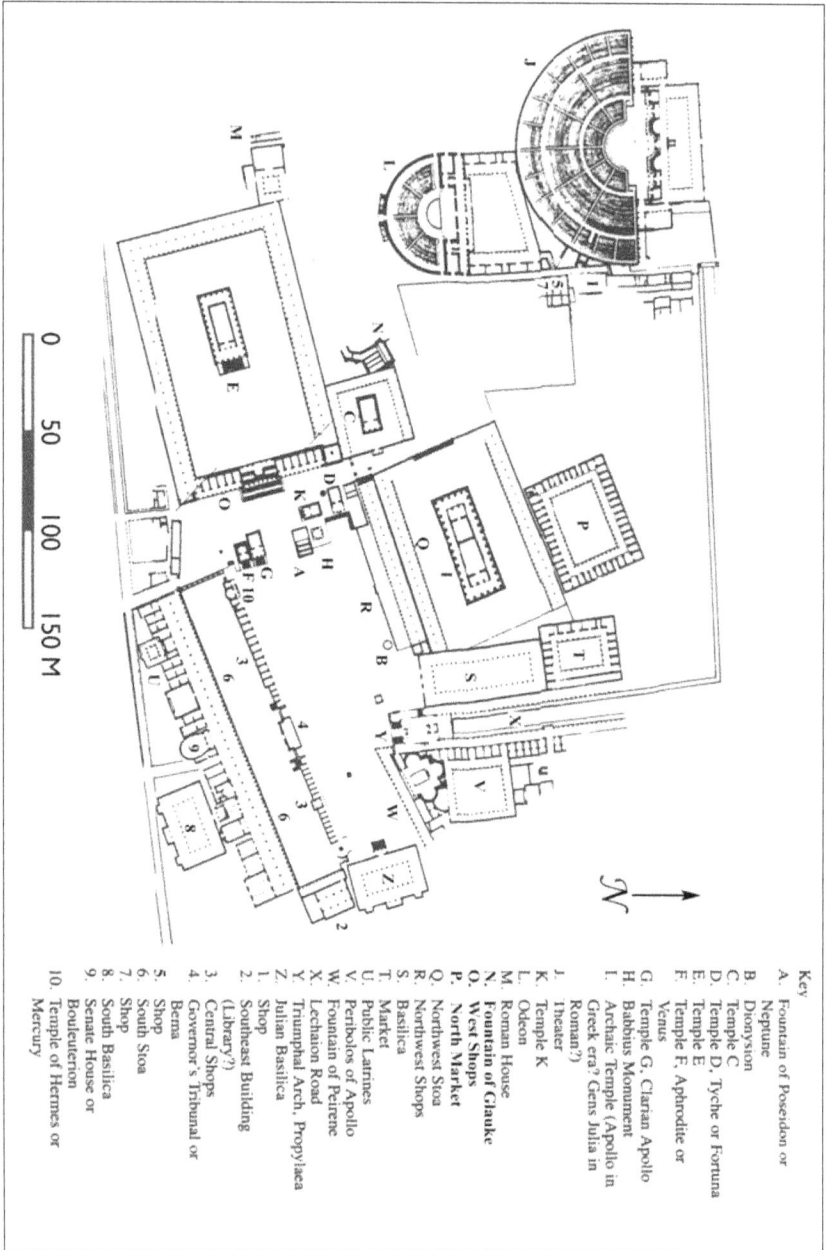

Key
A. Fountain of Poseidon or Neptune
B. Dionysion
C. Temple C
D. Temple D, Tyche or Fortuna
E. Temple E
F. Temple F, Aphrodite or Venus
G. Temple G, Clarian Apollo
H. Babbius Monument
I. Archaic Temple (Apollo in Greek era? Gens Julia in Roman?)
J. Theater
K. Temple K
L. Odeon
M. Roman House
N. **Fountain of Glauke**
O. **West Shops**
P. **North Market**
Q. Northwest Stoa
R. Northwest Shops
S. Basilica
T. Market
U. Public Latrines
V. Peribolos of Apollo
W. Fountain of Peirene
X. Lechaion Road
Y. Triumphal Arch, Propylaea
Z. Julian Basilica
1. Shop
2. Southeast Building (Library?)
3. Central Shops
4. Governor's Tribunal or Bema
5. Shop
6. South Stoa
7. Shop
8. South Basilica
9. Senate House or Bouleuterion
10. Temple of Hermes or Mercury

FIGURE 10.3

Plan of the forum area of the Roman colony of Corinth. (Source: Williams and Zervos 1989; courtesy of the American School of Classical Studies at Athens) to the inhabitants of the northeast Peloponnese and beyond, not least as a symbolic sign of Roman control (Purcell 1990; Clavel-Leveque 1983). Such regional evidence, of course, makes ignoring the Caesarian birth of Corinth far more difficult. The subsequent growth of individual wealthy estates seems attested by the discovery of large and lavishly decorated villas in the city's hinterland, although this is a development seen in other parts of the province, not just in colonial territories.

Turning to the urban center of the colony, meticulous archaeological excavation has clearly revealed Corinth's civic plan in early imperial times (fig. 10.3). Notable monuments include Roman-style temples at the west end of the forum, dedicated to such Roman-oriented cults as Venus (mother of the Julian family; F in fig. 10.3) and Apollo (patron god of Augustus; G in fig. 10.3). Construction techniques and architectural details of these temples have been described as "Italic" (C. K. Williams 1987:26). The forum also saw the early construction of a basilica (the quintessential Roman civic building form) decorated with statues of the imperial family (hence its name, the Julian basilica; Z in fig. 10.3). In the early first century A.D., a new, impressive complex (Temple E) was added to the west of the forum in order to house the imperial cult (the complex labeled E in fig.10.3; Walbank 1989; C. K. Williams 1989). Major preconquest cult sites, such as the Temple of Apollo (I in fig. 10.3) in the forum and of Aphrodite on the height of Acrocorinth above the city, were renewed and rebuilt in a Roman manner, and in the former case perhaps rededicated (C. K. Williams 1987:31–32). Finally, a very unusual sculptural depiction of Rome and the Seven Hills was found in the city (H. S. Robinson 1974), and the colony possessed a rare eastern example of a purpose-built amphitheater (Welch 1999).

All of these features have been taken to point to an early westward-looking emphasis in urban design (see Engels 1990:43–65; C. K. Williams 1987, 1989, 1993). These renewals and new constructions, together with a galaxy of other statues and dedications, were initially sponsored by the wealthy and notable members of the colony, men of freedmen status. Coinage, dedications, and display all featured the imperial cult, the imperial family, or associations with wealthy individual Roman patrons; some colonial families, such as the Gellii, were mildly derided for making "a hobby of setting up monuments to their friends of high rank" (Spawforth 1994:228 n. 70; Engels 1990:101–2). In sum, it has been argued that, for the first century or so of its existence, Corinth offered an assertive "centre of Romanitas" for the province as a whole (Cartledge and Spawforth 1989:104; Amandry 1988; Spawforth and Walker 1985).

Whether the rest of the province wanted to acknowledge, let alone enjoy, such Romanitas is another matter. Achaia, in ways violent and nonviolent, made clear some initial rejection of Roman domination. For example, an epigram of Augustan date by the Greek poet Krinagoras of Mytilene sneers at the "shop-soiled slaves" who made up the new Corinthian population, and there is a significant gap in time before neighboring Greek cities began truly to interact with the colony. It is only around the reign of Claudius and Nero (circa mid-first century A.D.) that the first dedications from important figures outside Corinth appear and Greek communities join with the Corinthians in celebration of the imperial cult. Hostility and disdain for the "jumped up" colony at Corinth on the part of older, prestigious, "truly Greek" cities lingered on through the first century A.D. and was even expressed directly to Roman authorities, who apparently tolerated such Greek impudence on account of their past greatness (Spawforth 1994, 1996).

Despite such resentments, from the second half of the first century A.D. onward Corinth became increasingly integrated with neighboring poleis, and indeed came to serve as a more general showcase for elite displays of loyalty to Rome (Alcock 1993:156; Spawforth 1974, 1978). This is usually attributed to the passage of time and to a growing realization of the advantages (and inevitabilities) of Roman rule on the part of the Achaian elite. Elite families, recognizing the potential benefits of Roman patronage and Roman friendships, came to view Corinth, "seat of Roman officialdom in the province," as an important place to cultivate (Spawforth 1996:173). To an extent, the stress here on elite actors reflects the nature of our sources. On the other hand, in the decentralized administration of the Roman Empire, this group—wealthy, well born, and increasingly connected with one another and with their peers across the empire—provided the preeminent decision-makers in provincial life.

In some ways, the early decades of colonial Corinth (until, say, the reign of Hadrian, A.D. 117–138) describe a certain trajectory, with the colony established to serve imperial dictates and needs, to promote communication and trade, to anchor a not entirely enthusiastic Greece to the Roman world, and to provide a focal point for the expression of elite loyalties. But matters did not rest there. By the second century A.D., a Greek orator could remark to the Corinthians, "You have become thoroughly hellenized, even as your city has" (Ps.-Dio Chrysostom, *Oration* 37 [*The Corinthian Oration*] 26). This might be taken as mere pro-Hellenic rhetoric, but certain material and epigraphic indicators point in this direction as well. The Italic building elements noted in the early stages of forum reconstruction disappear, in favor of more traditional Greek designs. In the second century A.D., eastern ceramic imports begin for the first time to outnumber their western counterparts in excavated assemblages, and the names of recorded local potters shift from Latin to Greek (Engels 1990:72; Slane 1989). The official language of the colony, as reflected in surviving inscriptions, also switches from Latin to Greek. Of those inscriptions prior to the rule of Hadrian, 97 percent (n = 104) had been in Latin; of those dating from his reign through the third century A.D., 70 percent (n = 56) were now in Greek (Kent 1966:18–19; Engels 1990:71; C. K. Williams 1987:37 n. 20; Wiseman 1979:507–8). Admittedly, these are public inscriptions that can tell us little of languages spoken or of less formal communications, but in terms of colonial self-representation, the change is striking. Accompanying this (at least on present evidence) was a move away from the colony's early emphasis on the imperial cult and Roman deities in favor of more indigenous gods. Of those inscriptions concerned with priesthoods or dedications in the first century A.D., 81 percent (n = 47) are to more centrally oriented divinities; in the second century this drops to 27 percent (n = 11); in the third century to 25 percent (n = 4) (Engels 1990:228–29 n. 48). The data are not superb, but something is happening here.

What is happening, it has repeatedly been said, is that after a strong Roman start, Corinth "goes native"—a phenomenon usually explained through the inevitable resurgence of an indomitable Hellenic culture. "Native" is obviously a problematic term here: what is "native" to the descendants of Greek freedmen from Rome in a Roman colony in Greece? Proclaiming the triumph of "Hellenization," moreover, is just as annoying as heralding an uncheckable "Romanization" elsewhere in the empire, or indeed as any other form of what van Dommelen terms "colonial representations" (van Dommelen 1998:18–20). Yet aspects of life in Corinth unquestionably alter over time and do seem to move toward a more local, provincial orientation and less toward a westward-looking, imperial link. This may simply reflect the increasing stability of Rome's control over the province and indeed over the entire eastern Mediterranean. It may also reflect, however, the pressures of civic rivalries endemic in the Greek half of the Roman Empire, rivalries over status and prestige invested deeply in associations with the Hellenic past but also aimed at attracting Roman interest and favor (Alcock 2002: 35–98; Bowie 1974; Swain 1996; Woolf 1994). To compete, Corinth needed to reach back and to stress its indigenous Greek heritage and mythic genealogies. It is intriguing that being Colonia Laus Iulia Corinthiensis may not have been enough (at least in the eyes of the Corinthian aristocracy) to ensure the city's reputation and eminence. These complexities in colonial identity will be discussed further below.

Patras: Colonia Aroe Augusta Patrensis

Lying at the west end of the Peloponnese, along the shores of the Corinthian Gulf, the community of Patras had, in precolonial times, been a somewhat minor player, at least when compared with neighboring Corinth. In the geopolitical shifts of the first century B.C., however, its position became increasingly key, for Patras was a port through which traffic connecting Greece and Italy naturally flowed. A general early imperial interest in encouraging and supporting the western half of the Greek mainland has been argued on many grounds: not only by the Augustan foundation of Patras (in 15 B.C.), but by the creation of an earlier colony (by Caesar) at Dyme just to its west, by the creation of the free city (*civitas libera*) of Nikopolis (Victory City) by Augustus to its north, and by imperial interest in the panhellenic sanctuary at Olympia to its south (fig. 10.1). This support was called for by the severe depredations suffered in this area during the Roman Civil Wars and by the economic interests of Roman nobles who possessed large landholdings along the Balkan west coast—a coast that was, after all, geographically very proximate to the Italian peninsula. A "special relationship" between Italy and western Greece was thus promoted by Augustan-period propaganda, placing the foundation at Patras within a wider agenda for provincial reorganization (Alcock 1993:141–43; Doukellis 1990; Rizakis 1988).

It has been argued that Julius Caesar had originally planned to place a colony at Patras, before being dissuaded by Cicero who spoke for his clients in that city; Caesar chose Dyme instead. Whether Augustus overrode similar antagonisms in his turn is unrecorded, but there may well have been some opposition to his decision. On the other hand, the people of Patras had lost the emperor's favor by allying with his enemy, Mark Antony (Rizakis 1990b, 1997:18). The coloni, veterans of the *legio* XII *fulminata* and legio X *equestris*, took their place at the top of the colony's social hierarchy, with the former, indigenous inhabitants of the city somewhat lower in that sequence. Citizens of communities attached to the colony (see below) would probably have been treated as *perigrini*, inferior in status to the coloni or incolae dwelling in the colony itself. The creation of Patras, in other words, led to a very complex political and juridical situation and to the existence of various status hierarchies within the colony and its broader hinterland (Rizakis 1989, 1997:22–26).

As noted earlier, the archaeology of Patras is poorly understood compared with that of Corinth; the modern sprawling city (still a jumping-off point for Italy and points west) rests atop the ancient remains. A regular, gridlike expansion visible in the modern-day city plan does suggest, however, that the settlement was enlarged at the time of the colonial foundation (fig. 10.4; Papapostolou 1971; Rizakis 1989:181). One first-century A.D. author, Strabo, avers that Patras was "exceptionally populous at present, since it is a Roman colony" (8.7.5) and, although it never grew to the size and scale of Corinth, there seems no reason to doubt that the community flourished. The second-century A.D. traveler Pausanias enumerates many standard urban features: baths, temples, sanctuaries, and civic festivals. Patras, like Corinth, had a purpose-built amphitheater for gladiatorial games and animal contests (Rizakis 1989:185; Spawforth 1994:217).

The colonial foundation of Patras affected a large swath of the surrounding countryside, in a fashion even more intrusive than the steps taken at Corinth. Signs of centuriation have been traced around the city (Rizakis 1990a), and rural survey has observed new patterns of settlement, including the creation of "villa" establishments, most marked

FIGURE 10.4

Patras, with the grid plan showing the Roman-period enlargement of the city (after Papastolou 1971).

along the coast (Petropoulos and Rizakis 1994). Beyond that, there is evidence that large tracts of land on either side of the Corinthian Gulf (in western Achaia, southern Aetolia, and west Lokris) were assigned to the colony, including the urban centers and territories of previously independent poleis. Augustus outright destroyed the community at Rhypes, moving its inhabitants to Patras (Pausanias 7.18.7), and Pausanias notes elsewhere (7.22.1, 6) that two other formerly independent cities (Pharai and Triteia) now "belonged to" Patras, becoming dependent villages (*komai*), with their inhabitants assigned perigrini status. In the indigenous Greek value system, this kind of political subordination was no small demotion. Along with this web of varying categories of political status, the development of growing social and economic inequality within the region goes without saying. This was reinforced by the granting of other economic resources, including a well-stocked lake near Kalydon in Aetolia (on the north side of the Corinthian Gulf), to "the Romans who live in Patras" (Strabo 10.2.21; Kahrstedt 1950). Such individuals could, with such advantages, consolidate their fortunes and "take their place among the elite of the empire" (Rizakis 1997:21).

Interventions on behalf of the colony were not restricted to pragmatic realignments of territory or economic resources. The religious landscape of the region was also affected—for example, by the transplantation of the ancient cult of Artemis Laphria from Aetolian Kalydon to Patras:

> On the acropolis of Patras is a sanctuary of Artemis Laphria. The surname of the goddess is a foreign one, and her image too was brought in from elsewhere. For after Kalydon with the rest of Aetolia had been laid waste by the Emperor Augustus in order that the Aetolian people might be incorporated into Nikopolis above Actium, the people of Patras thus secured the image of Laphria...which even in my time was still worshipped on the acropolis of Patras...(Pausanias 7.18.8–9).

Cult images from the new satellite settlements of Pharai and Triteia were also moved, not to Patras, but to Rome itself (Pausanias 7.22.5, 9). Such transferals of sacred images, often taken as a sign of imperial connoisseurship, need instead to be considered as acts marking a clear redefinition of central places and local allegiances. The new foci of the region were Colonia Aroe Augusta Patrensis and Nikopolis, the free city founded to celebrate Augustus's victory at Actium. As this quote from Pausanias suggests, Nikopolis also received—by imperial dictate—land, population, and cult images from surrounding polities.

Pisidian Antioch: Colonia Caesarea Antiochia

Antioch originated in a third-century foundation by the Hellenistic royal dynasty of the Seleucids (for whom "Antiochus" was a royal name); it was often called "Pisidian" after its neighboring region, in order to distinguish it from the numerous other Antiochs dotting the Seleucid Empire. The placement of Antioch, and other Seleucid cities in Anatolia, was very much dictated by strategic concerns; south-central Anatolia in particular was the mountainous home to numerous indigenous tribes who long resisted attempts at imperial incorporation. In the late first century B.C., this area was the province of a Celtic client king of Rome, Amyntas, whose death while battling one such tribe (the fierce Homonadeis) led to direct annexation by Augustus in 25 B.C. (Sherwin-White 1976). Augustus created the province of Galatia and founded a cluster of colonies, probably shortly after that date (Levick 1967:29–41; Calder 1912; compare Bowie 1970:204–6). This cluster included, apart from the two examples to be discussed here, the colonies at Olbasa, Comama, Parlais, and Lystra (fig. 10.1; A. H. M. Jones 1937:135). Antioch seems initially to have been the chief of this group, as well as the *caput viae* (center point of the road) for the via Sebaste, a major imperial highway inaugurated in 6 B.C. to connect this region to the outside world.

The Antiochan colonists were veterans from legio VII, which had been moved to this area at the time of the annexation. As at Patras, the decision reflects Augustus's need to reward and permanently settle large numbers of demobilized soldiers. One major difference, however, is that the seventh legion remained in the area as a garrison force for some time after the colony's foundation (S. Mitchell 1976). Unlike the provincia inermis of Achaia, an unmistakable Roman military presence can be observed in this part of Galatia. Although varying in intensity over time, this presence would never entirely disappear. The established colonies themselves would almost certainly have continued to bear military obligations (A. H. M. Jones 1940:142; S. Mitchell 1976, 1993a:74–76). Hints of constant, if low-level, acts of Roman repression have been noted for the first century B.C./first century A.D., and a violent third-century A.D. rebellion (in which the colony at Cremna became directly involved) indicates ongoing tribal unrest and resistance (Shaw 1990). The motivation for Augustus's rapid foundation of these Anatolian colonies has been attributed—with little hesitation—to his need to establish order in a volatile, newly acquired zone; Levick speaks of throwing a "cordon...round the whole of Pisidia" (1967:38; Syme 1995:225–41; compare Bowie 1970:205–6). Subsequent imperial foundations in the following century (although now not taking the form of colonies) points to a continued concern, if not outright anxiety, about this area's stability.

The population of Antioch, as in all Roman colonies, would have been formally divided into at least two groups: coloni with Roman citizenship and incolae with lesser political status (Mitchell and Waelkens 1998:8; Levick 1967:68–91). It would also have been an ethnic mixture, from the Italian veterans, to the Greek settlers of the previous Hellenistic foundation, to the so-called substratum of indigenous Anatolian peoples, such as Phrygians and Pisidians. The epigraphic record makes clear that Antioch's political and economic life was dominated for centuries by the coloni and their descendants, following a constitution laid down along Roman precedents and broadly similar to colonies elsewhere in the empire, east and west (S. Mitchell 1993a: 89–90).

The colony was established upon the Hellenistic settlement, unfortunately eradicating most earlier architectural traces, but indigenous styles in burial markers and ritual objects attest to continuing traditions of self-expression and religious worship in the wake of the colonial foundation. Indeed, the principal deity of the city (apart from the worship of the imperial cult) was the Anatolian moon god Mên Askaênos, who possessed a large sanctuary (of Hellenistic date) outside the urban center (Hardie 1912; S. Mitchell 1993a:90, 1993b:9–10). No major traces of Roman-period building have been observed at this sanctuary, but it manifestly continued to flourish until its later violent destruction at Christian hands. Epigraphic and archaeological evidence indicates that the colonial immigrants readily adopted the worship of Mên Askaênos and maintained his position as patron deity (*patrios theos*) of the city; the most distinguished of colonial families offered him dedications (Mitchell and Waelkens 1998:37–90; Levick 1970, 1971). On the other hand, somewhat ironically, Strabo reports that one of the first steps in the colony's foundation was the confiscation of the sanctuary's ample landholdings (worked by sacred slaves), which were converted into the necessary colonial allotments (Strabo 12.8.14; Syme 1995:237, 344). In the end, Antioch's assigned territory extended over some 540 square miles, swallowing up many outlying villages—although this did not involve the "demotion" of free communities, as happened at Patras.

The urban center of Antioch was dominated by a religious complex almost certainly dedicated to Augustus and the imperial cult (figs. 10.5 and 10.6). Built in a canonically Roman style—in the Corinthian order, with a frontal emphasis, on a high podium, on axial alignment within a larger complex—the temple would have been visible for many miles around (Lyttelton 1987:41–43; S. R. F. Price 1984:269–70). The cult complex was entered through a triple-arched gateway lavishly decorated with images of imperial victory, including kneeling captives who could be taken either as generic "barbarians" or as losers in the region's Roman subjugation (S. Mitchell 1993a:105–7; Mitchell and Waelkens 1998:113–73). Before this sanctuary stood an open colonnaded avenue (the *Tiberia Platea*; see fig. 10.5) where a copy (in Latin) of Augustus's *Res Gestae* was placed: a document erected outside his tomb in Rome and at various select points, not all colonial, across the empire (D. M. Robinson 1928).

The entire complex—from its architectural prototypes, to the *Res Gestae*, to the symbolism of victory and of the Golden Age typical of Augustan propaganda—seems extraordinarily "central" in its inspirations and aspirations (compare Zanker 1988). For example, the complex's long axial development, with the temple awaiting the visitor at its end, has been linked to the design of the Forum of Augustus dedicated in 2 B.C. in downtown Rome. Equally provocative is the fact that the colony was divided into seven *vici*, or neighborhoods, all of which shared their names with counterparts in the imperial capital itself (Levick 1967:76–77).

Antioch, at least in its early years, has been interpreted very much as a little piece of Rome—indeed a new Rome—set down in the highlands of Anatolia: "Julio-Claudian Antioch, in the fullest sense of the adjective, was an imperial city" (Mitchell and Waelkens 1998:11; Levick 1967:188). Public inscriptions continued to be written in Latin until the fourth century A.D.; as at Corinth, this reveals nothing of actual languages spoken, but it can be taken as "a mark of pride in Roman origins.... Pride and ostentation ensured that Latin was inscribed..." (Bowie 1970:206). Yet here too signs of "creeping Hellenization" have been identified: the appearance of the Greek title *gymnasiarch*, the deification (against the custom of Rome) of living emperors, the growth of interregional links to other Greek, noncolonial cities

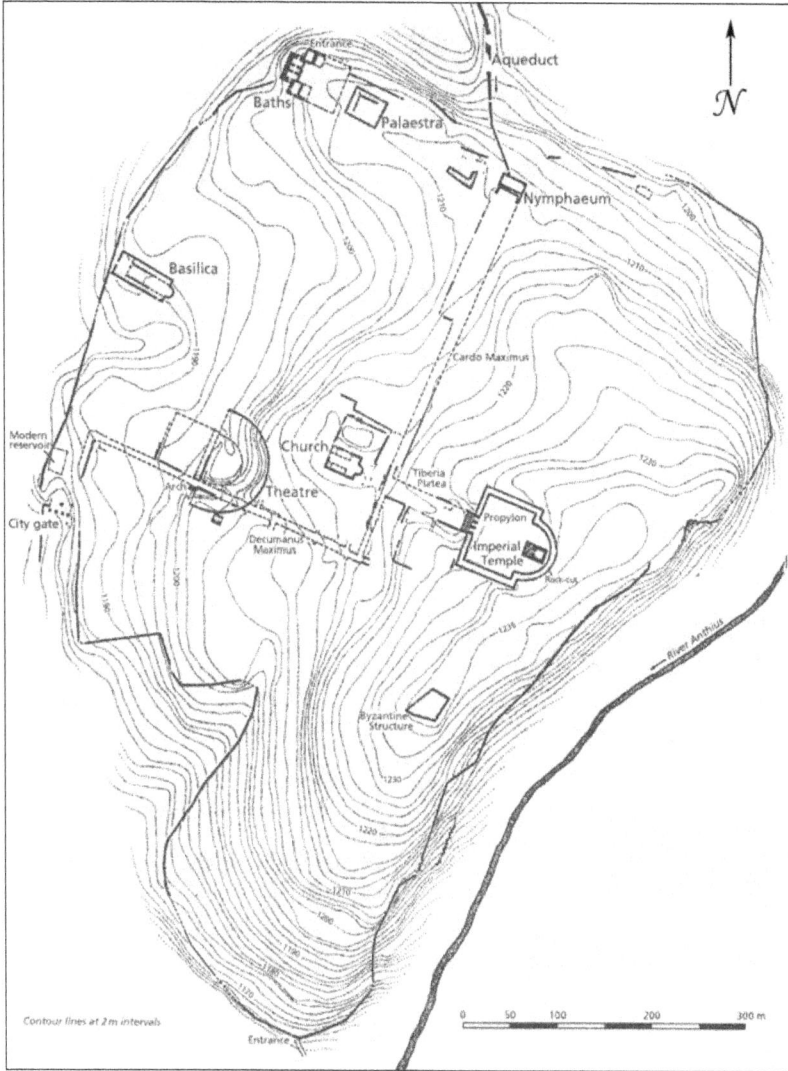

FIGURE 10.5

City plan of Pisidian Antioch (after Mitchell and Waelkens 1998).

through marriage and cultural associations, the ultimate "decline" of Latin (A. H. M. Jones 1937:140; Levick 1967:121–44; S. R. F. Price 1984:89; compare Bowie 1970:206–7).

The problems of envisioning a simple trajectory from "Roman" to "Greek" behavior will be discussed further below. Apart from the inherent

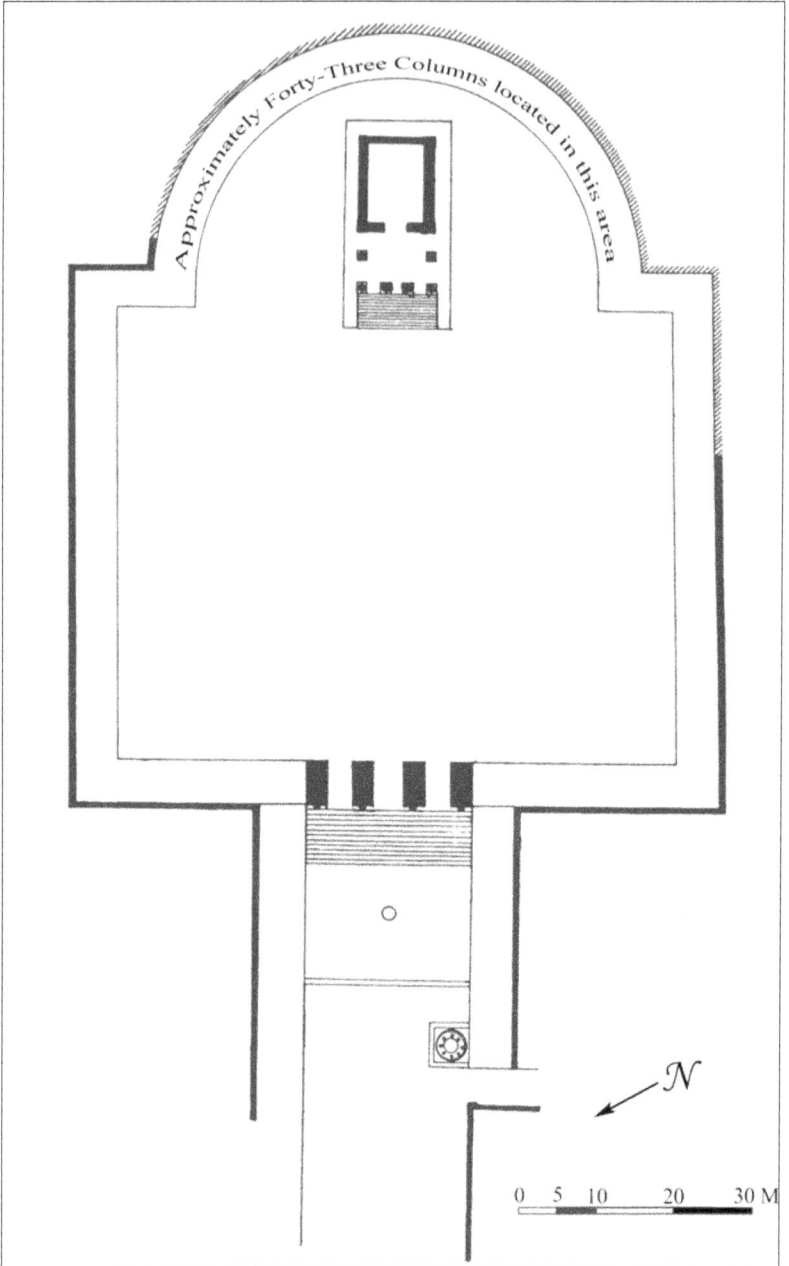

Figure 10.6

Ground plan of the imperial sanctuary and the Tiberia Platea at Pisidian Antioch (after Mitchell and Waelkens 1998).

unlikelihood of such a straightforward cultural divide, other factors complicate the picture. The nomenclature of the original veteran colonists suggests they were drawn from central and northern Italy, not from Rome itself, and it is increasingly clear that different ways of "being Roman" held sway across the Italian peninsula itself (Terranato 1998). The dominance of Mên Askaênos and the still poorly understood, but unmistakable, endurance of Phrygian and Pisidian symbols, practices, and—most likely—languages requires further exploration (A. H. M. Jones 1940:289). Finally, we have the testimony of no less a source than the *Acts of the Apostles* about a visit by Saint Paul to Pisidian Antioch (A.D. 45–49), when he preached to the civic elite and came in conflict with the colony's powerful Jewish synagogue. The very individual who served as Paul's patron on that visit, the proconsul and convert Sergius Paullus, wonderfully destabilizes the category of "Roman" in the colony:

> The person of Sergius Paullus himself—Italian in origin, Asiatic in domicile, from a family who had freedmen active in Rome and estates in central Anatolia, who was commemorated by inscriptions set up in Latin and in Greek, and who combined the public functions of a Roman magistrate with a demonstrable receptiveness to the persuasion of a new eastern cult—points to some of the complexities of Paul's earliest congregations (S. Mitchell 1993b:8).

It also points to some of the complexities of social life and cultural identity within Colonia Caesarea Antiochia.

Cremna: Colonia Iulia Augusta Felix Cremna

In many ways the history of Cremna's foundation parallels that of Pisidian Antioch, which lies some 100 kilometers to the north-northeast (fig. 10.1). It too was a veteran's settlement, also with colonists drawn from Italy, also founded shortly after 25 B.C. by Augustus. Cremna, however, was settled on the site of a preexisting Pisidian settlement that, unlike the Seleucid foundation of Antioch, had maintained an existence independent of Hellenistic imperial control. The community was captured only by Amyntas, that client king whose death in 25 B.C. inaugurated the Roman annexation of the region (Strabo 12.6.3–5; A. H. M. Jones 1937:133; Levick 1967:29–41; Syme 1995:237).

Another difference is in the colony's location. Antioch, and most of the other Augustan colonies, had not been set directly within the wilder mountainous zones of southern Anatolia, but instead had been placed in positions skirting, and observing, the high uplands. Cremna, by contrast, lies in the heart of potentially rebellious tribal territory, being set in a very high and precipitous place. The decision to found a colony at Cremna must reflect a reluctance to risk losing such a strategic base, but it also evinces a willingness to use colonies in a more aggressively vigilant fashion (Levick 1967:37; S. Mitchell 1993a:77).

The settlement history of the colony also diverges significantly from that of Antioch, or indeed of the other two colonies discussed. If Antioch witnessed an early efflorescence of civic building, such as the imperial cult center, Cremna can offer no equivalent. Indeed, detailed architectural mapping and survey of the site have failed to find any trace of significant public structures from the first century or so of the colony's existence. In its early years Cremna appears to lack coinage, building activity, and the usual "urban furniture" one expects of a Roman-period city; we possess only a scant handful of inscriptions. Indeed, without its colonial titulature, and without the attestation of a handful of literary sources, it is unlikely that Cremna would be recognized as an Augustan colonia. One explanation for this "slow start" is that the colony, with its unusual position, was in its early years more a fortress than a colonial settlement. Although no evidence supports this assumption outright, it seems a stronger argument than the alternative offered—that all traces of Augustan/Julio-Claudian building have merely been removed by later settlement activity (S. Mitchell 1995:54).

Only beginning in the reign of the emperor Hadrian (A.D. 117–138) would local donors add to the existing Hellenistic cityscape of Cremna. This took the form of several second-century A.D. temples (some clearly devoted to the imperial cult) and a forum-basilica complex whose best parallels come from the western half of the empire (fig. 10.7; S. Mitchell 1995:53–139, 1993b:13; Owens 1991; S. R. F. Price 1984:270; Ward-Perkins and Ballance 1958). This complex—with the open space of the forum framed on three sides by colonnades and on the fourth by a basilica—is

> virtually a cliche of Roman or romanised town-planning....
> When Lucius Fabricius Longus and the councilors of the

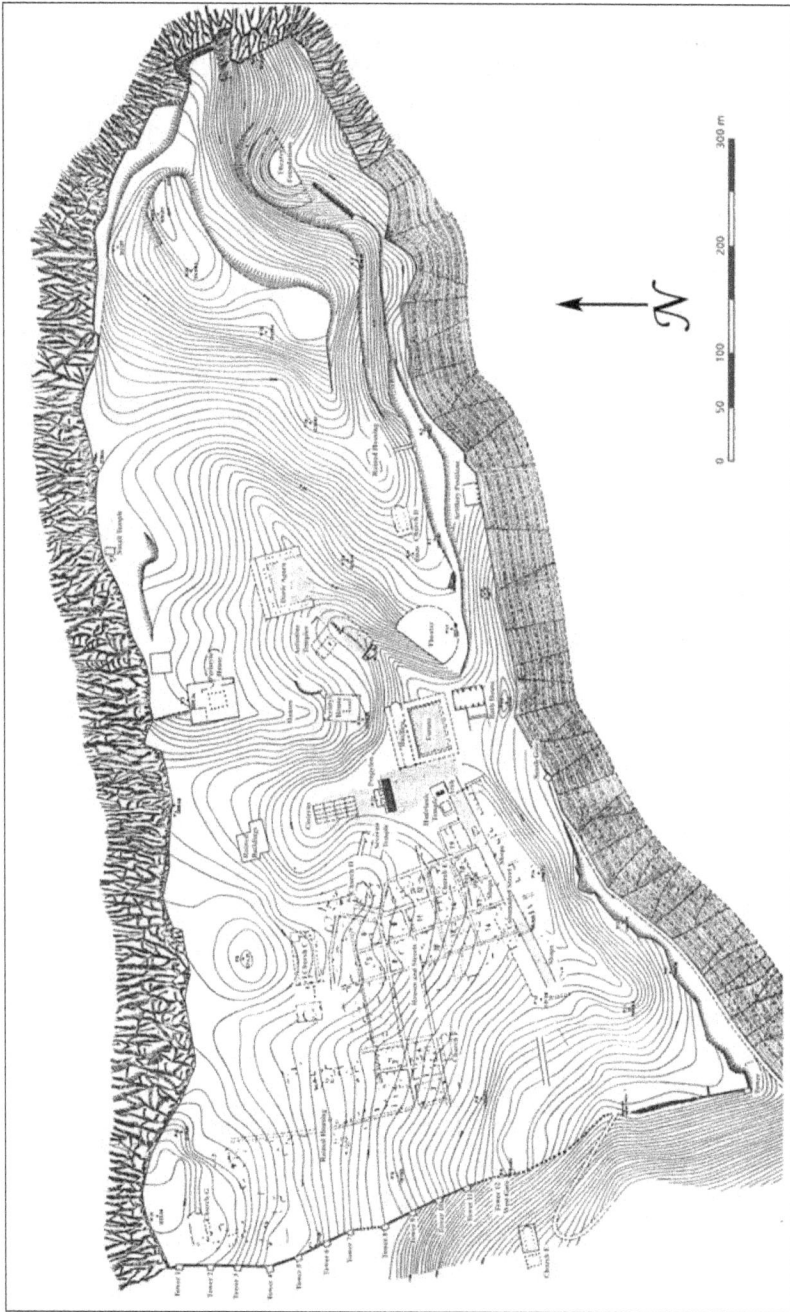

Figure 10.7
City plan of Cremna (after S. Mitchell 1995).

Roman colony at Cremna approved the design for their new
forum they knew exactly what they were doing, namely creating a building of Roman design and reflecting a Roman
political idea at the heart of a hellenistic city (S. Mitchell
1995:68–69).

As at all other colonies reviewed so far, there is evidence that the
colonists at Cremna achieved a degree of integration, through intermarriage and cultural ties, with the wider Greek world of the early
empire; indigenous practices too are seen continuing—for example, in
local forms of augury. Yet, as the second-century construction of the
forum suggests, this colony always maintained close links to its origins,
cults with strong Roman associations appear throughout on coin types;
and Latin endured as the language of public inscriptions (S. Mitchell
1995:4). The gridlike layout of Cremna's residential zone, more regular in its features and more like a canonical Roman colony than the
other Anatolian examples, has also been commented on (fig. 10.7).
The argument has been made—although the evidence is not the best—
that domestic architecture at Cremna follows more "empire-wide"
norms, rather than demonstrating overt signs of local influence or tradition. Simple and relatively modest houses, as far as can be told, were
preferred here, unlike the more varied and often elaborate domestic
architecture of other parts of the Greek east (S. Mitchell 1995:175;
compare Wallace-Hadrill 1994). Another intriguing pattern is the
apparent lack of Cremnian interest in prize games (*themides*)—competitions that were wildly popular in the Greek cities of Anatolia yet seem
absent in this colony (S. Mitchell 1993a:224-25). All these indicators
may be mere straws in the wind, but the argument could tentatively be
made that, at least in certain aspects of civic behavior, Cremna
remained more deliberately "Roman" in its self-presentation than the
other coloniae reviewed (see Millar 1990 for similar arguments about
the Roman colony at Berytus).

That loyalty, however, was no more etched in stone than any other
colonial position. The best-known historical incident associated with
Cremna occurred in the third century A.D. (A.D. 278), when the empire
as a whole and Anatolia in particular began to experience upsurges of
local rebellion and loss of centralized control. As part of an attack on
the low-lying province of Lycia/Pamphylia, Cremna was seized by

Lydius, a local leader (usually called a "brigand leader") of the highland Isaurians. Lydius's aims—for example, whether this was a specifically anti-Roman insurrection—are poorly understood; unfortunately, the most detailed version of this episode appears in a late and highly colored account (Zosimus, *New History* I.69–70). Roman authorities and Roman troops quickly became involved, however, and Cremna withstood a massive bombardment and siege. The most remarkable monument at the site today is the mound raised, stone by stone, to aid the Roman artillery attack; a countering mound can be seen within the besieged town (S. Mitchell 1989, 1993a:234–35, 1995:177–218). It is possible that Cremna, just before Lydius's rebellion, had been employed as a military base by the emperor Aurelian in opposition to the separatist movement of Queen Zenobia of Palmyra. Military-civilian interactions—at such close quarters—seem often in Anatolia to have resulted in friction; potential ill treatment of the inhabitants of Cremna may have made them more open to the overtures of Lydius, bringing this Roman attack down upon their heads (although see Lenski 1999:446 n. 169). Whatever the truth of the situation, the fact that the siege mound was never destroyed (and thus always posed a threat to the city) suggests that, although the community of Colonia Iulia Augusta Felix Cremna lived on, it lost its claim to independent civic status (S. Mitchell 1989:323).

CONVERGENCES, DIVERGENCES, AND IDENTITY POLITICS

What do these four coloniae share in common? All involved the introduction of an alien resident population, at the cost of disruption to a host people and their territory. All served central needs and priorities, at least in their initial decades, not least by providing a safety valve for excess or potentially unruly populations. All introduced new patterns of internal civic administration, with coloni dominating the social and economic life of their communities. All likewise introduced new systems of regional organization, permanently affecting patterns of landholding and settlement, as well as cultic distribution: by no means did the impact of these places stop at the city limits. Material culture and textual evidence alike speak to close and continual contact and interaction with indigenous practices and peoples.

Once one pushes past such bald statements, however, divergences begin to emerge. Although all reflected central concerns in their foundation, these were far from identical in every case. The Achaian colonies worked primarily to ensure channels of communication and to develop economic and administrative infrastructure; the Anatolian colonies seem more fundamentally aimed at defensive postures and keeping order, in conjunction with a military presence. The sites selected ranged from relatively empty space (the sacked city of Corinth) to existing, but quite different types of cities (Patras, Pisidian Antioch, Cremna). Nor was the cultural and ethnic matrix into which the colonies were inserted the same from case to case, with Achaia being the "heartland" of Hellenism (and where Corinth had been a far more venerable city than Patras), and with the Anatolian colonies added to an already-layered social world and to a more complex blend of indigenous traditions. Nor need distinctions necessarily follow straight geographic (Achaian versus Anatolian) lines. Corinth and Antioch both seem to have begun with a significant florescence of imperially oriented building and propaganda, with signs of apparent later slackening (leading to scholarly praise or blame for "going native"). The situation at Patras and Cremna is less clear but may not indicate (especially at the more remote and threatened Cremna) the same trajectory of development, the same loosening of ties to home.

In the end, what these four cities—so similar in some ways, quite distinct in others—may offer is a very simple lesson. It would seem that the terms of analysis can be transferred from one to another: an endless triangulation between colonists (and their miscellaneous backgrounds), indigenous peoples (and their existing structures of life), and the central authority that sets the process in motion (and its global priorities). Because of the variability possible to each of these categories, however—in the Roman case perhaps most marked in that middle category of indigenous conditions—it seems wise not to predict, or to expect, the same outcome from any two colonial experiments.

If those are points of convergence and divergence, what about identity politics? At this point, it becomes necessary to take on the deeply embedded, and deeply constraining, issue of dualist conceptions: in this case Greek versus Roman, but present (to a greater or lesser extent) in all colonial situations between colonizer and colonized. In many senses, this study's most fundamental impediment is past scholarship's constant focus on the battle of Greek versus Roman for the soul of these colonies. Not only does this eliminate other indigenous voices (most markedly in the Anatolian cases), but it reifies a notion of static and unitary cultures with which few today would agree. The warping effect on the minds of Roman archaeologists—who pick apart these communities looking for traces of one or the other, rather than considering colonial culture as a whole or as a hybrid—is obvious; equally obvious is the fact that this effect has not been entirely escaped in the present discussion either. The prescription is clear: we must abandon strictly dualist assessments, leaving more room for other associations and identifications (gender, class, faction) to be considered (see van Dommelen 1997a, 1998:20–22). The development of a kind of supra-civic elite—demarcated by education, artistic self-representation, marriage, wealth, friendships—bound together fortunate individuals throughout the Greek provinces and across the empire, all at the expense of a growing social divide within the provinces themselves (Alcock 2002:123–31). Distinguishing "Greek" from "Roman" (themselves obviously shifting and developing categories) was by no means always the primary issue in dispute.

Having said all that, the baby cannot be allowed to go out with the bathwater. Categories of Greek and Roman did possess meaning and power; in particular, Hellenic culture was clearly employed as a form of symbolic capital, to garner approbation from philhellenic Roman authorities, to delineate boundaries between civic elites and the hoi polloi, to maintain a sense of separate regional identity. The Greek provinces never became an indistinguishable part of the Roman Empire, and the constant practice and display of Greek rhetoric, art, and literature worked to negotiate distance from the ruling power.

Where do the four Roman colonies examined here fit within this framework? The evidence suggests, if chiefly at the better understood instances of Corinth and Antioch, that they increasingly (if never exclusively) adopted Greek styles in architecture, writing, cult, and cultural interests. Rather than praising (or decrying!) this as "Hellenization" or "re-Hellenization," however, it should instead be seen as part of a wider negotiation of the colony's position within their dominantly Greek cultural matrix. These Roman colonies did not remain isolated enclaves (although Corinth may at least initially have been shunned as such). This meant, as suggested above for Corinth, that they had to compete for prestige and status in more local terms, terms rooted in the antiquity and purity of Hellenic culture. To play this game, colonies would need to invoke public vocabularies that would resonate with other cities of the eastern Mediterranean.

This is not the same phenomenon as "going native." These colonies never fully relinquished their Roman identity (seen in titulature, coinage, and other public display), an identity that no doubt remained appropriate and helpful in other contexts and competitions. The hypothesized adherence of Cremna, a more isolated and potentially endangered colony, to imperial norms is worth remembering. At this juncture, it might be fruitful to think about the articulation of individual identities in the Roman east. Plutarch, a Greek author of the Roman period, could bemoan Roman control of his homeland; he could travel to and teach in Rome; he could swear never to leave his small hometown in central Greece; he could—and did—become a Roman citizen (Alcock 2002:86–88; C. P. Jones 1971). Saint Paul, a Christian missionary who escaped certain brutal punishments thanks to his Roman citizenship, is another example. Polyphonic identities, with different contexts determining choices made in self-presentation and cultural allegiance, would seem to have become the elite norm at this time, rather than any strict exclusivity between Greek and Roman positions (compare R. R. R. Smith 1998). One productive way to consider Roman colonial foundations in the east would be similarly to think, not in terms of absolute movement from one cultural mode to another, but of colonial identity as being a more multiple and flexible domain. These communities could see themselves, and sell themselves, as both Roman coloniae and Greek poleis, as context and need demanded.

Overemphasis on dualist categories, all would agree, is a common evil in colonial analysis. On the other hand, we must be careful in its eradication; we cannot erase cultural distinctions held as vital and defining by past peoples themselves. Stein has introduced the notion of "distance-parity" into conceptions of long-distance contact and control, arguing "that the leveling effects of distance give rise to a highly variable social landscape" (Stein 1998:247). One is tempted, in the case of Roman colonies in the Greek east, to consider also "culture-parity"—

where colonial trajectories and relationships would be shaped by the cultural world in which they were placed and by imperial attitudes to that world. This too would help to explain the highly variable social landscape we can see emerging across the Roman empire, or any other empire you might care to name, or to study.

CONCLUSION

Given the ideological investment of the west in the ancient cultures of Greece and Rome, both Dietler and van Dommelen have spoken to the need for special sensitivity on the part of Mediterranean scholars of colonialism (Dietler 1998:290; van Dommelen 1998:15). Although agreeing completely that Mediterranean models have provided justification for subsequent colonial operations (as Rome has served nobly as archetype for later imperial systems; see MacCormack 2001; Moreland 2001), there is a flip side to the story. The mastery of modern colonization, with its military and technological superiorities, has arguably been projected back into the Roman world, with exaggerating effect. Although these colonies, notably the Anatolian examples, were meant to play a strategic role, they could hardly be called powerful instruments of domination; though the colonies consolidated provincial infrastructures, they were not tireless engines of imperial prosperity. Their roles and influence were more limited, perhaps, than the term "colony" tends immediately to suggest. If we must beware of viewing modern European colonialism through an ancient veil, the reverse is also true.

In this light, it is provocative to contemplate how much of what has here been treated as "colonial" behavior in the Roman east is actually seen elsewhere, in other categories of settlement. The free city of Nikopolis, founded to commemorate Augustus's victory over the forces of Antony and Cleopatra, was granted large tracts of land, the subordination of previously free cities, and the gift of cult images; it pairs neatly with its close neighbor, Patras. Similar imperial benefactions for favored, or useful, cities can be enumerated across the eastern provinces. Groups of Italian or Roman businessmen (*negotiatores*) moved into numerous eastern communities, taking a prominent part in civic affairs and ultimately intermarrying or otherwise associating themselves with indigenous families (Hatzfeld 1919; C. P. Jones 1970).

Veterans were also settled within Greek cities other than colonies (A. H. M. Jones 1940:64). Many Greek cities could thus boast *Rhomaioi* ("Romans") in their midst and in their decision-making processes; this was not limited to colonial settings.

Parallels for the artistic and architectural forms noted in the colonies are also very widespread. Structures such as Roman-style temples and basilicas were built in very great numbers across the eastern Mediterranean, with such temples being dedicated to Greek as well as to Roman gods; the ubiquity of such structures has been downplayed through classical archaeology's concentration on more purely Hellenic monuments (Macready and Thompson 1987; S. R. F. Price 1984:168). Nor are celebrations of the imperial cult or monuments celebrating imperial glory confined to colonies. The astonishing Sebasteion (imperial cult center) recently discovered in the free city of Aphrodisias in Asia Minor, where semi-nude Roman emperors are depicted abusing the female personifications of various provinces, is only one flamboyant example of identification with the center (Alcock 2000; R. R. R. Smith 1987, 1988). In general, it could be argued that Roman preference for the widespread co-optation of local elites—and the imperial reliance on that group to keep order, to collect taxes, and so on—led to the rejection of other possible governing strategies, such as ubiquitous military garrisons or multiple colonial foundations. All cities of the empire, to an extent, played a "colonial" role; all became implicated, if not seamlessly, into an imperial web of control and integration.

That is not to say that nothing distinguishes Roman colonies from a more general backdrop of elite collaboration and civic accommodation. The act of colonial imposition, with its reordering of so many aspects of local territories, loyalties, and memories, cannot be minimized, nor can it be assumed that time would automatically heal all wounds. Another obvious distinction is the way colonies governed themselves; the effect of colonial administration, with its automatic status distinctions, upon the life of the community remains to be further investigated. It seems a shame to end on a note of frustration but, although many future avenues for investigation could be highlighted, at the moment they are largely stymied by the type of research done to date. Archaeological approaches to these eastern colonies remain far too "top-down," limiting the tales our four cities can tell. Other papers in this volume amply demonstrate the desirability of systematic research into other domains of life—burial practices, domestic architecture, foodways, and minor cults. Such research could not only clarify all-important differences within a colonial body and between colonial foundations, but would help us to distinguish just how far, and for how long, colonies stood out from the peoples who surrounded and engaged with them.

Acknowledgments

I would like to thank Gil Stein for his original invitation to the 2000 SAR session, "The Archaeology of Colonization in Cross-Cultural Perspective," as well as the other participants both for their collegiality and their advice about this paper. All problems remain my own.

11

Archaeology and the Interpretation
of Colonial Encounters

J. Daniel Rogers

In the colony, a new cultural landscape is constructed from the intertwined frames of reference brought together by differing groups. The following chapter makes explicit the implications of this sort of interaction, shows its key components, and develops an archaeological methodology that brings together areas of analysis that have traditionally been separated. Although we may define the colony and its participants as an object of analysis, to the actors it was not a concrete thing. Instead, it was a series of overlapping perceptions and events with contradictory outcomes, each relevant as a separate theme of study. But, the colony, its genesis, and transformation also represent a process that can reveal the workings of even more broadly relevant social constructs, such as the creation of meaning and cultural order.

Observing how people confront the disruptions and ambiguities produced by colonial encounters opens a window onto a host of themes fundamental to understanding cultural interactions and the more encompassing aspects of culture change. The reasons anthropologists, historians, and others have spent so much time studying what happens when different groups of people come into contact is because of the often profound implications of these encounters. For instance, the European expansion of the sixteenth century was immensely significant in structuring the dimensions of the modern world. We are able to study fruitfully these histories of encounter to extract the outlines and even interpret the content of our present world. From a more analytical point of view, a variety of processes become apparent through culture contacts that operate more overtly than in other circumstances. This allows a clearer reading of processes of change than otherwise might be possible. For the archaeologist, there is also the potential for theory building offered by circumstances where written record exists in tandem with the material remains. These issues have a significant place in linking colonization to other forms of interaction and to fundamental processes of change so vividly at work in a variety of encounter contexts. In particular, patterns of change evident in the context of colonialism are central to developing the linking arguments necessary to connect social theory with archaeological analysis of long-term change and stability. In essence, these are change contexts that have the potential of contributing to the development of social theory and a culturally informed theory of the object.

For the ancient and not so ancient past, however, the archaeological interpretation of colonialism is still largely unexplored territory. In the next section, a critical look at the broader study of colonialism over the last forty years serves to highlight several key themes with implications for archaeological practice and theory building. These themes include the construction of power relations, identity in the context of agency, and the reformulation of viable histories through the construction of memory. Interactions between peer-based and hierarchically dissimilar social groups reveal how different modes of colonialism expose patterns inherent in the maintenance and reconstruction of personal and group identity. To apply these concepts to the archaeology of colonialism requires methodologies to identify meaningful linkages with changes in material assemblages and their contexts. What constitutes change in a material assemblage, how the assemblage itself is conceptualized, and how objects are linked to the motivations revealed in individual and group actions become crucial issues.

FINDING THE COLONIZER AND COLONIZED

The terms "colonizer" and "colonized" are often used to represent a simple interpretive dichotomy. The contrasting of players and their roles, however, turns out to mask a complex range of interactions. To even describe these terms as a coherent opposition is suspect (Stoler 1989; van Dommelen 1998:18), although they are clearly enshrined as such in a wide range of anthropological and historical studies. The military, economic, and cultural interactions that develop in the environment of the colony and colonialism are not unique to this type of interaction. Differing forms of migration, trade interactions, explorations, and other cultural contacts may produce the types of cultural institutions and power relations often ascribed to the colonizer/colonized dichotomy. The range of interactions that develop and diverge almost immediately upon contact is too broad to be contained by any simple dichotomy. Although it may be a simple and convenient contrast, it has served as a rigid framework and has come to imply outcomes that are themselves reflective of the modern experiences of the nineteenth and twentieth centuries. The implied outcomes are linked to a duality of domination and resistance so important to contemporary anthropological interpretations of the colonial experience. Concepts of domination and resistance are likewise limiting and should be placed in a broader context that does not restrict colonialism to a mere reflection of the European expansion of the last 500, and especially the last 100, years.

Colonization, as discussed in this book, is closely associated with the existence and growth of states, and the forms of organizational control that ruling hierarchies use to meet their needs. The formal existence of colonies derives largely from centralized decision-making processes, which are usually opaque from an archaeological point of view. In fact, other movements of people such as migrations (Rouse 1986) also produced culture-contact encounters similar to those noted at the frontiers of expansionistic states. How to sort out the differences in cultural encounters, especially in purely prehistoric cases, continues to be a source of debate. The contributors to this volume have entered that debate and developed new perspectives on recognizing and analyzing the existence and role of colonies.

We can observe the growth and eventual decline of a range of political and social systems over the course of thousands of years. The historical record from the ancient Mediterranean world, medieval Inner Asia, or nineteenth-century North America, for instance, is often very explicit (and sometimes equally misleading) about these changes, even if the causal relationships we may ascribe are somewhat more suspect (see Comaroff and Comaroff 1991). For instance, Chinese historians introduced enduring biases when they wrote about the expanding states of the nomadic pastoralists living beyond China's northern frontier. Of the Hsiung Nu steppe empire (circa 200 B.C.–A.D. 155), the historian Sima Chien reports that Han Dynasty advisor Chu-fu Yen wrote, "They make a business of pillage and plunder, and indeed this would seem their inborn nature. Ever since the times of Emperor Shun and the rulers of the Hsia, Shang, and Chou dynasties, no attempt has ever been made to order or control them; rather, they have been regarded as beasts to be pastured, not as members of the human race" (Watson 1961:196). Chu-fu Yen's perspective derives from a centuries-old bias that saw the Hsiung Nu, Turks, Mongols, and others as essentially warlike tribes that only sustained themselves by raiding China, the true center of the world. The orientations of early Chinese historians continue to influence interpretations of the steppe empires, like the Hsiung Nu, as marginal and ephemeral phenomena. Only within the last few years have other aspects of steppe economy and organization received due attention, such as extensive irrigation agriculture supporting large urban centers and important trade networks with regions other than China (Barfield 2001; Di Cosmo 1994; Rogers 2004).

Colonies were seldom part of the expanding steppe empires, but in other regions of the world they constituted one of the standard strategies for incorporating new resources. The politics and ideology of control used by expanding states must factor in the implications of encountering cultural and political diversity. If ignored, such diversity becomes one of the foundations for the loss of control by centralized elites. For heuristic purposes, strategies for expansion can be broken down into four categories: (1) attempts at elimination of diversity through warfare, ethnocide, and the displacement of populations; (2) the creation of continuity or affiliation by "developing" shared history and cultural symbols; (3) overlay mechanisms that attempt to bypass or ignore diversity by importing new administrative structures; and (4) the marginal incorporation of conquered or dependent regions through minimal administrative contact and the payment of tribute (Rogers 2004).

Not all colonies are about fostering the ambitions of expanding states. Some colonies are established as trade contacts; others exist as a way for a circumscribed population to avoid political or religious control. But among the four strategies listed above, colonies are integral to at least the first three and are one of the chief mechanisms that states use to establish control in new regions. Several chapters in this book have illustrated how the differing roles of colonies can be identified archaeologically.

The domains set forth by the documentary record, as in Chu-fu Yen's comments on the Hsiung Nu, have typically defined the range and content for our explorations of archaic as well as modern states. In other words, there are things we typically say about states and their expansion when the documentary record is rich that we do not say when information is lacking. Such a situation also tends to determine the analytical perspective applied to archaic states in which the documentary record is poor or nonexistent. This was the observation of an earlier advanced seminar on archaic states likewise held at the School of American Research. The participants in that seminar concurred that "refined archaeological tools, both conceptual and methodological," were needed to understand the workings of states and would go a long way toward resolving many basic problems (Feinman and Marcus 1998:13). A new archaeological focus on colonialism fits well with an objective centered on state-level social and economic practice. This chapter, however, does not explore the political economy mega-models relating to world-systems theory (Wallerstein 1974, 1980). These models are not in the foreground of contemporary sociocultural anthropology, and they have been extensively challenged in archaeology (Kohl 1989; Stein 1999b), although the debate on their utility is far from over (for example, M. E. Smith 2001).

Rather than models like world-systems theory, the approach taken here is to determine, at a very basic level, the social and individual mechanisms that must be identified in order to construct comparative models. In particular, the focus is on developing an archaeological methodology that contributes to understanding the range of interactions evident in colonial encounters. The archaeological tools are the linking arguments and methodologies themselves that allow us to interpret situations that are not explicit in a documentary record, but can also make possible new interpretations even when supporting information is strong. Creating these tools first depends on conceptualizing the key factors that organize the differing forms of interaction. An archaeology of colonialism should not proceed without taking into account contemporary dialogues on the subject and acknowledging the genesis of certain concepts relevant to all colonialisms, past and present. The modern anthropological study of colonialism is largely focused on the European expansion of the last 500 years and is a late-twentieth-century invention that provides a context for the study of dominance, resistance, subjugation, and relativism (Dietler 1998:289; Dirks, ed. 1992:9; Gellner 1995:245–47). In essence, the term "colonialism" has taken on a certain set of meanings that relate to strategies of control. Because of the dialogue on domination currently implied by the word "colonialism," one might question whether its conceptual utility can be fully explored for any era other than the modern. Some contributors to this volume have argued on these grounds that the word "colonialism" should be set aside in favor of a view that equates colonial relationships with cultural processes that do not imply a particular set of outcomes (see N. Thomas 1994:2).

A further and equally well-known product of the study of colonialism is the wide variety of critical, self-reflective theoretical and methodological stances that have challenged many of the assumptions held dear by generations of ethnographers and other anthropologist (Bradburd 1998:153). As a postmodernist critique, "traditional" ethnography, as the distinguishing feature of modern anthropology, bears the brunt of revisionist thinking. In this newer, but no longer new approach, the ethnographer, as a member of the colonialist-dominating group, is developing a body of information about the "other" that serves to foster repression. It is further argued that the mere presence of the ethnographer is an unjustifiable enigma for the people under study (Pratt 1986:42). Likewise, the critique claims that classical ethnography does a disservice to indigenous peoples by defining them with a tribal or group name and then presuming that all members of the group think and behave the same. Indigenous voices are lost and individuals become categories reified only within the disconnected perceptions of intrusive observers serving a faraway audience (for example, Clifford 1983:133; Tyler 1986:126–27). One genre of scholarly product that addresses these concerns is a type of intersubjective dialogue between the anthropologist and the informant/partner that essentially acknowledges the heteroglossia, or multiple points of view, likely to exist in any cultural setting. This brand of ethnography places a high value on cultural relativism and advocacy for the "powerless" (Ortner 1995:186).

Ethnography as situated communication is a reaction to the almost invisible role of the individual in earlier studies. Whether or not such ethnography actually brings us closer to understanding the consequences of colonialism, it does seem clear that such debates are entrenched in the ambiguities spun from colonial encounters and are therefore relevant to the theme at hand. The dialectic of a relationship between "externally generated events and local reactions" (J. Webster 1997:328) should be something with which we are all directly concerned. The critical approach is also a reaction to other earlier styles of writing and analysis that still have relevance for how we consider the history of colonialism (Comaroff and Comaroff 1992).

Taking the long view, we know that colonialism happens, and we know that our understanding of the European expansion that has its roots in the Renaissance and earlier eras (see J. Webster 1997:331) is as much a product of anthropology and its sister disciplines as these forms of scholarship are a product of the expansion itself. In whatever way we may define the entanglement of the subject and its interpreters, there is no question that colonialism has shaped the modern world, and in this anthropology has found fertile ground for advocacy and analysis of basic human agendas. There are multiple ways to read history, and the critical assessments offered in recent years highlight the complexities of the task. A reassessment of our own ways of thinking about colonial encounters in prehistory and what it is we actually want to know would seem to be in order. As J. Webster (1997:330) points out, modern as well as ancient colonial encounters must be assessed with an awareness of our own place in history. To do this requires a comparative, yet reflective approach and not one defined principally by relativistic criteria (such as Hollis and Lukes 1982:5–12).

Several important issues for archaeological analysis emerge from the last twenty-five years of colonial reassessment and redefinition coupled with an awareness of our own status in a postcolonial world. Two issues, in particular, are fundamental to the interpretation of a wide range of contact events and processes. First, a Eurocentric bias in the ethnographic and archaeological analysis of culture contacts is commonplace in the study of the European expansion (Trigger 1980; Wilson and Rogers 1993:5). This interpretive bias exists as well in studies of other state expansions. In the Mediterranean world, a center-based approach has dominated the orientation used in the study of Phoenician, Carthaginian, and Roman empires, among others (van Dommelen 1998:17–18). As traditionally studied and interpreted in classical archaeology, the colonies and colonization process were approached from the perspective of the colonizer. This view of ancient colonialism is evident in the justifications used in the European establishment of nineteenth- and twentieth-century colonies (Dietler this volume). Recognizing a colonizer bias draws attention to key deficiencies inherent in earlier studies. Second, native cultural logics and perceptions of events play an essential role in how interactions have been structured. In effect, reflecting on the first point makes it possible to consider the second (Kaplan 1983; Wilson and Rogers 1993:3–6; see also Linton, ed. 1940:470). Likewise, the interpretive shifts implied by these two points move the scope of the argument conceptually from the center to the periphery. Such an interpretive shift is indeed part of a larger trend in Western society to focus on the pluralistic rights and privileges of the individual. The social sciences participate in this trend through concepts of practice and *habitus* as further embodied in the notion of "local practice" (N. Thomas 1994:58). Many new studies in archaeology are considering these issues, especially as they pertain to the individual and the concept of agency (for example, Bell 1992; Dietler 1998:298; Dobres and Robb 2000).

Colonization as a Structure of Interaction

Colonial relationships are the outcome of practices embedded within interactive cultural processes. The study of colonies and colonization, therefore, cannot be limited to the study of a duality of oppressor and oppressed. The cultures that emerge from the process of interaction are more than an ideology that sanctions or disguises oppression. The forms of colonial interaction are dynamic and replete with unexpected outcomes. Furthermore, the interactions exist in meaningful ways at both the individual and social levels and can be interpreted as historically situated interactions and as comparative cultural processes. Whereas much of contemporary analysis defines themes of local practice as contradictory, if not in direct opposition, to comparative approaches, the objective here is to instead build both methods into a single interpretive framework (see also Wylie 1989). To do this requires the development of linking arguments that contextualize meaning and practice at multiple levels.

Development of the linking arguments is ultimately dependent on at least a partial reconciliation of relativist approaches deriving from the individual subject with analyses of comparative social systems and the search for universals. But is the reconciliation of these two approaches of value? To be sure, the widespread use of simplistic scientific models in which reified categories took the place of dynamic interactions was a key motivator in shifting the focus away from the study of social universals (Coppet 1992:72; compare Fiske 1992; J. H. Turner 1992). Yet in the final analysis one must ask whether our more recent approaches bring us better understanding of how the human world operates. Collective social action is based on individual actions, but there is also a reality that cannot be approached through only one level of analysis. At the minimum, insights must be derived from exploration of a broad spectrum of interactions, whether parts or wholes. The solution proposed here defines multiple levels of analysis that link collective agency as discussed by Bell (1992) with the individual's participation in broader social formations in the colonial or culture contact frame of reference (compare Barraud and Platenkamp 1990:103). These are the realms in which archaeology operates—the generalized outcomes of long spans of change interpreted from the debris left behind by the actions of individuals and small groups (Hodder 2000:21).

To operationalize multiple levels of analysis, it is worthwhile to identify some particulars of the diversity of cultural encounters. The interactions between multiple cultural system can be broken down into two matrices: the conditions matrix, composed of external and internal conditions; and the structural matrix, composed of the interrelationships of those sets of conditions. Within the conditions matrix, the first set of factors, or external conditions, include such things as the biological consequences of interaction, differential resource availability, and climate. Referring to these as external conditions does not imply that they are less central to the interpretive process, nor that they are less interconnected to the social formations. Internal conditions consist of the types of social formations involved, existing economic and productive systems, relative size of contacting groups, and differentials of social and technological complexity. Many of these external and internal conditions have been used as the bases for acculturation theory (Broom et al. 1954; Redfield, Linton, and Herskovits 1936). Acculturation as a concept has been rightly criticized (for example Rogers 1993a:17); however, some of the cross-cultural variables defined as early as the 1930s may in another context deserve reexamination.

The structural matrix provides the interrelationships between the external and internal conditions and consists of a complex of factors including the regularizing principles of identity formation and the construction of ethnicity (Comaroff and Comaroff 1992:54; Kottak 1980:4–5), as mechanisms for both differentiation and integration. Additional aspects of the structural matrix include culturally invented memory (for hegemonic and ideological reasons), especially the conflation of events in memory (related to conceptions of time), and the creation of tradition; historical contextualization, or the reflexive nature of historical discourse; and the construction of authority. The structural matrix factors are largely about the formation of group and individual identity and the differential application of power. In this regard, both holistic and individualistic explanations of the role of agency are relevant.

Cultural order is always at risk in action (Keane 1997; Sahlins 1985:ix; N. Thomas 1989:103). In particular, at the level of individual action there is a constant alternation between conflation and expansion of time. As will be discussed later, this is an important concept for applications of archaeological analysis. Differing cultural systems of time constrain the role of memory in an ideal sense, but the individual's use of memory to make sense of a lifetime always has a certain linearity, no matter how predetermined, circular, or reciprocal the ideological view of past and future time may be. As part of memory in this constantly shifting use of time, there is a vision of the past as stable, synchronic, and normative. But this stable vision of the past, as a normative outline for cultural action, is not used in a static sense. The actor draws upon it in a very selective way, allowing all sorts of manipulations and inversions (M. H. Johnson 1989:207). Memory exists at the level of action, but it is connected in time and space through a series of relationships with material and social constructs through object associations defined below as "iconic structures."

When it comes to colonial encounters, the construction and maintenance of power is especially important, as it relates to control of or access to cosmological forces and differential authority in social hierarchies. Power can take many forms, including differentials derived from such things as technology and relative group size (that is, from some of the internal conditions mentioned earlier). In culture contact, the social groups involved in the encounter often exercise very different levels of power, the stronger of which is capable of controlling labor and achieving desired outcomes, thus producing patterns of colonial domination decidedly different from the use of power as it existed prior to the encounter (compare Giddens 1979:88).

Newly created power structures are one of the most visible aspects of colonialism. Using analogies based on the historical record and twentieth-century ethnography, archaeologically discernible differentials of power are visible in such things as changes in trade routes, settlement locations, concentrations of exotic or presumed high-value items, segregated enclaves, military establishments, and elite architecture. Ethnographically, domination of the colonizer finds expression in a wide range of social and individual forms, typically associated with economic and social subjugation.

Beyond the coercive powers evident through subjugation and associated forms of resistance, other types of power transfers can take place. At least in the early phases of colonial and other encounters, cosmological power and powers associated with legitimation of existing cultural practices were acquired by direct contact or exchange of goods between the contacting groups (Rogers 1990:54, 57–58; N. Thomas 1991:83–124). These types of power transfers were an extremely important part of the creation of new systems of interaction and set the stage for unanticipated outcomes. In reference to the European expansion of the fifteenth century, in many parts of the world the exchange of power was not balanced; however, where the contacting groups were relatively similar, transitions of power structures and their bureaucracies still took different shapes. And even where European-imposed structures of domination held sway, differential power transfers produced, at least for some time, outcomes consistent with the differential objectives of the contacting groups. All regions of the world for which we have evidence of colonial encounters provide examples of how indigenous and intruder interactions are structured by competing agendas (for example, this volume; Cusick, ed. 1998; Gosden, ed. 1997).

As argued above, the structure of individual and group action and the associated issue of contextualization of meaning, power relations, identity in agency, and the creation of history are important to the interpretation of contact interactions; in fact, they are equally essential as components of a theory of social action. The fundamental operation of colonization interactions is an aspect of all of these intertwined and admittedly complex issues.

Identifying Outcomes in Indigenous/Colonizer Encounters

Much of the foregoing discussion has described the factors at work in an interaction process—specifically, how meaning takes shape in relation to place, object, time, and the actor. One set of object/time relationships especially relevant to the approach advocated here is referred to as "iconic structures." These are the guideposts that partially link dynamic social activity and ideological constructs and represent part of the structure matrix discussed earlier. The concept of an iconic structure is derived from Peirce's (1931–1935, vol. 4:447) semiotics research in which he defined three types of signs—indexes, symbols, and icons. Each type of sign provides a means of conceptualizing links between objects or other forms of materiality and a temporal placement. Stated simply, indexes form a direct relationship between object and expression and are anchored to present action. Symbols are connected to future time because they always imply some further interpretation. Icons embody a direct resemblance between the expression and the physical object and therefore inherently refer to past time because the meaning functions without the presence of the object. Parmentier's (1985, 1987:107–26) ethnological work in Belau used semiotic analysis to connect patterns and meanings with their physical referents and is important here as a basis for these observations.

Although this analysis is concerned with the three types of signs, it is clear that other aspects of Peirce's analysis are relevant to the study of material culture and have the potential of providing an even more comprehensive analytical framework (Parmentier 1997; Preucel and Bauer 2001).

The semiotic networks that emerge from consideration of indexes, symbols, and icons represent a powerful tool for archaeological analysis, especially the study of social change over time. Peirce's work provides a dynamic set of relationships that can be identified and charted, and although his intent was to build understandings of complex relationships from very small-scale examples, it is possible to generalize the concept of signs and to identify iconic structures within particular cultural domains of activity that have visibility both archaeologically and in the historical record. Although signs are integral to a wide variety of cultural activities, expression of ritual, social structure, and the materiality of architecture and settlement organization are especially relevant for archaeology. All three types of signs serve to regularize time, although icons are associated with past time and serve as a conceptual anchor through concrete associations. Such things as the physical construction and organization of a house and its cosmological associations can be among the many vehicles for presentation, indexically anchored to other spatial relationships (for example, Cunningham 1973; Donley 1982; Kuper 1980; Swanton 1946:393). Over time, the degree to which a group maintains coherence in preexisting iconic structures is a good indicator of the level and types of change in operation. Likewise, the overlapping or integrated nature of icons can serve as a predictor of the relative degree of "success" a society may have in maintaining coherence in the face of powerful disruptive forces. The indexical structures are particularly important for archaeology because of the durable physical associations among object, place, and sets of meaning.

The maintenance of cultural coherence in iconic structures is actually an ever-changing activity. To maintain coherence does not mean a one-dimensional avoidance or rejection of change. Yet, the "success" a society may have in maintaining a broadly integrated and understood series of cultural meanings is often associated with attempting to control the disruptions associated with rapid changes in the conditions matrix.

Three divergent cases of colonial encounters derived from the documentary and ethnographic record—the Arikara, the !Kung San, and the Aztecs—illustrate contrasts in interaction outcomes relating to iconic structures. The conditions and structures described earlier serve as a footing for interpreting a variety of contact situations. All three cases are presented here because of the great differences in the circumstances of their respective encounters with Europeans, yet there are strong similarities that can be discovered through analysis of structure and power relations.

The Arikara (Sahnish) were a village-dwelling agricultural group from the northern Great Plains of North America. Today the Arikara are members of the Three Affiliated Tribes, principally living in North Dakota. From the middle of the seventeenth century through the middle of the nineteenth century, they were significant participants in the fur trade that developed with the arrival of primarily French and American traders. They did not experience a significant missionizing influence until the 1860s and no colonization efforts until somewhat later. Among the Arikara, every person knew his or her place within the limited number of roles that an individual was born to or might aspire to. Social relations were organized hierarchically and along significant gender and kinship lines. Iconic structures existed at many overlapping levels—in the individual and group bundle system that used mnemonic devices to represent historical events and cosmological relationships, in the layout of circular houses, in ritual, in secular performance, and in the ways the landscape was used (Rogers 1993b:77). Both architectural and landscape patterning are useful in archaeological analyses because of the relative clarity in which changes over time may be recognized. In one sense it can be said that Arikara cosmology depended on the discovery of order, its replication, and its representation in house architecture and village patterning. Individuals often had a significant role in multiple aspects of this system of relationships, thus producing for the individual a secure sense of place and obligation. All of these things functioned as tradition. Obviously, the same could be said for many peoples from anywhere in the world. Even so, there are many differences in the degree to which iconic structures functioned as integrative mechanisms within the long-standing system of beliefs.

The degree to which these structures were integrative is reflective of aspects of social cohesion. In studying a particular history of encounter, observations may be made on where gaps occur in the iconic structures. For the Arikara, important gaps developed because of the conflation of authority hierarchies associated with population loss, amalgamation of villages, and increasing European control of trading opportunities. The result was a less hierarchically organized system with more emphasis on achieved status (Rogers 1993b:85). This formulation of authority essentially allowed Arikara individuals to take advantage of changing circumstances, even as the upper levels of the authority hierarchy became occupied by European traders and missionaries (by the 1860s). While these drastic changes were taking place, continuity was maintained, for a time, in iconic structures, principally in the sacred bundle system and a conception, if not a reality, of the geographical organization of village clusters and their cosmological associations. This allowed the Arikara to perpetuate a distinct cultural identity in the face of massively destructive external conditions— although only for a time. Eventually the remnants of the Arikara population were forced to take up residence with the Mandan and Hidatsa. From the middle to the late twentieth century, a cultural rebirth process began to redefine "traditional" culture.

In another part of the world, the sweeping changes among the !Kung San and other groups of the Kalahari during the last three decades provide a further example of the implications of iconic structures. Especially since the 1960s, several San groups have undergone an accelerated rate of culture change, due largely to the intrusion of "modern" society (R. B. Lee 1976:20). Much of the encroachment can be attributed to neighboring groups under the influence of colonial regimes. From an archaeological point of view, an important part of the San experience is their increasing level of sedentism (Hitchcock 1982), associated with new settlement patterns (Yellen 1977), new concepts of property ownership (Gelburd 1978), and adoption of agriculture, where environment permits. Among the !Kung San, for instance, change brought extensive social disruption through a disjuncture between traditionally valued modes of behavior and new demands and opportunities, based on a shift to wage labor and a multitude of other factors. The effects of pressures exerted on the San continue to result in a major departure from the traditional social patterns and values, toward a shift to the types of practices of neighboring sedentary agricultural groups. San society lacks the political and social mechanisms necessary to control the consequences of contact with a drastically different and puissant social system. For now, and probably for some time to come, social disruption will be a way of life for the San.

The process of culture change that the !Kung San are now undergoing may be anticipated, in part, due to the comparatively few linkages between components of their indexical and iconic structures and the sharp contrast between traditional social concerns and new concerns generated from external pressures. In gatherer-hunter societies, like the !Kung San, the material linkages with the supernatural are relatively fewer and more polysemic in nature (that is, a single object tends to have several symbolic connotations depending on context [V. W. Turner 1977:186, 190]). The socially institutionalized linkages with the supernatural are also fewer, and therefore there is less potential for filling "gaps" resulting from disruptive interactions. Consequently, alterations in even a few areas of material and social linkage can have a major disruptive effect.

The Aztec case offers some important contrasts to the two examples of relatively small-scale societies discussed thus far. The Aztecs—or, more properly, the Mexica—developed a hegemonic empire during the fifteenth and early sixteenth centuries, with an imperial ideology based on the core pantheon of Central Mexican gods and associated beliefs. The creation of this ideology is a classic example of the invention of tradition, given the reasonably clear appropriation of the prestigious Toltec heritage by the Mexica (Conrad and Demarest 1984; compare Hobsbawm and Ranger 1983). Through conquest and the associated creation of subordinate political and ethnic affiliations, the Mexica empire expanded rapidly. The Mexica empire was in turn conquered in the infamous encounters following the arrival of Cortez in 1519.

In terms of complexity, there is little similarity between the Arikara, San, and Aztec cultural systems. The Aztec were a highly compartmentalized, market-based empire that integrated, on differing levels, hundreds of thousands of individuals. Integrated as it may have been, individuals generally participated in the overall system in relatively restricted ways. The most important linkages were through participation in state religion and especially through a reciprocal notion of time that served to predetermine an individual's actions—from birth to death (Durán 1967, vol. 2:2). The individual lived a life determined by the positive or negative connotations attached to the month and day under which he or she was born. Along with the characteristics of any particular day of the calendar, omens and divinations were part of the reading of divine intent.

Several authors have recognized that Aztec notions of time and cosmology are a fundamental prelude to reading the historical record of Spain–Mexico interactions. Todorov (1984), in particular, presents an integrated analysis of Aztec discourses in the context of the Spanish arrival in the early sixteenth century. Todorov's (1984:84–87) ideas contrast somewhat with those of León-Portilla (1963), who does not assign the same level of fatalistic orientation to Aztec thought. However, like Todorov, he does confirm the Mexica notion of time as having strong linear as well as reciprocal aspects. These two aspects of Mexica time are represented by the linear historiography and by the constant re-creation of events evident in the recording of happenings in the codices. Hassig's (2001) recent reanalysis of the calendric system and its role in Aztec society goes further, placing less emphasis on the cyclical nature of time while stressing elite use of the calendar for political purposes. Even so, it is reasonable to assert that Aztec cosmology is characterized by the establishment of first order and its periodic active re-creation as monitored by a complex calendric system (Durán 1967, vol. 1:22; Florescano 1994:19–20).

For the Aztecs, the arrival of the Spanish produced an event that was predestined as the return of the god Quetzalcoatl. The Spanish conquest resulted in the conflation of the authoritative hierarchy as in the Arikara case, as well as an almost instantaneous expansion of it. Much has been said about Spanish appropriation of existing tribute arrangements, and in some ways this is true. However, those arrangements quickly evolved to service the complex of Spanish interests generated by the church and the colonizing efforts of Spanish elites. These forces created new authority structures that the native populace was forced to serve. As the Aztec priests said, "Our gods are already dead" (Léon-Portilla 1963:63), presaging a capitulation to Spanish civil and religious authority, if not ideals. A materialist reading of these events might emphasize the fact that people are not easily duped by the logic of state ideologies. Nevertheless, the predetermined existence of the individual under the Aztec religion collapsed, and so did the associated iconic structures.

One might hypothesize a crisis of identity for the individual in Aztec society, if it were not for the fact that the vast majority of families, whether urban or rural, maintained some semblance of continuity in their daily labor and relations to local authority structures. Even in the face of massive population decline and congregation into new population centers, there was continuity on the local level. The compartmentalized nature of the Aztec empire was key to providing individual continuities very different from that experienced by the Arikara or !Kung San. The gaps that may have appeared in the Aztec iconic structure could be filled or circumvented by a complex web of other linkages in their sociomaterial cosmological hierarchy of relations.

If we simply say that peoples wherever encountered by Europeans suffered massive changes in the native order of things, or if we describe these encounters as disjointed histories unconnected to other similar colonial occurrences, then we miss the interpretive implications of society and the structure of interactions (see Coppet 1992). The purpose of contrasting groups like the Arikara, the !Kung San, and the Aztec is not to determine which type of formation was most successful in withstanding the pressures of culture contact, but instead to examine individual action and the contextualization of meaning as forces for change and continuity.

Culture contact is ongoing, and the iconic structures, plus constructs of memory/time and authority, provide points of departure for understanding long-term change for both the individual and larger social formations. The complexity of the semiotic structures and their interconnectedness provides a crucial reading of the consequences of colonial encounters. Other factors, however—such as disease or the hostile intent of intruding groups (especially in the New World)—must also be considered. Even so, within limits, cultural systems determine the nature of the response to a context of change. Some may accept change, like the Batak of Indonesia (Bruner 1973); others may reject outside influences, as did the Erromango and groups on the Isle of Pines in the South Pacific (Sahlins 1982); and others, like the !Kung San, Yir Yoront of Australia (Sharp 1952), and many groups in the

Americas, may face drastic social consequences. Cultural perceptions orient responses to further the goals of individuals or subgroups in the society along themes of general social concern. These goals, when operating within a context of change, may carry a largely unforeseen trajectory of their own. The trajectory instigated by cultural perceptions may have the long-term effect of keeping change within manageable proportions or of fostering a cycle of social disruption. This point, however, is well beyond the scope of this discussion, but could be usefully investigated to provide insight into additional consequences of internally structured change.

The iconic structures, in the context of semiotics, are part of the broader object connection—the relation between places and things and their social, political, and cosmological referents. The establishment of this link is largely methodological here but is the crucial step for archaeological analysis. Meaning as attached to objects is context- and function-specific (Hodder 1985:14). Archaeologically, we can identify some contexts that have solid material implications and relatively unambiguous functional interpretations. As part of a cultural context, objects serve to bind experience into meaningful parcels (Csikszentmihalyi and Rochberg-Halton 1981:16), whereas the construction of meaning as it involves objects centers on the creation of value as a political process (Appadurai, ed. 1986:3). The best way we have of addressing this observation is through contextual interpretation.

AN ARCHAEOLOGICAL METHODOLOGY

Considering the components of the conditions and structure matrices and the specific examples of iconic structures, we are ready to return to issues of an archaeological methodology informed by, but not contingent on, historically documented cases. Five propositions can be advanced that articulate the observations developed thus far:

1. The forms of response engendered by interaction are meaningfully constructed. This includes the creation of meaning through objects (see Douglas and Isherwood 1979) that serve to substantiate and regularize the construction of knowledge and practice. Likewise, objects as a principal, but not sole, medium of exchange relations are key to the related process of value definition.

2. Contacting groups each operate in accordance with their respective cultural logics to achieve their own version of autonomy, security, and other culturally defined goals. Although a region might be colonized or an indigenous people subjugated, encounter outcomes are predicated on the disjuncture between the multiple cultural logics, regardless of power differentials. Although there are patterns in the way that encounter outcomes are structured, predictability is at least partially dependent on the uniquely ordered qualities of particular culture histories.

3. Historical observations, as the reflexive nature of historical discourse, are key to understanding the disjuncture in cultural logics as a "rationalization" of interaction processes and outcomes, especially through the construction of cultural memory. Essentially, events are placed in time and interpreted and reinterpreted according to individual and social contingencies.

4. Meaningful constructs are context-specific, both historical and physical. This is a key proposition for archaeological analysis, because it allows the assignment of meaningful relationships without having to know the intricacies of specific cultural meanings. If, for example, this way of looking at contexts is correct, then the presence of exotic goods alone is not a good indicator of the level or type of interaction taking place. Nor are such items a good indicator of broader change processes that may be the result of such interactions.

5. Although the cultural and social meaning of an object may vary with context, the physical properties of the item are not arbitrary. Some materials are better at performing a particular function than others. An iron knife is manifestly stronger and more durable than a stone knife.

These five propositions lay the groundwork for an archaeological methodology that allows the interpretation of colonial encounters.

The question is this: What are the material culture components of cultural meaning relevant to specific instances and types of colonial interactions? Through several iterations, an approach has been developed and applied to the analysis of changes in native societies (primarily Arikara) associated with the arrival of Europeans on the North American Great Plains (Rogers 1990, 1993b). These studies produced a methodology to allow the crucial linkage to be established. The approach is summarized below as a sequence of analysis, with notations on key considerations about how data are conceptualized and interpreted.

In order to link the object with cultural practice, the archaeological methodology must begin with the fundamentals of chronology. For a particular case, any existing chronology should be evaluated in terms of whether it reflects "meaningful" changes in the society under study. A chronology based largely on changes in ceramic typology may need to be reconstructed. Studies of typologies, especially chronologies, in archaeology have illustrated the technical and cultural biases inherent in the production of any sequence of events or time periods. The chronology is the first-level hypothesis, and it must be congruent with relevant changes spanning a particular colonial encounter time frame. Likewise, the basis for the chronology should be made explicit.

Given a useful chronology, defining sets of unambiguous archaeological contexts for comparison between periods represents the next task. For instance, domestic structures, public structures, burials, or middens associated with activities that can reasonably be inferred are among the most likely contexts for comparison. These types of contexts often produce a wide range of material associations that can be utilized as context assemblages. Depending on the particular case, other archaeological contexts may be usable, but must be consistently definable for each time period.

Assuming that comparable contexts can be identified, while also considering depositional history and sample validity, it then becomes possible to consider issues of the iconic structures and to characterize the materials that have been or may be recovered from the context. Characterizing the materials refers to what we do when we infer that a small, sharp, flaked piece of stone is an arrowhead. At several levels this piece of stone has meaning. It is a technology of weaponry, and it contains cultural messages through style, value, and through contexts of use and archaeological discovery, all of which may or may not change over time. These many functions can be inferred through specific or generalized knowledge of cultural practices. Even so, it is not enough to characterize one object as simply a projectile point and another as only a knife. The object is made up of overlapping and simultaneous meanings. These meanings cannot be parceled out effectively, as in a tree diagram (dendrogram), but can be presented as an overlapping cover set model (Gould 1981; Rogers 1990:148). Use of this type of model produces a distinctively different form of analysis that emphasizes the connectedness of meanings rather than their separateness (Beaumont and Gatrell 1982).

With a chronology and characterizations of the artifacts, specific material-change propositions with definable cultural implications can be advanced. In an earlier study, these propositions were described as *maintenance, addition, replacement, rejection,* and *transformation* (Rogers 1990:105). Each ties a simple social implication to an observable material change in the artifact categories. Although the processes define simple relationships, when taken together interpretations can be built that reveal disruptions in social organization, the meaningful construction of practice, and disjunctures that reveal the construction of outcomes. The change propositions are then used to construct a hypothesized set of relationships derived from the chronological sequence. Expected relationships between change propositions, specific archaeological contexts, artifact categories, and each chronological period can be compared with actual data. This is the heart of the analysis, as the actual numerical and distributional observations serve to confirm or reject expected relationships.

Constructing the analysis through the process described here provides the potential to explore how different contexts change over time and how the composition of artifact assemblages relate to a variety of differential meanings. This type of analysis requires some significant shifts in thinking, principally about the role of the object in interpretation; however, other aspects of the analysis are more traditional. That is, the study relies on explicit objectives, well-defined chronologies, comparable data sets, and quantifiable results.

CONCLUSIONS

This book is about colonies, colonizers, and the people who had the peculiar fate of being on the receiving end of colonization.

Colonies and the process by which they are established, maintained, expanded, or abandoned represent an exceedingly complex yet important set of issues. Without question, our world was, and continues to be, shaped by events and processes derived from colonialism. All of the people involved in colonial interactions, from the first encounters through long stretches of time, played a role in establishing the direction of change. Histories written solely from the perspective of powerful empires and their colonial enterprises fail to understand the process as it impacted the colonizers or the colonized. In recent decades, much of anthropology has taken up the challenge of analyzing colonialism and its consequences as it existed in the nineteenth and twentieth centuries and continues to exist today. The focus has principally been the colonized peoples of the world and their individual struggles for self-determination. These studies have revealed much about how the world operates and what our individual and collective roles are.

For archaeology, the study of the colonial landscape has not dealt with the immediacy of colonialism as it exists in the modern world. However, where study has expanded to encompass all times and places, it has begun to approach the implications of the diversity of cases. Care must be taken to allow room for colonial interactions that do not conform to any known modern forms. Archaeology is particularly sensitized to the potential for more varied forms than exist currently or in the recent past, considering the well-articulated concerns already voiced about the limitations of the ethnographic record (H. M. Wobst 1978). Whereas the limitations of the documentary and ethnographic records may be recognized, the means necessary to go beyond these sources is generally lacking. This chapter attempts to address this particular concern by developing the theoretical and methodological tools for investigating the colony, and other forms of interaction, when the sources of information are largely archaeological. Likewise, the goal has been to place archaeological data on a sounder footing, even when other sources of information are available.

Colonies, by their very nature, are associated with states and empires, especially during periods of expansion. Colonies invariably provide points of contact for trade, exchange of information, technological innovation, and a context for the rapid creation of new forms of cultural practice. In this way colonies are among the most effective, yet difficult to control tools of complex power hierarchies. In a pragmatic sense, the political economy of colonies is often associated with conquest and rests on the creation of opportunity for individuals, the lure of profit, the extension of control, and effective competition with rivals. In an ideational sense, the colony and the justification for conquest is often associated with the expansion of state religions, which also provides a point of motivation for the individual participants.

The colony is one of the places where collective meaning is made. Humans try to make sense of the world and inhabit their surroundings in ways that are logical, within a particular cultural system (Kegan 1982). This is done in part by creating forms of meaning linked to particular contexts. Objects are integral to this process, as both an extension of the body itself and as part of meaning packages that make the world around us stable and knowable. Archaeology has the tremendous potential to explore the diversity of ways in which meaning is constructed in different places and times. This work, however, requires both theories that link objects to the realms of ideology as well as praxis, and also methodologies that are rigorous and comparative and can make use of the vast amounts of information at our disposal.

References

Abascal, R., G. Harbottle, and E. Sayre

1974   Correlation between Terra Cotta Figurines and Pottery from the Valley of Mexico and Source Clays by Activation Analysis. In *Archaeological Chemistry*, edited by C. Beck, pp. 81–99. Washington, DC: Chemical Society.

Abu El-Haj, N.

1998   Translating Truths: Nationalism, the Practice of Archaeology, and the Remaking of Past and Present in Contemporary Jerusalem. *American Ethnologist* 25:166–88.

2001   *Facts on the Ground: Archaeological Practice and Territorial Self Fashioning in Israeli Society.* Chicago: University of Chicago Press.

Acosta, J. de

1985–   *Historia natural y moral de las Indias.* Mexico City: Biblioteca Americana,
[1590]   Fondo de Cultura Económica.

Acquaro, E.

1983   Nuove ricerche a Tharros. In *Atti del I congresso internazionale di studi fenici e punici, Roma 5–10 Novembre 1979*, pp. 624–31. Rome: Istituto di studi fenici (CNR).

1991   Tharros tra Fenicia e Cartagine. In *Atti del II congresso internazionale di studi fenici e punici*, pp. 547–58. Collezione di studi fenici 30. Rome: Istituto di studi fenici (CNR)

Adams, R. McC.

1974   Anthropological Perspectives on Ancient Trade. *Current Anthropology* 15 (2):239–58.

1981   *Heartland of Cities.* Chicago: University of Chicago Press.

Adams, R. N.

1994   Guatemalan Ladinization and History. *The Americas* 50 (4):527–43.

Adams, W.

1984   The First Colonial Empire: Egypt in Nubia, 3200–1200 B.C. *Comparative Studies in Society and History* 26 (1):36–71.

Adorno, R.

1993   Reconsidering Colonial Discourse for Sixteenth- and Seventeenth-Century Spanish America. *Latin American Research Review* 28 (3):135–45.

1994   The Indigenous Ethnographer: The "Indio Ladino" as Historian and Cultural Mediation. In *Implicit Understandings,* edited by Stuart B. Schwartz, pp. 378–402. Cambridge: Cambridge University Press.

Aginsky, B. W.

1949   The Interaction of Ethnic Groups: A Case Study of Indians and Whites. *American Sociological Review* 14 (2):288–93.

Aguayo, P., M. Carrilero, and G. Martinez

1991   La presencia fenicia y el proceso de acculturación de las communidades del Bronce Final de la depresión de Ronda (Málaga). In *Atti del II congresso internazionale di studi fenici e punici,* pp. 559–71. Collezione di studi fenici 30. Rome: Istituto di studi fenici (CNR).

Akkermans, P. M. M. G., and I. Rossmeisl

1990   Excavations at Tell Sabi Abyad, Northern Syria: A Regional Centre on the Assyrian Frontier. *Akkadica* 66:13–60.

Albeck, M. E.

1992–   Areas agrícolas y densidad de ocupación prehispánica en la quebrada de
1993   Humahuaca. *Avances en arqueología* 2:56–77.

Albeck, M. E., and M. C. Scattolin

1991   Cálculo fotogramétrico de superficies de cultivo en Coctaca y Rodero, quebrada de Humahuaca. *Avances en arqueología* 1:43–58.

Alcock, S. E.

1989   Archaeology and Imperialism: Roman Expansion and the Greek City. *Journal of Mediterranean Archaeology* 2:87–135.

1993   *Graecia Capta: The Landscapes of Roman Greece.* Cambridge: Cambridge University Press.

2000   Classical Order and the Uses of Nostalgia. In *Order, Legitimacy and Wealth in Early States,* edited by J. Richards and M. Van Buren, pp. 110–19. Cambridge: Cambridge University Press.

2001   The Reconfiguration of Memory in the Eastern Roman Empire. In *Empires: Perspectives from Archaeology and History,* edited by S. E. Alcock, T. N. D'Altroy, K. D. Morrison, and C. M. Sinopoli, pp. 323–50. Cambridge: Cambridge University Press.

2002   *Archaeologies of the Greek Past: Landscapes, Monuments and Memories.* Cambridge: Cambridge University Press.

Alconini, S.

2001   Dynamics and Settlement Patterns of the Imperial Inka Frontier against the Chiriguanos, Southeastern Bolivia. Paper presented at the Annual Meeting of the Society for American Archaeology, New Orleans.

Algaze, G.

1986   Habuba on the Tigris: Archaic Nineveh Reconsidered. *Journal of Near Eastern Studies* 45:125–37.

1989   The Uruk Expansion: Cross Cultural Exchange in Early Mesopotamian Civilization. *Current Anthropology* 30 (1):571–608.

1993a   Expansionary Dynamics of Some Early Pristine States. *American Anthropologist* 95 (2):304–33.

1993b   *The Uruk World System: The Dynamics of Expansion of Early Mesopotamian Civilization.* Chicago: University of Chicago Press.

Allen, R.

1998   *Native Americans at Mission Santa Cruz, 1791–1834: Interpreting the Archaeological Record.* Perspectives in California Archaeology 5. Los Angeles: Institute of Archaeology, UCLA.

Altman, I., and J. Lockhart, eds.

1976   *Provinces of Early Mexico.* Los Angeles: Latin American Center, UCLA.

Alva, W., and C. B. Donnan

1994   *Royal Tombs of Sipán.* 2nd ed. Los Angeles: Fowler Museum of Cultural History, UCLA.

Amandry, M.

1988   *Le monnayage des duovirs corinthiens.* Paris: Diffusion de Boccard.

Amselle, J.

1998   *Mestizo Logics: Anthropology of Identity in Africa and Elsewhere.* Stanford, CA:
[1990] Stanford University Press.

Anderson, A. J. O., F. Berdan, and J. Lockhart

1976   *Beyond the Codices.* Berkeley: University of California Press.

Anderson, B.

1991   *Imagined Communities: Reflections on the Origin and Spread of Nationalism.* 2nd ed. London: Verso.

Appadurai, A.

1986   Introduction: Commodities and the Politics of Value. In *The Social Life of Things: Commodities in Cultural Perspective,* edited by A. Appadurai, pp. 3–63. Cambridge: Cambridge University Press.

1996   *Modernity at Large: Cultural Dimensions of Globalization.* Minneapolis: University of Minnesota Press.

Appadurai, A., ed.

1986   *The Social Life of Things: Commodities in Cultural Perspective.* Cambridge: Cambridge University Press.

Arriaga, P. J. de

1968   La extirpación de la idolatría del Pirú. In *Crónicas peruanas de interés*
[1621] *indígena,* edited by F. E. Barba. *Biblioteca de autores españoles (continuación),* vol. 209, pp. 191–275. Madrid: Ediciones Atlas.

REFERENCES

Ascher, M., and R. Ascher

1981   *Code of the Quipu.* Ann Arbor: University of Michigan Press.

Ashcroft, B., G. Griffiths, and H. Tiffin

1995   *The Post-Colonial Studies Reader.* London: Routledge.

Aubet, M.-E.

1991   Notas sobre las colonias del sur de España y su función en el marco terri-
        torial: El ejemplo del Cerro del Villar. In *Atti del II congresso internazionale
        di studi fenici e punici*, pp. 617–28. Collezione di studi fenici 30. Rome:
        Istituto di studi fenici (CNR).

1993   *The Phoenicians and the West: Politics, Colonies and Trade.* Cambridge:
        Cambridge University Press.

1997a   Introducción: Los Fenicios en Málaga. In *Los Fenicios en Málaga*, edited by
        M.-E. Aubet, pp. 5–10. Thema. Málaga: Universidad de Málaga.

1997b   Un lugar de mercado en el Cerro del Villar. In *Los Fenicios en Málaga*, edit-
        ed by M.-E. Aubet, pp. 197–213. Thema. Málaga: Universidad de Málaga.

**Aubet, M.-E., P. Carmona, E. Curià, A. Delgado, A. Fernández Cantos, and
M. Pàrraga**

1999   *Cerro del Villar: I. El asentamiento fenicio en la desembocadura del Río
        Guadalhorce y su interacción con el hinterland.* Arqueología monografías.
        Seville: Junta de Andalucía.

Auslander, L.

1996   *Taste and Power: Furnishing Modern France.* Berkeley: University of California
        Press.

BAHD

1983   *Boletín del archivo histórico diocesano.* Boletín 5. Instituto de asesoria
        antropológica para la region Maya, A.C. San Cristóbal de las Casas,
        Chiapas, Mexico.

Baines, J., and N. Yoffee

1998   Order, Legitimacy, and Wealth in Ancient Egypt and Mesopotamia. In
        Archaic States, edited by G. Feinman and J. Marcus, pp. 199–260. Santa Fe:
        School of American Research Press.

Bairoch, P.

1988   *Cities and Economic Development.* Chicago: University of Chicago Press.

Baker, B. J., and L. Kealhofer, eds.

1996   *Bioarchaeology of Native American Adaptation in the Spanish Borderlands.*
        Gainesville: University Press of Florida.

Balandier, G.

1951   La situation coloniale: Approche théorique. *Cahiers internationaux de soci-
        ologie* 11:44–79.

Ballard, H. S.

1997   Ethnicity and Chronology at Metini, Fort Ross State Historic Park,

California. In *The Archaeology of Russian Colonialism in the North and Tropical Pacific*, edited by P. R. Mills and A. Martinez, pp. 116–40. Kroeber Anthropological Society Papers 81. Berkeley, CA.

Bandelier, A. F.

1910   *The Islands of Titicaca and Coati.* New York: Hispanic Society of America.

Barandas, J. M.

1984   The Catholic Church in Colonial Spanish America. In *Cambridge History of Latin America*, vol. 1, edited by L. Bethell, pp. 511–40. Cambridge: Cambridge University Press.

Barba, L., and J. L. Córdova

1999   Estudios energéticos de la producción de cal en tiempos teotihuacanos y sus implicaciones. *Latin American Antiquity* 10:168–79.

Barcelò, P.

1988   Karthago und die iberische Halbinsel vor den Barkiden. *Antiquitas* 1–37. Bonn.

1989   Zur karthagischen Überseepolitik im VI. und V. Jahrhundert v. Chr. *Gymnasium* 96:13–37.

Barfield, T. J.

2001   The Shadow Empires: Imperial State Formation along the Chinese-Nomad Frontier. In *Empires: Perspectives from Archaeology and History*, edited by S. E. Alcock, T. N. D'Altroy, K. D. Morrison, and C. M. Sinopoli, pp. 10–41. Cambridge: Cambridge University Press.

Barker, F., P. Hulme, and M. Iversen, eds.

1994   *Colonial Discourse/Postcolonial Theory.* Manchester: Manchester University Press.

Barraud, C., and J. D. M. Platenkamp

1990   Rituals and the Comparison of Societies. *Bijdragen tot de Taal-, Land- en Volkenkunde* 146:103–23.

Bartel, B.

1985   Comparative Historical Archaeology and Archaeological Theory. In *Comparative Studies in the Archaeology of Colonialism*, edited by S. L. Dyson, pp. 8–37. BAR International Series 233. Oxford: British Archaeological Reports.

Bats, M.

1988   La logique de l'écriture d'une société à l'autre en Gaule méridionale protohistorique. *Revue archéologique de Narbonnaise* 21:121–48.

Baudrillard, J.

1968   *Le système des objets.* Paris: Gallimard.

Bauer, B. S.

1998   *The Sacred Landscape of the Inca: The Cusco Ceque System.* Austin: University of Texas Press.

REFERENCES

Bauer, B. S., and C. Stanish

2001   *Ritual and Pilgrimage in the Ancient Andes.* Austin: University of Texas Press.

Bawden, G.

1982   Community Organization Reflected by the Household: A Study of Pre-Columbian Social Dynamics. *Journal of Field Archaeology* 9:165–82.

Beaumont, J. R., and A. C. Gatrell

1982   *An Introduction to Q-Analysis.* Concepts and Techniques in Modern Geography 34. Norwich, UK: Geo Abstracts.

Behm-Blancke, M. R.

1981   Hassek Höyük. Vorläufiger Bericht über die Ausgrabungen der Jahre 1978–1980. *Istanbuler Mitteilungen* 31:5–82.

1992   Hassek Höyük eine Uruk Station im Grenzland zu Anatolien. *Nürnberger Blätter zur Archäologie* 8:82–94.

Bell, J.

1992   On Capturing Agency in Theories about Prehistory. In *Representations in Archaeology,* edited by J.-C. Gardin and C. S. Peebles, pp. 30–55. Bloomington: Indiana University Press.

Bénabou, M.

1976   *La résistance africaine à la romanisation.* Paris: Maspéro.

Benavides C., M.

1978   *Yacimientos arqueológicos en Ayacucho.* Huamanga: Universidad Nacional de San Cristóbal de Huamanga.

1991   Cheqo Wasi, Huari. In *Huari Administrative Structure: Prehistoric Monumental Architecture and State Government,* edited by W. H. Isbell and G. F. McEwan, pp. 55–69. Washington, DC: Dumbarton Oaks.

Benoit, F.

1965   *Recherches sur l'hellénisation du Midi de la Gaule.* Publications des Annales de la faculté des lettres 43. Aix-en-Provence.

Berberián, E. E., and R. A. Raffino

1991   *Culturas indígenas de los Andes meridionales.* Madrid: Alhambra.

Berdan, F. F.

1996   The Tributary Provinces. In *Aztec Imperial Strategies,* by F. F. Berdan et al., pp. 115–36. Washington, DC: Dumbarton Oaks.

Berdan, F. F., R. E. Blanton, E. H. Boone, M. G. Hodge, M. E. Smith, and E. Umberger

1996   *Aztec Imperial Strategies.* Washington, DC: Dumbarton Oaks.

Berdan, F. F., M. A. Masson, J. Gasco, and M. E. Smith

2003   An International Economy. In *The Postclassic Mesoamerican World,* edited by M. E. Smith and F. F. Berdan, pp. 96–108. Salt Lake City: University of Utah Press.

Berdan, F. F., and M. E. Smith

1996   Imperial Strategies and Core-Periphery Relations. In *Aztec Imperial Strategies*, by F. F. Berdan et al., pp. 209–17. Washington, DC: Dumbarton Oaks.

2003   The Aztec Empire. In *The Postclassic Mesoamerican World*, edited by M. E. Smith and F. F. Berdan, pp. 67–72. Salt Lake City: University of Utah Press.

Bermann, M.

1994   *Lukurmata: Household Archaeology in Prehispanic Bolivia.* Princeton: Princeton University Press.

Betanzos, J. de

1996   *Narrative of the Incas.* 1st ed., edited by R. Hamilton and D. Buchanan.
[1557]   Austin: University of Texas Press.

Bhabha, H.

1985   Signs Taken for Wonders: Questions of Ambivalence and Authority under
[1994]   a Tree outside Dehli, May 1817. In *The Location of Culture*, by H. Bhabha, pp. 102–22. London: Routledge.

1992   The Postcolonial and the Postmodern. In *The Location of Culture*, by
[1994]   H. Bhabha, pp. 171–97. London: Routledge.

Billman, B. R., and G. M. Feinman, eds.

1999   *Settlement Pattern Studies in the Americas: Fifty Years since Virú.* Washington, DC: Smithsonian Institution Press.

Bintliff, J.

1984   Iron Age Europe in the Context of Social Evolution from the Bronze Age through to Historic Times. In *European Social Evolution: Archaeological Perspectives*, edited by J. Bintliff, pp. 157–226. Bradford: University of Bradford Press.

Blake, E.

1998   Sardinia's Nuraghi: Four Millennia of Becoming. *World Archaeology* 30 (1):59–71.

Blanton, R. E.

1996   The Basin of Mexico Market System and the Growth of Empire. In *Aztec Imperial Strategies*, by F. F. Berdan et al., pp. 47–84. Washington, DC: Dumbarton Oaks.

Blanton, R. E., and G. M. Feinman

1984   The Mesoamerican World System. *American Anthropologist* 86:673–82.

Blanton, R., G. Feinman, S. Kowalewski, and P. Peregrine

1996   A Dual-Processual Theory for the Evolution of Mesoamerican Civilization. *Current Anthropology* 37:1–14.

Blanton, R. E., S. A. Kowalewski, and G. M. Feinman

1992   The Mesoamerican World-System. *Review* 15:419–26.

Blanton, R. E., S. A. Kowalewski, G. M. Feinman, and L. M. Finsten

1993   *Ancient Mesoamerica: A Comparison of Change in Three Regions.* 2nd ed. Cambridge: Cambridge University Press.

Blaut, J.

1993   *The Colonizer's Model of the World.* New York: Guilford Press.

Boardman, J.

1980   *The Greeks Overseas.* London: Thames and Hudson.

Boese, J.

1996   Tell Sheikh Hassan in Nordsyrien. Eine Stadt des 4. Jahrtausends v. Chr. am Euphrat. *Nürnberger Blätter zur Archäologie* 12:157–72.

Boman, E.

1908   *Antiquités de la region Andine de la République Argentine et du Desert d'Atacama.* 2 vols. Paris: Imprimerie Nationale.

Boone, E. H.

1998   Introduction. In *Native Traditions in the Postconquest World*, edited by E. H. Boone and T. Cummins, pp. 1–11. Washington, DC: Dumbarton Oaks Research Library and Collection.

2003   A Web of Understanding: Pictorial Codices and the Shared Intellectual Culture of Late Postclassic Mesoamerica. In *The Postclassic Mesoamerican World*, edited by M. E. Smith and F. F. Berdan, pp. 207–21. Salt Lake City: University of Utah Press.

Bouloumié, B.

1981   Le vin étrusque et la première hellénisation du Midi de la Gaule. *Revue Archéologique de l'Est et du Centre-Est* 32:75–81.

1987   Le rôle des Étrusques dans la diffusion des produits étrusques et grecs en milieu préceltique et celtique. In *Hallstatt-Studien, Tübinger Kolloquium zur westeuropäischen Hallstatt-Zeit, 1980*, pp. 20–43. Weinheim: VCH Acta Humaniora.

Bourdieu, P.

1977   *Outline of a Theory of Practice.* Cambridge: Cambridge University Press.

1984   *Distinction: A Social Critique of the Judgement of Taste.* Cambridge, MA:
[1979]   Harvard University Press.

1990   *The Logic of Practice.* Stanford, CA: Stanford University Press.
[1980]

Bowen, J.

1989   Education, Ideology and the Ruling Class: Hellenism and English Public Schools in the Nineteenth Century. In *Rediscovering Hellenism: The Hellenic Inheritance and the English Imagination*, edited by G. W. Clarke, pp. 161–86. Cambridge: Cambridge University Press.

Bowie, E. L.

1970   Review of B. Levick, *Roman Colonies in Southern Asia Minor. Journal of Roman Studies* 60:202–7.

1974 Greeks and Their Past in the Second Sophistic. In *Studies in Ancient Society*, edited by M. I. Finley, pp. 166–209. London: Routledge and Kegan Paul.

Bradburd, D.

1998 *Being There: The Necessity of Field Work.* Washington, DC: Smithsonian Institution Press.

Brandes, M.

1979 *Siegelabrollungen aus den Archäischen Bauschichten in Uruk-Warka.* Freiburger Altorientalischen Studien 3. Weisbaden: Franz Steiner.

Braudel, F.

1992 *The Perspective of the World,* Vol. 3: *Civilization and Capitalism, 15th–18th*
[1984] *Century.* Berkeley: University of California Press.

Bray, W., ed.

1993 *The Meeting of Two Worlds: Europe and the Americas 1492–1650.* Oxford: Oxford University Press.

Broneer, O.

1941 Colonia Laus Iulia Corinthiensis. *Hesperia* 10:388–90.

Broom, L., B. J. Siegel, E. Z. Vogt, and J. B. Watson

1954 Acculturation: An Exploratory Formulation. *American Anthropologist* 56:973–1000.

Browman, D. L.

1970 Early Peruvian Peasants: The Culture History of a Central Highlands Valley. Ph.D. dissertation, Department of Anthropology, Harvard University.

Brown, F. E.

1980 *Cosa: The Making of a Roman Town.* Ann Arbor: University of Michigan Press.

Brumfiel, E. M.

1980 Specialization, Market Exchange, and the Aztec State: A View from Huexotla. *Current Anthropology* 21:459–78.

1987 Elite and Utilitarian Crafts in the Aztec State. In *Specialization, Exchange, and Complex Societies,* edited by E. Brumfiel and T. Earle, pp. 102–18. Cambridge: Cambridge University Press.

1994 Ethnic Groups and Political Development in Ancient Mexico. In *Factional Competition and Political Development in the New World,* edited by E. M. Brumfiel and J. W. Fox, pp. 89–102. Cambridge: Cambridge University Press.

Brumfiel, E., and T. Earle

1987 Specialization, Exchange, and Complex Societies: An Introduction. In *Specialization, Exchange, and Complex Societies,* edited by E. Brumfiel and T. Earle, pp. 1–9. Cambridge: Cambridge University Press.

Brun, P.

1987   *Princes et princesses de la Celtique: Le Premier Age du Fer en Europe, 850–450 av. J.-C.* Paris: Editions Errance.

1992   L'influence grecque sur la société celtique non-méditerranéenne. In *Marseille grecque et la Gaule,* edited by M. Bats, G. Bertucchi, G. Congès, and H. Tréziny, pp. 389–99. Lattes, France: A.D.A.M. Editions.

Bruner, E. M.

1973   The Missing Tins of Chicken: A Symbolic Interactionist Approach to Culture Change. *Ethos* 1:219–38.

Brunt, P. A.

1965   Reflections on British and Roman Imperialism. *Comparative Studies in Society and History* 7:267–88.

Bryce, J.

1901   The Roman Empire and the British Empire in India. In *Studies in History and Jurisprudence,* vol. 1, pp. 1–71. London: Oxford University Press.

Bureau of Indian Affairs

2002   Indian Entities Recognized and Eligible to Receive Services from the United States Bureau of Indian Affairs; Notice. *Federal Register* 67 (134) (July 12, 2002): 46328–46333.

Burger, R., and L. Salazar, eds.

2004   *Machu Picchu: Unveiling the Mystery of the Incas.* New Haven: Yale University Press.

Burger, R. L., K. J. Schreiber, M. D. Glascock, and J. Ccencho

1998   The Jampatilla Obsidian Source: Identifying the Geological Source of Pampas Type Obsidian Artifacts from Southern Peru. *Andean Past* 5:225–39.

Burkhart, L. M.

1989   *The Slippery Earth: Nahua-Christian Moral Dialogue in Sixteenth-Century Mexico.* Tucson: University of Arizona Press.

1998   Pious Performances: Christian Pageantry and Native Identity in Early Colonial Mexico. In *Native Traditions in the Postconquest World,* edited by E. H. Boone and T. Cummins, pp. 361–81. Washington, DC: Dumbarton Oaks.

Burkhart, L. M., and J. Gasco

1996   The Colonial Period in Mesoamerica. In *The Legacy of Mesoamerica: History and Culture of a Native American Civilization,* edited by R. M. Carmack, J. Gasco, and G. Gossen, pp. 122–53. Englewood Cliffs: Prentice-Hall.

Butler, E. M.

1935   *The Tyranny of Greece over Germany.* Cambridge: Cambridge University Press.

Byland, B. E., and J. M. D. Pohl

1994   *In the Realm of 8 Deer: The Archaeology of the Mixtec Codices.* Norman: University of Oklahoma Press.

Cabrera, R.

1998   Teotihuacan: Nuevos datos para el estudio de las rutas de comunicación. In *Rutas de intercambio en Mesoamérica: III Coloquio Pedro Bosch Gimpera*, edited by E. Rattray, pp. 57–75. Mexico, DF: Universidad Nacional Autónoma de México.

Calder, W. M.

1912   Colonia Caesareia Antiocheia. *Journal of Roman Studies* 2:79–109.

Callapiña, S., y Otros Quipucamayos

1974   *Relación de los Quipucamayos*, edited by J. J. Vega. Lima: Biblioteca universitaria.

Campbell, L.

1988   *The Linguistics of Southeast Chiapas, Mexico.* Papers of the New World Archaeological Foundation, No. 50. Provo: Brigham Young University.

Campus, A.

1997   Appunti e spunti per un'analisi dei complessi votivi punici in Sardegna. In *Phoinikes b shdn. I Fenici in Sardegna*, edited by P. Bernardini, R. D'Oriano, and P. Spano, pp. 166–75. Oristano, Italy: S'Alvure.

Carmack, R. M.

1981   *The Quiche Mayas of Utatlan: The Evolution of a Highland Guatemala Kingdom.* Norman: University of Oklahoma Press.

1996   Mesoamerica at Spanish Contact. In *The Legacy of Mesoamerica: History and Culture of a Native American Civilization*, edited by R. M. Carmack, J. Gasco, and G. Gossen, pp. 80–121. Englewood Cliffs: Prentice-Hall.

Carmack, R. M., J. Gasco, and G. Gossen, eds.

1996   *The Legacy of Mesoamerica: History and Culture of a Native American Civilization.* Englewood Cliffs: Prentice-Hall.

Carmagnani, M.

1985   The Intertia of Clio: The Social History of Colonial Mexico. *Latin American Research Review* 20 (1):149–66.

Carr, C.

1995   Mortuary Practices: Their Social, Philosophical-Religious, Circumstantial, and Physical Determinants. *Journal of Archaeological Method and Theory* 2:105–99.

Carrasco, D.

1990   *Religions of Mesoamerica: Cosmovision and Ceremonial Centers.* New York: Harper and Row.

1998   *Daily Life of the Aztecs.* Westport, CT: Greenwood Press.

Carrasco, P.

1997   Indian-Spanish Marriages in the First Century of the Colony. In *Indian Women of Early Mexico*, edited by S. Schroeder, S. Wood, and R. Haskett, pp. 87–103. Norman: University of Oklahoma Press.

1999 *The Tenochca Empire of Ancient Mexico: The Triple Alliance of Tenochtitlan, Tetzcoco, and Tlacopan.* Norman: University of Oklahoma Press.

Carrasco, P., and J. Broda, eds.

1976 *Estratificación social en a mesoamerica prehispánica.* México, DF: Instituto nacional de antropología e historia.

Carrilero Millán, M.

2000 Economía y sociedad en el sur peninsular en el periodo orientalizante: La Serranía de Ronda. In *Intercambio y comercio preclásico en el Mediterráneo,* edited by P. Fernández Uriel, C. González Wagner, and F. López Pardo, pp. 203–14. Actas del I coloquio del CEFYP. Madrid: Centro de estudios fenicio y púnicos.

Carrilero Millán, M., P. Aguayo de Hoyos, O. Garrido Vílchez, and B. Padial Robles

2002 Autóctonos y fenicios en la Andalucía mediterránea. In *La colonización fenicia en Occidente. Estado de la investigación en los inicios del siglo XXI,* edited by B. Costa and J. Fernández, pp. 69–125. XVI Jornadas de arqueología fenicio-púnica (Eivissa, 2001). Eivissa, Ibiza: Museu arqueològic d'Eivissa.

Cartledge, P., and A. Spawforth

1989 *Hellenistic and Roman Sparta: A Tale of Two Cities.* London: Routledge.

Caso, A., I. Bernal, and J. Acosta

1967 *La Cerámica de Monte Albán.* Memorias 13. Mexico DF: Instituto nacional de antropología e historia.

Castillo, E. D.

1989 The Assassination of Padre Andres Quintana by the Indians of Mission Santa Cruz in 1812: The Narrative of Lorenzo Asisara. *California History* 68 (3):116–25.

Ccencho Huamaní, J. E.

1991 Informe de los estudies arqueológicos del proyecto "El Periodo Intermedio Tardio en la margen derecha del Río Sondondo, Lucanas-Ayacucho." Final report submitted to the National Institute of Culture, Lima. Manuscript in possession of the author.

Céspedes Paz, R.

1982 La arqueología del area de Pocona. *Cuadernos de investigación, Serie Arqueología* 1:89–99.

Chakrabarty, D.

2000 *Provincializing Europe.* Princeton: Princeton University Press.

Champagne, D.

1994 Change, Continuity, and Variation in Native American Societies as a Response to Conquest. In *Violence, Resistance, and Survival in the Americas: Native Americans and the Legacy of Conquest,* edited by W. B. Taylor and F. Pease G.Y., pp. 208–25. Washington, DC: Smithsonian Institution Press.

Champion, T., ed.

1989   *Centre and Periphery: Comparative Studies in Archaeology.* London: Unwin Hyman.

Chance, J. K.

1986   Colonial Ethnohistory of Oaxaca. In *Handbook of Middle American Indians,* Supplement 4: Ethnohistory, edited by R. Spores, pp. 165–89. Austin: University of Texas Press.

1989   *Conquest of the Sierra: Spaniards and Indians in Colonial Oaxaca.* Norman: University of Oklahoma Press.

Chapa Brunet, T.

1997   Models of Interaction between Punic Colonies and Native Iberians: The Funerary Evidence. In *Encounters and Transformations. The Archaeology of Iberia in Transition,* edited by M. Balmuth, A. Gilman, and L. Prados-Torreira, pp. 141–50. Monographs in Mediterranean Archaeology 7. Sheffield: Sheffield Academic Press.

1998   Iron Age Iberian Sculptures as Territorial Markers: The Córdoban Example (Andalusía). *European Journal of Archaeology* 1 (1):71–90.

Charlton, T. H.

1972   *Post-Conquest Developments in the Teotihuacan Valley, Mexico.* Part I: *Excavations.* Iowa City: Office of State Archaeologist of Iowa.

1977   Final Report of a Surface Survey of Preconquest Trade Networks in Mesoamerica. Report to the National Endowment for the Humanities, Washington, DC.

1979   Historical Archaeology in the Valley of Mexico. In *Actes du XLII congres international des americanistes,* vol. 8, pp. 21–33. Paris.

1987   Teotihuacan Non-urban Settlements: Functional and Evolutionary Implications. In *Teotihuacan: Nuevos datos, nuevas síntesis, nuevos problemas,* edited by E. McClung de Tapia and E. Rattray, pp. 473–88. Mexico, DF: Universidad nacional autónoma de México.

Chase, A. F., and P. M. Rice, eds.

1985   *The Lowland Maya Postclassic.* Austin: University of Texas Press.

Chase-Dunn, C., and T. D. Hall

1997   *Rise and Demise: Comparing World-Systems.* Boulder, CO: Westview Press.

Cieza de León, Pedro de

1967   *El señorio de los Incas. Segunda parte de la Crónica del Perú.* Lima: Instituto de
[1553]   estudios peruanos.

Clark, J. E.

1989   Obsidian Tool Manufacture. In *Ancient Trade and Tribute: Economies of the Soconusco Region of Mesoamerica,* edited by B. Voorhies, pp. 215–28. Salt Lake City: University of Utah Press.

Clavel-Lévêque, M.

1983   Pratiques impérialistes et implantations cadastrales. *Ktema* 8:185–251.

Clendinnen, I.

1987   *Ambivalent Conquests: Maya and Spaniard in Yucatan, 1517–1570.*
Cambridge: Cambridge University Press.

Cleuziou, S., and T. Berthoud

1982   Early Tin in the Near East: A Reassessment in the Light of New Evidence
from Western Afghanistan. *Expedition* 25 (1):14–25.

Clifford, J.

1983   On Ethnographic Authority. *Representations* 1:118–46.

Cline, H. F.

1949   Civil Congregations of the Indians in New Spain, 1598–1606. *Hispanic
American Historical Review* 39 (3):348–69.

Cline, S. L.

1986   *Colonial Culhuacan, 1580–1600: A Social History of an Aztec Town.*
Albuquerque: University of New Mexico Press.

Cobo, B.

1979   *History of the Incas.* Translated by R. Hamilton. Austin: University of Texas
[1653]   Press.

Cock, G.

2002   Inca Rescue. *National Geographic Magazine* 201 (5):78.

Coe, M. D.

1994   *Mexico: From the Olmecs to the Aztecs.* 4th ed. New York: Thames and Hudson.

Coe, S. D.

1994   *America's First Cuisines.* Austin: University of Texas Press.

Cohen, A.

1969   *Custom and Politics in Urban Africa: A Study of Hausa Migrants in Yoruba
Towns.* Berkeley: University of California Press.

1971   Cultural Strategies in the Organization of Trading Diasporas. In *The
Development of Indigenous Trade and Markets in West Africa,* edited by
C. Meillassoux, pp. 266–81. Oxford: Oxford University Press.

Cohen, S.

1973   Enmerkar and the Lord of Aratta. Ph.D. dissertation, Near Eastern
Languages and Literature, University of Pennsylvania.

Cohen, W. B.

1971   *Rulers of Empire: The French Colonial Service in Africa.* Stanford: Hoover
Institution Press.

Cohn, B. S.

1987   *An Anthropologist among the Historians and Other Essays.* Delhi: Oxford
University Press.

1996   *Colonialism and Its Forms of Knowledge: The British in India.* Princeton:
Princeton University Press.

Collier, G. A., R. I. Rosaldo, and J. D. Wirth, eds.

1982   *The Inca and Aztec States, 1400–1800: Anthropology and History.* New York: Academic Press.

Collins, Roger

1995   *Early Medieval Spain: Unity in Diversity, 400–1000.* 2nd ed. New York: St. Martin's Press.

Comaroff, J[ean].

1983   On Ethnographic Authority. *Representations* 1:118–46.

1996   The Empire's Old Clothes: Fashioning the Colonial Subject. In *Cross-Cultural Consumption: Global Markets, Local Realities,* edited by D. Howes, pp. 19–38. London: Routledge.

Comaroff, J[ean]., and J[ohn]. L. Comaroff

1991   *Of Revelation and Revolution,* Vol. 1: *Christianity, Colonialism, and Consciousness in South Africa.* Chicago: University of Chicago Press.

Comaroff, J[ohn]. L.

1997   Images of Empire, Contests of Conscience: Models of Colonial Domination in South Africa. In *Tensions of Empire: Colonial Cultures in a Bourgeois World,* edited by F. Cooper and A. L. Stoler, pp. 163–97. Berkeley: University of California Press.

Comaroff, J[ohn]. L., and J[ean]. Comaroff

1992   *Ethnography and the Historical Imagination.* Boulder, CO: Westview Press.

1997   *Of Revelation and Revolution,* Vol. 2: *The Dialectics of Modernity on a South African Frontier.* Chicago: University of Chicago Press.

Conrad, G. W., and A. A. Demarest

1984   *Religion and Empire: The Dynamics of Aztec and Inca Expansionism.* Cambridge: Cambridge University Press.

Constantine, D.

1984   *Early Greek Travellers and the Hellenic Ideal.* Cambridge: Cambridge University Press.

Cook, A. G.

1994   *Wari y Tiwanaku: Entre el estilo y la imagen.* Lima: Fondo Editorial Pontificia, Universidad Católica del Perú.

2001   Wari D-Shaped Structure, Sacrificial Offerings, and Divine Rulership. In *Ritual Sacrifice in Ancient Peru,* edited by E. P. Benson and A. G. Cook, pp. 137–63. Austin: University of Texas Press.

Cook, N. D.

1998   *Born to Die: Disease and New World Conquest, 1492–1650.* Cambridge: Cambridge University Press.

Cook, N. D., and G. Lovell

1992   *"Secret Judgments of God": Old World Disease in Colonial Spanish America.* Norman: University of Oklahoma Press.

Cook, S. F., and W. Borah
1971– *Essays in Population History: Mexico and the Caribbean.* 3 vols. Berkeley:
1979   University of California Press.

Cooper, F., and A. L. Stoler, eds.
1997   *Tensions of Empire: Colonial Cultures in a Bourgeois World.* Berkeley: University
        of California Press.

de Coppet, D.
1992   Comparison, A Universal for Anthropology: From "Re-Presentation" to the
        Comparison of Hierarchies of Values. In *Conceptualizing Society,* edited by
        A. Kuper, pp. 59–74. London: Routledge.

Cornejo Guerrero, M. A.
2000   An Archaeological Analysis of an Inka Province: Pachacamac and the
        Ischma Nation of the Central Coast of Peru. Ph.D. dissertation,
        Department of Archaeology, Australian National University, Canberra.

Costa, B., and J. Fernández
2000   El establecimiento de los Fenicios en Ibiza. Algunas cuestiones actual-
        mente en debate. In *Actas del IV congreso internacional de estudios fenicios e
        púnicos, Cádiz, 2–6 Octubre 1995,* edited by M.-E. Aubet and M. Barthélemy,
        pp. 91–101. Cádiz: Servicio de publicaciones de la universidad de Cádiz.

Costello, J., and D. Hornbeck
1989   Alta California: An Overview. In *Columbian Consequences,* Vol. 1:
        Archaeological and Historical Perspectives on the Spanish Borderlands West,
        edited by D. H. Thomas, pp. 303–31. Washington, DC: Smithsonian
        Institution Press.

Cowgill, G. L.
1997   State and Society at Teotihuacan, Mexico. *Annual Review of Anthropology*
        26:129–61.

Cowgill, G. L., J. Altschul, and R. Sload
1984   Spatial Analysis of Teotihuacan: A Mesoamerican Metropolis. In *Intrasite
        Spatial Analysis in Archaeology,* edited by H. Hietala, pp. 154–95.
        Cambridge: Cambridge University Press.

Crawford, H. E. W.
1973   Mesopotamia's Invisible Exports in the Third Millennium. *World
        Archaeology* 5 (2):232–241.

Crespo, A., and A. G. Mastache
1981   La presencia en el área de Tula, Hidalgo, de grupos relacionados con el
        barrio de Oaxaca en Teotihuacan. In *Interacción cultural en México Central,*
        edited by E. Rattray, J. Litvak King, and C. Díaz, pp. 99–106. Mexico, DF:
        Universidad nacional autónoma de México.

Cromer, E. O.
1910   *Ancient and Modern Imperialism.* New York: Longmans, Green and Co.

Crosby, A. W.

1972   *The Columbian Exchange: Biological and Cultural Consequences of 1492.* Westport, CT: Greenwood Press.

1986   *Ecological Imperialism: The Biological Expansion of Europe, 900–1900.* Cambridge: Cambridge University Press.

Crowell, A. L.

1997   *Archaeology and the Capitalist World System: A Study from Russian America.* New York: Plenum Press.

Csikszentmihalyi, M., and E. Rochberg-Halton

1981   *The Meaning of Things: Domestic Symbols and the Self.* Cambridge: Cambridge University Press.

Culbert T. P., ed.

1991   *Classic Maya Political History: Hieroglyphic and Archaeological Evidence.* Cambridge: Cambridge University Press.

Cunliffe, B.

1988   *Greeks, Romans and Barbarians: Spheres of Interaction.* London: Batsford.

Cunningham, C. E.

1973   Order in the Atoni House. In *Right and Left: Essays on Dual Symbolic Classification,* edited by R. Needham, pp. 204–38. Chicago: University of Chicago Press.

Curtin, P.

1984   *Cross-Cultural Trade in World History.* Cambridge: Cambridge University Press.

Cusick, J. G.

1998a   Introduction. In *Studies in Culture Contact: Interaction, Culture Change, and Archaeology,* edited by J. G. Cusick, pp. 1–20. Occasional Paper 25. Carbondale: Center for Archaeological Investigations, Southern Illinois University.

1998b   Historiography of Acculturation: An Evaluation of Concepts and their Application in Archaeology. In *Studies in Culture Contact: Interaction, Culture Change, and Archaeology,* edited by J. G. Cusick, pp. 126–45. Occasional Paper 25. Carbondale: Center for Archaeological Investigations, Southern Illinois University.

Cusick, J. G., ed.

1998   *Studies in Culture Contact: Interaction, Culture Change, and Archaeology.* Occasional Paper 25. Carbondale: Center for Archaeological Investigations, Southern Illinois University.

D'Altroy, T. N.

1992   *Provincial Power in the Inka Empire.* Washington, DC: Smithsonian Institution Press.

371

2001   *The Incas.* Oxford: Blackwell Publishers.

D'Altroy, T. N., C. A. Hastorf, and Associates

2001   *Empire and Domestic Economy.* New York: Kluwer Academic / Plenum Press.

D'Altroy, T. N., A. M. Lorandi, and V. I. Williams

1998   Production and Use of Ceramics in the Inka Political Economy. In *Andean Ceramics: Technology, Organization and Approaches,* edited by I. Shimada. MASCA Research Papers in Science and Archaeology, Supplement to vol. 15, pp. 283–312. Philadelphia: University of Pennsylvania Museums.

D'Altroy, T. N., and V. I. Williams

1998   Provisioning the Inka Economy in Kollasuyu: Production and Distribution of Ceramics at Inka Sites in the Southern Andes. Final Report to National Science Foundation of Project SBR-97-07962.

Daneels, A.

2002   Presencia de Teotihuacan en el Centro y Sur de Veracruz. In *Ideología y política a través de materiales, imágenes y símbolos: Memoria de la Primera Mesa Redonda de Teotihuacan,* edited by M. E. Ruiz Gallut, pp. 655–83. Mexico, DF: Instituto nacional de antropología e historia.

Davies, N.

1977   *The Toltecs until the Fall of Tula.* Norman: University of Oklahoma Press.

Deagan, K.

1983   *Spanish St. Augustine: The Archaeology of a Colonial Creole Community.* New York: Academic Press.

1990   Sixteenth-Century Spanish-American Colonization in the Southeastern United States and the Caribbean. In *Columbian Consequences,* Vol. 2: *Archaeological and Historical Perspectives in the Spanish Borderlands East,* edited by D. H. Thomas, pp. 225–50. Washington, DC: Smithsonian Institution Press.

1995a   After Columbus: The Sixteenth-Century Spanish-Caribbean Frontier. In *Puerto Real: The Archaeology of a Sixteenth-Century Spanish Town in Hispaniola,* edited by K. Deagan, pp. 419–56. Gainesville: University Press of Florida.

1995b   *Puerto Real: The Archaeology of a Sixteenth-Century Spanish Town in Hispaniola.* Gainesville: University Press of Florida.

1998   Transculturation and Spanish American Ethnogenesis: The Archaeological Legacy of the Quincentenary. In *Studies in Culture Contact: Interaction, Culture Change, and Archaeology,* edited by J. G. Cusick, pp. 23–43. Occasional Paper 25. Carbondale: Center for Archaeological Investigations, Southern Illinois University.

2001   Dynamics of Imperial Adjustment in Spanish America: Ideology and Social Integration. In *Empires: Perspectives from Archaeology and History,* edited by S. E. Alcock, T. N. D'Altroy, K. D. Morrison, and C. M. Sinopoli, pp. 179–94. Cambridge: Cambridge University Press.

De Angelis, F.

1998   Ancient Past, Imperial Present: The British Empire in T. J. Dunbabin's *The Western Greeks. Antiquity* 72 (277):539–49.

De Graef, K.

1999a   Les étrangers dans les textes Paléobabyloniens tardifs de Sippar (premier partie). *Akkadica* 111:1–48.

1999b   Les étrangers dans les textes Paléobabyloniens tardifs de Sippar. *Akkadica* 112:1–17.

de Jesus, P. S.

1980   *The Development of Prehistoric Mining and Metallurgy in Anatolia.* BAR International Series 74. Oxford: British Archaeological Reports.

Dercksen, J. G.

1996   *The Old Assyrian Copper Trade in Anatolia.* Leiden: Nederlands Historisch-Archaeologisch Instituut te Istanbul.

Descoeudres, J.-P.

1990   Introduction. In *Greek Colonists and Native Populations. Proceedings of the First Australian Congress of Classical Archaeology Held in Honour of Emeritus Professor A. D. Trendall, Sydney 9–14 July 1985*, edited by J.-P. Descoeudres, pp. 1–12. Oxford: Clarendon.

Descoeudres, J.-P., ed.

1990   *Greek Colonists and Native Populations. Proceedings of the First Australian Congress of Classical Archaeology Held in Honour of Emeritus Professor A. D. Trendall, Sydney 9–14 July 1985.* Oxford: Clarendon.

Díaz, C.

1980   *Chingú, un sitio Clásico del área de Tula, Hgo.* Mexico, DF: Instituto nacional de antropología e historia.

1981   Chingú. In *Interacción cultural en México Central*, edited by E. Rattray, J. Litvak King, and C. Díaz, pp. 112–20. Mexico, DF: Universidad national autónoma de México.

Díaz del Castillo, B.

1956   *The True History of the Conquest of Mexico.* New York: Farrar, Straus and Cudahy.

Di Cosmo, N.

1994   Ancient Inner Asian Nomads: Their Economic Basis and Its Significance in Chinese History. *Journal of Asian Studies* 53:1092–1126.

Diehl, R. A.

1983   *Tula: The Toltec Capital of Ancient Mexico.* New York: Thames and Hudson.

Dietler, M.

1989   Greeks, Etruscans and Thirsty Barbarians: Early Iron Age Interaction in the Rhône Basin of France. In *Centre and Periphery: Comparative Studies in Archaeology*, edited by T. Champion, pp. 127–41. London: Unwin Hyman.

1990a   Driven by Drink: The Role of Drinking in the Political Economy and the
         Case of Early Iron Age France. *Journal of Anthropological Archaeology*
         9:352–406.

1990b   Exchange, Consumption, and Colonial Interaction in the Rhône Basin of
         France: A Study of Early Iron Age Political Economy. Ph.D. dissertation,
         University of California, Berkeley.

1994   "Our Ancestors the Gauls": Archaeology, Ethnic Nationalism, and the
         Manipulation of Celtic Identity in Modern Europe. *American Anthropologist*
         96:584–605.

1995   The Cup of Gyptis: Rethinking the Colonial Encounter in Early Iron Age
         Western Europe and the Relevance of World-Systems Models. *Journal of
         European Archaeology* 3 (2):89–111.

1997   The Iron Age in Mediterranean France: Colonial Encounters,
         Entanglements, and Transformations. *Journal of World Prehistory*
         11:269–357.

1998   Consumption, Agency, and Cultural Entanglement: Theoretical
         Implications of a Mediterranean Colonial Encounter. In *Studies in Culture
         Contact: Interaction, Culture Change and Archaeology*, edited by J. G. Cusick,
         pp. 288–315. Occasional Paper 25. Carbondale: Center for Archaeological
         Investigations, Southern Illinois University.

1999a   Consumption, Cultural Frontiers, and Identity: Anthropological
         Approaches to Greek Colonial Encounters. In *Confini e frontiera nella
         Grecità d'Occidente, Atti del XXXVII convegno di studi sulla Magna Grecia,
         Taranto, 3–6 Ottobre, 1997*, pp. 475–501. Naples: Arte tipographica.

1999b   Rituals of Commensality and the Politics of State Formation in the
         "Princely" Societies of Early Iron Age Europe. In *Les princes de la
         Protohistoire et l'émergence de l'état*, edited by P. Ruby, pp. 135–52. Cahiers du
         Centre Jean Bérard, Institut Français de Naples 17. Naples: Collection de
         l'École Française de Rome 252.

2001   Theorizing the Feast: Rituals of Consumption, Commensal Politics, and
         Power in African Contexts. In *Feasts: Archaeological and Ethnographic
         Perspectives on Food, Politics, and Power*, edited by M. Dietler and B. Hayden,
         pp. 65–114, Washington, DC: Smithsonian Institution Press.

2004   *Consumption and Colonial Encounters in the Rhône Basin of France: A Study of
         Early Iron Age Political Economy*. Monographies d'archéologie med-
         itéranéenne, 20. Lattes, France.

n.d.   Archaeologies of Colonialism: Disentangling an Ancient Mediterranean
         Encounter. Book manuscript.

Dietler, M., and B. Hayden, eds.
2001   *Feasts: Archaeological and Ethnographic Perspectives on Food, Politics, and Power.*
         Washington, DC: Smithsonian Institution Press.

Dietler, M., and I. Herbich

1998   *Habitus*, Techniques, Style: An Integrated Approach to the Social
        Understanding of Material Culture and Boundaries. In *The Archaeology of
        Social Boundaries*, edited by M. Stark, pp. 232–69. Washington, DC:
        Smithsonian Institution Press.

Diez de San Miguel, G.

1964   *Visita hecha a la Provincia de Chucuito por Garci Diez de San Miguel en el año
        1567*, edited by W. Espinoza Soriano. Lima: Casa de la cultura del Perú.

Dillehay, T. D., and P. Netherly, eds.

1988   *La frontera del estado Inca. Proceedings, 45 Congreso internacional de american-
        istas, Bogotá, Colombia, 1985*. BAR International Series 442. Oxford: British
        Archaeological Reports.

Dirks, N. B.

1992   Introduction: Colonialism and Culture. In *Colonialism and Culture*, edited
        by N. B. Dirks, pp. 1–25. Ann Arbor: University of Michigan Press.

Dirks, N. B., ed.

1992   *Colonialism and Culture*. Ann Arbor: University of Michigan Press.

Dobres, M.-A., and J. Robb, eds.

2000   *Agency in Archaeology*. London: Routledge.

Dobyns, H. F.

1983   *Their Number Become Thinned: Native American Populations Dynamics in
        Eastern North America*. Knoxville: University of Tennessee Press.

1991   New Native World: Links between Demographic and Cultural Changes. In
        Columbian Consequences, Vol. 3: *The Spanish Borderlands in Pan-American
        Perspective*, edited by D. H. Thomas, pp. 541–60. Washington, DC:
        Smithsonian Institute Press.

1993   Disease Transfer at Contact. *Annual Review of Anthropology* 22:273–91.

Donley, L. W.

1982   House Power: Swahili Space and Symbolic Markers. In *Symbolic and
        Structural Archaeology*, edited by Ian Hodder, pp. 63–73. Cambridge:
        Cambridge University Press.

Donnan, C. B., and D. McClelland

1999   *Moche Fineline Painting: Its Evolution and Its Artists*. Los Angeles: Fowler
        Museum of Cultural History, UCLA.

Dougherty, C.

1993   *The Poetics of Colonization. From City to Text in Archaic Greece*. Oxford and
        New York: Oxford University Press.

Douglas, M., and B. Isherwood

1979   *The World of Goods: Towards an Anthropology of Consumption*. New York:
        Norton.

REFERENCES

Doukellis, P.

1990   Actia Nicopolis: idéologie impériale, structures urbaines et développement régional. *Journal of Roman Archaeology* 3:399–406.

Dreyfus, H., and P. Rabinow

1982   *Michel Foucault: Beyond Structuralism and Hermeneutics.* Hassocks, UK: Harvester Press.

Dubuisson, M.

1991   Graecus, Graeculus, Gracari: L'emploi pejoratif du nom des Grecs en Latin. In *Ellenismos: Quelques jalons pour une histoire de l'identité grecque,* edited by S. Said, pp. 315–35. Leiden: E. J. Brill.

Dunbabin, T. J.

1948   *The Western Greeks: The History of Sicily and South Italy from the Foundations of the Greek Colonies to 480 B.C.* Oxford: Oxford University Press.

Durán, D.

1967   *Historia de las Indias de la Nueva España e islas de la tierra firme.* Compiled by A. M. Garibay. Mexico, DF: Editorial Porrúa.

Dyson, S.

1989   The Role of Ideology and Institutions in Shaping Classical Archaeology in the Nineteenth and Twentieth Centuries. In *Tracing Archaeology's Past,* edited by A. L. Christenson, pp. 127–35. Carbondale: Southern Illinois University Press.

Dyson, S., ed.

1985   *Comparative Studies in the Archaeology of Colonialism.* BAR International Series 233. Oxford: British Archaeological Reports.

Earle, T. K., T. N. D'Altroy, C. A. Hastorf, C. J. Scott, C. L. Costin, G. S. Russell, and E. Sandefur

1987   *Archaeological Field Research in the Upper Mantaro, Peru, 1982–1983: Investigations of Inka Expansion and Exchange.* Monograph 28. Los Angeles: Institute of Archaeology, UCLA.

Eber, C.

2000   *Women and Alcohol in a Highland Maya Town.* Rev. ed. Austin: University of Texas Press.

Edens, C.

1992   The Dynamics of Trade in the Ancient Mesopotamian "World System." *American Anthropologist* 94 (1):118–39.

Efrén Fernández, L., J. Suárez, J. Mayorga, A. Rambla, I. Navarro, A. Arancibia, and M. del Mar Escalante

1997   Un poblado indígena del siglo VIII a.C. en la bahía de Málaga. La intervención de urgencia en la Plaza de San Pablo. In *Los Fenicios en Málaga,* edited by M.-E. Aubet, pp. 216–51. Thema. Málaga: Universidad de Málaga.

Elliott, J. H.

1963 *Imperial Spain, 1469–1716.* London: Edward Arnold Ltd.

1990 *Spain and Its World 1500–1700.* New Haven: Yale University Press.

Emberling, G.

1997 Ethnicity in Complex Societies: Archaeological Perspectives. *Journal of Archaeological Research* 5:295–344.

Emberling, G., and N. Yoffee

1999 Thinking about Ethnicity in Mesopotamian Archaeology and History. *Fluchtpunkt Uruk. Archäologische Einheit aus Methodischer Vielfalt,* edited by H. Kühne, R. Bernbeck, and K. Bartl, pp. 272–81. Rahden/Westfalia: Verlag Marie Leidorf.

Emerson, R., and D. K. Fieldhouse

1968 Colonialism. In *International Encyclopedia of the Social Sciences,* pp. 1–12. New York: MacMillan.

Engels, D.

1990 *Roman Corinth: An Alternative Model for the Classical City.* Chicago: University of Chicago Press.

Espinoza Soriano, W.

1970 Los mitmas yungas de Collique en Cajamarca, siglos XV, XVI, y XVII. *Revista del Museo Nacional* 36:9–57. Lima.

1973 Las colonias de mitmas múltiples en Abancay, siglos XV y XVI. *Revista del Museo Nacional* 39:225–99. Lima.

1975 Los mitmas huayacuntu en Quito o guarniciones para larepresión armada, siglos XV y XVI. *Revista del Museo Nacional* 41:351–94. Lima.

1980 Acerca de la historia militar Inca. *Allpanchis Phuturinqa* 14 (16):171–86. Cuzco.

1983 Los mitmas plateros de Ishma en le país de los Ayamarca, siglos XV–XIX. *Boletín de Lima* 30 (5):38–52. Lima.

1987 Migraciones internas en el Reino Colla. Tejedores, plumeros, y alfareros del estado imperial Inca. *Chungará* 19:243–89.

1993 Los mitmas ajiceros-maniceros y los plateros de Ica en Cochabamba. *Historia y Cultura* 22:47–74.

Fabian, J.

1986 *Time and the Other: How Anthropology Makes Its Object.* New York: Columbia University Press.

Farnsworth, P.

1987 The Economics of Acculturation in the California Missions: A Historical and Archaeological Study of Mission Nuestra Senora de la Soledad. Ph.D. dissertation, Department of Anthropology, University of California, Los Angeles.

1989 The Economics of Acculturation in the Spanish Missions of Alta California. *Research in Economic Anthropology* 11:217–49.

Farnsworth, P., and J. S. Williams, eds.

1992   The Archaeology of the Spanish Colonial and Mexican Republican Periods. *Historical Archaeology* 26 (1).

Farris, G. J.

1991   Archaeological Testing in the Neophyte Housing Area at Mission San Juan Bautista, California. Resource Protection Division, California Departments of Parks and Recreation, Sacramento, California.

1997   Historical Archaeology of the Native Alaskan Village Site. In *The Archaeology and Ethnohistory of Fort Ross, California*, Vol. 2: *The Native Alaskan Neighborhood: A Multiethnic Community at Colony Ross*, edited by K. G. Lightfoot, A. M. Schiff, and T. A. Wake, pp. 129–35. Contributions of the University of California Archaeological Research Facility 55. Berkeley: Archaeological Research Facility.

Farriss, N. M.

1983   Indians in Colonial Yucatan: Three Perspectives. In *Spaniards and Indians in Southeastern Mesoamerica*, edited by M. MacLeod and R. Wasserstrom, pp. 1–39. Lincoln: University of Nebraska Press.

1984   *Maya Society under Colonial Rule: The Collective Enterprise of Survival.* Princeton: Princeton University Press.

1986   Indians in Colonial Northern Yucatan. *Handbook of Middle American Indians*, Supplement 4: *Ethnohistory*, edited by R. Spores, pp. 88–102. Austin: University of Texas Press.

Fedorova, S. G.

1973   *The Russian Population in Alaska and California Late 18th Century—1867.* Edited and translated by R. Pierce and A. Donnelly. Kingston, Ontario: Limestone Press.

Feinman, G. M., and J. Marcus

1998   *Archaic States.* Santa Fe: School of American Research Press.

Feinman, G., L. Nicholas, and S. Upham

1996   A Macroregional Comparison of the American Southwest and Highland Mesoamerica in Pre-Columbian Times: Preliminary Thoughts and Implications. In *Pre-Columbian World Systems*, edited by P. Peregrine and G. Feinman, pp. 65–76. Madison, WI: Prehistory Press.

Fentress, L.

2000   Introduction: Frank Brown, Cosa, and the Idea of a Roman City. In *Romanization and the City: Creation, Dynamics and Failures*, edited by L. Fentress, pp. 11–24. Journal of Roman Archaeology Supplementary Vol. 38. Portsmouth, RI: Journal of Roman Archaeology.

Fernández Jurado, J.

2000   Tartessos. La memoria contada. In *Fenicios y indígenas en el Mediterraneo y Occidente: Modelos y interacción*, edited by D. Ruiz Mata, pp. 99–105.

Encuentros de primavera en El Puerto 3. El Puerto de Santa María, Spain: Ayuntamiento de El Puerto de Santa María.

Fernández-Miranda, M.

1997   Aspects of Talayotic Culture. In *Encounters and Transformations. The Archaeology of Iberia in Transition*, edited by M. Balmuth, A. Gilman, and L. Prados-Torreira, pp. 59–68. Monographs in Mediterranean Archaeology 7. Sheffield: Sheffield Academic Press.

Ferro, M.

1997   *Colonization: A Global History.* London: Routledge.

Fieldhouse, D. K.

1981   *Colonialism 1870–1945: An Introduction.* London: Weidenfeld and Nicolson.

Finley, M. I.

1976   Colonies—An Attempt at a Typology. *Transactions of the Royal Historical Society* 26 (5th Series):167–88.

Fish, S. K., and S. A. Kowalewski

1990   *The Archaeology of Regions: A Case for Full-Coverage Survey.* Washington, DC: Smithsonian Institution Press.

Fiske, A. P.

1992   The Four Elementary Forms of Sociality: Framework for a Unified Theory of Social Relations. *Psychological Review* 99:689–723.

Florescano, E.

1994   *Memory, Myth, and Time in Mexico: From the Aztecs to Independence.* Translated by A. G. Bork and K. R. Bork. Austin: University of Texas Press.

Fock, Nils

1961   Inka Imperialism in Northwest Argentina, and Chaco Burial Forms. *Folk* 3:67–90.

Foster, B.

1977   Commercial Activity in Sargonic Mesopotamia. *Iraq* 39:31–43.

1993   "International" Trade at Sargonic Susa. *Altorientalische Forschungen* 20:59–68.

Foster, G.

1960   *Culture and Conquest: America's Spanish Heritage.* New York: Wenner-Gren Foundation for Anthropological Research.

Foucault, M.

1971   Nietzsche, Genealogy, History. In *Michel Foucault: Language, Counter-Memory, Practice*, edited by D. F. Bouchard, pp. 139–64. New York: Cornell University Press

1979   *Discipline and Punish. The Birth of the Prison.* Harmondsworth: Peregrine.

1982   Afterword. The Subject and Power. In *Michel Foucault: Beyond Structuralism and Hermeneutics*, by H. Dreyfus and P. Rabinow, pp. 208–26. Hassocks: Harvester Press.

Fox, D. S.

1978   *Mediterranean Heritage.* London: Routledge and Kegan Paul.

Frangipane, M.

1993   Local Components in the Development of Centralized Societies in Syro-Anatolian Regions. In *Between the Rivers and Over the Mountains,* edited by M. Frangipane, H. Hauptmann, M. Liverani, P. Matthiae, and M. Mellink, pp. 133–61. Rome: Università di Roma "La Sapienza."

1994   The Record Function of Clay Sealings in Early Administrative Systems as Seen from Arslantepe, Malatya. In *Archives before Writing,* edited by P. Ferioli and others, pp. 125–36. Turin: Scriptorium.

1997   A 4th Millennium Temple/Palace Complex at Arslantepe-Malatya. North-South Relations and the Formation of Early States in the Northern Regions of Greater Mesopotamia. *Paléorient* 23 (1):45–73.

Frangipane, M., and A. Palmieri

1987   Urbanization in Perimesopotamian Areas: The Case of Eastern Anatolia. In *Studies in the Neolithic and Urban Revolutions,* edited by L. Manzanilla, pp. 295–318. BAR International Series 349. Oxford: British Archaeological Reports.

1989   Aspects of Centralization in the Late Uruk Period in Mesopotamian Periphery. *Origini* 14:539–60.

Frank, A. G.

1993   Bronze Age World System Cycles. *Current Anthropology* 34:383–429.

Frankenstein, S.

1979   The Phoenicians in the Far West: A Function of Assyrian Neo-Imperialism. In *Power and Propaganda. A Symposium on Ancient Empires,* edited by M. T. Larsen, pp. 263–94. Mesopotamia 7. Copenhagen: Akademisk Forlag.

1994   Regional Development in the First Millennium B.C.: The Phoenicians in Iberia. In *Europe in the First Millennium B.C.,* edited by K. Kristiansen and J. Jensen, pp. 41–44. Sheffield Archaeological Monographs 6. Sheffield: J. R. Collis Publications.

1997   *Arqueología del colonialismo. El impacto fenicio y griego en el sur de la Península Ibérica y el suroeste de Alemania.* Barcelona.

Frankenstein, S., and M. J. Rowlands

1978   The Internal Structure and Regional Context of Early Iron Age Society in Southwestern Germany. *Bulletin of the Institute of Archaeology* 15:73–112. London.

Friedman, J.

1995   Global System, Globalization and the Parameters of Modernization. In *Global Modernities. Theory, Culture and Society,* edited by M. Featherstone, L. Lash, and R. Robertson, pp. 69–90. London: Sage.

Furst, J. L. McKeever

1995   *The Natural History of the Soul in Ancient Mexico.* New Haven: Yale University Press.

Galton, F.

1869   *Hereditary Genius: An Inquiry into Its Laws and Consequences.* London: MacMillan.

Gamboa, L.

1995   Proyecto San Juan Teotihuacan: Drenaje Sanitario. Report to the Instituto nacional de antropología e historia, Mexico.

Garelli, P.

1963   *Les Assyriens en Cappadoce.* Paris: Librairie Adrien-Maisonneuve.

Garnsey, P. D. A., and C. R. Whittaker, eds.

1978   *Imperialism in the Ancient World.* Cambridge: Cambridge University Press.

Garr, D.

1972   Planning, Politics and Plunder: The Missions and Indian Pueblos of Hispanic California. *Southern California Quarterly* 54:291–312.

Gasco, J.

1987a   Cacao and the Economic Integration of Native Society in Colonial Soconusco, New Spain. Ph.D. dissertation, University of California, Santa Barbara. Ann Arbor: University Microfilms.

1987b   Economic Organization in Colonial Soconusco, New Spain: Local and External Influences. *Research in Economic Anthropology* 8:105–137. Greenwich, CT: JAI Press.

1989a   Economic History of Ocelocalco, A Colonial Soconusco Town. In *Ancient Trade and Tribute: Economies of the Soconusco Region of Mesoamerica,* edited by B. Voorhies, pp. 304–25. Salt Lake City: University of Utah Press.

1989b   The Colonial Economy in the Province of Soconusco. In *Ancient Trade and Tribute: Economies of the Soconusco Region of Mesoamerica,* edited by B. Voorhies, pp. 283–303. Salt Lake City: University of Utah Press.

1991   Indian Survival and Ladinoization in Colonial Soconusco. In *Columbian Consequences,* vol. 3: *The Spanish Borderlands in Pan-American Perspective,* edited by D. H. Thomas, pp. 301–18. Washington, DC: Smithsonian Institution Press.

1992   Material Culture and Colonial Indian Society in Southern Mesoamerica: The View from Coastal Chiapas, Mexico. *Historical Archaeology* 26:67–74.

1993   Socioeconomic Change within Native Society in Colonial Soconusco, New Spain. In *Ethnohistory and Archaeology: Approaches to Postcontact Change in the Americas,* edited by J. D. Rogers and S. M. Wilson, pp. 163–80. New York: Plenum Press.

1996   Cacao and Economic Inequality in Colonial Soconusco, Chiapas, Mexico. *Journal of Anthropological Research* 52 (4):385–409.

1997   Consolidation of the Colonial Regime: Native Society in Western Central America. *Historical Archaeology* 31 (1):55–63.

2003a   The Polities of Xoconochco. In *The Postclassic Mesoamerican World,* edited by M. E. Smith and F. Berdan, pp. 50–54. Salt Lake City: University of Utah Press.

2003b   Soconusco in the Postclassic Period. In *The Postclassic Mesoamerican World*, edited by M. E. Smith and F. Berdan, pp. 282–96. Salt Lake City: University of Utah Press.

2005   Beyond the Indio/Ladino Dichotomy: Shifting Identities in Colonial and Contemporary Chiapas, Mexico. In *New World, First Nations: Native Peoples of Mesoamerica and the Andes under Colonial Rule*, edited by D. Cahill and B. Tovías. Brighton, UK: Sussex Academic Press.

Gasco, J., and B. Voorhies

1989   The Ultimate Tribute: The Role of the Soconusco as an Aztec Tributary. In *Ancient Trade and Tribute: Economies of the Soconusco Region of Mesoamerica*, edited by B. Voorhies, pp. 48–94. Salt Lake City: University of Utah Press.

Gasco, J., G. C. Smith, and P. Fournier-García, eds.

1997   *Approaches to the Historical Archaeology of Mexico, Central, and South America.* Los Angeles: Institute of Archaeology, UCLA.

Gasparini, G., and L. Margolies

1980   *Inca Architecture.* Translated by P. J. Lyon. Bloomington: Indiana University Press.

Geiger, M., and C. W. Meighan, eds.

1976   *As the Padres Saw Them: California Indian Life and Customs as Reported by the Franciscan Missionaries 1813–1815.* Santa Barbara, CA: Santa Barbara Mission Archive Library.

Gelburd, D. E.

1978   Indicators of Culture Change among the Dobe: Kung San. M. A. thesis, Department of Anthropology, George Washington University.

Gellner, E.

1995   *Anthropology and Politics: Revolutions in the Sacred Grove.* Oxford: Blackwell.

Gerard, A.

1982   La vision de la défaite gauloise dans l'enseignement secondaire (particulièrement entre 1870 et 1914). In *Nos ancêtres les Gaulois*, edited by P. Viallaneix and J. Ehrard, pp. 357–65. Clermont-Ferrand: Faculté des lettres et sciences humaines de l'université de Clermont-Ferrand II.

Gerhard, P.

1993   *The Southeast Frontier of New Spain.* Rev. ed. Norman: University of Oklahoma Press.

Gibbs, K.

2001   Time and Ethnicity in the Oaxaca Barrio, Teotihuacan: The TL6 Ceramics. M.A. thesis, University of Western Ontario, London.

Gibson, C.

1964   *The Aztecs under Spanish Rule.* Stanford: Stanford University Press.

1984   Indian Societies under Spanish Rule. In *Cambridge History of Latin America*, vol. 2, edited by L. Bethel, pp. 381–419. Cambridge: Cambridge University Press.

Giddens, A.

1979 *Central Problems in Social Theory.* London: Macmillan.

Gills, B. K., and A. G. Frank

1991 5,000 Years of World System History: The Cumulation of Accumulation. In *Core/Periphery Relations in Precapitalist Worlds,* edited by C. Chase-Dunn and T. D. Hall, pp. 67–112. San Francisco: Westview Press.

Girault, A.

1921 *Principes de colonisation et de législation coloniale.* Paris: Larose.

Gladstone, W. E.

1858 *Studies in Homer and the Homeric Age.* Oxford: Oxford University Press.

Glass, J. B.

1975 A Survey of Native Middle American Pictorial Manuscripts. In *Handbook of Middle American Indians,* vol. 14, edited by R. Wauchope, pp. 3–80. Austin: University of Texas Press.

Glick, T. F.

1979 *Islamic and Christian Spain in the Early Middle Ages: Comparative Perspectives on Social and Cultural Formation.* Princeton: Princeton University Press.

1995 *From Muslim Fortress to Christian Castle: Social and Cultural Change in Medieval Spain.* Manchester: Manchester University Press.

Goldstein, P.

1993 Tiwanaku Temples and State Expansion: A Tiwanaku Sunken Court Temple in Moquegua, Peru. *Latin American Antiquity* 4 (3):22–47.

2000 Communities without Borders: The Vertical Archipelago and Diaspora Communities in the Southern Andes. In *The Archaeology of Communities,* edited by M. Canuto and J. Yaeger, pp. 182–209. New York: Routledge.

Gómez, S.

1998 Nuevos datos sobre la relación de Teotihuacan y el Occidente de México. In *Antropología e historia del Occidente de México* III: *1461–1493.* XXIV Mesa Redonda, Sociedad Mexicana de Antropología, Mexico, DF.

Gómez Bellard, C.

1986 Asentamientos rurales en la Ibiza púnica. In *Los fenicios en la península Ibérica,* edited by M.-E. Aubet and G. del Olmo, pp. 177–92. Aula Orientalis 3 (1985). Sabadell, Spain: Ausa.

1991 La fondation phénicienne d'Ibiza et son développement aux VIIe et VIe s. avant J.C. In *Atti del II congresso internazionale di studi fenici e punici,* pp. 109–12. Collezione di studi fenici 30. Rome: Istituto di studi fenici (CNR).

1995a The First Colonization of Ibiza and Formentera (Balearic Islands, Spain): Some More Islands out of the Stream? *World Archaeology* 26 (3):442–55.

1995b Baléares. In *La civilisation phénicienne et punique. Manuel de recherche,* edited by V. Krings, pp. 763–75. Handbuch der Orientalistik 1.20. Leiden: Brill.

1996 Agricultura fenicio-púnica: Algunos problemas y un caso de estudio. *Complutum extra* 6 (1):389–400.

2003   Colonos sin indígenas: El campo ibicenco en época fenicio-púnica. In *Ecohistoria del paesaje agrario. La agricoltura fenicio-púnica en el Mediterráneo*, edited by C. Gómez Bellard, pp. 205–18. Valencia: Universitat de València.

González, A. R.

1983   Inca Settlement Patterns in a Marginal Province of the Empire: Sociocultural Implications. In *Prehistoric Settlement Patterns: Essays in Honor of Gordon R. Willey*, edited by E. Z. Vogt and R. M. Leventhal, pp. 337–60. Cambridge, MA: Harvard University.

González Carré, E., E. Bragayraq Dávila, C. Vivanco Pomacanchari, V. Tiesler Blos, and M. Lopez Quispe

1996   *El Templo Mayor en al ciudad de Wari: Estudios arqueológicos en Vegachayoq Moqo-Ayacucho.* Huamanga: Laboratorio de Arqueología, Universidad Nacional San Cristóbal de Huamanga.

Gosden, C.

1985   Gifts and Kin in Early Iron Age Europe. *Man* 20:475–93.

1999   *Anthropology and Archaeology. A Changing Relationship.* London and New York: Routledge.

2001   Postcolonial Archaeology: Issues of Culture, Identity, and Knowledge. In *Archaeological Theory Today*, edited by I. Hodder, pp. 241–61. Cambridge: Polity Press.

2004   *Archaeology and Colonialism. Cultural Contact from 5000 B.C. to the Present.* Cambridge: Cambridge University Press.

Gosden, C., ed.

1997   Culture Contact and Colonialism. *World Archaeology* 28:275–460.

Gossen, G. H.

1996   The Religious Traditions of Mesoamerica. In *The Legacy of Mesoamerica: History and Culture of a Native American Civilization,* edited by R. M. Carmack, J. Gasco, and G. H. Gossen, pp. 290–319. Englewood Cliffs: Prentice-Hall.

Goudineau, C.

1990   *César et la Gaule.* Paris: Editions Errance.

Gould, P.

1981   A Structural Language of Relations. In *Future Trends in Geomathematics*, edited by R. G. Craig and M. Labowitz, pp. 121–34. London: Pion.

Grafton, A.

1992   Germany and the West 1830–1900. In *Perceptions of the Ancient Greeks*, edited by K. J. Dover, pp. 225–44. Oxford: Blackwell.

Graham, E.

1998   Mission Archaeology. *Annual Review of Anthropology* 27:25–62.

Graham, A. J.
1964   *Colony and Mother City in Ancient Greece.* Manchester: Manchester University Press.

Gras, M., P. Rouillard, and J. Teixidor
1991   The Phoenicians and Death. *Berytus* 39:127–76.

Green, M. D.
1996   The Expansion of European Colonization to the Mississippi Valley, 1780–1880. In *The Cambridge History of the Native Peoples of the Americas,* Vol. 1, *North America, Part 1,* edited by B. G. Trigger and W. E. Washburn, pp. 461–538. Cambridge: Cambridge University Press.

Grosboll, S.
1993   ...And He Said in the Time of the Ynga, They Paid Tribute and Served the Ynga. In *Provincial Inca: Archaeological and Ethnohistorical Assessment of the Impact of the Inca State,* edited by M. Malpass, pp. 44–76. Iowa City: University of Iowa Press.

Gruzinski, S.
1989   *Man-Gods in the Mexican Highlands: Indian Power and Colonial Society, 1520–1800.* Translated by E. Corrigan. Stanford: Stanford University Press.

Guerrero, V.
2000   Intercambios y comercio precolonial en las Baleares (c. 1100–600 Cal. BC). In *Intercambio y comercio preclásico en el Mediterráneo,* edited by P. Fernández Uriel, C. González Wagner, and F. López Pardo, pp. 35–57. Actas del I coloquio del CEFYP, Madrid, 9–12 de noviembre, 1998. Madrid: Centro de estudios fenicios y púnicos.

Guerrero Ayuso, V.
1991   Naturaleza y función de los asentamientos púnicos en Mallorca. In *Atti del II congresso internazionale di studi fenici e punici,* pp. 923–30. Collezione di studi fenici 30. Rome: Istituto di studi fenici (CNR).

Guest, F. F.
1966   The Indian Policy under Fermín Francisco de Lasuén, California's Second Father President. *The California Historical Society Quarterly,* September: 195–224.

1978   Mission Colonization and Political Control in Spanish California. *The Journal of San Diego History* 24:97–116.

Guha, R.
1997   *Dominance without Hegemony: History and Power in Colonial India.* Cambridge, MA: Harvard University Press.

Gyarmati, J., and A. Varga
1999   *The Chacaras of War: An Inka State Estate in the Cochabamba Valley, Bolivia.* Translated by M. Seleanu. Budapest: Museum of Ethnography.

Haas, L.

1995   *Conquests and Historical Identities in California, 1769–1936.* Berkeley: University of California Press.

Hall, T., and C. Chase-Dunn

1993   The World-Systems Perspective and Archaeology: Forward into the Past. *Journal of Archaeological Research* 1(2):121–43.

Hannerz, U.

1987   The World in Creolization. *Africa* 57:546–59.

Hanson, V. D., and J. Heath

1998   *Who Killed Homer? The Demise of Classical Education and the Recovery of Greek Wisdom.* New York: The Free Press.

Hardie, M. M.

1912   The Shrine of Mên Askaênos at Pisidian Antioch. *Journal of Hellenic Studies* 32:111–50.

Haselgrove, C.

1987   Culture Process on the Periphery: Belgic Gaul and Rome During the Late Republic and Early Empire. In *Centre and Periphery in the Ancient World*, edited by M. Rowlands, M. Larsen, and K. Kristiansen, pp. 104–24. Cambridge: Cambridge University Press.

Haskell, F., and N. Penny

1981   *Taste and the Antique: The Lure of Classical Sculpture, 1500–1900.* New Haven: Yale University Press.

Haskett, R.

1991   *Indigenous Rulers: An Ethnohistory of Town Government in Colonial Cuernavaca.* Albuquerque: University of New Mexico Press.

Hassig, R.

1985   *Trade, Tribute, and Transportation: The Sixteenth-Century Political Economy of the Valley of Mexico.* Norman: University of Oklahoma Press.

2001   *Time, History, and Belief in Aztec and Colonial Mexico.* Austin: University of Texas Press.

Hatzfeld, J.

1919   *Les trafiquants italiens dans l'orient hellénique.* New York: E. de Boccard.

Haun, S. J.

2004   A Local Perspective of Late Horizon Imperial Effect in the Rimac Valley. Paper presented at the Annual Meeting of the Society for American Archaeology, in the Symposium "The Inkas at the Margins," Montreal.

Hernández, C.

1994   Rescate de una Tumba Zapoteca en Tepeji del Rio. In *Simposium sobre arqueología en el estado de Hidalgo. Trabajos recientes, 1989*, edited by

E. Fernández, pp. 125–42. Mexico, DF: Instituto nacional de antropología e historia.

Herrmann, G.

1968   Lapis Lazuli: The Early Phases of Its Trade. *Iraq* 30:21–57.

Hill, J. D.

1998   Violent Encounters: Ethnogenesis and Ethnocide in Long-Term Contact Situations. In *Studies in Culture Contact: Interaction, Culture Change, and Archaeology*, edited by J. G. Cusick, pp. 146–71. Occasional Paper 25. Carbondale: Center for Archaeological Investigations, Southern Illinois University.

Hillgarth, J. N.

1976   *The Spanish Kingdoms, 1250–1516.* Vol. 1. Oxford: Clarendon Press.

1978   *The Spanish Kingdoms, 1250–1516.* Vol. 2. Oxford: Clarendon Press.

Hingley, R.

1994   Britannia, Origin Myths and the British Empire. In *Trac 94: Proceedings of the Fourth Annual Theoretical Roman Archaeology Conference, Durham 1994*, edited by S. Cottam, D. Dungworth, S. Scott, and J. Taylor, pp. 11–23. Oxford: Oxbow Books.

Hirth, K.

1993   The Household as an Analytical Unit: Problems in Method and Theory. In *Prehispanic Domestic Units in Western Mesoamerica*, edited by R. Santley and K. Hirth, pp. 21–36. Boca Raton, FL: CRC Press.

Hirth, K., and W. Swezey

1976   The Changing Nature of the Teotihuacan Classic: A Regional Perspective from Manzanilla, Puebla. In *Las Fronteras de Mesoamérica*, pp. 12–23. XIV Mesa Redonda of the Sociedad Mexicana de Antropología, Mexico, DF.

Hitchcock, R. K.

1982   Patterns of Sedentism among the Bosarwa of Eastern Botswana. In *Politics and History in Band Societies*, edited by E. Leacock and R. B. Lee, pp. 223–68. Cambridge: Cambridge University Press.

Hobsbawn, E., and T. Ranger, eds.

1983   *The Invention of Tradition.* Cambridge: Cambridge University Press.

Hobson, J. A.

1902   *Imperialism.* Ann Arbor: University of Michigan Press.

Hodder, I.

2000   Agency and Individuals in Long-Term Processes. In *Agency in Archaeology*, edited by M.-A. Dobres and J. Robb, pp. 21–33. London: Routledge.

1985   Boundaries as Strategies: An Ethnoarchaeological Study. In *The Archaeology of Frontiers and Boundaries*, edited by S. W. Green and S. M. Perlman, pp. 141–59. New York: Academic Press.

Hoekstra, R.

1990   A Different Way of Thinking: Contrasting Spanish and Indian Social and Economic Views in Central Mexico 1550–1600. In *The Indian Community of Colonial Mexico: Fifteen Essays on Land Tenure, Corporate Organization, Ideology, and Village Politics*. Amsterdam: Centro de estudios y documentación latinoamericanos.

Hoffman, K.

1997   Cultural Development in La Florida. *Historical Archaeology* 31 (1):24–35.

Holl, A.

1990   West African Archaeology: Colonialism and Nationalism. In *A History of African Archaeology*, edited by P. Robertshaw, pp. 296–308. Portsmouth, NH: Heineman.

Hollis, M., and S. Lukes

1982   Introduction. In *Rationality and Relativism*, edited by M. Hollis and S. Lukes. Cambridge, MA: MIT Press.

Hoover, R.

1989   Spanish-Native Interaction and Acculturation in the Alta California Missions. In *Columbian Consequences*, Vol. 1: *Archaeological and Historical Perspectives on the Spanish Borderlands West*, edited by D. H. Thomas, pp. 395–406. Washington, DC: Smithsonian Institution Press.

Hoover, R. L., and J. G. Costello

1985   *Excavations at Mission San Antonio, 1976–1978*. Monograph 26. Los Angeles: Institute of Archaeology, UCLA.

Hopkins, K.

1978   *Conquerors and Slaves*. Cambridge: Cambridge University Press.

Hosler, D.

1994   *The Sounds and Colors of Power: The Sacred Metallurgical Technology of Ancient West Mexico*. Cambridge, MA: MIT Press.

2003   Metal Production. In *The Postclassic Mesoamerican World*, edited by M. E. Smith and F. Berdan, pp. 158–71. Salt Lake City: University of Utah Press.

Hovarth, R.J.

1972   A Definition of Colonialism. *Current Anthropology* 13:45–57.

Howes, D., ed.

1996   *Cross-Cultural Consumption: Global Markets, Local Realities*. London: Routledge.

Hurtado, A. L.

1988   *Indian Survival on the California Frontier*. New Haven: Yale University Press.

Hyslop, J.

1984   *The Inka Road System*. New York: Academic Press.

1990   *Inka Settlement Planning.* Austin: University of Texas Press.

Idrovo Urigüen, J.

1988   Tomebamba: primera fase de conquista incaica en los Andes septentri-onales: Los Cañaris y la conquista incasica del austro ecuatoriano. In *La frontera del estado Inca, Proceedings, 45 Congreso internacional de americanistas, Bogotá, Colombia, 1985,* edited by T. D. Dillehay and P. J. Netherly, pp. 87–104. BAR International Series 442. Oxford: British Archaeological Reports.

Ingham, J. M.

1986   *Mary, Michael, and Lucifer: Folk Catholicism in Central Mexico.* Austin: University of Texas Press.

Isbell, W. H., C. Brewster-Wray, and L. E. Spickard

1991   Architecture and Spatial Organization at Huari. In *Huari Administrative Structure: Prehistoric Monumental Architecture and State Government,* edited by W. H. Isbell and G. F. McEwan, pp. 19–53. Washington, DC: Dumbarton Oaks.

Isbell, W. H., and G. F. McEwan, eds.

1991   *Huari Administrative Structure: Prehistoric Monumental Architecture and State Government.* Washington, DC: Dumbarton Oaks.

Isbell, W. H., and K. J. Schreiber

1978   Was Huari a State? *American Antiquity* 43 (3):372–89.

Istomin, A. A.

1992   *The Indians at the Ross Settlement according to the Censuses by Kuskov, 1820–1821.* Fort Ross, CA: Fort Ross Interpretive Association, Inc.

Jackson, R. H.

1994   *Indian Population Decline, The Missions of Northwestern New Spain, 1687–1840.* Albuquerque: University of New Mexico Press.

Jackson, R. H., and E. Castillo

1995   *Indians, Franciscans, and Spanish Colonization: The Impact of the Mission System on California Indians.* Albuquerque: University of New Mexico Press.

Jacobs, J.

1996   *Edge of Empire. Postcolonialism and the City.* London: Routledge.

Jacobsthal, P., and E. Neuffer

1933   Gallia Graeca. Recherches sur l'hellénisation de la Provence. *Préhistoire* 2:1–64.

James, L.

1994   *The Rise and Fall of the British Empire.* London: Little, Brown and Company.

Jenkyns, R.

1980   *The Victorians and Ancient Greece.* Cambridge, MA: Harvard University Press.

Jiménez, P., and J. A. Darling

2000   Archaeology of Southern Zacatecas: The Malpaso, Juchipila, and Valparaiso-Bolaños Valleys. In *Greater Mesoamerica: The Archaeology of West and Northwest Mexico*, edited by M. S. Foster and S. Gorenstein, pp. 155–80. Salt Lake City: University of Utah Press.

Johnson, G.

1973   *Local Exchange and Early State Development in Southwestern Iran.* Anthropological Paper 51. Ann Arbor: Museum of Anthropology, University of Michigan.

1980a   Rank-Size Convexity and System Integration: A View from Archaeology. *Economic Geography* 56 (3):234–47.

1980b   Spatial Organization of Early Uruk Settlement Systems. In *L'archéologie de l'Iraq du debut de l'epoque Néolithique à 333 avant Notre Ere: Perspectives et limites de l'interpretation anthropologique des documents*, edited by M.-T. Barrelet, pp. 233–63. Colloques internationaux du CNRS, vol. 580. Paris: Editions de CNRS.

1988–   Late Uruk in Greater Mesopotamia: Expansion or Collapse? *Origini*
1989   14:595–613.

Johnson, J. R.

1989   The Chumash and the Missions. In *Columbian Consequences*, Vol. 1: *Archaeological and Historical Perspectives on the Spanish Borderlands West*, edited by D. H. Thomas, pp. 365–76. Washington, DC: Smithsonian Institution Press.

Johnson, M. H.

1989   Conceptions of Agency in Archaeological Interpretation. *Journal of Anthropological Archaeology* 8:189–211.

Jones, A. H. M.

1937   *Cities of the Eastern Roman Provinces.* Oxford: Clarendon Press (repr. 1998).

1998   *The Greek City: From Alexander to Justinian.* Oxford: Clarendon Press.
[1940]

Jones, C. P.

1970   A Leading Family from Roman Thespiae. *Harvard Studies in Classical Philology* 74:223–55.

1971   *Plutarch and Rome.* Oxford: Clarendon Press.

Jones, G. D.

1989   *Maya Resistance to Spanish Rule: Time and History on a Colonial Frontier.* Albuquerque: University of New Mexico Press.

1998   *The Conquest of the Last Maya Kingdom.* Stanford: Stanford University Press.

Jones, S.

1997   *The Archaeology of Ethnicity: Constructing Identities in the Past and Present.* New York: Routledge.

Joyce, R. A.

2001   *Gender and Power in Prehispanic Mesoamerica.* Austin: University of Texas Press.

Julien, C. J.

1983   *Hatungolla: A View of Inca Rule from the Lake Titicaca Region.* Berkeley: University of California Press.

1988   How Inca Decimal Administration Worked. *Ethnohistory* 35:257–79.

1993   Finding a Fit: Archaeology and Ethnohistory of the Incas. In *Provincial Inca: Archaeological and Ethnohistorical Assessment of the Impact of the Inca State,* edited by M. Malpass, pp. 177–233. Iowa City: University of Iowa Press.

2000   *Reading Inca History.* Iowa City: University of Iowa Press.

Kahrstedt, U.

1950   Die Territorien von Patrai und Nikopolis in der Kaiserzeit. *Historia* 1:549–61.

Kammeyer, D., G. Emberson, and G. D. Singleton

2002   *2002 Field Directory of the California Indian Community.* Sacramento: California Indian Assistance Program, Department of Housing and Community Development, State of California.

Kaplan, S. A.

1983   Economic and Social Change in Labrador Neo-Eskimo Culture. Ph.D. dissertation, Department of Anthropology, Bryn Mawr College.

Kardulias, P. N., ed.

1999   *World-Systems Theory in Practice.* Lanham, MD: Rowman and Littlefield.

Karttunen, F.

1997   Rethinking Malinche. In *Indian Women of Early Mexico,* edited by S. Schroeder, S. Wood, and R. Haskett, pp. 291–312. Norman: University of Oklahoma Press.

Kealhofer, L.

1996   The Evidence for Demographic Collapse in California. In *Bioarchaeology of Native American Adaptation in the Spanish Borderlands,* edited by B. J. Baker and L. Kealhofer, pp. 56–92. Gainesville: University Press of Florida.

Keane, W.

1997   *Signs of Recognition: Powers and Hazards of Representation in an Indonesian Society.* Berkeley: University of California Press.

Keesing, R.

1994   Colonial and Counter-Colonial Discourse in Melanesia. *Critique of Anthropology* 14:41–58.

Kegan, R.

1982   *The Evolving Self: Problems and Process in Human Development.* Cambridge, MA: Harvard University Press.

Kellogg, S.

1995   *Law and the Transformation of Aztec Culture, 1500–1700.* Norman: University of Oklahoma Press.

1997   From Parallel and Equivalent to Separate but Unequal: Tenochca Mexica Women, 1500–1700. In *Indian Women of Early Mexico*, edited by S. Schroeder, S. Wood, and R. Haskett, pp. 123–43. Norman: University of Oklahoma Press.

Kelsey, H.

1985   European Impact on the California Indians, 1530–1830. *The Americas* 41 (4):494–511.

Kennedy, M. J.

1955   Culture Contact and Acculturation of the Southwestern Pomo. Ph.D. dissertation, Department of Anthropology, University of California, Berkeley.

Kent, J. H.

1966   *The Inscriptions* (Corinth 8.3). Princeton: American School of Classical Studies at Athens.

Kepecs, S., and M. A. Masson

2003   Political Organization in Yucatan and Belize. In *The Postclassic Mesoamerican World*, edited by M. E. Smith and F. Berdan, pp. 40–44. Salt Lake City: University of Utah Press.

Kicza, J.

1997   Native American, African, and Hispanic Communities during the Middle Period in the Colonial Americas. *Historical Archaeology* 31 (1):9–17.

Kimmig, W.

1983   Die griechische Kolonisation im westlichen Mittelmeergebiet und ihre Wirkung auf die Landschaften des Westlichen Mitteleuropa. *Jahrbuch des Römisch-Germanischen Zentralmuseums Mainz* 30:5–78.

Kirch, P. V., and M. Sahlins

1992   *Anahulu: The Anthropology of History in the Kingdom of Hawaii.* 2 vols. Chicago: University of Chicago Press.

Kirchhoff, P.

1943   Mesoamérica, sus limites geográficos, composición étnica y caracteres culturales. *Acta Americana* I:92–107.

Klor de Alva, J. J.

1982   Spiritual Conflict and Accommodation in New Spain: Toward a Typology of Aztec Responses to Christianity. In *Inca and Aztec States, 1400–1800: Anthropology and History*, edited by G. A. Collier, R. I. Rosaldo, and J. D. Wirth, pp. 345–66. New York: Academic Press.

1992   Colonialism and Postcolonialism as (Latin) American Mirages. *Colonial Latin American Review* 1 (1–2):3–23.

1995   The Postcolonization of the (Latin) American Experience: A Reconsideration of "Colonialism," "Postcolonialism," and "Mestizaje." In

After Colonialism: Imperial Histories and Postcolonial Displacements, edited by
G. Prakesh, pp. 241–75. Princeton: Princeton University Press.

Knobloch, P. J.

1976   A Study of the Huarpa Ceramic Style of the Andean Early Intermediate
Period. M.A. thesis, Department of Anthropology, SUNY Binghamton.

Koebner, R., and H. D. Schmidt

1964   *Imperialism: The Story and Significance of a Political Word, 1840–1960*.
Cambridge: Cambridge University Press.

Kohl, P. L.

1978   The Balance of Trade in Southwest Asia in the Mid-Third Millennium B.C.
Current Anthropology 19:463–92.

1987   The Use and Abuse of World Systems Theory: The Case of the Pristine
West Asian State. *Advances in Archaeological Method and Theory* 11:1–35.

1989   The Use and Abuse of World Systems Theory: The Case of the Pristine West
Asian State. In *Archaeological Thought in America*, edited by C. C. Lamberg-
Karlovsky, pp. 218–40. Cambridge: Cambridge University Press.

Kostof, S.

1995   *A History of Architecture: Settings and Rituals*. Oxford: Oxford University
Press.

Kottak, C. P.

1980   *The Past in the Present: History, Ecology, and Cultural Variation in Highland
Madagascar*. Ann Arbor: University of Michigan Press.

Kramer, S. N.

1952   *Enmerkar and the Lord of Aratta*. Philadelphia: The University Museum.

Krey, A. C.

1921   *The First Crusade: The Accounts of Eyewitnesses and Participants*. Princeton:
Princeton University Press.

Kristiansen, K.

1994   The Emergence of the European World System in the Bronze Age:
Divergence, Convergence and Social Evolution during the First and
Second Millennia B.C. in Europe. In *Europe in the First Millennium B.C.*,
edited by K. Kristiansen and J. Jensen, pp. 7–30. Sheffield: Sheffield
Archaeological Monographs.

Kroeber, A. L.

1925   *Handbook of the Indians of California*. Bulletin 78, Bureau of American
Ethnology, Smithsonian Institution. Washington, DC: U.S. Government
Printing Office.

1966   The Nature of Land-Holding Groups in Aboriginal California. In
Aboriginal California: Three Studies in Culture History, edited by R. F. Heizer,
pp. 82–120. Berkeley: Archaeological Research Facility, University of
California.

REFERENCES

Kuhrt, A.

1995   *The Ancient Near East ca. 3000–330 B.C.* 2 vols. London: Routledge.

Kuper, A.

1980   Symbolic Dimensions of the Southern Bantu Homestead. *Africa* 50:8–23.

La Lone, M. B., and D. E. La Lone

1987   The Inka State in the Southern Highlands: State Administrative and
        Production Enclaves. *Ethnohistory* 34:47–62.

Lamberg-Karlovsky, C. C.

1972   Trade Mechanisms in Indus-Mesopotamian Interrelations. *Journal of the
        American Oriental Society* 92 (2):222–30.

1996   The Archaeological Evidence for International Commerce: Public and/or
        Private Enterprise in Mesopotamia? In *Privatization in the Ancient Near East
        and the Classical World*, edited by M. Hudson and B. Levine, pp. 73–108.
        Peabody Museum Bulletin 5. Cambridge, MA: Harvard University,
        Peabody Museum of Archaeology and Ethnology.

Lang, J.

1975   *Conquest and Commerce.* New York: Academic Press.

Larsen, C. S.

1994   In the Wake of Columbus: Native Population Biology in the Postcontact
        Americas. *Yearbook of Physical Anthropology* 37:109–54.

Larsen, M.

1974   Review Article: The Old Assyrian Colonies in Anatolia. *Journal of the
        American Oriental Society* 94 (4):468–75.

1976   *The Old Assyrian City-State and Its Colonies.* Copenhagen Studies in
        Assyriology 4. Copenhagen: Akademisk Forlag.

1987   Commercial Networks in the Ancient Near East. In *Centre and Periphery in
        the Ancient World*, edited by M. Rowlands, M. Larsen, and K. Kristiansen,
        pp. 47–56. Cambridge: Cambridge University Press.

Lee, R. B.

1976   Introduction. In *Kalahari Hunter-Gatherers: Studies of the !Kung San and
        Their Neighbors*, edited by R. B. Lee and I. DeVore, pp. 3–24. New York:
        Aldine.

Lee, T. A.

1979   Early Colonial Coxoh Maya Syncretism in Chiapas, Mexico. *Estudios de
        Cultura Maya* 11:93–109.

Lee, T. A., and S. Markman

1979   Coxoh Maya Acculturation in Colonial Chiapas: A Necrotic Archaeological
        Ethnohistorical Model. In *Actes du XLII congres international des
        americanistes*, vol. 8, pp. 57–66. Paris.

Lenski, N.

1999   Assimilation and Revolt in the Territory of Isauria, from the 1st Century
B.C. to the 6th Century A.D. *Journal of the Economic and Social History of the
Orient* 42:413–65.

León-Portilla, M.

1963   *Aztec Thought and Culture.* Norman: University of Oklahoma Press.

1980   *Native American Spirituality.* New York: Paulist Press.

1992   *The Broken Spears: The Aztec Account of the Conquest of Mexico.* Boston: Beacon
Press.

Levick, B.

1967   *Roman Colonies in Southern Asia Minor.* Oxford: Clarendon Press.

1970   Dedications to Mên Askaênos. *Anatolian Studies* 20:37–50.

1971   The Table of Mên. *Journal of Hellenic Studies* 91:80–84.

Lightfoot, K. G.

1995   Culture Contact Studies: Redefining the Relationship between Prehistoric
and Historic Archaeology. *American Antiquity* 60 (2):199–217.

1997   Russian Colonialism in the North and Tropical Pacific: An Introduction.
In *The Archaeology of Russian Colonialism in the North and Tropical Pacific,*
edited by P. R. Mills and A. Martinez, pp. 1–9. Kroeber Anthropological
Society Papers 81. Berkeley, CA.

n.d.   *Indians, Missionaries, and Merchants: The Legacy of Colonial Encounters on the
California Frontiers.* Berkeley: University of California Press. In press.

Lightfoot, K. G., and A. Martinez

1997   Interethnic Relationships in the Native Alaskan Neighborhood:
Consumption Practices, Cultural Innovations and the Construction of
Household Identities. In *The Archaeology and Ethnohistory of Fort Ross,
California.* Vol. 2: *The Native Alaskan Neighborhood: A Multiethnic Community
at Colony Ross,* edited by K. G. Lightfoot, A. M. Schiff, and T. A. Wake,
pp. 1–22. Contributions of the University of California Archaeological
Research Facility 55. Berkeley: Archaeological Research Facility, University
of California.

Lightfoot, K. G., A. Martinez, and A. M. Schiff

1998   Daily Practice and Material Culture in Pluralistic Social Settings: An
Archaeological Study of Culture Change and Persistence from Fort Ross,
California. *American Antiquity* 63:199–222.

Lightfoot, K. G., A. M. Schiff, and T. A. Wake

1997   *The Archaeology and Ethnohistory of Fort Ross, California.* Vol. 2: *The Native
Alaskan Neighborhood: A Multiethnic Community at Colony Ross.* Contributions
of the University of California Archaeological Research Facility 55.
Berkeley: Archaeological Research Facility, University of California.

Lightfoot, K. G., T. A. Wake, and A. M. Schiff

1991   *The Archaeology and Ethnohistory of Fort Ross, California*, Vol. 1: *Introduction.* Contributions of the University of California Archaeological Research Facility 49. Berkeley: Archaeological Research Facility, University of California.

Lilliu, G.

1988   *La civiltà dei Sardi dal Paleolitico all'età dei nuraghi.* 3rd ed. Turin: Nuova ERI.

Linton, R.

1940   The Distinctive Aspects of Acculturation. In *Acculturation in Seven American Indian Tribes,* edited by R. Linton, pp. 501–19. New York: Appleton-Century-Crofts.

Linton, R., ed.

1940   *Acculturation in Seven American Indian Tribes.* New York: Appleton-Century-Crofts.

Liss, Peggy K.

1992   *Isabel the Queen.* Oxford: Oxford University Press.

Liverani, M., ed.

1993   *Akkad: The First World Empire.* Padua: Sargon.

Livingstone, R. W.

1935   *Greek Ideals and Modern Life.* Cambridge, MA: Harvard University Press.

Lizárraga, Y., and A. Ortiz

1993   Hacia una reinterpretación de los "Pulidores de Estuco." In *Anatomía de un conjunto residencial Teotihuacano en Oztoyahualco I,* edited by L. Manzanilla, pp. 468–93. Mexico, DF: Universidad national autónoma de México.

Lockhart, J.

1992   *The Nahuas after the Conquest: A Social and Cultural History of the Indians of Central Mexico, Sixteenth through Eighteenth Centuries.* Stanford: Stanford University Press.

1994   Sightings: Initial Nahua Reactions to Spanish Culture. In *Implicit Understandings: Observing, Reporting, and Reflecting on the Encounters between Europeans and Other Peoples in the Early Modern Era,* edited by S. B. Schwartz, pp. 218–48. Cambridge: Cambridge University Press.

Lomax, D. W.

1978   *The Reconquest of Spain.* London: Longham.

Loomba, A.

1998   *Colonialism/Postcolonialism: The New Critical Idiom.* London and New York: Routledge.

López Pardo, F., and J. Suárez Padilla

2003   Aproximación al conocimiento del paleoambiente, poblamiento y aprovechamiento de los recursos durante el primer milenio a.C. en el litoral occidental de Málaga. In *Ecohistoria del paesaje agrario. La agricoltura fenicio-púnica en el Mediterráneo*, edited by C. Gómez Bellard, pp. 75–91. Valencia: Universitat de València.

Lorandi, A. M.

1984 Soñocamayoc: Los olleros del Inka en los centros manufactureros del Tucumán. *Revista del Museo de la Plata, Sección Antropología* 7 (62):303–27. La Plata, Argentina: Universidad Nacional de la Plata, Facultad de Ciencias Naturales y Museo.

1988 Los Diaguitas y el Tawantinsuyu: Una hipótesis de conflicto. In *La frontera del estado Inca. Proceedings, 45 Congreso internacional de americanistas, Bogotá, Colombia, 1985*, edited by T. D. Dillehay and P. J. Netherly, pp. 235–59. BAR International Series 442. Oxford: British Archaeological Reports.

Lorandi, A. M., and L. Rodríguez

n.d. Yana y mitimaes. Alteraciones incaicas al mapa étnico andino. Manuscript.

Lucas, C. P.

1912 *Greater Rome and Greater Britain*. Oxford: Clarendon Press.

Luttwak, E.

1976 *The Grand Strategy of the Roman Empire*. Baltimore: Johns Hopkins University Press.

Lutz, C. H.

1994 *Santiago de Guatemala, 1541–1773*. Norman: University of Oklahoma Press.

Lyons, C. L., and J. Papadopoulos

2002 Archaeology and Colonialism. In *The Archaeology of Colonialism*, edited by C. L. Lyons and J. Papadopoulos, pp. 1–23. Issues and Debates. Los Angeles: Getty Research Institute.

Lyons, C. L., and J. K. Papadopoulos, eds.

2002 *The Archaeology of Colonialism*. Issues and Debates. Los Angeles: Getty Research Institute.

Lyttelton, M.

1987 The Design and Planning of Temples and Sanctuaries in Asia Minor in the Roman Imperial Period. In *Roman Architecture in the Greek World*, edited by S. Macready and F. H. Thompson, pp. 38–49. Society of Antiquaries of London Occasional Papers 10. London: Society of Antiquaries of London.

Macarthur, J. R.

1943 *Ancient Greece in Modern America*. Caldwell, ID: Caxton Printers.

MacCormack, S.

2001 Cuzco, Another Rome? In *Empires: Perspectives from Archaeology and History*, edited by S. E. Alcock, T. D'Altroy, K. Morrison, and C. Sinopoli, pp. 419–35. Cambridge: Cambridge University Press.

MacKay, A.

1977   *Spain in the Middle Ages: From Frontier to Empire, 1000–1500.* New York: St. Martin's Press.

MacLachlan, C. M.

1988   *Spain's Empire in the New World: The Role of Ideas in Institutional and Social Change.* Berkeley: University of California Press.

MacLeod, M. J.

1973   *Spanish Central American: A Socioeconomic History 1520–1720.* Berkeley: University of California Press.

MacLeod, M. J., and R. Wasserstrom, eds.

1983   *Spaniards and Indians in Southeastern Mesoamerica.* Lincoln: University of Nebraska Press.

MacNeish, R., F. Peterson, and K. Flannery

1970   *The Prehistory of the Tehuacan Valley,* Vol. 3: *Ceramics.* Austin: University of Texas Press.

Macready, S., and F. H. Thompson, eds.

1987   *Roman Architecture in the Greek World.* Society of Antiquaries of London Occasional Papers 10. London: Society of Antiquaries of London.

Madsen, W.

1967   Religious Syncretism. In *Handbook of Middle American Indians*, vol. 6, edited by M. Nash, pp. 369–91. Austin: University of Texas Press.

Mallowan, M. E. L.

1936   Excavations at Tell Chagar Bazar and the Archaeological Survey of the Habur. *Iraq* 3:1–86.

Manzanilla, L., ed.

1986   *Unidades habitacionales mesoamericanas y sus áreas de actividad.* Mexico, DF: Universidad national autónoma de México.

Manzanilla, L.

2004   Social Identity and Daily Life at Classic Teotihuacan. In *Mesoamerican Archaeology,* edited by J. Hendon and R. Joyce, pp. 124–47. Oxford: Blackwell Publishing.

Marchand, S. L.

1996   *Down from Olympus: Archaeology and Philhellenism in Germany, 1750–1970.* Princeton: Princeton University Press.

Marcus, J.

1983   Teotihuacan Visitors on Monte Albán Monuments and Murals. In *The Cloud People: Divergent Evolution of the Zapotec and Mixtec Civilizations,* edited by K. Flannery and J. Marcus, pp. 175–81. New York: Academic Press.

1992   *Mesoamerican Writing Systems: Propaganda, Myth, and History in Four Ancient Civilizations.* Princeton: Princeton University Press.

Marcus, J., and K. Flannery
1996   *Zapotec Civilization.* London: Thames and Hudson.

Marfoe, L.
1987   Cedar Forest to Silver Mountain: Social Change and the Development of Long Distance Trade in Early Near Eastern Societies. In *Centre and Periphery in the Ancient World*, edited by M. Rowlands, M. Larsen, and K. Kristiansen, pp. 25–35. Cambridge: Cambridge University Press.

Martín Córdoba, E., and A. Recio Ruiz
2002   *Los Fenicios en la costa de Vélez-Málaga.* Vélez-Málaga: Axarmedia.

Martinez, A.
1997   View from the Ridge: The Kashaya Pomo in a Russian-American Company Conext. In *The Archaeology of Russian Colonialism in the North and Tropical Pacific*, edited by P. R. Mills and A. Martinez, pp. 141–56. Kroeber Anthropological Society Papers 81. Berkeley, CA.

1998   An Archaeological Study of Change and Continuity in the Material Remains, Practices and Cultural Identities of Native California Women in a Nineteenth Century Pluralistic Context. Ph.D. dissertation, Department of Anthropology, University of California, Berkeley.

Mason, W.
1984   Indian-Mexican Cultural Exchange in the Los Angeles Area, 1781–1834. *Aztlan* 15 (1):123–44.

Mattingly, D. J.
1996   From One Imperialism to Another. Imperialism in the Maghreb. In *Roman Imperialism: Post-Colonial Perspectives*, edited by J. Webster and N. Cooper, pp. 49–69. Leicester Archaeology Monographs 3. Leicester: Leicester University Press.

Maxwell-Hyslop, R.
1977   Sources of Sumerian Gold. *Iraq* 39:83–86.

McAlister, L. N.
1984   *Spain and Portugal in the New World 1492–1700.* Minneapolis: University of Minnesota Press.

McCracken, G.
1988   *Culture and Consumption.* Bloomington: Indiana University Press.

McEwan, B. G.
1995   Spanish Precedents and Domestic Life at Puerto Real: The Archaeology of Two Spanish Homesites. In *Puerto Real: The Archaeology of a Sixteenth-Century Spanish Town in Hispaniola*, edited by K. Deagan, pp. 197–230. Gainesville: University Press of Florida.

REFERENCES

McGuire, R.

1986   Economies and Modes of Production in the Prehistoric Southwestern Periphery. In *Ripples in the Chichimec Sea: New Considerations of Southwestern-Mesoamerican Interactions*, edited by F. Mathien and R. McGuire, pp. 243–69. Carbondale: Southern Illinois University Press.

McLendon, S., and R. L. Oswalt

1978   Pomo: Introduction. In *Handbook of North American Indians*, Vol. 8: *California*, edited by R. F. Heizer, pp. 274–88. Washington, DC: Smithsonian Insitution.

Menzel, D.

1964   Style and Time in the Middle Horizon. *Ñawpa Pacha* 2:1–106

Mignolo, W. D.

1995   *The Darker Side of the Renaissance: Literacy, Territoriality, and Colonization.* Ann Arbor: University of Michigan Press.

Milanich, J. T.

1995   *Florida Indians and the Invasion from Europe.* Gainesville: University Press of Florida.

Millar, F.

1981   *The Roman Empire and Its Neighbours.* 2nd ed. London: Duckworth.

1990   The Roman *coloniae* of the Near East: A Study of Cultural Relations. In *Roman Eastern Policy and Other Studies in Roman History*, Proceedings of a Colloquium at Tvärminne, 2–3 October 1987, edited by H. Solin and M. Kajava, pp. 7–58. Helsinki: Finnish Society of Sciences and Letters.

Miller, D.

1987   *Material Culture and Mass Consumption.* Oxford: Blackwell.

1995   Consumption and Commodities. *Annual Review of Anthropology* 24:141–61.

Millett, M.

1990   *The Romanization of Britain.* Cambridge: Cambridge University Press.

Milliken, R.

1995   *A Time of Little Choice: The Disintegration of Tribal Culture in the San Francisco Bay Area 1769–1810.* Menlo Park, CA: Ballena Press.

Millon, R.

1973   *The Teotihuacan Map*, Part 1, *Text.* Austin: University of Texas Press.

1976   Social Relations in Ancient Teotihuacan. In *The Valley of Mexico: Studies in Pre-Hispanic Ecology and Society*, edited by E. Wolf, pp. 205–48. Albuquerque: University of New Mexico Press.

1981   Teotihuacan: City, State, and Civilization. In *Supplement to the Handbook of Middle American Indians*, Vol. 1: *Archaeology*, edited by J. Sabloff, pp. 198–243. Austin: University of Texas Press.

1988   The Last Years of Teotihuacan Dominance. In *The Collapse of Ancient States and Civilizations,* edited by N. Yoffee and G. L. Cowgill, pp. 102–64. Tucson: University of Arizona Press.

Mills, C. W.

1959   *The Sociological Imagination.* New York: Oxford University Press.

Mintz, S.

1977   The So-Called World System: Local Initiative and Local Response. *Dialectical Anthropology* 1:253–70.

Mitchell, S.

1976   Legio VII and the Garrison of Augustan Galatia. *Classical Quarterly* 26:298–308.

1989   The Siege of Cremna A.D. 278. In *The Eastern Frontier of the Roman Empire,* edited by D. H. French and C. S. Lightfoot, pp. 311–28. BAR International Series 553. Oxford: British Archaeological Reports.

1993a   *Anatolia: Land, Men and Gods in Asia Minor.* Vol. I: *The Celts and the Impact of Roman Rule.* Oxford: Clarendon Press.

1993b   *Anatolia: Land, Men and Gods in Asia Minor.* Vol. II: *The Rise of the Church.* Oxford: Clarendon Press.

1995   *Cremna in Pisidia: An Ancient City in Peace and War.* London: Duckworth.

Mitchell, S., and M. Waelkens

1998   *Pisidian Antioch: The Site and Its Monuments.* London: Duckworth.

Mitchell, T.

1988   *Colonising Egypt.* Berkeley: University of California Press.

Molina, C. de (el Cuzqueño)

1988   Relación de la fábulas y ritos de la Incas. In *Fabulas y mitos de los Incas,*
[1575]   edited by H. Urbano and P. Duviols, pp. 47–134. Historia 16. Madrid.

Monaghan, J. D.

2000   Theology and History in the Study of Mesoamerican Religions. In *Handbook of Middle American Indians,* Supplement 6: *Ethnology,* edited by John D. Monaghan, pp. 24–49. Austin: University of Texas Press.

Monroy, D.

1990   *Thrown among Strangers: The Making of Mexican Culture in Frontier California.* Berkeley: University of California Press.

Moorey, P. R. S.

1976   The Late Prehistoric Administrative Building at Jemdet Nasr. *Iraq* 38:95–106.

1978   *Kish Excavations 1923–1933.* Oxford: Clarendon Press.

1993   Iran: A Sumerian El Dorado? *Early Mesopotamia and Iran. Contact and Conflict c. 3500–1600 B.C.,* edited by J. Curtis, pp. 31–43. London: British Museum Press.

1994   *Ancient Mesopotamian Materials and Industries.* Oxford: Clarendon Press.

REFERENCES

Morel, J. P.

1983   Greek Colonization in Italy and in the West (Problems of Evidence and
        Interpretation). In *Crossroads of the Mediterranean*, edited by T. Hackens,
        N. D. Holloway, and R. R. Holloway, pp. 123–61. Louvain-la-Neuve:
        Université Catholique de Louvain.

Moreland, J.

2001   The Carolingian Empire: Rome Reborn? In *Empires: Perspectives from
        Archaeology and History*, edited by S. E. Alcock, T. D'Altroy, K. Morrison,
        and C. Sinopoli, pp. 392–418. Cambridge: Cambridge University Press.

Mörner, M.

1967   *Race Mixture in the History of Latin America.* Boston: Little Brown.

Morris, C.

1972   State Settlements in Tawantinsuyu: A Strategy of Compulsory Urbanism. In
        Contemporary Archaeology, edited by M. P. Leone, pp. 393–401. Carbondale:
        Southern Illinois University Press.

1988   Mas allá de las fronteras de Chincha. In *La frontera del estado Inca.
        Proceedings, 45 Congreso internacional de americanistas, Bogotá, Colombia, 1985*,
        edited by T. D. Dillehay and P. J. Netherly, pp. 131–40. BAR International
        Series 442. Oxford: British Archaeological Reports.

1991   Signs of Division, Symbols of Unity: Art in the Inka Empire. In *Circa 1492:
        Art in the Age of Exploration*, edited by J. A. Levenson, pp. 521–28.
        Washington, DC: National Gallery of Art; New Haven and London: Yale
        University Press.

1995   Symbols to Power: Styles and Media in the Inka State. In *Style, Society, and
        Person: Archaeological and Ethnological Perspectives,* edited by C. Carr and
        J. E. Neitzel, pp. 419–33. New York: Plenum Press.

1998   Inka Strategies of Incorporation and Governance. In *Archaic States*, edited
        by G. M. Feinman and J. Marcus, pp. 293–309. Santa Fe: School of
        American Research Press.

Morris, C., and D. Thompson

1985   *Huánuco Pampa: An Inca City and Its Hinterland.* London: Thames and
        Hudson.

Morris, I.

1994   Archaeologies of Greece. In *Classical Greece: Ancient Histories and Modern
        Archaeologies*, edited by I. Morris, pp. 8–47. Cambridge: Cambridge
        University Press.

Moscati, S.

1992   *Il santuario dei bambini.* Itinerari 11. Rome: Libreria dello stato.

Muhly, J.

1973   *Copper and Tin: The Distribution of Mineral Resources and the Nature of the*

Metals Trade in the Early Bronze Age. Transactions of the Connecticut Academy of Arts and Sciences 43. Hamden, CT.

Mukerji, C.

1997   *Territorial Ambitions and the Gardens of Versailles.* Cambridge: Cambridge University Press.

Mulhare, E. M.

2000   Mesoamerican Social Organization and Community after 1960. In *Handbook of Middle American Indians,* Supplement 6: *Ethnology,* edited by John D. Monaghan, pp. 9–23. Austin: University of Texas Press.

Muller, F.

1948   Chimalacatlán. *Acta Antropológica* III:1. Mexico City: Alumnos de la Escuela nacional de antropología e historia.

Mulvany de Peñaloza, E., and S. Soria

1998   Sitios y caminos en los bosques serranos de los Andes meridionales. *Tawantinsuyu* 5:120–26.

Murra, J. V.

1958   On Inca Political Structure. *Proceedings of the Annual Spring Meeting of the American Ethnological Society,* pp. 30–41. Seattle: University of Washington.

1972   El "control vertical" de un máximo de pisos ecológicos en la economía de las sociedades andinas. In *Visita de la Provincia de León de Huánuco en 1562, Iñigo Ortiz de Zúñiga, visitador,* vol. 2, edited by J. V. Murra, pp. 427–76. Huánuco, Perú: Universidad Nacional Hermilio Valdizán.

1978   Los olleros del Inka: Hacia una historia y arqueología del Qollasuyu. In *Historia, problema, y promesa: Homenaje a Jorge Basadre,* edited by F. Miro Quesada, F. Pease G. Y., and D. Sobrevilla, pp. 415–23. Lima: Pontificia Universidad Católica del Perú.

1986   The Expansion of the Inka State: Armies, War, and Rebellions. In *Anthropological History of Andean Polities,* edited by J. V. Murra, N. Wachtel, and J. Revel, pp. 49–58. Cambridge: Cambridge University Press.

Murray, G.

1953   *Hellenism and the Modern World.* London: George Allen and Unwin.

Napoléon III

1866   *Histoire de Jules César,* vol. 2. Paris: Imprimerie impériale.

Nash, J.

1981   Ethnographic Aspects of the World Capitalist System. *Annual Review of Anthropology* 10:393–423.

Nelson, B.

1997   Chronology and Stratigraphy at La Quemada, Zacatecas, Mexico. *Journal of Field Archaeology* 24:85–109.

REFERENCES

Newson, L.
1985   Indian Population Patterns in Colonial Spanish America. *Latin American Research Review* 20 (3):41–74.

Nichols, D. L., M. W. Spence, and M. Borland
1991   Watering the Fields of Teotihuacan: Early Irrigation at the Ancient City. *Ancient Mesoamerica* 2:119–29.

Nicholson, H. B.
1975   Middle American Ethnohistory: An Overview. In *Handbook of Middle American Indians,* vol. 14, edited by R. Wauchope, pp. 487–505. Austin: University of Texas Press.

Nielsen, A.
1996   Demografía y cambio social en Quebrada de Humahuaca (Jujuy, Argentina) 700–1535 d.C. *Relaciones de la Sociedad Argentina de Antropología* 21:307–85. Buenos Aires.

Niemeyer, H.-G.
1990   The Phoenicians in the Mediterranean: A Non-Greek Model for Expansion and Settlement in Antiquity. In *Greek Colonists and Native Populations. Proceedings of the First Australian Congress of Classical Archaeology Held in Honour of Emeritus Professor A. D. Trendall, Sydney, 9–14 July 1985,* edited by J.-P. Descoeudres, pp. 469–89. Oxford: Oxford University Press.
1999   Die frühe phönizische Expansion im Mittelmeer. Neue Beiträge zu ihrer Beschreibung und ihren Ursachen. *Saeculum* 50 (2):153–75.

Nissen, H.
1985   The Emergence of Writing in the Ancient Near East. *Interdisciplinary Science Reviews* 10 (4):349–61.

Nissen, H., P. Damerow, and R. Englund
1993   *Archaic Bookkeeping. Early Writing and Techniques of Economic Administration in the Ancient Near East.* Chicago: University of Chicago Press.

Noguera, E.
1940   Excavations at Tehuacan. In *The Maya and Their Neighbors,* pp. 306–19. Salt Lake City: University of Utah Press.
1945   Excavaciones en el estado de Puebla. *Anales del Instituto nacional de antropología e historia* I:31–74.

Noyola, A.
1993   Unidades habitacionales prehispánicas excavadas en el estado de Puebla. *Notas mesoamericanas* 14:19–36.

Nuñez de la Vega, F.
1988   *Constituciones diocesanas del obispado de Chiapa,* edited by M. Leon Cazares and M. H. Ruz. Mexico, D.F.: Centro de estudios mayas and Universidad autónoma de México.

Nuttall, Z.

1922 Royal Ordinances Concerning the Laying Out of New Towns. *Hispanic American Historical Review* 5 (2):249–54.

Oates , J.

1993 Trade and Power in the Fifth and Fourth Millennia B.C.: New Evidence from Northern Mesopotamia. *World Archaeology* 24 (3):403–22.

Oates, J., and D. Oates

1997 An Open Gate: Cities of the Fourth Millennium B.C. (Tell Brak 1997). *Cambridge Archaeological Journal* 7:287–97.

O'Crouley, P. A.

1972 *A Description of the Kingdom of New Spain*. Edited and translated by Sean Galvin. San Francisco: John Howell Books.

Oded, B.

1992 *War, Peace, and Empire: Justifications for War in Assyrian Royal Inscriptions.* Wiesbaden: Dr. Ludwig Reichert Verlag.

Oppenheim, A. L.

1954 Seafaring Merchants of Ur. *Journal of the American Oriental Society* 74:6–17.

Orellana, S. L.

1984 *The Tzutujil Mayas: Continuity and Change, 1250–1630.* Norman: University of Oklahoma Press.

Orlin, L.

1970 *Assyrian Colonies in Cappadocia.* The Hague: Mouton.

Ortega, V., and T. Palomares

2003 Nuevas evidencias sobre el barrio Oaxaqueño de Teotihuacan. *Arqueología mexicana* 61:6.

Ortiz de Zúñiga, I.

1967 *Visita de la Provincia de León de Huánuco en 1562, Iñigo Ortiz de Zúñiga,*
[1562] *visitador,* , vol. 1, edited by J. V. Murra. Huánuco. Perú: Universidad Nacional Hermilio Valdizán.

1972 *Visita de la Provincia de León de Huánuco en 1562, Iñigo Ortiz de Zúñiga,*
[1562] *visitador,* vol. 2, edited by J. V. Murra. Huánuco, Perú: Universidad Nacional Hermilio Valdizán.

Ortner, S. B.

1995 Resistance and the Problem of Ethnographic Refusal. *Comparative Studies in History and Society* 37:173–93.

Osborn, S. K.

1997 Death in the Daily Life of the Ross Colony: Mortuary Behavior in Frontier Russian America. Ph.D. dissertation, Department of Anthropology, University of Wisconsin, Milwaukee.

Osborne, R.

1998   Early Greek Colonization? The Nature of Greek Settlement in the West. In *Archaic Greece: New Approaches and New Evidence*, edited by N. Fisher and H. van Wees, pp. 251–69. London: Duckworth.

Osterhammel, J.

1997   *Colonialism: A Theoretical Overview.* Princeton: Marcus Wiener Publishers.

Oswalt, R. L.

1957   Russian Loanwords in Southwestern Pomo. *International Journal of American Linguistics* 23:123–31.

Ouweneel, A., and S. Miller, eds.

1990   *The Indian Community of Colonial Mexico: Fifteen Essays on Land Tenure, Corporate Organization, Ideology, and Village Politics.* Amsterdam: Centro de estudios y documentación latinoamericanos.

Owens, E. J.

1991   The Kremna Aqueduct and Water Supply in Roman cities. *Greece and Rome* 38:41–58.

Özgüç, T.

1963   An Assyrian Trading Outpost. *Scientific American* 207 (3):235–42.

1986   *Kültepe-Kanis II: New Researches at the Center of the Assyrian Trading Colonies.* Ankara: Türk Tarih Kurumu.

Pagden, A.

1995   *Lords of All the World: Ideologies of Empire in Spain, Britain and France, c. 1500–c. 1800.* New Haven: Yale University Press.

Pailes, R., and J. Whitecotton

1979   The Greater Southwest and the Mesoamerican "World" System: An Exploratory Model of Frontier Relationships. In *The Frontier: Comparative Studies II*, edited by W. Savage and S. Thompson, pp. 105–21. Norman: University of Oklahoma Press.

Papapostolou, J.

1971   Topographikia ton Patron. *Athens Annals of Archaeology* 4:305–19.

Papastergiadis, N.

1997   Tracing Hybridity in Theory. In *Debating Cultural Hybridity: Multi-Cultural Identities and the Politics of Anti-Racism*, edited by P. Werbner and T. Modood, pp. 257–81. Postcolonial Encounters. London: Zed Books.

Pare, C.

1991   Fürstensitze, Celts and the Mediterranean world: Developments in the West Hallstatt Culture in the 6th and 5th centuries B.C. *Proceedings of the Prehistoric Society* 57:183–202.

Parkman, E. B.

1996   Fort and Settlement: Interpreting the Past at Fort Ross State Historic Park.
/1997   *California History* 75 (4):354–69.

Parmentier, R. J.

1985   Diagrammatic Icons and Historical Processes in Belau. *American Anthropologist* 87:840–52.

1987   *The Sacred Remains: Myth, History, and Polity in Belau.* Chicago: University of Chicago Press.

1997   The Pragmatic Semiotics of Cultures. *Semiotica* (special issue), vol. 116 (1).

Parpola, S., A. Parpola, and R. H. Brunswig

1977   The Meluhha Village. Evidence of Acculturation of Harappan Traders in Late Third Millennium Mesopotamia? *Journal of the Economic and Social History of the Orient* 20 (2):129–65.

Parry, B.

1987   Problems in Current Theories of Colonial Discourse. *Oxford Literary Review* 9 (1–2):27–58.

Parry, J. H.

1966   *The Spanish Seaborne Empire.* New York: Alfred Knopf.

Parsons, E. C.

1936   *Mitla, Town of the Souls, and Other Zapoteco-Speaking Pueblos of Oaxaca, Mexico.* Chicago: University of Chicago Press.

Parsons, J. R., C. M. Hastings, and R. Matos Mendieta

2000   *Prehispanic Settlement Patterns in the Upper Mantaro and Tarma Drainages, Junín, Peru.* Ann Arbor: Museum of Anthropology, University of Michigan.

Pärssinen, M.

1992   *Tawantinsuyu: The Inca State and Its Political Organization.* Helsinki: Societas Historica Finlandiae.

Paso y Troncoso, F. del, ed.

1939–   *Epistolario de Nueva España,* 16 vols. Biblioteca historica mexicana de obras
1942   ineditas, segunda serie. Porrua, Mexico, DF.

Pastrana, A.

1998   *La explotación azteca de la obsidiana en la Sierra de las navajas.* Colección scientífica, vol. 383. Mexico, DF: Instituto nacional de antropología e historia.

Pasztory, E.

1997   *Teotihuacan: An Experiment in Living.* Norman: University of Oklahoma Press.

Patch, R. W.

1993   *Maya and Spaniard in Yucatan, 1648–1812.* Stanford: Stanford University Press.

Pease, F.

1982   The Formation of Tawantinsuyu: Mechanisms of Colonization and Relationship with Ethnic Groups. In *The Inca and Aztec States, 1400–1800,* edited by G. A. Collier, R. I. Rosaldo, and J. D. Wirth, pp. 173–98. New York: Academic Press.

Peeler, D., and M. Winter

1993   *Tiempo sagrado, espacio sagrado: Astronomía, calendario y arquitectura en Monte Albán y Teotihuacán.* Monte Albán Proyecto Especial 1992–1994, Contribución 1. Oaxaca City: Instituto Oaxaqueño de las Culturas.

Peirce, C. S.

1931–   *Collected Papers of Charles Sanders Peirce.* 8 vols. Edited by C. Hartshorne and
1935   P. Weiss. Cambridge, MA: Harvard University Press.

Pels, P.

1997   The Anthropology of Colonialism: Culture, History, and the Emergence of Western Governmentality. *Annual Review of Anthropology* 26:163–83.

1999   *A Politics of Presence: Contacts between Missionaries and Waluguru in Late Colonial Tanganyika.* History and Anthropology 22. Amsterdam: Harwood Academic Publishers.

Peregrine, P. N., and G. M. Feinman, eds.

1996   *Pre-Columbian World Systems.* Madison, WI: Prehistory Press.

Pérez Calderón, I.

1999   *Huari: Misteriosa ciudad de piedra.* Ayacucho, Peru: Gráfica Bendezú.

Perrault, C.

1979   *Parallèle des anciens et des modernes.* Geneva: Slatkin Reprints.
[1692]

Petropoulos, M., and A. D. Rizakis

1994   Settlement Patterns and Landscape in the Coastal Area of Patras. Preliminary Report. *Journal of Roman Archaeology* 7:183–207.

Phillips, G. H.

1975   *Chiefs and Challengers: Indian Resistance and Cooperation in Southern California.* Berkeley: University of California Press.

1990   *The Enduring Struggle: Indians in California History.* Sparks, NV: Materials for Today's Learning, Inc.

Planella, M. T., and R. Stehberg

1994   Etnohistoria y arqueología en el estudio de la fortaleza indigena de Cerro Grande de la Compañia. *Revista Chungará* 26:1:65–78. Arica, Chile: Universidad de Tarapacá.

Plaza Schuller, F.

1976   *La incursión inca en el septentrión andino ecuatoriano.* Serie Arqueología, no. 2. Otavalo, Ecuador: Instituto otavaleño de antropología.

1980   *El complejo de fortalezas de Pambamarca.* Serie Arqueología, no. 3. Otavalo, Ecuador: Instituto Otavaleño de Antropología.

Plunket, P., and G. Uruñuela

1998   Cholula y Teotihuacan: Una consideración del Occidente de Puebla durante el Clásico. In *Rutas de intercambio en Mesoamérica: III Coloquio Pedro*

Bosch Gimpera, edited by E. Rattray, pp. 101–14. Mexico, DF: Universidad national autónoma de México.

Pohl, J. M. D.

2003 Royal Marriage and Confederacy Building among the Eastern Nahuas, Mixtecs, and Zapotecs. In *The Postclassic Mesoamerican World*, edited by M. E. Smith and F. Berdan, pp. 243–48. Salt Lake City: University of Utah Press.

Polanyi, K.

1963 Ports of Trade in Early Societies. *Journal of Economic History* 23:30–45.

Pollard, H.

1993 *Tariacuri's Legacy: The Prehispanic Tarascan State*. Norman: University of Oklahoma Press.

2003 Development of a Tarascan Core: The Lake Pátzcuaro Basin. In *The Postclassic Mesoamerican World*, edited by M. E. Smith and F. Berdan, pp. 227–37. Salt Lake City: University of Utah Press.

Polo de Ondegardo, J.

1916 Relación de los fundamentos acerca del notable daño que resulta de no
[1571] guardar a los indios sus fueros. In *Colección de libros y documentos referentes a la historia del Perú*, vol. 3, edited by H. H. Urteaga, pp. 45–188. Lima: Sanmartí.

Porada, E.

1980 Kanis. Karum. C. Die Glyptik. *Reallexikon der Assyriologie* 5:383–89.

Postgate, J. N.

1979 The Economic Structure of the Assyrian Empire. In *Power and Propaganda. A Symposium on Ancient Empires*, edited by M. Larsen, pp. 193–221. Copenhagen Studies in Assyriology 7. Copenhagen: Akademisk Forlag.

1992 *Early Mesopotamia. Society and Economy at the Dawn of History*. London: Routledge.

Potts, T.

1994 *Mesopotamia and the East*. Oxford University Committee for Archaeology Monograph 37. Oxford.

Pratt, M. L.

1986 Fieldwork in Common Places. In *Writing Culture: The Poetics and Politics of Ethnography*, edited by J. Clifford and G. E. Marcus, pp. 27–50. Berkeley: University of California Press.

Preucel, R. W., and A. A. Bauer

2001 Archaeological Pragmatics. *Norwegian Archaeological Review* 34:85–96.

Price, B.

1986 Teotihuacan as World System: Concerning the Applicability of Wallerstein's Model. In *Origen y formación del estado en Mesoamérica*, edited by A. Medina, A. López Austin, and M. C. Serra Puche, pp. 169–94. Mexico, DF: Universidad national autónoma de México.

Price, S. R. F.

1984 *Rituals and Power: The Roman Imperial Cult in Asia Minor.* Cambridge: Cambridge University Press.

Price, T. D., L. Manzanilla, and W. D. Middleton

2000 Immigration and the Ancient City of Teotihuacan in Mexico: A Study using Strontium Isotope Ratios in Human Bone and Teeth. *Journal of Archaeological Science* 27:903–13.

Purcell, N.

1990 The Creation of Provincial Landscape: The Roman Impact. In *The Early Roman Empire in the West,* edited by T. F. C. Blagg and M. Millett, pp. 7–29. Oxford: Oxbow Books.

Quilter, J., and G. Urton, eds.

2002 *Narrative Threads.* Austin: University of Texas.

Quinn, D. B.

1976 Renaissance Influences in English Colonization. *Transactions of the Royal Historical Society* 26:73–93.

Quintanilla, P.

1982 Estructura 69. In *Memoria del Proyecto Arqueológico Teotihuacan 80–82,* edited by R. Cabrera, I. Rodríguez, and N. Morelos, pp. 355–60. Colección científica 132. Mexico, DF: Instituto nacional de antropología e historia.

1993 Superposición de estructuras habitacionales en San Juan Teotihuacan. Thesis, Escuela nacional de antropología e historia, Mexico DF.

Raffino, R.

1983 *Los Inkas del Kollasuyu.* 2nd ed. La Plata, Argentina: Ramos Americana Editora.

1993 *Inka. Arqueología, historia, y urbanismo del altiplano andino.* Buenos Aires: Corregidor.

Ramenofsky, A. F.

1987 *Vectors of Death: The Archaeology of European Contact.* Albuquerque: University of New Mexico Press.

Ramos Gavilán, A.

1988 *Historia de Nuestra Senora de Copacabana.* Edited by R. Sans. La Paz:
[1621] Imprenta de la Unión Católica.

Ramsey, J. F.

1973 *Spain: The Rise of the First World Power.* Tuscaloosa: University of Alabama Press.

Rattray, E.

1987 Los Barrios Foráneos de Teotihuacan. In *Teotihuacan: Nuevos datos, nuevas síntesis, nuevos problemas,* edited by E. McClung de Tapia and E. Rattray, pp. 243–73. Mexico, DF: Universidad national autónoma de México.

1990a   New Findings on the Origins of Thin Orange Ceramics. *Ancient Mesoamerica* 1:181–95.

1990b   The Identification of Ethnic Affiliation at the Merchant's Barrio, Teotihuacan. In *Etnoarqueología: Coloquio Bosch-Gimpera*, edited by Y. Sugiura and M. C. Serra Puche, pp. 113–38. Mexico, DF: Universidad national autónoma de México.

1992   *The Teotihuacan Burials and Offerings: A Commentary and Inventory.* Publications in Anthropology 42. Nashville: Vanderbilt University.

1993   *The Oaxaca Barrio at Teotihuacan.* Monografías mesoamericanas 1. Cholula: Universidad de las Américas-Puebla.

1998   Rutas de intercambio en el periodo Clásico en Mesoamérica. In *Rutas de intercambio en Mesoamérica: III Coloquio Pedro Bosch Gimpera*, edited by E. Rattray, pp. 153–84. Mexico, DF: Universidad national autónoma de México.

Redfield, R., R. Linton, and M. J. Herskovits

1936   Memorandum for the Study of Acculturation. *American Anthropologist* 38:149–52.

Reindel, M., and J. Isla C.

1998   Proyecto arqueológico Palpa: Iinforme final, temporada setiembre 1997–marzo 1998. Report submitted to the National Institute of Culture, Lima. Manuscript in possession of the author.

Restall, M.

1997   *The Maya World: Yucatec Culture and Society, 1550–1850.* Stanford: Stanford University Press.

Reyes, L.

1961   Documentos Nahuas sobre el estado de Chiapas. In *Los Mayas del sur y sus relaciones con las Nahuas meridionales*, pp. 167–93. VIII Mesa Redonda, Sociedad Mexicana de Antropología, Mexico, DF.

RGI (Relaciones Geográficas de Indias)

1965   *Biblioteca de autores españoles (continuación)*, vols. 183–185. Madrid: Ediciones Atlas.
[1557–1586]

Ricard, R.

1966   *The Spiritual Conquest of Mexico.* Translated by L. B. Simpson. Berkeley: University of California Press.

Ricoeur, P.

1992   *Oneself as Another.* Chicago: University of Chicago Press.
[1990]

Ridley, R.

1992   *The Eagle and the Spade: Archaeology in Rome during the Napoleonic Era.* Cambridge: Cambridge University Press.

Ringer, F. K.

1992   *Fields of Knowledge: French Academic Culture in Comparative Perspective, 1890–1920.* Cambridge: Cambridge University Press.

1979 *Education and Society in Modern Europe.* Bloomington: Indiana University Press.

Rizakis, A. D.

1988 Le port de Patras et les communications avec l'Italie sous la République. *Cahiers d'histoire* 33:453–72.

1989 La colonie romaine de Patras en Achaie: Le témoignage épigraphique. In *The Greek Renaissance in the Roman Empire,* edited by S. Walker and A. Cameron, pp. 180–96. London: University of London, Institute of Classical Studies.

1990a Cadastres et espace rural dans le nord-ouest du Péloponnese. *Dialogues d'histoire ancienne* 16:259–80.

1990b Sumbole ste melete tou romaikou apoikismou tes BD Peloponnesou. *Meletemata* 10:321–37.

1997 Roman Colonies in the Province of Achaia: Territories, Land and Population. In *The Early Roman Empire in the East,* edited by S. E. Alcock, pp. 15–36. Oxford: Oxbow Books.

Robertson, D.

1959 *Mexican Manuscript Painting of the Early Colonial Period: The Metropolitan Schools.* Norman: University of Oklahoma Press.

Robinson, D. M.

1928 The *Res Gestae Divi Augusti* as Recorded on the Monumentum Antiochenum. *American Journal of Philology* 47:1–54.

Robinson, H. S.

1974 A Monument of Roma at Corinth. *Hesperia* 43:470–84.

Rogers, J. D.

1990 *Objects of Change: The Archaeology and History of Arikara Contact with Europeans.* Washington, DC: Smithsonian Institution Press.

1993a Theoretical Orientations on Culture Contact. In *Ethnohistory and Archaeology: Approaches to Postcontact Change in the Americas,* edited by J. D. Rogers and S. M. Wilson, pp. 17–18. New York: Plenum Press.

1993b The Social and Material Implications of Culture Contact on the Northern Plains. In *Ethnohistory and Archaeology: Approaches to Postcontact Change in the Americas,* edited by J. D. Rogers and S. M. Wilson, pp. 73–88. New York: Plenum Press.

2004 The Contingencies of State Formation in Eastern Inner Asia. Manuscript on file, Department of Anthropology, National Museum of Natural History.

Romano, D. G.

1993 Post-146 B.C. Land Use in Corinth, and Planning of the Roman Colony of 44 B.C. In *The Corinthia in the Roman Period,* edited by T. E. Gregory, pp. 9–30. Journal of Roman Archaeology Supplementary Vol. 8. Ann Arbor: Journal of Roman Archaeology.

2000   A Tale of Two Cities: Roman Colonies at Corinth. In *Romanization and the City: Creation, Dynamics and Failures*, edited by L. Fentress, pp. 83–104. Journal of Roman Archaeology Supplementary Vol. 38. Portsmouth, RI: Journal of Roman Archaeology.

Romano, D. G., and B. Schoenbrun
1994   A Computerized Architectural and Topographical Survey of Ancient Corinth. *Journal of Field Archaeology* 29:177–90.

Ronda, J. P.
1984   *Lewis and Clark among the Indians.* Lincoln: University of Nebraska Press.

Roseberry, W.
1988   Political Economy. *Annual Review of Anthropology* 17:161–85.

1989   *Anthropologies and Histories: Essays in Culture, History, and Political Economy.* New Brunswick, NJ: Rutgers University Press.

Rosenbaum, B.
1996   Women and Gender in Mesoamerica. In *The Legacy of Mesoamerica: History and Culture of a Native American Civilization*, edited by R. M. Carmack, J. Gasco, and G. Gossen, pp. 322–52. Englewood Cliffs: Prentice-Hall.

Rostworowski de Diez Canseco, M.
1999   *History of the Inca Realm.* Translated by H. B. Iceland. Cambridge: Cambridge University Press.

Rothman, M., ed.
2001   *Uruk Mesopotamia and Its Neighbors: Cross Cultural Interactions in the Era of State Formation.* Santa Fe: School of American Research Press.

Rouse, I.
1986   *Migrations in Prehistory.* New Haven: Yale University Press.

Rowe, J. H.
1946   Inca Culture at the Time of the Spanish Conquest. In *Handbook of South American Indians*, edited by J. Steward. Bulletin 143, vol. 2, pp. 183–330. Washington, DC: Bureau of American Ethnology.

1967   What Kind of a Settlement Was Inca Cuzco? *Ñawpa Pacha* 5:59–77.

1982   Inca Policies and Institutions relating to the Cultural Unification of the Empire. In *The Inca and Aztec States, 1400–1800: Anthropology and History*, edited by G. A. Collier, R. I. Rosaldo, and J. D. Wirth, pp. 93–118. New York: Academic Press.

Rowe, J. H., D. Collier, and G. R. Willey
1950   Reconnaissance Notes on the Site of Huari, Near Ayacucho, Peru. *American Antiquity* 16 (2):120–37.

Rowlands, M.
1998   The Archaeology of Colonialism. In *Social Transformations in Archaeology. Global and Local Perspectives*, edited by K. Kristiansen and M. Rowlands, pp. 327–33. London: Routledge.

Rowlands, M. J., M. T. Larsen, and K. Kristiansen, eds.

1987 *Centre and Periphery in the Ancient World.* Cambridge: Cambridge University Press.

Rowton, M.

1967 The Woodlands of Ancient Asia. *Journal of Near Eastern Studies* 26:261–77.

Rubin, N.

1991 *Isabella of Castile: The First Renaissance Queen.* New York: St. Martin's Press.

Ruhl, D. L., and K. Hoffman

1997 Diversity and Social Identity in Colonial Spanish America: Native American, African, and Hispanic Communities during the Middle Period. *Historical Archaeology* 31 (1):1–3.

Ruiz Rodríguez, A.

1997 The Iron Age Iberian Peoples of the Upper Guadalquivir Valley. In *The Archaeology of Iberia: The Dynamics of Change. Selected Papers from the Theoretical Archaeology Group,* edited by M. Díaz-Andreu and S. Keay, pp. 175–91. London: Routledge.

Sabloff, J. A., and E. W. Andrews V, eds.

1986 *Late Lowland Maya Civilization: Classic to Postclassic.* Albuquerque: University of New Mexico Press.

Sahlins, M.

1985 *Islands of History.* Chicago: University of Chicago Press.

1992 The Economics of Develop-man in the Pacific. *Res* 21:12–25.

1994 Cosmologies of Capitalism: The Trans-Pacific Sector of "the World System." In *Culture/Power/History: A Reader in Contemporary Social Theory,* edited by N. B. Dirks, G. Eley, and S. B. Ortner, pp. 412–55. Princeton: Princeton University Press.

1995 *How "Natives" Think: About Captain Cook, For Example.* Chicago: University of Chicago Press.

Said, E. W.

1978 *Orientalism.* New York: Vintage Books.

1993 *Culture and Imperialism.* New York: Vintage Books.

Saignes, T.

1985 *Los Andes orientales: Historia de un olvido.* Cochabamba, Bolivia: Instituto francés de estudios andinos and Centro de estudios de la realidad económica y social.

1999 The Colonial Condition in the Quechua-Aymara Heartland (1570–1780). In *The Cambridge History of the Native Peoples of the Americas,* Vol. 3, *South America, Part 2,* edited by F. Salomon and S. B. Schwartz, pp. 59–137. Cambridge: Cambridge University Press.

Salisbury, N.

1996   Native People and European Settlers in Eastern North America,
        1600–1783. In *The Cambridge History of the Native Peoples of the Americas*,
        Vol. 1, *North America, Part 1*, edited by B. G. Trigger and W. E. Washburn,
        pp. 399–460. Cambridge: Cambridge University Press.

Salmon, E. T.

1969   *Roman Colonization under the Republic*. London: Thames and Hudson.

Salomon, F. L.

1986   *Native Lords of Quito in the Age of the Incas*. Cambridge: Cambridge
        University Press.

2001   How an Andean "Writing without Words" Works. *Current Anthropology*
        42:1:1–27.

Sandos, J. A.

1997   Between Crucifix and Lance: Indian-White Relations in California,
        1769–1848. *California History* 76 (2–3):196–229.

Sandstrom, Alan R.

1991   *Corn is our Blood: Culture and Ethnic Identity in a Contemporary Aztec Indian
        Village*. Norman: University of Oklahoma Press.

San Nicolas, M.

2000   Interrelación de los santuarios fenicios y púnicos de Ibiza. In *Actas del IV
        congreso internacional de estudios fenicios e púnicos, Cádiz, 2–6 Octubre 1995*,
        edited by M.-E. Aubet and M. Barthélemy, pp. 675–90. Cádiz: Servicio de
        publicaciones de la universidad de Cádiz.

Santley, R., and R. Alexander

1992   The Political Economy of Core-Periphery Systems. In *Resources, Power, and
        Interregional Interaction*, edited by E. M. Schortman and P. A. Urban,
        pp. 23–49. New York: Plenum Press.

1996   Teotihuacan and Middle Classic Mesoamerica: A Precolumbian World
        System? In *Arqueología Mesoamericana: Homenaje a William T. Sanders*, edited
        by A. G. Mastache, J. Parsons, R. Santley, and M. C. Serra Puche,
        pp. 173–94. Mexico, DF: Universidad national autónoma de México.

Santley, R., C. Yarborough, and B. Hall

1987   Enclaves, Ethnicity, and the Archaeological Record at Matacapan. In
        Ethnicity and Culture, edited by R. Auger, M. Glass, S. MacEachern, and
        P. McCartney, pp. 85–100. Calgary: University of Calgary Archaeological
        Association.

Sarmiento de Gamboa, P.

1960   Historia de los Incas. In *Biblioteca de Autores Españoles (continuación)*, vol.
[1572] 135, pp. 193–297. Madrid: Ediciones Atlas.

Sauer, C. O.

1966   *The Early Spanish Main*. Berkeley: University of California Press.

Schjellerup, I.

1997   Incas and Spaniards in the Conquest of the Chachapoyas: Archaeological and Ethnohistorical Research in the North-Eastern Andes of Peru. Archaeological Theses, no. 7, Series B. Gothenberg: Gothenberg University, Department of Archaeology.

Schnapp, A.

1996   *The Discovery of the Past: The Origins of Archaeology*. London: British Museum Press.

Scholes, F. V., and R. L. Roys

1968   *The Maya Chontal Indians of Acalan-Tixchel*. Norman: University of Oklahoma Press.

Schortman, E. M., and P. A. Urban

1998   Culture Contact Structure and Process. In *Studies in Culture Contact: Interaction, Culture Change, and Archaeology*, edited by J. G. Cusick, pp.102–25. Occasional Paper 25. Carbondale: Center for Archaeological Investigations, Southern Illinois University.

Schortman, E., and P. Urban, eds.

1992   *Resources, Power, and Interregional Interaction*. New York: Plenum.

Schreiber, K. J.

1978   Planned Architecture of Middle Horizon Peru: Implications for Social and Political Organization. Ph.D. dissertation, Department of Anthropology, SUNY Binghamton.

1987   Conquest and Consolidation: A Comparison of the Wari and Inka Occupations of a Highland Peruvian Valley. *American Antiquity* 52 (2):266–84.

1992   *Wari Imperialism in Middle Horizon Peru*. Anthropological Paper 87. Ann Arbor: Museum of Anthropology, University of Michigan.

1993   The Inca Occupation of the Province of Andamarca Lucanas, Peru. In *Provincial Inca*, edited by M. A. Malpass, pp. 77–116. Iowa City: University of Iowa Press.

1998   Regional Approaches to the Study of Prehistoric Empires: Examples from Ayacucho and Nasca, Peru. In *Settlement Pattern Studies in the Americas: Fifty Years since Virú*, edited by B. R. Billman and G. M. Feinman, pp. 160–71. Washington, DC: Smithsonian Institution Press.

2001   The Wari Empire of Middle Horizon Peru: The Epistemological Challenge of Documenting an Empire without Documentary Evidence. In *Empires: Perspectives from Archaeology and History*, edited by S. E. Alcock, T. N. D'Altroy, K. D. Morrison, and C. M. Sinopoli, pp. 70–92. Cambridge: Cambridge University Press.

Schreiber, K. J., and J. Lancho R.

1995   The Puquios of Nasca. *Latin American Antiquity* 6 (3):229–54.

2003   *Irrigation and Society in the Peruvian Desert: The Puquios of Nasca*. Lanham: Lexington Books.

Schroeder, S., S. Wood, and R. Haskett, eds.

1997   *Indian Women of Early Mexico.* Norman: University of Oklahoma Press.

Schubart, H.

1982   Phönizische Niederlassungen an der iberischen Südküste. In *Phönizier im Westen. Die Beiträge des internationalen Symposiums über 'die phönizische Expansion im westlichen Mittelmeerraum' in Köln 1979,* edited by H.-G. Niemeyer, pp. 207–31. Mainz: Römisch-Germanisches Zentral Museum.

1998   Phönizische Eisenschmiede auf dem Morro de Mezquitilla. In *Archaologische Studien in Kontaktzonen der antiken Welt.* Veroffentlichung der Joachim Jungius-Gesellschaft der Wissenschaften Hamburg 87, edited by R. Rolle and D. Schmidt, pp. 545–58. Gottingen: Vandenhoeck and Ruprecht.

Schwaller, J. F.

1987   *The Church and Clergy in Sixteenth-Century Mexico.* Albuquerque: University of New Mexico Press.

Schwartz, G.

1988   Excavations at Karatut Mevkii and Perspectives on the Uruk/Jemdet Nasr Expansion. *Akkadica* 56:1–41.

Schwartz, G. M., and S. E. Falconer, eds.

1994   *Archaeological Views from the Countryside: Village Communities in Early Complex Societies.* Washington, DC: Smithsonian Institution Press.

Schwartz, S. B.

1994   Introduction. In *Implicit Understandings: Observing, Reporting, and Reflecting on the Encounters between Europeans and Other Peoples in the Early Modern Era,* edited by S. B. Schwartz, pp. 1–19. Cambridge: Cambridge University Press.

Schwartz, S. B., and F. Salomon

1999   New Peoples and New Kinds of People: Adaptation, Readjustment, and Enthnogenesis in South American Indigenous Societies (Colonial Era). In *The Cambridge History of the Native Peoples of the Americas,* Vol. 3, *South America, Part 2,* edited by F. Salomon and S. B. Schwartz, pp. 59–137. Cambridge: Cambridge University Press.

Seed, P.

1991   Colonial and Postcolonial Discourse. *Latin American Research Review* 26 (3):181–200.

1995   *Ceremonies of Possession in Europe's Conquest of the New World, 1492–1640.* Cambridge: Cambridge University Press.

Seifert, D. J.

1977   *Archaeological Majolicas of the Rural Teotihuacan Valley, Mexico.* Ph.D. dissertation, University of Iowa. Ann Arbor: University Microfilms.

Séjourné, L.

1966   *El lenguaje de las formas en Teotihuacán.* Mexico DF.: Fondo de cultura económica.

Shanks, M.

1995   *Classical Archaeology of Greece: Experiences of the Discipline.* London: Routledge.

Sharer, R. J.

1994   *The Ancient Maya.* Stanford: Stanford University Press.

Sharp, L.

1952   Steel Axes for Stone Age Australians. In *Human Problems in Technological Change: A Casebook*, edited by E. H. Spicer, pp. 69–90. New York: Russell Sage Foundation.

Shaw, B.

1990   Bandit Highlands and Lowland Peace: The Mountains of Isauria-Cilicia. *Journal of the Economic and Social History of the Orient* 43:199–233, 237–70.

Shelley, P. B.

1822   *Hellas: A Lyrical Drama.* London: C. and J. Ollier.

Sherratt, A.

1993   What Would a Bronze-Age World System Look Like? Relations between Temperate Europe and the Mediterranean in Later Prehistory. *Journal of European Archaeology* 1 (2):1–57.

Sherwin-White, A. N.

1976   Rome, Pamphylia and Cilicia. *Journal of Roman Studies* 66:1–14.

Shipek, F. C.

1977   A Strategy for Change: The Luiseño of Southern California. Ph.D. dissertation, Department of Anthropology, University of Hawaii.

Silliman, S.

2000   Colonial Worlds, Indigenous Practices: The Archaeology of Labor on a 19th-Century California Rancho. Ph.D. dissertation, Department of Anthropology, University of California, Berkeley.

Silverman, H.

1993   Cahuachi in the Ancient Nasca World. Iowa City: University of Iowa Press.

Simmons, W. S.

1988   Culture Theory in Contemporary Ethnohistory. *Ethnohistory* 35:1–14.

1997   Indian Peoples of California. *California History* 76 (2–3):48–77.

Simpson, L. B.

1934   *Studies in the Administration of the Indians of New Spain.* Ibero-Americana 7. Berkeley: University of California Press.

1950   *The Encomienda in New Spain.* Berkeley: University of California Press.

Singleton, T. A.

1998   Cultural Interaction and African American Identity in Plantation Archaeology. In *Studies in Culture Contact: Interaction, Culture Change, and Archaeology*, edited by J. G. Cusick, pp. 172–88. Occasional Paper 25. Carbondale: Center for Archaeological Investigations, Southern Illinois University.

Slane, K.

1989   Corinthian Ceramic Imports: The Changing Pattern of Provincial Trade in the First and Second Centuries A.D. In *The Greek Renaissance in the Roman Empire*, edited by S. Walker and A. Cameron, pp. 219–25. London: University of London, Institute of Classical Studies.

Smith, C.

1978   Beyond Dependency Theory: National and Regional Patterns of Underdevelopment in Guatemala. *American Ethnologist* 5:574–617.

1984   Local History and Global Context: Social and Economic Transition in Western Guatemala. *Comparative Studies in Society and History* 26:193–228.

Smith, M. E.

1996   *The Aztecs*. Malden, MA: Blackwell Publishers.

2001   The Aztec Empire and the Mesoamerican World System. In *Empires: Comparative Perspectives from Archaeology and History*, edited by S. E. Alcock, T. N. D'Altroy, K. D. Morrison, and C. M. Sinopoli, pp. 128–54. Cambridge: Cambridge University Press.

2003   Small Polities in Postclassic Mesoamerica. In *The Postclassic Mesoamerican World*, edited by M. E. Smith and F. Berdan, pp. 35–39. Salt Lake City: University of Utah Press.

Smith, M. E., and F. F. Berdan

1996   Appendix 4: Province Descriptions. In *Aztec Imperial Strategies*, by F. Berdan et al., pp. 265–349. Washington, DC: Dumbarton Oaks.

2000   The Postclassic Mesoamerican World System. *Current Anthropology* 41 (2):283–87.

2003   Postclassic Mesoamerica. In *The Postclassic Mesoamerican World*, edited by M. E. Smith and F. Berdan, pp. 3–13. Salt Lake City: University of Utah Press.

Smith, M. E., and J. Gasco

1996   Origins and Development of Mesoamerican Civilization. In *The Legacy of Mesoamerica: History and Culture of a Native American Civilization*, edited by R. M. Carmack, J. Gasco, and G. Gossen, pp. 40–79. Englewood Cliffs: Prentice-Hall.

Smith, R. R. R.

1987   The Imperial Reliefs from the Sebasteion at Aphrodisias. *Journal of Roman Studies* 77:88–138.

1988   Simulacra Gentium: The Ethne from the Sebasteion at Aphrodisias. *Journal of Roman Studies* 78:50–77.

1998   Cultural Choice and Political Identity in Honorific Portrait Statues in the Greek East in the Second Century A.D. *Journal of Roman Studies* 88:56–93.

Smith, S. T.

1998   Nubia and Egypt: Interaction, Acculturation, and Secondary State Formation from the Third to the First Millennium B.C. In *Studies in Culture Contact. Interaction, Culture Change, and Archaeology*, edited by J. Cusick, pp. 256–87. Occasional Paper 25. Carbondale: Center for Archaeological Investigations, Southern Illinois University Press.

Spalding, K.

1999   The Crises and Transformations of Invaded Societies: Andean Area (1500–1580). In *The Cambridge History of the Native Peoples of the Americas*, Vol. 3, *South America, Part 1*, edited by F. Salomon and S. B. Schwartz, pp. 59–137. Cambridge: Cambridge University Press.

Spawforth, A.

1974   The Appaleni of Corinth. *Greek, Roman and Byzantine Studies* 15:295–303.

1978   Balbilla, the Euryclids and Memorials for a Greek Magnate. *Annals of the British School at Athens* 73:249–60.

1994   Corinth, Argos, and the Imperial Cult: Pseudo-Julian, *Letters* 198. *Hesperia* 63:211–32.

1996   Roman Corinth: The Formation of a Colonial Elite. In *Roman Onomastics in the Greek East: Social and Political Aspects*, edited by A. D. Rizakis, pp. 167–82. Meletemata 21. Paris: Diffusion de Boccard.

Spawforth, A., and S. Walker

1985   The World of the Panhellenion: I. Athens and Eleusis. *Journal of Roman Studies* 75:78–104.

Spence, M. W.

1976   Human Skeletal Material from the Oaxaca Barrio in Teotihuacan, Mexico. In *Archaeological Frontiers: Papers on New World High Cultures in Honor of J. Charles Kelley*, edited by R. Pickering, pp. 129–48. University Museum Research Records 4. Carbondale: Southern Illinois University.

1989   Excavaciones recientes en Tlailotlacan, el Barrio Oaxaqueño de Teotihuacan. *Arqueología* 5:81–104.

1992   Tlailotlacan, A Zapotec Enclave in Teotihuacan. In *Art, Ideology, and the City of Teotihuacan*, edited by J. C. Berlo, pp. 59–88. Washington, DC: Dumbarton Oaks Research Library and Collection.

1994   Human Skeletal Material from Teotihuacan. In *Mortuary Practices and Skeletal Remains at Teotihuacan*, by M. Sempowski and M. W. Spence, pp. 312–427. *Urbanization at Teotihuacan, Mexico*, vol. 3, edited by R. Millon. Salt Lake City: University of Utah Press.

1996a   Commodity or Gift: Teotihuacan Obsidian in the Maya Region. *Latin American Antiquity* 7:21–39.

1996b   A Comparative Analysis of Ethnic Enclaves. In *Arqueología Mesoamericana: Homenaje a William T. Sanders*, edited by A. G. Mastache, J. Parsons, R. Santley, and M. C. Serra Puche, pp. 333–53. Mexico, DF: Universidad national autónoma de México.

1998   La cronología de radiocarbono de Tlailotlacan. In *Los ritmos de cambio en Teotihuacán: Reflexiones y discusiones de su cronología*, edited by R. Cabrera and R. Brambila, pp. 283–97. Colección científica 366. Mexico, DF: Instituto nacional de antropología e historia.

2000   From Tzintzuntzan to Paquimé: Peers or Peripheries in Greater Mesoamerica? In *Greater Mesoamerica: The Archaeology of West and Northwest Mexico*, edited by M. S. Foster and S. Gorenstein, pp. 255–61. Salt Lake City: University of Utah Press.

2002   Domestic Ritual in Tlailotlacan, Teotihuacan. In *Domestic Ritual in Ancient Mesoamerica*, edited by P. Plunket, pp. 53–66. Monograph 46. Los Angeles: Cotsen Institute of Archaeology, UCLA.

Spence, M. W., and L. Gamboa
1999   Mortuary Practices and Social Adaptation in the Tlailotlacan Enclave. In *Prácticas funerarias en la Ciudad de los Dioses: Los enterramientos humanos de la antigua Teotihuacan*, edited by L. Manzanilla and C. Serrano, pp. 173–201. Mexico, DF: Universidad national autónoma de México.

Spicer, E. H.
1962   *Cycles of Conquest: The Impact of Spain, Mexico, and the United States on the Indians of the Southwest, 1533–1960.* Tucson: University of Arizona Press.

Spickard, L.
1983   The Development of Huari Administrative Architecture. In *Investigations of the Andean Past*, edited by D. H. Sandweiss, pp. 136–60. Ithaca: Latin American Studies Program, Cornell University Press.

Šprajc, I. Š.
2000   Astronomical Alignments at Teotihuacan. *Latin American Antiquity* 11:403–15.

Spurling, Geoffrey E.
1992   *The Organization of Craft Production in the Inka State: The Potters and Weavers of Milliraya.* Ph.D. dissertation, Cornell University. Ann Arbor: University Microfilms.

Stanish, C.
1989   Household Archaeology: Testing Models of Zonal Complementarity in the South Central Andes. *American Anthropologist* 91:7–24.

Stark, B.
1986   Perspectives on the Peripheries of Mesoamerica. In *Ripples in the Chichimec Sea: New Considerations of Southwestern-Mesoamerican Interactions*, edited by F. Mathien and R. McGuire, pp. 270–90. Carbondale: Southern Illinois University Press.

Stech, T., and V. Pigott

1986   The Metals Trade in Southwest Asia in the Third Millennium B.C. *Iraq* 48:39–64.

Stein, G. J.

1998   World Systems Theory and Alternative Modes of Interaction in the Archaeology of Culture Contact. In *Studies in Culture Contact: Interaction, Culture Change and Archaeology*, edited by J. G. Cusick, pp. 220–55. Occasional Paper 25. Carbondale: Center for Archaeological Investigations, Southern Illinois University.

1999a   Material Culture and Social Identity: The Evidence for a 4th Millennium B.C. Uruk Mesopotamian Colony at Hacınebi, Turkey. *Paléorient* 25:11–22.

1999b   *Rethinking World-Systems: Diasporas, Colonies, and Interaction in Uruk Mesopotamia.* Tucson: Arizona University Press.

2002a   Colonies without Colonialism: A Trade Diaspora Model of Fourth Millennium B.C. Mesopotamian Enclaves in Anatolia. In *The Archaeology of Colonialism*, edited by C. Lyons and J. Papadopoulos, pp. 27–64. Los Angeles: Getty Research Institute.

2002b   Distinguished Lecture: From Passive Periphery to Active Agents: Emerging Perspectives in the Archaeology of Interregional Interaction. *American Anthropologist* 104:903–16.

Stein, G., and M. J. Blackman

1993   The Organizational Context of Specialized Craft Production in Early Mesopotamian States. *Research in Economic Anthropology* 14:29–59.

Stein, G., C. Edens, J. Pearce Edens, K. Boden, N. Laneri, H. Özbal, B. Earl, M. Adriaens, and H. Pittman

1998   Southeast Anatolia before the Uruk Expansion: Preliminary Report on the 1997 Excavations at Hacınebi, Turkey. *Anatolica* 24:143–93.

Steinkeller, P.

1993   Early Political Development in Mesopotamia and the Origins of the Sargonic Empire. In *Akkad: The First World Empire*, edited by M. Liverani, pp. 105–27. Parua: Sargon.

Stocking, G., ed.

1991   *Colonial Situations: Essays on the Contextualization of Ethnographic Knowledge.* History of Anthropology 7. Madison: University of Wisconsin Press.

Stoler, A. L.

1989   Rethinking Colonial Categories: European Communities and the Boundaries of Rule. *Comparative Studies in Society and History* 31:134–61.

1992   Rethinking Colonial Categories: European Communities and the Boundaries of Rule. In *Colonialism and Culture*, edited by N. B. Dirks, pp. 319–52. Ann Arbor: University of Michigan Press.

1997   Sexual Affronts and Racial Frontiers: European Identities and the Cultural Politics of Exclusion in Colonial Southeast Asia. In *Tensions of Empire:*

Colonial Cultures in a Bourgeois World, edited by F. Cooper and A. Stoler, pp. 198–237. Berkeley: University of California Press.

Stoler, A., and F. Cooper
1997   Between Metropole and Colony. Rethinking a Research Agenda. In *Tensions of Empire: Colonial Cultures in a Bourgeois World*, edited by F. Cooper and A. Stoler, pp. 1–56. Berkeley: University of California Press.

Strommenger, E.
1980   *Habuba Kabira, Eine Stadt vor 5000 Jahren.* Mainz am Rhein: Phillip von Zabern.

Sürenhagen, D.
1986   The Dry-Farming Belt: The Uruk Period and Subsequent Developments. In *The Origins of Cities in Dry Farming Syria and Mesopotamia in the Third Millennium B.C.*, edited by H. Weiss, pp. 7–43. Guilford, CT: Four Quarters Publishing Co.

Swagerty, W. R.
1988   Indian Trade in the Trans-Mississippi West to 1870. In *Handbook of North American Indians*, Vol. 4: *History of Indian-White Relations*, edited by W. E. Washburn, pp. 351–74. Washington, DC: Smithsonian Institution Press.

Swain, S.
1996   Hellenism and Empire: Language, Classicism and Power in the Greek World, A.D. 50–250. Oxford: Clarendon Press.

Swanton, J. R.
1946   *The Indians of the Southeastern United States.* Bureau of American Ethnology Bulletin 137. Washington, DC: Smithsonian Institution Press.

Syme, R.
1995   *Anatolica: Studies in Strabo.* Oxford: Clarendon Press.

Symonds, J. A.
1880   *Studies of the Greek Poets.* Vol. 1. New York: Harper and Brothers.

Tadmor, H.
1975   Assyria and the West: The Ninth Century and Its Aftermath. In *Unity and Diversity: Essays in the History, Literature, and Religion of the Ancient Near East*, edited by H. Goedicke and J. J. M. Roberts. Baltimore: Johns Hopkins University Press.

Terraciano, Kevin
2001   *The Mixtecs of Colonial Oaxaca: Nudzahui History, Sixteenth through Eighteenth Centuries.* Stanford: Stanford University Press.

Terranato, N.
1998   *Tam Firmum Municipium:* The Romanization of Volaterrae and Its Cultural Implications. *Journal of Roman Studies* 88:94–114.

Thomas, D. H., ed.

1991　　*Columbian Consequences*, Vol. 3: *The Spanish Borderlands in Pan-American Perspective*. Washington, DC: Smithsonian Institution Press.

Thomas, N.

1989　　*Out of Time: History and Evolution in Anthropological Discourse*. Cambridge: Cambridge University Press.

1990　　Partial Texts. *Journal of Pacific History* 25:139–58.

1991　　*Entangled Objects: Exchange, Material Culture, and Colonialism in the Pacific*. Cambridge, MA: Harvard University Press.

1994　　*Colonialism's Culture: Anthropology, Travel and Government*. Princeton: Princeton University Press.

1997　　Partial Texts. In *In Oceania: Vision, Artifacts, Histories*, by N. Thomas, pp. 23–49. Durham and London: Duke University Press.

Thompson, D. E.

1967　　Investigaciones arqueológicas en las aldeas chupachu de Ichu y Auquimarka. In *Visita de la Provincia de León de Huánuco en 1562: Iñigo Ortiz de Zúñiga, visitador*, vol. 1, edited by J. V. Murra, pp. 357–62. Huánuco, Peru: Universidad Nacional Hermilio Valdizán.

Todorov, T.

1984　　*The Conquest of America: The Question of the Other*. Translated by R. Howard. New York: Harper and Row.

Toledo, Franciso de

1940　　Información hecha en el Cuzco por orden del Virrey Toledo, con respuestas
[1571]　　al mismo interrogatorio utilizado en las cuatro informaciones anteriores: Añádese un auto del año 1563 del Conde de Nieva, en el cual otorga ese Virrey investidura a un cacique en la misma forma en que antes la daban los Incas a los curacas. In *Don Francisco del Toledo, Supremo organizador del Perú, su vida, su obra* [1515–1582], vol. 2, edited by R. Levillier, pp. 65–98. Buenos Aires: Espasa-Calpe.

Townsend, R. F.

1992　　*The Aztecs*. New York: Thames and Hudson.

Tozzer, A. M., ed. and trans.

1941　　*Landa's* Relación de las Cosas de Yucatán. Papers of the Peabody Museum of American Archaeology and Ethnology 18. Cambridge, MA: Harvard University.

Trigger, B.

1980　　Archaeology and the Image of the American Indian. *American Antiquity* 45:662–76.

1984　　Alternative Archaeologies: Nationalist, Colonialist, Imperialist. *Man* 19:355–70.

Trigger, B. G., and W. R. Swagerty

1996   Entertaining Strangers: North America in the Sixteenth Century. In *The Cambridge History of the Native Peoples of the Americas*, Vol. 1, *North America, Part 1*, edited by Bruce G. Trigger and Wilcomb E. Washburn, pp. 461–538. Cambridge: Cambridge University Press.

Truhan, D. L.

2004   An Ethnohistorical Introduction to the Inka Occupation of Cañari Territory. Paper presented at the Annual Meeting of the Society for American Archaeology, in the Symposium "The Inkas at the Margins," Montreal.

Tsetskhladze, G., and F. De Angelis, eds.

1994   *The Archaeology of Greek Colonisation. Essays Dedicated to Sir John Boardman.* Oxford University Committee for Archaeology Monograph 40. Oxford: Oxbow Books.

Tulard, J.

1997   Introduction. In *Les empires occidentaux de Rome à Berlin*, edited by J. Tulard, pp. 9–16. Paris: Presses Universitaires de France.

Turgeon, L., ed.

1998   *Les entre-lieux de la culture.* Quebec: Presses de l'Université Laval.

Turgeon, L., D. Delâge, and R. Ouellet, eds.

1996   *Transferts culturels et métissages, Amérique/Europe XVIe–XXe siècle.* Quebec: Presses de l'Université de Laval.

Turner, F. M.

1981   *The Greek Heritage in Victorian Britain.* New Haven: Yale University Press.

Turner, J. H.

1992   Overcoming Humanities Babble: Searching for Universal Types of Human Social Relations. *Contemporary Sociology* 21:126–28.

Turner, L

1995   Consuming Colonialism. *Critique of Anthropology* 15:203–12.

Turner, V. W.

1977   Symbols in African Ritual. In *Symbolic Anthropology*, edited by J. L. Dolgin, D. S. Kemnitzer, and D. M. Schneider, pp. 183–94. New York: Columbia University Press.

Tyler, S. A.

1986   Post-modern Ethnography: From Document of the Occult to Occult Document. In *Writing Culture: The Poetics and Politics of Ethnography*, edited by J. Clifford and G. E. Marcus, pp. 122–40. Berkeley: University of California Press.

Uhle, M.

1903   Pachacamac—Report of the William Pepper, M.D., LL.D., Peruvian Expedition of 1896. Department of Archaeology, University of Pennsylvania, Philadelphia.

Urcid, J.

1983   The Tombs and Burials from Lambityeco: A Prehistoric Community in the Valley of Oaxaca, Mexico. M.A. thesis, University of the Americas, Puebla, Cholula.

Urton, G.

2003   *Signs of the Inka Khipu.* Austin: University of Texas.

van Dommelen, P.

1997a   Colonial Constructs: Colonialism and Archaeology in the Mediterranean. *World Archaeology* 28:305–23.

1997b   Some Reflections on Urbanization in a Colonial Context: West Central Sardinia in the 7th to 5th centuries B.C. In *Urbanization in the Mediterranean in the 9th–6th Centuries B.C., Copenhagen,* edited by H. Damgaard Andersen, H. Horsnæs, and A. Rathje, pp. 243–78. Acta Hyperborea 7. Copenhagen: Tusculanum Press.

1998   *On Colonial Grounds: A Comparative Study of Colonialism and Rural Settlement in First Millennium B.C. West Central Sardinia.* Archaeological Studies, no. 2. Leiden: Faculty of Archaeology, Leiden University.

2002   Ambiguous Matters: Colonialism and Local Identities in Punic Sardinia. In *The Archaeology of Colonialism,* edited by C. Lyons and J. Papadopoulos, pp. 121–47. Issues and Debates. Los Angeles: Getty Research Institute.

Van Driel, G.

1977   The Uruk Settlement at Jebel Aruda: A Preliminary Report. In *Le Moyen Euphrate: Zone de Contact et d'Echanges,* edited by J.C. Margueron, pp. 75–93. Leiden: E. J. Brill.

Van Driel, G., and C. Van Driel-Murray

1979   Jebel Aruda 1977–1978. *Akkadica* 12:2–28.

1983   Jebel Aruda, the 1982 Season of Excavation. Interim Report. *Akkadica* 33:1–26.

Van Dyke, R., and S. Alcock

2003   Archaeologies of Memory: An Introduction. In *Archaeologies of Memory,* edited by R. Van Dyke and S. Alcock, pp. 1–13. Oxford: Blackwell Publishing.

Vance, N.

1997   *The Victorians and Ancient Rome.* Oxford: Blackwell.

Veenhof, K.

1972   *Aspects of Old Assyrian Trade and Its Terminology.* Leiden: E. J. Brill.

1977   Some Social Effects of Old Assyrian Trade. In *Trade in the Ancient Near East,* edited by J. D. Hawkins, pp. 109–18. XXIII Rencontre Assyriologique Internationale. Berlin.

1982   The Old Assyrian Merchants and their Relations with the Native
        Population of Anatolia. In *Mesopotamien und Seine Nachbarn*, edited by
        H. Nissen and J. Renger. XXV Rencontre Assyriologique Internationale.
        Berlin.

1995   Kanesh: An Assyrian Colony in Anatolia. In *Civilizations of the Ancient Near
        East*, vol. 2, edited by J. Sasson, pp. 859–73. New York: Hendrickson
        Publishers.

Verano, J. W.

2003   Human Skeletal Remains from Machu Picchu: A Reexamination of the
        Yale Peabody Museum's Collections. In *The 1912 Yale Peruvian Scientific
        Expedition Collections from Machu Picchu: Human and Animal Remains*, edited
        by R. L. Burger and L. C. Salazar, pp. 65-118. New Haven: Yale University
        Publications in Anthropology.

Vicens Vives, J.

1969   *An Economic History of Spain*. Princeton: Princeton University Press.

Voorhies, B.

1989   A Model of the Pre-Aztec Political System of the Soconusco. In *Ancient
        Trade and Tribute: Economies of the Soconusco Region of Mesoamerica*, edited by
        B. Voorhies, pp. 95–129. Salt Lake City: University of Utah Press.

Voorhies, B., and J. Gasco

2004   *Postclassic Soconusco Society: The Late Prehistory of the Coast of Chiapas, Mexico.*
        Albany: Institute for Mesoamerican Studies, State University of New York.

Wachtel, N.

1982   The Mitimas of the Cochabamba Valley: The Colonization Policy of
        Huayna Capac. In *The Inca and Aztec States, 1400–1800: Anthropology and
        History*, edited by G. A. Collier, R. I. Rosaldo, and J. D. Wirth, pp. 199–235.
        New York: Academic Press.

Wade, M.

1988   French Indian Policies. In *Handbook of North American Indians*, Vol. 4:
        History of Indian-White Relations, edited by W. E. Washburn, pp. 20–28.
        Washington, DC: Smithsonian Institution Press.

Wagner, C.

1989   The Carthaginians in Ancient Spain from Administrative Trade to
        Territorial Annexation. In *Punic War*, edited by H. Devijver and
        E. Lipinski, pp. 145–56. Studia Phoenicia 10. Leuven.

2000   Comercio lejano, colonización e intercambio desigual en la expansión
        fenicia arcaica. In *Intercambio y comercio preclásico en el Mediterráneo*, edited
        by P. Fernández Uriel, C. González Wagner, and F. López Pardo, pp.
        79–91. Actas del I coloquio del CEFYP, Madrid, 9–12 de noviembre, 1998.
        Madrid: Centro de estudios fenicios y púnicos.

Wagner, M. J.

1998   Some Think It Impossible to Civilize Them at All: Cultural Change and Continuity among the Early Nineteenth-Century Potawatomi. In *Studies in Culture Contact: Interaction, Culture Change, and Archaeology*, edited by J. G. Cusick, pp. 430–56. Occasional Paper 25. Carbondale: Center for Archaeological Investigations, Southern Illinois University.

Wake, T. A.

1995   Mammal Remains from Fort Ross: A Study in Ethnicity and Culture Change. Ph.D. dissertation, Department of Anthropology, University of California, Berkeley.

1997   Bone Artifacts and Tool Production in the Native Alaskan Neighborhood. In *The Archaeology and Ethnohistory of Fort Ross, California*. Vol. 2: *The Native Alaskan Neighborhood: A Multiethnic Community at Colony Ross*, edited by K. G. Lightfoot, A. M. Schiff, and T. A. Wake, pp. 248–78. Contributions of the University of California Archaeological Research Facility 55. Berkeley: Archaeological Research Facility, University of California.

Walbank, M.

1989   Pausanias, Octavia and Temple E at Corinth. *Annual of the British School at Athens* 84:361–94.

Walker, P. L., and J. R. Johnson

1992   Effects of Contact on the Chumash Indians. In *Disease and Demography in the Americas*, edited by J. W. Verano and D. H. Ubelaker, pp. 127–39. Washington, DC: Smithsonian Institution Press.

1994   The Decline of the Chumash Indian Population. In *In the Wake of Contact: Biological Responses to Conquest*, edited by C. S. Larsen and G. Milner, pp. 109–20. New York: John Wiley and Sons.

Wallace-Hadrill, A.

1994   *Houses and Society in Pompeii and Herculaneum*. Princeton: Princeton University Press.

Wallerstein, I.

1974   *The Modern World-System*, Vol. 1: *Capitalist Agriculture and the Origin of the European World-Economy in the Sixteenth Century*. New York: Academic Press.

1980   *The Modern World-System*, Vol. 2: *Mercantilism and the Consolidation of the European World-Economy, 1600–1750*. New York: Academic Press.

1989   *The Modern World-System*, Vol. 3: *The Second Era of Great Expansion of the Capitalist World-Economy, 1730's–1840's*. New York: Academic Press.

Ward-Perkins, J., and M. H. Balance

1958   The Caesarium at Cyrene and the Basilica at Cremna. *Papers of the British School at Rome* 26:137–94.

Watson, B., trans.

1961   *Records of the Grant Historian of China by Ssuma Ch'ien,* Vol. 2: *The Age of Emperor Wu 140 to circa 100 B.C.* New York: Columbia University Press.

Weaver, M. P.

1993   *The Aztecs, Maya, and Their Predecessors.* 3rd ed. New York: Academic Press.

Webb, T.

1982   *English Romantic Hellenism, 1700–1824.* New York: Barnes and Noble.

Weber, D. J.

1992   *The Spanish Frontier in North America.* New Haven: Yale University Press.

Webster, G.

1996   *A Prehistory of Sardinia 2300–500 B.C.* Monographs in Mediterranean Archaeology 5. Sheffield: Sheffield Academic Press.

Webster, J.

1996   Roman Imperialism and the Post-Imperial Age. In *Roman Imperialism: Post-Colonial Perspectives,* edited by J. Webster and N. Cooper, pp. 1–18. Leicester Archaeology Monographs 3. Leicester: Leicester University Press.

1997   Necessary Comparisons: A Post-Colonial Approach to Religious Syncretism in the Roman Provinces. *World Archaeology* 28 (3):324–38.

Weigand, P.

1982   Mining and Mineral Trade in Prehispanic Zacatecas. *Anthropology* 6:87–134.

Weiss, H., and T. Cuyler Young

1975   The Merchants of Susa: Godin V and Plateau-Lowland Relations in the Late Fourth Millennium B.C. *Iran* 13:1–17.

Welch, K.

1999   Negotiating Roman Spectacle Architecture in the Greek World: Athens and Corinth. In *The Art of Ancient Spectacle,* edited by B. Bergmann and C. Kondoleon, pp. 125–45. New Haven and London: National Gallery of Art.

Wells, P.

1992   Tradition, Identity, and Change Beyond the Roman Frontier. In *Resources, Power, and Interregional Interaction,* edited by E. Schortman and P. Urban, pp. 175–88. New York: Plenum.

1998   Culture Contact, Identity, and Change in the European Provinces of the Roman Empire. In *Studies in Culture Contact: Interaction, Culture Change, and Archaeology,* edited by J. Cusick, pp. 316–34. Occasional Paper 25. Carbondale: Center for Archaeological Investigations, Southern Illinois University.

Werbner, R., and T. Ranger, eds.

1996   *Postcolonial Identities in Africa.* Postcolonial Encounters. London: Zed Books.

Whelan, M. K.

1993   Dakota Indian Economics and the Nineteenth-Century Fur Trade. *Ethnohistory* 40:246–76.

White, C. D., M. W. Spence, F. J. Longstaffe, and K. Law

2003   Demography and Ethnic Continuity in the Tlailotlacan Enclave of Teotihuacan: The Evidence from Stable Oxygen Isotopes. Manuscript on file with the authors.

White, C. D., M. W. Spence, F. Longstaffe, E. Rattray, and K. Law

2000   Un análisis de las proporciones de los isótopos del oxígeno en los entierros del Barrio de los Comerciantes. Paper presented at the Segunda Mesa Redonda de Teotihuacan, Centro de Estudios Teotihuacanos, Teotihuacan.

White, C. D., M. W. Spence, H. Le Q. Stuart-Williams, and H. P. Schwarcz

1998   Oxygen Isotopes and the Identification of Geographical Origins: The Valley of Oaxaca versus the Valley of Mexico. *Journal of Archaeological Science* 25:643–55.

White, R.

1991   *The Middle Ground: Indians, Empires, and Republics in the Great Lakes Region, 1650–1815.* Cambridge: Cambridge University Press.

Whitecotton, J., and R. Pailes

1986   New World Precolumbian World Systems. In *Ripples in the Chichimec Sea: New Considerations of Southwestern-Mesoamerican Interactions*, edited by F. Mathien and R. McGuire, pp. 183–204. Carbondale: Southern Illinois University Press.

Whitehouse, R. D., and J. B. Wilkins

1989   Greeks and Natives in South-east Italy: Approaches to the Archaeological Evidence. In *Centre and Periphery: Comparative Studies in Archaeology*, edited by T. Champion, pp. 102–26. London: Unwin Hyman.

Williams, C. K. II

1987   The Refounding of Corinth: Some Roman Religious Atittudes. In *Roman Architecture in the Greek World*, edited by S. Macready and F. H. Thompson, pp. 26–37. Society of Antiquaries of London Occasional Papers 10. London: Society of Antiquaries of London.

1989   A Re-Evaluation of Temple E and the West End of the Forum at Corinth. In *The Greek Renaissance in the Roman Empire*, edited by S. Walker and A. Cameron, pp. 156–62. London: University of London, Institute of Classical Studies.

1993   Roman Corinth as a Commercial Center. In *The Corinthia in the Roman Period*, edited by T. E. Gregory, pp. 31–46. Journal of Roman Archaeology Supplementary Vol. 8. Ann Arbor: Journal of Roman Archaeology.

Williams, C. K. II, and O. Zervos

1989   Corinth 1988: East of the Theater. *Hesperia* 58: 1–50.

Williams, V. I.

1996   La ocupación inka en la región central de Catamarca (República Argentina). Ph.D. dissertation. Universidad Nacional de La Plata, Argentina.

Williams, V. I., and A. M. Lorandi

1986   Evidencias funcionales de un establecimiento incaico del Noroeste argentino. *Comechingonia*, Vol. Homenaje al 450 Congreso Internacional de Americanistas (Bógota), pp. 133–49. Córdoba.

Wilson, A.

1966   *Emigration from Italy in the Republican Age of Rome.* Manchester: Manchester University Press.

Wilson, S. M., and J. D. Rogers

1993   Historical Dynamics in the Contact Era. In *Ethnohistory and Archaeology: Approaches to Postcontact Change in the Americas,* edited by J. D. Rogers and S. M. Wilson, pp. 3–15. New York: Plenum Press.

Winckelmann, J. J.

1987   *Reflections on the Imitation of Greek Works in Painting and Sculpture*
[1755]   *(Gedanken über die Nachahmung der griechischen Werke in der Malerei und Bildhauerkunst).* German text with translation by E. Heyer and R. C. Norton. La Salle, IL: Open Court.

Winter, M. C.

1986   Unidades habitacionales prehispánicas en Oaxaca. In *Unidades habitacionales mesoamericanas y sus áreas de actividad,* edited by L. Manzanilla, pp. 325–74. Mexico, DF: Universidad national autónoma de México.

1998   Monte Alban and Teotihuacan. In *Rutas de intercambio en Mesoamérica: III Coloquio Pedro Bosch Gimpera,* edited by E. Rattray, pp. 153–84. Mexico, DF: Universidad national autónoma de México.

Wiseman, J.

1978   *The Land of the Ancient Corinthians.* Göteborg: Paul Åstrom.

1979   Corinth and Rome, I. *Aufstieg und Niedergang der römischen Welt* 7 (1):438–548.

Wobst, H. M.

1978   The Archaeo-Ethnology of Hunter-Gatherers or the Tyranny of the Ethnographic Record in Archaeology. *American Antiquity* 43 (2):303–9.

Wobst, M.

1977   Stylistic Behavior and Information Exchange. In *For the Director: Research Essays in Honor of James B. Griffin,* edited by C. Cleland, pp. 317–42. Anthropological Paper 61. Ann Arbor: Museum of Anthropology, University of Michigan.

REFERENCES

Wohlleben, J.

1992   Germany 1750–1830. In *Perceptions of the Ancient Greeks*, edited by
K. J. Dover, pp. 170–202. Oxford: Blackwell.

Wolf, E. R.

1982   *Europe and the People without History*. Berkeley: University of California
Press.

Woolf, G.

1990   World-Systems Analysis and the Roman Empire. *Journal of Roman
Archaeology* 3:44–58.

1994   Becoming Roman, Staying Greek: Culture, Identity and the Civilizing
Process in the Roman East. *Proceedings of the Cambridge Philological Society*
40:116–43.

1997   The Roman Urbanization of the East. In *The Early Roman Empire in the East*,
edited by S. E. Alcock, pp. 1–14. Oxford: Oxbow Books.

1998   *Becoming Roman: The Origins of Provincial Civilization in Gaul*. Cambridge:
Cambridge University Press.

Woolley, L.

1934   *Ur Excavations*, Vol. II: *The Royal Cemetery*. London and Philadelphia: The
British Museum and The University of Pennsylvania University Museum.

Wrangell, F. P. V.

1969   Russia in California, 1833, Report of Governor Wrangell. Edited and
translated by J. Gibson. *Pacific Northwest Quarterly* 60:205–15.

Wright, G.

1969   *Obsidian Analysis and Prehistoric Near Eastern Trade: 7500 to 3500 B.C.*
Anthropological Paper 37. Ann Arbor: Museum of Anthropology,
University of Michigan.

Wright, H.

1972   A Consideration of Interregional Exchange in Greater Mesopotamia:
4000–3000 B.C. In *Social Exchange and Interaction*, edited by E. Wilmsen,
pp. 95–147. Anthropology Paper 46, Ann Arbor: Museum of
Anthropology, University of Michigan.

Wright, H., and G. Johnson

1975   Population, Exchange, and Early State Formation in Southwestern Iran.
American Anthropologist 77:267–89.

Wright, H., N. Miller, and R. Redding

1980   Time and Process in an Uruk Rural Center. In *L'archéologie de l'Iraq du
début de l'epoque Neolithique à 333 avant Notre Ere: Perspectives et limites de
l'interpretation anthropologique des documents*, edited by M.-T. Barrelet,
pp. 265–84. Colloques internationaux du CNRS, vol. 580. Paris: Editions
de CNRS.

Wright, H., R. Redding, and S. Pollock

1989   Monitoring Interannual Variability: An Example from the Period of Early State Development in Southwestern Iran. In *Bad Year Economics: Cultural Responses to Risk and Uncertainty*, edited by P. Halstead and J. O'Shea, pp. 106–13. Cambridge: Cambridge University Press.

Wright, J., J. F. Cherry, J. L. Davis, E. Mantzourani, S. B. Sutton, and R. F. Sutton, Jr.

1990   The Nemea Valley Archaeological Project: A Preliminary Report. *Hesperia* 59:579–659.

Wylie, A.

1989   Matters of Fact and Matters of Interest. In *Archaeological Approaches to Cultural Identity*, edited by S. J. Shennan, pp. 94–109. London: Unwin Hyman.

Yarborough, C.

1992   Teotihuacan and the Gulf Coast: Ceramic Evidence for Contact and International Relationships. Ph.D. dissertation, University of Arizona, Tucson.

Yellen, J.

1977   *Archaeological Approaches to the Present.* New York: Academic Press.

Yener, K. A.

1982   A Review of Interregional Exchange in Southwest Asia. *Anatolica* 9:33–75.

1983   The Production, Exchange, and Utilization of Silver and Lead Metals in Ancient Anatolia. *Anatolica* 10:1–15.

2000   *The Domestication of Metals: The Rise of Complex Metal Industries in Anatolia.* Leiden: Brill.

Yener, A., H. Özbal, et al.

1989   Kestel: An Early Bronze Age Source of Tin Ore in the Taurus Mountains, Turkey. *Science* 244:220–30.

Yener, A., A. E. Geckinli, et al.

1996   A Brief Survey of Anatolian Metallurgy prior to 500 B.C. *Archaeometry 94. Proceedings of the 29th International Symposium on Archaeometry*, edited by S. Demirci, A. M. Özer, and G. Summers, pp. 375–91. Ankara: Tübitak.

Yoffee, N.

1981   *Explaining Trade in Ancient Western Asia.* Monographs on the Ancient Near East 2 (2):1–40.

1993   Too Many Chiefs? (Or, Safe Texts for the 90's). In *Archaeological Theory: Who Sets the Agenda?*, edited by N. Yoffee and A. Sherratt, pp. 60–78. Cambridge: Cambridge University Press.

1995   Political Economy in Early Mesopotamian States. *Annual Review of Anthropology* 24:281–311.

REFERENCES

Young, R. J. C.

1995   *Colonial Desire. Hybridity in Theory, Culture and Race.* London and New York: Routledge.

1998   Ideologies of the Postcolonial. *Interventions* 1 (1):4–8.

2001   *Postcolonialism: An Historical Introduction.* Oxford: Blackwell.

2003   *Postcolonialism. A Very Short Introduction.* Very Short Introductions 98. Oxford: Oxford University Press.

Young, T. C.

1986   Godin Tepe VI/V and Central Western Iran at the End of the Fourth Millennium. In *Gamdat Nasr: Period or Regional Style?*, edited by U. Finkbeiner and W. Röllig, pp. 212–28. Wiesbaden: Dr. Ludwig Reichert Verlag.

Zaccagnini, C.

1987   Aspects of Ceremonial Exchange in the Near East during the Second Millennium B.C. In *Centre and Periphery in the Ancient World*, edited by M. Rowlands, M. Larsen, and K. Kristiansen, pp. 57–65. Cambridge: Cambridge University Press.

Zanker, P.

1988   *The Power of Images in the Age of Augustus.* Ann Arbor: University of Michigan Press.

Zettler, R., and L. Horne, eds.

1998   *Treasures from the Royal Tombs of Ur.* Philadelphia: Museum of Archaeology and Anthropology, University of Pennsylvania.

Zuber, R.

1992   France, 1640–1790. In *Perceptions of the Ancient Greeks*, edited by K. J. Dover, pp. 147–169. Oxford: Blackwell.

Zucca, R.

1987   *Neapolis e il suo territorio.* Oristano, Italy: S'Alvure.

1991   La città punica di Neapolis in Sardegna. In *Atti del II congresso internazionale di studi fenici e punici*, pp. 1299–311. Collezione di studi fenici 30. Rome: Istituto di studi fenici (CNR).

Zuidema, T.

1983   Hierarchy and Space in Incaic Social Organization. *Ethnohistory* 30 (2):49–75.

Index

Abancay Valley (Peru), 280
acculturation: and emerging
  paradigms of interregional
  interaction, 9; and identity
  transformations in colonial
  encounters, 16, 28; and
  social landscape of Inka
  Empire, 287; and Spanish
  missions in California,
  229–30
Achaia (Greece), and
  Roman colonies, 300–303,
  304, 308, 323–29
Acoculco (Mexico), and
  Zapotec diaspora network
  in Classic period, 195, 198,
  200, 201, 202
administration: functions
  and definitions of colonies,
  11; *municipios* and Spanish
  colonialism in
  Mesoamerica, 92
Adorno, T., 71
Africa. *See* !Kung San; North
  Africa; Tswana
agency: and archaeological
  interpretation of colonialism in Iron Age France,
  61–67; and colonial strategies of Wari Empire,
  237–61; and concept of
  diaspora network, 175; and
  emerging paradigms of
  interregional interaction,
  9; as emerging theme in
  archaeology of colonial
  encounters, 30–31
agriculture: and functions of
  colonies, 12; and indigenous peoples of

Mesoamerica, 80–81; Inka
  Empire and state farms,
  277–81; and sedentism of
  !Kung San, 345–46;
  Spanish colonialism and
  introduction of new tech-
  nologies in Mesoamerica,
  89; and reverse movement
  of goods from New World
  to Europe, 89, 90. *See also*
  diet; terraces
Akkadian Empire, and
  Mesopotamian trade net-
  works, 147–48, 149, 151,
  153
Alcock, S., 22–23, 25, 28, 30,
  215, 273
Alconini, S., 287
Alexander, R., 239
Algaze, G., 13, 155, 238
Allen, R., 230, 232
alliance strategies, and comparative analysis of colonial
  encounters, 14
Alvarado, Jorge & Pedro, 104
American School of Classical
  Studies, 302
Amselle, J., 65
Anatolia: and Mesopotamian
  colonial network, 154,
  156–61, 162, 165–68; and
  Roman colonies, 300–303,
  313–29
anthropology, and European
  colonialism, 70. *See also*
  archaeology; ethnography
Antioch. *See* Pisidian
  Antioch
apoikia, and colonialism in
  ancient Greece, 110

Apuleius, 304
Arabs (Moors), and Spain as
  multiethnic society in fifteenth century, 75–77, 78
archaeology: and colonial
  strategies of Wari Empire
  in Middle Horizon,
  240–44; and cross-cultural
  analysis of Spanish and
  Russian colonization in
  California, 217–35; emerging themes in colonial
  encounters and, 23–31;
  and identification of diaspora communities, 175–77;
  and interpretation of colonial encounters, 331–54;
  postcolonial theory and
  colonization studies in
  Mediterranean, 112,
  114–15, 140; and recognition of colonies, 14–16;
  research issues involved in
  developing comparative
  model for colonial encounters, 5–23; and Roman
  colonies in Eastern
  Empire, 299, 311; and
  social landscape of Inka
  Empire, 272–77; study of
  ancient Mediterranean
  and colonization of, 33–68.
  See also architecture; burials; ceramics; material culture
architecture: and criteria for
  diaspora networks, 176;
  influence of ancient
  Greece and Rome on mod-
  ern European, 38, 42; and

School for Advanced Research Advanced Seminar Series

DEVELOPMENT & DISPOSSESSION: THE
CRISIS OF FORCED DISPLACEMENT AND
RESETTLEMENT
Anthony Oliver-Smith, ed.

GLOBAL HEALTH IN TIMES OF VIOLENCE
*Barbara Rylko-Bauer, Linda Whiteford, &
Paul Farmer, eds.*

THE EVOLUTION OF LEADERSHIP:
TRANSITIONS IN DECISION MAKING FROM
SMALL-SCALE TO MIDDLE-RANGE SOCIETIES
*Kevin J. Vaughn, Jelmer W. Eerkins, &
John Kantner, eds.*

ARCHAEOLOGY & CULTURAL RESOURCE
MANAGEMENT: VISIONS FOR THE FUTURE
Lynne Sebastian & William D. Lipe, eds.

ARCHAIC STATE INTERACTION: THE
EASTERN MEDITERRANEAN IN THE BRONZE
AGE
*William A. Parkinson & Michael L. Galaty,
eds.*

INDIANS & ENERGY: EXPLOITATION AND
OPPORTUNITY IN THE AMERICAN SOUTHWEST
Sherry L. Smith & Brian Frehner, eds.

ROOTS OF CONFLICT: SOILS, AGRICULTURE,
AND SOCIOPOLITICAL COMPLEXITY IN
ANCIENT HAWAI'I
Patrick V. Kirch, ed.

PHARMACEUTICAL SELF: THE GLOBAL
SHAPING OF EXPERIENCE IN AN AGE OF
PSYCHOPHARMACOLOGY
Janis Jenkins, ed.

FORCES OF COMPASSION: HUMANITARI-
ANISM BETWEEN ETHICS AND POLITICS
Erica Bornstein & Peter Redfield, eds.

ENDURING CONQUESTS: RETHINKING THE
ARCHAEOLOGY OF RESISTANCE TO SPANISH
COLONIALISM IN THE AMERICAS
Matthew Liebmann & Melissa S. Murphy, eds.

THE ARCHAEOLOGY OF LOWER CENTRAL
AMERICA
Frederick W. Lange & Doris Z. Stone, eds.

CHAN CHAN: ANDEAN DESERT CITY
Michael E. Moseley & Kent C. Day, eds.

DEMOGRAPHIC ANTHROPOLOGY:
QUANTITATIVE APPROACHES
Ezra B. W. Zubrow, ed.

THE DYING COMMUNITY
Art Gallaher, Jr. & Harlan Padfield, eds.

ELITES: ETHNOGRAPHIC ISSUES
George E. Marcus, ed.

ENTREPRENEURS IN CULTURAL CONTEXT
*Sidney M. Greenfield, Arnold Strickon,
& Robert T. Aubey, eds.*

LOWLAND MAYA SETTLEMENT PATTERNS
Wendy Ashmore, ed.

METHODS AND THEORIES OF
ANTHROPOLOGICAL GENETICS
M. H. Crawford & P. L. Workman, eds.

THE ORIGINS OF MAYA CIVILIZATION
Richard E. W. Adams, ed.

STRUCTURE AND PROCESS IN LATIN AMERICA
Arnold Strickon & Sidney M. Greenfield, eds.

Participants in the School of American Research advanced seminar "The Archaeology of Colonization in Cross-Cultural Perspective," Santa Fe, New Mexico, March 19–23, 2000.
Standing from left: Katharina Schreiber, Kent G. Lightfoot, Gil J. Stein, Peter van Dommelen, Michael W. Spence, Michael Dietler.
Seated from left: J. Daniel Rogers, Terence D'Altroy, Janine L. Gasco, Susan E. Alcock.